Lecture Notes in Computer Science 5501

Commenced Publication in 1973
Founding and Former Series Editors:
Gerhard Goos, Juris Hartmanis, and Jan van Leeuwen

Oege de Moor   Michael I. Schwartzbach (Eds.)

Compiler Construction

18th International Conference, CC 2009
Held as Part of the Joint European Conferences
on Theory and Practice of Software, ETAPS 2009
York, UK, March 22-29, 2009
Proceedings

 Springer

Volume Editors

Oege de Moor
Oxford University Computing Laboratory, Wolfson Building
Parks Road, Oxford OX1 3QD, UK
E-mail: oege@comlab.ox.ac.uk

Michael I. Schwartzbach
Aarhus University, Department of Computer Science
Aabogade 34, 8200 Aarhus N., Denmark
E-mail: mis@cs.au.dk

Library of Congress Control Number: Applied for

CR Subject Classification (1998): D.3.4, D.2.2, D.2.4, D.2.5, D.3.3

LNCS Sublibrary: SL 1 – Theoretical Computer Science and General Issues

ISSN	0302-9743
ISBN-10	3-642-00721-X Springer Berlin Heidelberg New York
ISBN-13	978-3-642-00721-7 Springer Berlin Heidelberg New York

springer.com

© Springer-Verlag Berlin Heidelberg 2009
Printed in Germany

Typesetting: Camera-ready by author, data conversion by Scientific Publishing Services, Chennai, India
Printed on acid-free paper   SPIN: 12630653   06/3180   5 4 3 2 1 0

Foreword

ETAPS 2009 was the 12th instance of the European Joint Conferences on Theory and Practice of Software. ETAPS is an annual federated conference that was established in 1998 by combining a number of existing and new conferences. This year it comprised five conferences (CC, ESOP, FASE, FOSSACS, TACAS), 22 satellite workshops (ACCAT, ARSPA-WITS, Bytecode, COCV, COMPASS, FESCA, FInCo, FORMED, GaLoP, GT-VMT, HFL, LDTA, MBT, MLQA, OpenCert, PLACES, QAPL, RC, SafeCert, TAASN, TERMGRAPH, and WING), four tutorials, and seven invited lectures (excluding those that were specific to the satellite events). The five main conferences received 532 submissions (including 30 tool demonstration papers), 141 of which were accepted (10 tool demos), giving an overall acceptance rate of about 26%, with most of the conferences at around 25%. Congratulations therefore to all the authors who made it to the final programme! I hope that most of the other authors will still have found a way of participating in this exciting event, and that you will all continue submitting to ETAPS and contributing towards making it the best conference on software science and engineering.

The events that comprise ETAPS address various aspects of the system development process, including specification, design, implementation, analysis and improvement. The languages, methodologies and tools which support these activities are all well within its scope. Different blends of theory and practice are represented, with an inclination towards theory with a practical motivation on the one hand and soundly based practice on the other. Many of the issues involved in software design apply to systems in general, including hardware systems, and the emphasis on software is not intended to be exclusive.

ETAPS is a confederation in which each event retains its own identity, with a separate Programme Committee and proceedings. Its format is open-ended, allowing it to grow and evolve as time goes by. Contributed talks and system demonstrations are in synchronised parallel sessions, with invited lectures in plenary sessions. Two of the invited lectures are reserved for 'unifying' talks on topics of interest to the whole range of ETAPS attendees. The aim of cramming all this activity into a single one-week meeting is to create a strong magnet for academic and industrial researchers working on topics within its scope, giving them the opportunity to learn about research in related areas, and thereby to foster new and existing links between work in areas that were formerly addressed in separate meetings.

ETAPS 2009 was organised by the University of York in cooperation with

▷ European Association for Theoretical Computer Science (EATCS)
▷ European Association for Programming Languages and Systems (EAPLS)
▷ European Association of Software Science and Technology (EASST)

and with support from ERCIM, Microsoft Research, Rolls-Royce, Transitive, and Yorkshire Forward.

The organising team comprised:

Chair	Gerald Luettgen
Secretariat	Ginny Wilson and Bob French
Finances	Alan Wood
Satellite Events	Jeremy Jacob and Simon O'Keefe
Publicity	Colin Runciman and Richard Paige
Website	Fiona Polack and Malihe Tabatabaie.

Overall planning for ETAPS conferences is the responsibility of its Steering Committee, whose current membership is:

Vladimiro Sassone (Southampton, Chair), Luca de Alfaro (Santa Cruz), Roberto Amadio (Paris), Giuseppe Castagna (Paris), Marsha Chechik (Toronto), Sophia Drossopoulou (London), Hartmut Ehrig (Berlin), Javier Esparza (Munich), Jose Fiadeiro (Leicester), Andrew Gordon (MSR Cambridge), Rajiv Gupta (Arizona), Chris Hankin (London), Laurie Hendren (McGill), Mike Hinchey (NASA Goddard), Paola Inverardi (L'Aquila), Joost-Pieter Katoen (Aachen), Paul Klint (Amsterdam), Stefan Kowalewski (Aachen), Shriram Krishnamurthi (Brown), Kim Larsen (Aalborg), Gerald Luettgen (York), Rupak Majumdar (Los Angeles), Tiziana Margaria (Göttingen), Ugo Montanari (Pisa), Oege de Moor (Oxford), Luke Ong (Oxford), Catuscia Palamidessi (Paris), George Papadopoulos (Cyprus), Anna Philippou (Cyprus), David Rosenblum (London), Don Sannella (Edinburgh), João Saraiva (Minho), Michael Schwartzbach (Aarhus), Perdita Stevens (Edinburgh), Gabriel Taentzer (Marburg), Dániel Varró (Budapest), and Martin Wirsing (Munich).

I would like to express my sincere gratitude to all of these people and organisations, the Programme Committee Chairs and PC members of the ETAPS conferences, the organisers of the satellite events, the speakers themselves, the many reviewers, and Springer for agreeing to publish the ETAPS proceedings. Finally, I would like to thank the Organising Chair of ETAPS 2009, Gerald Luettgen, for arranging for us to hold ETAPS in the most beautiful city of York.

January 2009

Vladimiro Sassone, Chair
ETAPS Steering Committee

Preface

This volume contains the papers presented at CC 2009, the 18th International Conference on Compiler Construction held on March 23-24 in York, UK as part of the Joint European Conference on Theory and Practice of Software (ETAPS 2009). Papers were solicited from a wide range of areas including traditional compiler construction, compiler analyses, runtime systems and tools, programming tools, techniques for specific domains, and the design and implementation of novel language constructs. The submissions and the papers in this volume reflect this variety.

There were 72 submissions. Each submission was reviewed by at least three Programme Committee members and was subjected to several rounds of thorough discussions, and in some cases additional expert reviews were obtained. The PC finally decided to accept 18 research papers.

Many people contributed to the success of this conference. First of all, we would like to thank the authors for submitting papers of high quality. We are also grateful to the members of the Programme Committee and to the external reviewers for their substantive and insightful reviews. Also, thanks go to the developers and supporters of the EasyChair conference management systems for making life so much easier for the authors and the Programme Committee.

CC 2009 was made possible by the ETAPS Steering Committee and the Local Organizing Committee. Finally, we are grateful to Vivek Sarkar for giving the CC 2009 invited talk entitled *Challenges in Code Optimization of Parallel Programs*.

January 2009

Michael Schwartzbach
Oege de Moor

Conference Organization

Programme Chairs

Oege de Moor
Michael I. Schwartzbach

Programme Committee

Silvia Breu	University of Cambridge, UK
Manuel Chakravarty	University of New South Wales, Australia
Satish Chandra	IBM Research, New York
Michael Franz	UC Irvine, USA
Jan Heering	CWI, The Netherlands
Paul Kelly	Imperial College, UK
Viktor Kuncak	EPFL, Switzerland
Sorin Lerner	University of California at San Diego, USA
Yanhong Annie Liu	SUNY at Stony Brook, USA
Ondrej Lhotak	University of Waterloo, Canada
Oege de Moor	Oxford University, UK
Pierre-Etienne Moreau	INRIA Nancy, France
Lori Pollock	University of Delaware, USA
Markus Pueschel	Carnegie Mellon University, USA
Mooly Sagiv	Tel-Aviv University, Israel
Wolfram Schulte	Microsoft Research Redmond, USA
Michael I. Schwartzbach	University of Aarhus, Denmark
Yannis Smaragdakis	University of Oregon, USA
Zhendong Su	UC Davis, USA
Don Syme	Microsoft Research Cambridge, UK

Reviewers

Amaral, J. Nelson	Cintra, Marcelo
Arnold, Mat	Cunei, Antonio
Balland, Emilie	Danvy, Olivier
Bird, Christian	Ditu, Gabriel
Bouchez, Florent	Dor, Nurit
Brauner, Paul	Edwards, Stephen A.
Bravenboer, Martin	Ernst, Erik
Burckel, Serge	Field, John
Chang, Mason	Fink, Stephen
Chugh, Ravi	Franchetti, Franz

Gabel, Mark
Gal, Andreas
Gfeller, Sebastian
Gorbovitski, Michael
Hu, Zhenjiang
Huang, Shan Shan
Jackson, Todd
Jiang, Lingxiao
Keller, Gabriele
Klint, Paul
Kopetz, Radu
Lashari, Ghulam
Lee, Sean
Leshchinskiy, Roman
Lev-Ami, Tal
Lindig, Christian
Liu, Xuezheng
Lokhmotov, Anton
Manevich, Roman
de Mesmay, Frederic
Message, Robin
Mullins, Robert
Naeem, Nomair
Parkinson, Matthew
Pearce, David
Piskac, Ruzica
Rabbah, Rodric

Reilles, Antoine
Rinetzky, Noan
Rothamel, Tom
Russell, Francis
Salamat, Babak
Seyster, Justin
Sittampalam, Ganesh
Sridharan, Manu
Suter, Philippe
Swierstra, Doaitse
Tatlock, Zachary
Tekle, Tuncay
Theoduloz, Gregory
Van Wyk, Eric
Vechev, Martin
Vinju, Jurgen
Voronenko, Yevgen
Wagner, Gregor
Wang, Liqiang
Wies, Thomas
Wilhelm, Reinhard
Wimmer, Christian
Winwood, Simon
Yahav, Eran
Yermolovich, Alexander
Yohan, Boichut

Table of Contents

Challenges in Code Optimization
of Parallel Programs

Vivek Sarkar

Rice University

Abstract. Code optimization has a rich history that dates back over half a century, and includes deep innovations that arose in response to changing trends in hardware and programming languages. These innovations have contributed significantly to programmer productivity by reducing the effort that programmers spend on hand-implementing code optimizations and by enabling code to be more portable. Often these innovations were accompanied by *paradigm shifts* in the foundations of compilers led by the introduction of new ideas such as interprocedural whole program analysis, coloring-based register allocation, static single assignment form, array dependence analysis, pointer alias analysis, loop transformations, adaptive profile-directed optimizations, and dynamic compilation.

In this talk, we claim that the current multicore trend in the computer industry is forcing a new paradigm shift in compilers to address the challenge of *code optimization of parallel programs*, regardless of whether the parallelism is implicit or explicit in the programming model. All computers — embedded, mainstream, and high-end — are now being built from multicore processors with little or no increase in clock speed per core. This trend poses multiple challenges for compilers for future systems as the number of cores per socket continues to grow, and the cores become more heterogeneous. In addition, compilers have to keep pace with a proliferation of new parallel languages and libraries.

To substantiate our claim, we first highlight some of the anomalies that arise when classical techniques from sequential code optimization are applied to parallel code. We then examine the historical foundations of code optimization including intermediate representations (IR's), abstract execution models, legality and cost analyses of IR transformations and identify paradigm shifts that will be necessary to support optimization of parallel code. We pay special attention to memory consistency models and their impact on code optimization. Finally, we summarize the approach to code optimization of parallel programs being taken in the Habanero Multicore Software Research project at Rice University.

O. de Moor and M. Schwartzbach (Eds.): CC 2009, LNCS 5501, p. 1, 2009.
© Springer-Verlag Berlin Heidelberg 2009

Extensible Proof-Producing Compilation

Magnus O. Myreen[1], Konrad Slind[2], and Michael J.C. Gordon[1]

[1] Computer Laboratory, University of Cambridge, Cambridge, UK
[2] School of Computing, University of Utah, Salt Lake City, USA

Abstract. This paper presents a compiler which produces machine code from functions defined in the logic of a theorem prover, and at the same time proves that the generated code executes the source functions. Unlike previously published work on proof-producing compilation from a theorem prover, our compiler provides broad support for user-defined extensions, targets multiple carefully modelled commercial machine languages, and does not require termination proofs for input functions. As a case study, the compiler is used to construct verified interpreters for a small LISP-like language. The compiler has been implemented in the HOL4 theorem prover.

1 Introduction

Compilers pose a problem for program verification: if a high-level program is proved correct, then the compiler's transformation must be trusted in order for the proof to carry over to a guarantee about the generated executable code. In practice there is also another problem: most source languages (C, Java, Haskell etc.) do not have a formal semantics, and it is therefore hard to formally state and verify properties of programs written in these languages.

This paper explores an approach to compilation aimed at supporting program verification. We describe a compiler which takes as input functions expressed in the logic of a theorem prover, compiles the functions to machine code (ARM, x86 or PowerPC) and also proves that the generated code executes the supplied functions. For example, given function f as input

$$f(r_1) = \text{if } r_1 < 10 \text{ then } r_1 \text{ else let } r_1 = r_1 - 10 \text{ in } f(r_1)$$

the compiler can generate ARM machine code

```
E351000A       L:   cmp r1,#10
2241100A            subcs r1,r1,#10
2AFFFFFC            bcs L
```

and automatically prove a theorem which certifies that the generated code executes f. The following theorem states, if register one (r1) initially holds value r_1, then the code will leave register one holding value $f(r_1)$. The theorem is expressed as a machine-code Hoare triple [17] where the separating conjunction '$*$' can informally be read as 'and'.

$$\{\text{r1 } r_1 * \text{pc } p * \text{s}\} \ p : \text{E351000A, 2241100A, 2AFFFFFC} \ \{\text{r1 } f(r_1) * \text{pc } (p+12) * \text{s}\}$$

O. de Moor and M. Schwartzbach (Eds.): CC 2009, LNCS 5501, pp. 2–16, 2009.

The fact that f is expressed as a function in the native language of a theorem prover means that it has a precise semantics and that one can prove properties about f, e.g. one can prove that $f(x) = x$ mod 10 (here mod is modulus over unsigned machine words). Properties proved for f carry over to guarantees about the generated machine code via the certificate proved by the compiler. For example, one can rewrite the theorem from above to state that the ARM code calculates r_1 mod 10:

$$\{r1\ r_1 * pc\ p * s\}\quad p : \texttt{E351000A, 2241100A, 2AFFFFFC}\quad \{r1\ (r_1 \bmod 10) * pc\ (p{+}12) * s\}$$

Proof-producing compilation from a theorem prover has been explored before by many, as will be discussed in Section 6. The contributions that distinguish the work presented here are that the compiler:

1. targets multiple, carefully modelled, commercial machine languages (namely ARM, PowerPC and x86, as modelled by Fox [7], Leroy [11] and Sarkar [6]);
2. does not require the user to prove termination of the input functions (a restriction posed by the theorem prover in similar work by Li et al. [12,13,14]);
3. can, without any added complexity to the certification proof, handle a range of optimising transformations (Section 4); and
4. supports significant user-defined extensions to its input language (Section 3.1); extensions which made it possible to compile interpreters for a small LISP-like language as a case study (Section 5).

The compiler[1] uses a functional input, which is meant to either be extended directly by the user, as discussed in Section 3.1, or used as a back-end in compilers with more general input languages, e.g. [8,13,14].

This paper builds on the authors' work on *post hoc* verification of realistically modelled machine code [16,17,18], and certifying compilation [8,12,13,14].

2   Core Functionality

The compiler presented in this paper accepts tail-recursive functions as input, functions defined as recursive equations '$f(\ldots) = \ldots$' in a format described in Section 2.1. As output the compiler produces machine code together with a correctness certificate, a theorem which states that the generated machine code executes the function given as input.

The overall compilation algorithm can be broken down into three stages:

1. code generation: generates, without proof, machine code from input f;
2. decompilation: derives, via proof, a function f' describing the machine code;
3. certification: proves $f = f'$.

The remaining subsections describe the input language and code generation that make proving $f = f'$ feasible, as well as the mechanism by which f' is derived. Section 3 describes extensions to the core algorithm.

---

[1] The HOL4 source is at http://hol.sf.net/ under HOL/examples/machine-code.

2.1 Input Language

The compiler's input language consists of let-expressions, if-statements and tail-recursion. The language restricts variable names to correspond to names of registers or stack locations.

The following grammar describes the input language. Let r range over register names, r_0, r_1, r_2, etc., and s over stack locations, s_1, s_2, s_3 etc., m over memory modelling functions (mappings from aligned 32-bit machine words to 32-bit machine words), f over function names, g over names of already compiled functions, and i_5, i_7, i_8 and i_{32} over unsigned words of size 5-, 7-, 8- and 32-bits, respectively. Bit-operators $\&$, $??$, $!!$, $\ll$, $\gg$ are and, xor, or, left-shift, right-shift. Operators suffixed with '.' are signed-versions of those without the suffix.

$$input ::= f(v, v, ..., v) = rhs$$

$$
\begin{aligned}
rhs ::= \ &\mathsf{let}\ r = exp\ \mathsf{in}\ rhs \\
| \ &\mathsf{let}\ s = r\ \mathsf{in}\ rhs \\
| \ &\mathsf{let}\ m = m[\,address \mapsto r\,]\ \mathsf{in}\ rhs \\
| \ &\mathsf{let}\ (v, v, ..., v) = g(v, v, ..., v)\ \mathsf{in}\ rhs \\
| \ &\mathsf{if}\ guard\ \mathsf{then}\ rhs\ \mathsf{else}\ rhs \\
| \ &f(v, v, ..., v) \\
| \ &(v, v, ..., v)
\end{aligned}
$$

$$exp ::= x \mid \neg\ x \mid s \mid i_{32} \mid x\ binop\ x \mid m\ address \mid x \ll i_5 \mid x \gg i_5 \mid x \gg. i_5$$
$$binop ::= +\ \mid\ -\ \mid\ \times\ \mid\ \mathsf{div}\ \mid\ \&\ \mid\ ??\ \mid\ !!$$
$$cmp ::= <\ \mid\ \leq\ \mid\ >\ \mid\ \geq\ \mid\ <.\ \mid\ \leq.\ \mid\ >.\ \mid\ \geq.\ \mid\ =$$
$$guard ::= \neg\ guard \mid guard \wedge guard \mid guard \vee guard \mid x\ cmp\ x \mid x\ \&\ x = 0$$
$$address ::= r \mid r + i_7 \mid r - i_7$$

$$x ::= r \mid i_8$$
$$v ::= r \mid s \mid m$$

This input language was designed to be machine independent; programs constructed from this grammar can be compiled to any of the target languages: ARM, x86 and PowerPC. However the input language differs for each target in the number of registers available ($r_0...r_{12}$ for ARM, $r_0...r_6$ for x86 and $r_0...r_{31}$ for PowerPC) and some detailed restrictions on the use of $\times$ and div.

2.2 Code Generation

The input language was designed to mimic the operations of machine instructions in order to ease code generation. Each let-expression usually produces a single instruction, e.g.

$$
\begin{array}{lll}
\mathsf{let}\ r_3 = r_3 + r_2\ \mathsf{in} & \text{generates ARM code} & \texttt{add r3,r3,r2} \\
\mathsf{let}\ r_3 = r_3 + r_2\ \mathsf{in} & \text{generates x86 code} & \texttt{add ebx,edx} \\
\mathsf{let}\ r_3 = r_3 + r_2\ \mathsf{in} & \text{generates PowerPC code} & \texttt{add 3,3,2}
\end{array}
$$

In some cases one let-expression is split into a few instructions, e.g.

$$\text{let } r_3 = r_0 - r_2 \text{ in} \quad \text{generates x86 code}$$

```
mov ebx,eax
sub ebx,edx
```

$$\text{let } r_3 = 5000 \text{ in} \quad \text{generates ARM code}$$

```
mov r3,#19
mov r3,r3,lsl 8
add r3,r3,#136
```

The code generator was programmed to use a few assembly tricks, e.g. on x86 certain instances of addition, which would normally require two instructions (mov followed by add), can be implemented as a single load-effective-address lea:

$$\text{let } r_3 = r_0 + r_2 \text{ in} \quad \text{generates x86 code} \quad \text{lea ebx,[eax+edx]}$$

A combination of compare and branch are used to implement if-statements, e.g.

$$\text{if } r_3 = 45 \text{ then } ... \text{ else } ... \quad \text{generates ARM code}$$

```
cmp r3,#45
bne L1
```

Function returns and function calls generate branch instructions.

The compiler generates a list of assembly instructions, which is translated into machine code using off-the-shelf assemblers: Netwide Assembler nasm [1] for x86 and the GNU Assembler gas [2] for ARM and PowerPC. Note that these tools do not need to be trusted. If incorrect code is generated then the certification phase, which is to prove the correctness certificate, will fail.

2.3 Proving Correctness Theorem

The theorem certifying the correctness of the generated machine code is proved by first deriving a function f' describing the effect of the generated code, and then proving that f' is equal to the original function to be compiled. Function f' is derived using proof-producing *decompilation* [18]. This section will illustrate how decompilation is used for compilation and then explain decompilation.

Example. Given function f, which traverses r_0 steps down a linked-list in m,

$$
\begin{aligned}
f(r_0, r_1, m) = \\
&\text{if } r_0 = 0 \text{ then } (r_0, r_1, m) \text{ else} \\
&\quad \text{let } r_1 = m(r_1) \text{ in} \\
&\quad \text{let } r_0 = r_0 - 1 \text{ in} \\
&\quad\quad f(r_0, r_1, m)
\end{aligned}
$$

Code generation produces the following x86 code.

```
0:  85C0        L1:  test eax, eax
2:  7405             jz L2
4:  8B09             mov ecx,[ecx]
6:  48               dec eax
7:  EBF7             jmp L1
            L2:
```

Proof-producing decompilation is applied to the generated machine code. The decompiler takes machine code as input and produces a function f' as output,

$$f'(eax, ecx, m) =$$
$$\text{if } eax \,\&\, eax = 0 \text{ then } (eax, ecx, m) \text{ else}$$
$$\text{let } ecx = m(ecx) \text{ in}$$
$$\text{let } eax = eax - 1 \text{ in}$$
$$f'(eax, ecx, m)$$

together with a theorem (expressed as a machine-code Hoare triple [17,18]) which states that f' accurately records the update executed by the machine code. The decompiler derives f' via proof with respect to a detailed processor model written by Sarkar [6]. Here eip asserts the value of the program counter.

$$f'_{pre}(eax, ecx, m) \Rightarrow$$
$$\{\, (\mathsf{eax}, \mathsf{ecx}, \mathsf{m}) \text{ is } (eax, ecx, m) * \mathsf{eip}\ p * \mathsf{s}\,\}$$
$$p : \texttt{85C074058B0948EBF7}$$
$$\{\, (\mathsf{eax}, \mathsf{ecx}, \mathsf{m}) \text{ is } f'(eax, ecx, m) * \mathsf{eip}\ (p{+}9) * \mathsf{s}\,\}$$

The decompiler also automatically defines f'_{pre}, which is a boolean-valued function that keeps track of necessary conditions for the Hoare triple to be valid as well as side-conditions that are needed to avoid raising hardware exceptions. In this case, ecx is required to be part of the memory segment modelled by function m and the underlying model requires ecx to be word-aligned $(ecx \,\&\, 3 = 0)$, whenever $eax \,\&\, eax \neq 0$.

$$f'_{pre}(eax, ecx, m) =$$
$$\text{if } eax \,\&\, eax = 0 \text{ then } \mathit{true} \text{ else}$$
$$f'_{pre}(eax{-}1, m(ecx), m) \,\wedge\, ecx \in \mathsf{domain}\ m \,\wedge\, (ecx \,\&\, 3 = 0)$$

Next the compiler proves $f = f'$. Both f and f' are recursive functions; thus proving $f = f'$ would normally require an induction. The compiler can avoid an induction since both f and f' are defined as instances of tailrec:

$$\mathsf{tailrec}\ x = \text{if } (G\ x) \text{ then } \mathsf{tailrec}\ (F\ x) \text{ else } (D\ x)$$

The compiler proves $f = f'$ by showing that the components of the tailrec instantiation are equal, i.e. for f and f', as given above, the compiler only needs to prove the following. (f'_{pre} is not needed for these proofs.)

$$G: \qquad (\lambda(r_0, r_1, m).\ r_0 \neq 0) = (\lambda(eax, ecx, m).\ eax \,\&\, eax \neq 0)$$
$$D: \qquad (\lambda(r_0, r_1, m).\ (r_0, r_1, m)) = (\lambda(eax, ecx, m).\ (eax, ecx, m))$$
$$F: \quad (\lambda(r_0, r_1, m).\ (r_0{-}1, m(r_1), m)) = (\lambda(eax, ecx, m).\ (eax{-}1, m(ecx), m))$$

The code generation phase is programmed in such a way that the above component proofs will always be proved by an expansion of let-expressions followed by rewriting with a handful of verified rewrite rules that undo assembly tricks, e.g. $\forall w.\ w \,\&\, w = w$.

The precondition f'_{pre} is not translated, instead f_{pre} is defined to be f'_{pre}. The compiler proves the certificate of correctness by rewriting the output from the decompiler using theorems $f' = f$ and $f'_{pre} = f_{pre}$. The example results in:

$$f_{pre}(eax, ecx, m) \Rightarrow$$
$$\{ (\mathsf{eax}, \mathsf{ecx}, \mathsf{m}) \text{ is } (eax, ecx, m) * \mathsf{eip}\ p * \mathsf{s} \}$$
$$p : \mathtt{85C074058B0948EBF7}$$
$$\{ (\mathsf{eax}, \mathsf{ecx}, \mathsf{m}) \text{ is } f(eax, ecx, m) * \mathsf{eip}\ (p{+}9) * \mathsf{s} \}$$

Decompilation. The proof-producing decompilation, which was used above, is explained in detail in [18]. However, a brief outline will be given here.

Decompilation starts by composing together Hoare triples for machine instructions to produce Hoare triples describing one pass through the code. For the above x86 code, successive compositions collapse Hoare triples of the individual instructions into two triples, one for the case when the conditional branch is taken and one for the case when it is not.

$$eax\ \&\ eax = 0 \Rightarrow$$
$$\{ (\mathsf{eax}, \mathsf{ecx}, \mathsf{m}) \text{ is } (eax, ecx, m) * \mathsf{eip}\ p * \mathsf{s} \}$$
$$p : \mathtt{85C074058B0948EBF7}$$
$$\{ (\mathsf{eax}, \mathsf{ecx}, \mathsf{m}) \text{ is } (eax, ecx, m) * \mathsf{eip}\ (p{+}9) * \mathsf{s} \}$$

$$eax\ \&\ eax \neq 0 \ \wedge\ ecx \in \mathsf{domain}\ m\ \wedge\ (ecx\ \&\ 3 = 0) \Rightarrow$$
$$\{ (\mathsf{eax}, \mathsf{ecx}, \mathsf{m}) \text{ is } (eax, ecx, m) * \mathsf{eip}\ p * \mathsf{s} \}$$
$$p : \mathtt{85C074058B0948EBF7}$$
$$\{ (\mathsf{eax}, \mathsf{ecx}, \mathsf{m}) \text{ is } (eax{-}1, m(ecx), m) * \mathsf{eip}\ p * \mathsf{s} \}$$

Using these one-pass theorems, the decompiler instantiates the following loop rule to produce function f' and the certificate theorem. If F describes a looping pass, and D is a pass that exits the loop, then $\mathsf{tailrec}\ x$ is the result of the loop:

$$\forall \mathsf{res}\ \mathsf{res'}\ c.\ \ (\forall x.\ P\ x \wedge G\ x \Rightarrow \{\mathsf{res}\ x\}\ c\ \{\mathsf{res}\ (F\ x)\}) \wedge$$
$$(\forall x.\ P\ x \wedge \neg(G\ x) \Rightarrow \{\mathsf{res}\ x\}\ c\ \{\mathsf{res'}\ (D\ x)\}) \Rightarrow$$
$$(\forall x.\ \mathsf{pre}\ x \Rightarrow \{\mathsf{res}\ x\}\ c\ \{\mathsf{res'}\ (\mathsf{tailrec}\ x)\})$$

Here pre is the recursive function which records the side-conditions that need to be met (e.g. in this case P is used to record that ecx needs to be aligned).

$$\mathsf{pre}\ x = P\ x \wedge (G\ x \Rightarrow \mathsf{pre}\ (F\ x))$$

For the above one-pass Hoare triples to fit the loop rule, the decompiler instantiates G, F, D, P, res and $\mathsf{res'}$ as follows:

$$G = \lambda(eax, ecx, m).\ (eax\ \&\ eax \neq 0)$$
$$F = \lambda(eax, ecx, m).\ (eax{-}1, m(ecx), m)$$
$$D = \lambda(eax, ecx, m).\ (eax, ecx, m)$$
$$P = \lambda(eax, ecx, m).\ (eax\ \&\ eax \neq 0) \Rightarrow ecx \in \mathsf{domain}\ m \wedge (ecx\ \&\ 3 = 0)$$
$$\mathsf{res} = \lambda(eax, ecx, m).\ (\mathsf{eax}, \mathsf{ecx}, \mathsf{m}) \text{ is } (eax, ecx, m) * \mathsf{eip}\ p * \mathsf{s}$$
$$\mathsf{res'} = \lambda(eax, ecx, m).\ (\mathsf{eax}, \mathsf{ecx}, \mathsf{m}) \text{ is } (eax, ecx, m) * \mathsf{eip}\ (p{+}9) * \mathsf{s}$$

3   Extensions, Stacks and Subroutines

The examples above illustrated the algorithm of the compiler based on simple examples involving only registers and direct memory accesses. This section describes how the compiler supports user-defined extensions, stack operations and subroutine calls.

3.1   User-Defined Extensions

The compiler has a restrictive input language. User-defined extensions to this input language are thus vital in order to be able to make use of the features specific to each target language.

  User-defined extensions to the input language are made possible by the proof method which derives a function f' describing the effect of the generated code: function f' is constructed by composing together Hoare triples describing parts of the generated code. By default, automatically derived Hoare triples for each individual machine instruction are used. However, the user can instead supply the proof method with alternative Hoare triples in order to build on previously proved theorems.

  An example will illustrate how this observation works in practice. Given the following Hoare triple (proved in Section 1) which shows that ARM code has been shown to implement "r_1 is assigned $r_1 \bmod 10$",

$$\{\text{r1 } r_1 * \text{pc } p * \text{s}\} \ \ p : \text{E351000A, 2241100A, 2AFFFFFC} \ \ \{\text{r1 } (r_1 \bmod 10) * \text{pc } (p{+}12) * \text{s}\}$$

the code generator expands its input language for ARM with the following line:

$$rhs \ ::= \ \text{let } r_1 = r_1 \bmod 10 \text{ in } rhs$$

Now when a function f is to be compiled which uses this feature,

$$
\begin{aligned}
f(r_1, r_2, r_3) = \ &\text{let } r_1 = r_1 + r_2 \text{ in} \\
&\text{let } r_1 = r_1 + r_3 \text{ in} \\
&\text{let } r_1 = r_1 \bmod 10 \text{ in} \\
&r_1
\end{aligned}
$$

the code generator implements "let $r_1 = r_1 \bmod 10$ in" using the machine code (underlined below) found inside the Hoare triple. The other instructions are E0811002 for add r1,r1,r2 and E0811003 for add r1,r1,r3.

E0811002 E0811003 <u>E351000A 2241100A 2AFFFFFC</u>

The compiler would now normally derive f' by composing Hoare triples for the individual machine instructions, but in this case the compiler considers the underlined code as a 'single instruction' whose effect is described by the supplied Hoare triple. It composes the following Hoare triples, in order to derive a Hoare triple for the entire code.

$$\{\text{r1 } r_1 * \text{r2 } r_2 * \text{pc } p\} \ \ p : \text{E0811002} \ \ \{\text{r1 } (r_1{+}r_2) * \text{r2 } r_2 * \text{pc } (p{+}4)\}$$

$$\{r1\ r_1 * r3\ r_3 * pc\ p\}\quad p : \text{E0811003}\quad \{r1\ (r_1{+}r_3) * r3\ r_3 * pc\ (p{+}4)\}$$

$$\{r1\ r_1 * pc\ p * s\}\quad p : \text{E351000A, 2241100A, 2AFFFFFC}\quad \{r1\ (r_1 \bmod 10) * pc\ (p{+}12) * s\}$$

The resulting f' is trivially equal to f and thus the resulting Hoare triple states that the generated code actually executes f.

$$\{r1\ r_1 * r2\ r_2 * r3\ r_3 * pc\ p * s\}$$
$$p : \text{E0811002, E0811003, E351000A, 2241100A, 2AFFFFFC}$$
$$\{r1\ f(r_1, r_2, r_3) * r2\ r_2 * r3\ r_3 * pc\ (p{+}20) * s\}$$

It is important to note that the Hoare triples supplied to the compiler need not concern registers or memory locations, instead more abstract Hoare triples can be supplied. For example, in Section 5, the compiler is given Hoare triples that show how basic operations over LISP s-expressions can be performed. The LISP operation car is implemented by ARM instruction E5933000. Here s-expressions are defined as a data-type with type-constructors Dot (pairs), Num (numbers) and Sym (symbols). Details are given in Section 5.

$$(\exists x\ y.\ v_1 = \text{Dot}\ x\ y)\ \Rightarrow$$
$$\{\ \text{lisp}\ (a, l)\ (v_1, v_2, v_3, v_4, v_5, v_6) * pc\ p\ \}$$
$$p : \text{E5933000}$$
$$\{\ \text{lisp}\ (a, l)\ (\text{car}\ v_1, v_2, v_3, v_4, v_5, v_6) * pc\ (p + 4)\ \}$$

The above specification extends the ARM code generator to handle assignments of car v_1 to s-expression variable v_1.

$$rhs\ ::=\ \text{let}\ v_1 = \text{car}\ v_1\ \text{in}\ rhs$$

3.2   Stack Usage

The stack can be used by assignments to and from variables s_0, s_1, s_2 etc., e.g. the following let-expressions correspond to machine code which loads register 1 from stack location 3 (three down from top of stack), adds 78 to register 1 and then stores the result in stack location 2.

$$f(r_1, s_2, s_3) = \text{let}\ r_1 = s_3\ \text{in}$$
$$\text{let}\ r_1 = r_1 + 78\ \text{in}$$
$$\text{let}\ s_2 = r_1\ \text{in}$$
$$(r_1, s_2, s_3)$$

Internally stack accesses are implemented by supplying the decompiler with specifications which specify stack locations using M-assertions (defined formally in [17], informally $M\ x\ y$ asserts that memory location x holds value y), e.g. the following is the specification used for reading the value of stack location 3 into register 1. Register 13 is the stack pointer.

$$\{r1\ r_1 * r13\ sp * M(sp{+}12)\ s_3 * pc\ p\}$$
$$p : \text{E59D100C}$$
$$\{r1\ s_3 * r13\ sp * M(sp{+}12)\ s_3 * pc\ (p{+}4)\}$$

The postcondition for the certification theorem proved for the above function f:

$$\{\ (r1, M(sp{+}8), M(sp{+}12))\ \text{is}\ f(r_1, s_2, s_3) * r13\ sp * pc\ (p{+}12)\ \}$$

3.3   Subroutines and Procedures

Subroutines can be in-lined or called as procedures. Each compilation adds a new let-expression into the input languages of the compiler. The added let-expressions describe the compiled code, i.e. they allow subsequent compilations to use the previously compiled code. For example, when the following function (which uses f from above) is compiled, the code for f will be in-lined as in Section 3.1.

$$g(r_1, r_2, s_2, s_3) = \text{let } (r_1, s_2, s_3) = f(r_1, s_2, s_3) \text{ in}$$
$$\text{let } s_2 = r_1 \text{ in}$$
$$(r_1, r_2, s_2, s_3)$$

Note that for simplicity, function calls must match the variable names used when compiling the called function was compiled, e.g. a function compiled as '$k(r_1) = ...$' cannot be called as 'let $r_2 = k(r_2)$ in' since the input is passed to code implementing k in register 1 not in register 2.

   If the compiler had been asked to compile f as a procedure, then the numbering of stack variables needs to be shifted for calls to f. Compiling f as a procedure sandwiches the code for f between a push and pop instruction that keep track of the procedure's return address. When f accesses stack locations 2 and 3 (counting in pop-order), these are for caller g locations 1 and 2.

$$g(r_1, r_2, s_1, s_2) = \text{let } (r_1, s_1, s_2) = f(r_1, s_1, s_2) \text{ in}$$
$$\text{let } s_2 = r_1 \text{ in}$$
$$(r_1, r_2, s_1, s_2)$$

4   Optimising Transformations

Given a function f, the compiler generates code, which it decompiles to produce function f' describing the behaviour of the generated code. The code generation phase can perform any optimisations as long as the certification phase can eventually prove $f = f'$. In particular, certain instructions can be reordered or removed, and the code's control flow can use special features of the target language.

4.1   Instruction Reordering

Instruction reordering is a standard optimisation applied in order to avoid unnecessary pipeline stalls. The compiler presented here supports instruction reordering as is illustrated by the following example. Given a function f which stores r_1 into stack location s_5, then loads r_2 from stack location s_6, and finally adds r_1 and r_2.

$$f(r_1, r_2, s_5, s_6) = \text{let } s_5 = r_1 \text{ in}$$
$$\text{let } r_2 = s_6 \text{ in}$$
$$\text{let } r_1 = r_1 + r_2 \text{ in}$$
$$(r_1, r_2, s_5, s_6)$$

The code corresponding directly to f might cause a pipeline stall as the result of the load instruction (let $r_2 = s_6$ in) may not be available on time for the add instruction (let $r_1 = r_1 + r_2$ in). It is therefore beneficial to schedule the load instructions as early as possible; the generated code reduces the risk of a pipeline stall by placing the load instruction before the store instruction:

$$f'(r_1, r_2, s_5, s_6) = \mathsf{let}\ r_2 = s_6\ \mathsf{in}$$
$$\mathsf{let}\ s_5 = r_1\ \mathsf{in}$$
$$\mathsf{let}\ r_1 = r_1 + r_2\ \mathsf{in}$$
$$(r_1, r_2, s_5, s_6)$$

Valid reorderings of instructions are unnoticeable after expansion of let-expressions, thus the proof of $f = f'$ does not need to be smarter to handle this optimisation.

4.2   Removal of Dead Code

Live-variable analysis can be applied to the code in order to remove unused or *dead code*. In the following definition of f, the first let-expression is unnecessary.

$$f(r_1, r_2, s_5, s_6) = \mathsf{let}\ r_1 = s_5\ \mathsf{in}$$
$$\mathsf{let}\ r_2 = s_6\ \mathsf{in}$$
$$\mathsf{let}\ r_1 = r_2 + 8\ \mathsf{in}$$
$$(r_1, r_2, s_5, s_6)$$

The generated code ignores the first let-expression and produces a function f' which is, after expansion of let-expressions, identical to f.

4.3   Conditional Execution

ARM machine code allows conditional execution of nearly all instructions in order to allow short forward jumps to be replaced by conditionally executed instructions (this reduces branch overhead). The compiler produces conditionally-executed instruction blocks where short forward jumps would otherwise have been generated. The functions decompiled from conditionally executed instructions are indistinguishable from those decompiled from code with normal jumps (as can be seen in the examples of Section 1 and 4.4).

x86 supports conditional assignment using the conditional-move instruction cmov. For x86, the compiler replaces jumps across register-register moves by conditional-move instructions.

4.4   Shared Tails

The compiler's input language supports if-statements that split control, but does not provide direct means for joining control-flow. For example, consider

```
(if r1 = 0 then r2 := 23 else r2 := 56); r1 := 4
```

which can be defined either directly as function f with 'shared tails'

$$f(r_1, r_2) = \text{if } r_1 = 0 \text{ then let } r_2 = 23 \text{ in let } r_1 = 4 \text{ in } (r_1, r_2)$$
$$\text{else let } r_2 = 56 \text{ in let } r_1 = 4 \text{ in } (r_1, r_2)$$

or as function g with auxiliary function g_2 compiled to be in-lined:

$$g(r_1, r_2) \ = \text{let } (r_1, r_2) = g_2(r_1, r_2) \text{ in let } r_1 = 4 \text{ in } (r_1, r_2)$$

$$g_2(r_1, r_2) = \text{if } r_1 = 0 \text{ then let } r_2 = 23 \text{ in } (r_1, r_2)$$
$$\text{else let } r_2 = 56 \text{ in } (r_1, r_2)$$

Generating code naively for f would result in two instructions for let $r_1 = 4$ in, one for each branch. The compiler implements an optimisation which detects 'shared tails' so that the code for f will be identical to that produced for g. The compiler generates the following ARM code for function g (using conditional execution to avoid inserting short jumps).

```
 0:   E3510000        cmp r1,#0
 4:   03A02017        moveq r2,#23
 8:   13A02038        movne r2,#56
12:   E3A01004        mov r1,#4
```

5   Compilation Example: Verified LISP Interpreter

The following example shows how one can utilise extensions to the input language. A verified interpreter for a LISP-like language is constructed using compilation. Details of the following section will be published as a separate paper.

The LISP interpreter constructed here operates over a simple date-type of s-expressions: Dot x y is a pair, Num n is a number n, and Sym s is a symbol s, in HOL4, s has type string. Basic operations are defined as follows:

$$\text{car } (\text{Dot } x \ y) \ = \ x$$
$$\text{cdr } (\text{Dot } x \ y) \ = \ y$$
$$\text{cons } x \ y \ = \ \text{Dot } x \ y$$

$$\text{plus } (\text{Num } m) \ (\text{Num } n) \ = \ \text{Num } (m + n)$$
$$\text{minus } (\text{Num } m) \ (\text{Num } n) \ = \ \text{Num } (m - n)$$

$$\text{size } (\text{Num } w) \ = \ 0$$
$$\text{size } (\text{Sym } s) \ = \ 0$$
$$\text{size } (\text{Dot } x \ y) \ = \ 1 + \text{size } x + \text{size } y$$

$$\cdots$$

A new resource assertion lisp is defined which relates LISP objects to concrete memory representations: lisp (a, l) $(v_1, v_2, v_3, v_4, v_5, v_6)$ states that a heap is located at address a, has capacity l, and that s-expressions v_1, v_2, v_3, v_4, v_5, v_6 are stored in this heap. The definition of lisp is omitted in this presentation.

Machine code for basic operations has been proved (in various ways using decompilation and compilation) to implement basic assertions, e.g. ARM code for storing car v_1 into v_1:

$$(\exists x\ y.\ v_1 = \mathsf{Dot}\ x\ y)\ \Rightarrow$$
$$\{\ \mathsf{lisp}\ (a, l)\ (v_1, v_2, v_3, v_4, v_5, v_6) * \mathsf{pc}\ p\ \}$$
$$p : \mathsf{E5933000}$$
$$\{\ \mathsf{lisp}\ (a, l)\ ((\mathsf{car}\ v_1), v_2, v_3, v_4, v_5, v_6) * \mathsf{pc}\ (p + 4)\ \}$$

A memory allocator with a built-in copying garbage collector (a Cheney garbage collector [4]) is used to implement creation of a new pair $\mathsf{Dot}\ v_1\ v_2$. The precondition of this operation requires the heap to have enough space to accommodate a new cons-cell.

$$(\mathsf{size}\ v_1 + \mathsf{size}\ v_2 + \mathsf{size}\ v_3 + \mathsf{size}\ v_4 + \mathsf{size}\ v_5 + \mathsf{size}\ v_6) < l\ \Rightarrow$$
$$\{\ \mathsf{lisp}\ (a, l)\ (v_1, v_2, v_3, v_4, v_5, v_6) * \mathsf{s} * \mathsf{pc}\ p\ \}$$
$$p : \dots \text{ the allocator code } \dots$$
$$\{\ \mathsf{lisp}\ (a, l)\ ((\mathsf{cons}\ v_1\ v_2), v_2, v_3, v_4, v_5, v_6) * \mathsf{s} * \mathsf{pc}\ (p + 328)\ \}$$

When the above specifications are supplied to the compiler it knows what machine code to generate for two new commands: one for calculating car of v_1 and one for storing cons $v_1\ v_2$ into v_1:

$$\mathsf{let}\ v_1 = \mathsf{car}\ v_1\ \mathsf{in} \qquad \mathsf{let}\ v_1 = \mathsf{cons}\ v_1\ v_2\ \mathsf{in}$$

Once the compilers language had been extended with sufficiently many such primitive operations, a LISP interpreter was compiled using our proof-producing compiler. The top-level specification function defining a simple LISP interpreter *lisp_eval* is listed in Figure 1. When *lisp_eval* is compiled, code is generated and a theorem is proved which state that this LISP interpreter is implemented by the generated machine code, in this case ARM code.

$$lisp\_eval\_pre(v_1, v_2, v_3, v_4, v_5, v_6, l)\ \Rightarrow$$
$$\{\ \mathsf{lisp}\ (a, l)\ (v_1, v_2, v_3, v_4, v_5, v_6) * \mathsf{s} * \mathsf{pc}\ p\ \}$$
$$p : \dots \text{ the generated code } \dots$$
$$\{\ \mathsf{lisp}\ (a, l)\ (lisp\_eval(v_1, v_2, v_3, v_4, v_5, v_6, l)) * \mathsf{s} * \mathsf{pc}\ (p + 3012)\ \}$$

Here *lisp_eval_pre* has collected the various side-conditions that need to be true for proper execution of the code.

6   Summary and Discussion of Related Work

This paper has described how an extensible proof-producing compiler can be implemented using decompilation into logic [18]. The implementation required only a light-weight certification phase (approximately 100 lines of ML code) to be programmed, but still proves functional equivalence between the source and target programs. In contrast to previous work [8,12,13,14], correctness proofs are here separated from code generation.

```
TASK_EVAL = Sym "nil"
TASK_CONT = Sym "t"

lisp_lookup (v1,v2,v3,v4,v5,v6) = ...
lisp_eval0 (v1,v2,v3,v4,v5,v6,l) = ...
lisp_eval1 (v1,v2,v3,v4,v5,v6,l) = ...

lisp_eval (v1,v2,v3,v4,v5,v6,l) =
  if v2 = TASK_EVAL then
    let v2 = TASK_CONT in
      if isSym v1 then (* exp is Sym *)
        let (v1,v2,v3,v4,v5,v6) = lisp_lookup (v1,v2,v3,v4,v5,v6) in
          lisp_eval (v1,v2,v3,v4,v5,v6,l)
      else if isDot v1 then (* exp is Dot *)
        let v2 = CAR v1 in
        let v1 = CDR v1 in
        let (v1,v2,v3,v4,v5,v6,l) = lisp_eval0 (v1,v2,v3,v4,v5,v6,l) in
          lisp_eval (v1,v2,v3,v4,v5,v6,l)
      else (* exp is Num *)
        lisp_eval (v1,v2,v3,v4,v5,v6,l)
  else (* if v2 = TASK_CONT then *)
    if v6 = Sym "nil" then (* evaluation complete *)
      (v1,v2,v3,v4,v5,v6)
    else (* something is still on the to-do list v6 *)
      let (v1,v2,v3,v4,v5,v6,l) = lisp_eval1 (v1,v2,v3,v4,v5,v6,l) in
        lisp_eval (v1,v2,v3,v4,v5,v6,l)
```

Fig. 1. The top-level definition of *lisp_eval* in HOL4

For each run, the compiler generates code and then proves that the code is correct. This is an idea for which Pnueli et al. [20] coined the term *translation valida-tion*. There are two basic approaches to translation validation: (1) code generation is instrumented to generate proofs, and (2) code generation proceeds as usual then the certification phase attempts to guess the proofs. Approach 1 is generally considered more feasible [21]. However, Necula [19] showed that approach 2 is feasible even for aggressively optimising compilers such as GNU gcc [2]. Necula built into his certification phase heuristics that attempt to guess which optimisations were performed. The compiler presented here also implements approach 2, but restricts the (initial) input language and the optimisations to such an extent that the cer-tification phase does not need any guesswork.

An alternative to producing a proof for each run is to prove the compiler correct. A recent, particularly impressive, milestone in compiler verification was achieved by Leroy [11], who proved the correctness of an optimising compiler which takes a significant subset of C as input and produces PowerPC assembly code[2] as output. As part of this project Tristan and Leroy [22] verified multiple

---

[2] The work presented here builds on Leroy's specification of PowerPC assembly code.

translation validators. Other recent work is [10,15,11,3,5]. We chose not to verify our compiler/translation validator, since our compiler constructs all of its proofs in the HOL4 theorem prover. The trusted computing base (TCB) of our compiler is HOL4 and the specifications of the target machine languages. It seems that the user-defined extensions such as those in the LISP example would have been much harder to implement in a verified compiler, since verifying a compiler involves defining a deep embedding of the input language.

The VLISP project [9], which produced verified on-paper proofs for an implementation of a larger subset of LISP, is related to the example above of constructing a verified LISP interpreter. The fact that the proof presented here is mechanised and goes down to detailed models of commercial machine languages distinguishes this work from the VLISP project which stopped at the level of verified algorithms.

Acknowledgements. We thank Anthony Fox, Xavier Leroy and Susmit Sarkar for allowing us to use their processor models for this work. We also thank Thomas Tuerk, Aaron Coble and the anonymous reviewers for comments on earlier drafts. The first author is grateful for funding from EPSRC, UK.

References

1. The Netwide Assembler, http://www.nasm.us/
2. The GNU Project. GCC, the GNU Compiler Collection, http://gcc.gnu.org/
3. Benton, N., Zarfaty, U.: Formalizing and verifying semantic type soundness of a simple compiler. In: Leuschel, M., Podelski, A. (eds.) Principles and Practice of Declarative Programming (PPDP), pp. 1–12. ACM, New York (2007)
4. Cheney, C.J.: A non-recursive list compacting algorithm. Commun. ACM 13(11), 677–678 (1970)
5. Chlipala, A.J.: A certified type-preserving compiler from lambda calculus to assembly language. In: Programming Language Design and Implementation (PLDI), pp. 54–65. ACM, New York (2007)
6. Crary, K., Sarkar, S.: Foundational certified code in a metalogical framework. Technical Report CMU-CS-03-108, Carnegie Mellon University (2003)
7. Fox, A.: Formal specification and verification of ARM6. In: Basin, D., Wolff, B. (eds.) TPHOLs 2003. LNCS, vol. 2758, pp. 25–40. Springer, Heidelberg (2003)
8. Gordon, M., Iyoda, J., Owens, S., Slind, K.: Automatic formal synthesis of hardware from higher order logic. Electr. Notes Theor. Comput. Sci. 145, 27–43 (2006)
9. Guttman, J., Ramsdell, J., Wand, M.: VLISP: A verified implementation of scheme. Lisp and Symbolic Computation 8(1/2), 5–32 (1995)
10. Klein, G., Nipkow, T.: A machine-checked model for a Java-like language, virtual machine, and compiler. ACM Trans. Program. Lang. Syst. 28(4), 619–695 (2006)
11. Leroy, X.: Formal certification of a compiler back-end, or: programming a compiler with a proof assistant. In: Principles of Programming Languages (POPL), pp. 42–54. ACM Press, New York (2006)
12. Li, G.-D., Owens, S., Slind, K.: Structure of a proof-producing compiler for a subset of higher order logic. In: De Nicola, R. (ed.) ESOP 2007. LNCS, vol. 4421, pp. 205–219. Springer, Heidelberg (2007)

13. Li, G.-D., Slind, K.: Compilation as rewriting in higher order logic. In: Pfenning, F. (ed.) CADE 2007. LNCS, vol. 4603, pp. 19–34. Springer, Heidelberg (2007)
14. Li, G., Slind, K.: Trusted source translation of a total function language. In: Ramakrishnan, C.R., Rehof, J. (eds.) TACAS 2008. LNCS, vol. 4963, pp. 471–485. Springer, Heidelberg (2008)
15. Meyer, T., Wolff, B.: Tactic-based optimized compilation of functional programs. In: Filliâtre, J.-C., Paulin-Mohring, C., Werner, B. (eds.) TYPES 2004. LNCS, vol. 3839, pp. 201–214. Springer, Heidelberg (2006)
16. Myreen, M.O., Fox, A.C.J., Gordon, M.J.C.: A Hoare logic for ARM machine code. In: Arbab, F., Sirjani, M. (eds.) FSEN 2007. LNCS, vol. 4767, pp. 272–286. Springer, Heidelberg (2007)
17. Myreen, M.O., Gordon, M.J.C.: A Hoare logic for realistically modelled machine code. In: Grumberg, O., Huth, M. (eds.) TACAS 2007. LNCS, vol. 4424, pp. 568–582. Springer, Heidelberg (2007)
18. Myreen, M.O., Slind, K., Gordon, M.J.C.: Machine-code verification for multiple architectures – An application of decompilation into logic. In: Formal Methods in Computer Aided Design (FMCAD). IEEE, Los Alamitos (2008)
19. Necula, G.C.: Translation validation for an optimizing compiler. In: Programming Language Design and Implementation (PLDI), pp. 83–94. ACM, New York (2000)
20. Pnueli, A., Siegel, M., Singerman, E.: Translation validation. In: Steffen, B. (ed.) TACAS 1998. LNCS, vol. 1384, pp. 151–166. Springer, Heidelberg (1998)
21. Rinard, M.C.: Credible compilation. In: Jähnichen, S. (ed.) CC 1999. LNCS, vol. 1575. Springer, Heidelberg (1999)
22. Tristan, J.-B., Leroy, X.: Formal verification of translation validators: a case study on instruction scheduling optimizations. In: Principles of Programming Languages (POPL), pp. 17–27. ACM, New York (2008)

From Specification to Optimisation: An Architecture for Optimisation of Java Bytecode

Richard Warburton[1] and Sara Kalvala[2]

[1] University of Warwick, Coventry, UK
R.L.M.Warburton@warwick.ac.uk
[2] University of Warwick, Coventry, UK
Sara.Kalvala@warwick.ac.uk

Abstract. We present the architecture of the Rosser toolkit that allows optimisations to be specified in a domain specific language, then compiled and deployed towards optimising object programs. The optimisers generated by Rosser exploit model checking to apply dataflow analysis to programs to find optimising opportunities. The transformational language is derived from a formal basis and consequently can be proved sound. We validate the technique by comparing the application of optimisers generated by our system against hand-written optimisations using the Java based Scimark 2.0 benchmark.

1 Introduction

An optimisation phase is an integral part of most real-world compilers, and significant effort in compiler development is spent in obtaining fast-running code. This effort must be balanced with the need to ensure that optimisations do not introduce errors into programs, and the desire to not worsen compilation time significantly. Several publications, such as [8] have described the use of domain specific languages, based on temporal logic, in order to describe optimisations. Rosser allows the application of specifications of compiler optimisations to Java Bytecode. Optimisations are matched against programs using model-checking, and graph rewriting is used to actually modify the programs.

The contributions from the design of Rosser to the design of compilers include:

- An implementation that automatically generates optimisations from specifications and can be practically used against a real world programming language.
- A novel intermediate representation of Java programs, that uses BDDs to aid in symbolic model checking.
- A method of interactively and visually rewriting the control flow graph (CFG) of Java programs using the Rosser system.
- A case-study backed analysis of the performance ramifications of using model checking for dataflow analysis compared with hand-written analysers.

O. de Moor and M. Schwartzbach (Eds.): CC 2009, LNCS 5501, pp. 17–31, 2009.

The remainder of this paper is structured as follows: we summarize the TRANS language, discuss the design of Rosser, provide a brief explanation of the verification of soundness, discuss some experimental results, compare with related work, and discuss ongoing work.

2   Background and Specification Language

2.1   Specification Language Overview

The design of a specification language for optimisations needs to satisfy many constraints: the optimisations should be expressed in such a way that they are easy to understand and their correctness verified, and it should be possible to clearly express the conditions in which the optimisations apply.

In the TRANS language [7], the optimisations are represented through two components: a rewrite rule and a side condition which indicates the situations in which the rewrite can be applied safely. The specification of dead code elimination is shown in Fig. 1. Other optimisations specified in TRANS include lazy code motion, constant propagation, strength reduction, branch elimination, skip elimination, loop fusion, and lazy strength reduction; further details of these can be found in [4].

$$n : x := e \;\Rightarrow\; skip$$
$$\mathtt{if} \;\neg\, \mathtt{EX} \;(\mathtt{E}\;(\;\neg\, \mathtt{def(x)}\; \mathtt{U}\; \mathtt{use(x)} \wedge \neg\, \mathtt{node(n)}\;))\; @\; n$$

Fig. 1. Dead Code Elimination in TRANS

In order to use this language towards optimisation of Java programs, we replaced the original syntax for program fragments with code in Jimple, one of the intermediate representations used in Soot [18]. As such, the core of the rewrite rules is based on standard programming syntax (assignment statements, go-to and if statements, etc) and will therefore not be explained here. The syntax is expanded with a few constructs to support meta-variables, representing either syntactic fragments of the program or nodes of the CFG.

The side condition language is an extension of first order CTL, where formulae are built up from basic predicates that describe properties of states. There are two types of these basic predicates used to obtain information about a node in the control flow graph; these are the *node* and *stmt* predicates. The formula $node(x)$ will hold at a node n in a valuation that maps n to x. The formula $stmt(s)$ will hold at a node n where the valuation makes the pattern s match the statement at node n. As well as judgements about states the language can make "global" judgements. For example, the formula $\phi @ n \wedge conlit(c)$ states that ϕ holds at n and c is a constant literal, throughout the program.

A logical judgement of the form: $\phi @ n$ states that the formula ϕ is *satisfied* at node n of the control flow graph. We base our language for expressing conditions on CTL [3], a path-based logic which can express many optimisations while still being efficient to model-check. However, we modify the logic slightly to make it easier to express properties of programs: we include past temporal operators ($\overleftarrow{E}$ and $\overleftarrow{A}$) and extend the next state operators (EX and AX) so that one can specify what kind of edge they operate over. For example, the operators EX_{seq} and AX_{branch} stand for "there exists a next state via a *seq* edge" and "for all next states reached via a *branch* edge" respectively.

It is also possible to make use of user defined predicates via a simple macro system. These can be used in the same way as core language predicates such as *use*. They are defined by an equality between a named binding and the temporal logic condition that the predicate should be 'expanded' into.

Actions. A simple rewrite merely replaces the code at one node with new code; however, most optimisations must actually change the structure of CFGs. These structural changes are supported by four types of action: the *replace* action which replaces a node with some sequence of nodes, the *remove_edge* and *add_edge* actions which add and remove edges respectively and the *split_edge* action which inserts a node between two other nodes joined by an edge. All the actions maintain the invariant that if the *Dimple* representation can generate Jimple before the action has been performed, then it must do afterwards. This motivates the choice of several specific actions, rather than unrestricted graph rewriting.

Strategies. The TRANS language contains three strategies, that offer operators for combining different transformation. The MATCH ϕ *IN* T strategy restricts the domain of information in the transformation T by the condition ϕ. The T_1 THEN T_2 strategy applies the sequential composition of T_1 and T_2. When actions are applied normally, ambiguity with respect to what node actions and rewrites are applied to are automatically resolved. In other words, if there are several bindings that have the same value for a Node attribute that is being used in a rewrite rule then only one of them is non-deterministically selected. The APPLY_ALL T strategy uses all of the valuations within transformation T, without this restriction.

2.2   Implementation Background

Since side conditions in TRANS specifications use temporal logic, a model checking based approach is used to obtain the results of the analyses. The use of Binary Decision Diagrams (BDDs), in both model-checking and data-flow analysis applications, has significantly reduced memory consumption [12], and improved runtime performance.

To facilitate the use of a BDD representation of object programs, Rosser generates code in Jedd, an extension to Java that allows a high level representation of BDDs [11]. Relations are introduced as a primitive type within Jedd, and several operations, such as union, intersection, difference and comparison are defined over them. BDDs can be directly coded as relations. Jedd has been used as the basis for implementing inter-procedural data flow analysis [2]. The operators of Jedd are summarised in Table 1.

Table 1. Jedd operations

Operation	Comment
$x = 0B$	Assigns the empty set to relation x
$x = 1B$	Assigns the set of all possible elements to relation x
$(x =>) \, r$	projects attribute x away from relation r
$(x => y) \, r$	renames attribute x, from relation r to y
$(x => x \, y) \, r$	copies attribute x, from relation r to y
$r1 \, \& \, r2$	Intersection of relations $r1$ and $r2$
$r1 \mid r2$	Union of relations $r1$ and $r2$
$r1 - r2$	Set Difference of relations $r1$ and $r2$
$r1\{x\} >< r2\{y\}$	Joins relations $r1$ and $r2$ where x equals y, projecting y
$r1\{x\} <> r2\{y\}$	Joins relations $r1$ and $r2$ where x equals y, projecting x and y

3 Architecture of Rosser

3.1 Architectural Overview

The Rosser compiler framework comprises three components. A meta-compiler, RosserC, translates TRANS specifications to produce the code for the optimising phase. Every optimisation specification is compiled into the general form of finding satisfying valuations for its side condition, by application of its side condition to the intermediate representation. The program generated (referred to as RosserS) is loaded into the runtime framework and applied to a program via the Soot framework.

Soot provides the program already translated into Jimple, where expressions are represented as trees, at a Java-like level, and control flow at a lower level utilising basic conditionals and goto statements [17]. We introduce *Dimple*—a representation equivalent to Jimple in overall structure, but using BDDs instead of Plain Old Java Objects (POJOs) in order to implement the optimisations. *Dimple* represents the relations between parents and children as Jimple expression trees. The translation between Jimple and *Dimple* is done through the RosserF framework. Only parts of the program that are relevant to the optimisations are translated, since only some components of the program need to be pattern-matched. For example since we specify no inter-procedural optimisations there is no representation of the class hierachy in our implementation.

These interactions are illustrated in Fig. 2.

3.2 Representation of Programs in *Dimple*

The *Dimple* representation introduced in this paper offers a novel approach to the intermediate representation of programs. Whilst BDDs have been used as the basis of representing sets of data during dataflow analysis [2], they haven't been used to represent entire programs before.

The type system of *Dimple* is described through several domains:

OP consists of all operators represented in Jimple, for example addition, and negation.

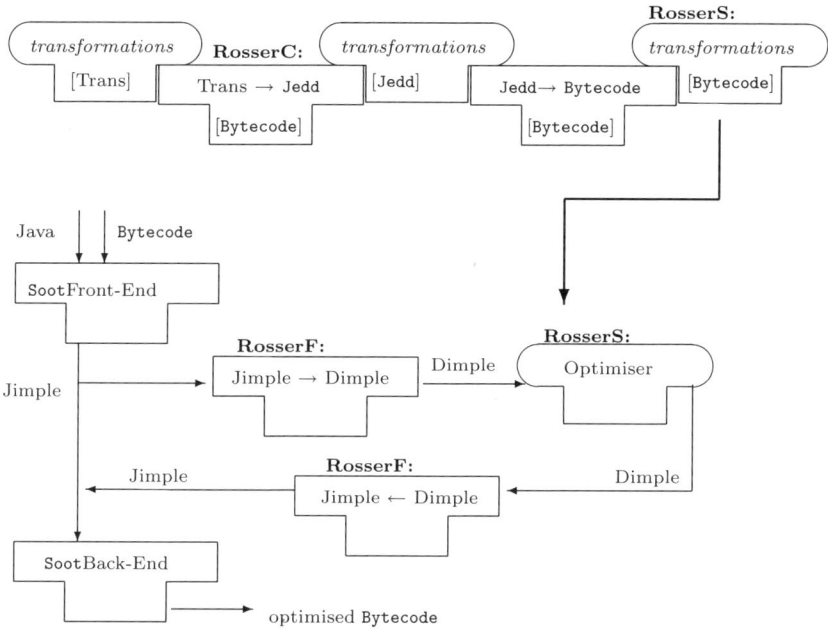

Fig. 2. Architecture of the Rosser framework

ET is the edge type domain and contains three possible values: sequential, branch and exception, and is used in pattern matching different edge.

Node lists every node in the control flow graph.

Call references every method invocation.

Value contains an entry for every possible value in the program, for example the expression $x + 1$, contains and entry for x, 1 and $x + 1$.

Table 2 summarises the translation of the syntactic components of programs in `Jimple`. Recall that `use` and `def` are predicates that hold true if their argument (a variable) is read from or written into at a given node. This fragment of the translation presents the `MustDef` relation, while similar treatment applies to `MayDef`, `MayUse` and `MustUse` relations, which all store information about different use/def chains in the same format. The next section describes these relations in more detail.

3.3   Use/def Analysis

The first phase in translation is the refinement of `use` and `def` predicates. These predicates hold true at statements where the variable that they refer to is either read or written to. In `Java`, as with other programming language, it is possible for several variables to alias the same heap object. This affects `use` and `def` predicates because it requires a refinement of the semantics to *variables that alias heap objects* that are either read or written to. Since assignment may differ

Table 2. Representing programs in *Dimple*

Name	Type	Comment/Example
Nodes	⟨Node⟩	All nodes in CFG
Skips	⟨Node⟩	All Noop instructions
Edges	⟨Node,Node,ET⟩	x = 1; y = x →⟨x = 1, y = x, SEQ⟩
ReturnValues	⟨Node,Value⟩	return x; →⟨return x, x⟩
Assign	⟨Node,Value,Value⟩	y = z + 1 →⟨y = z + 1,y,z + 1⟩
IfStmt	⟨Node,Value⟩	if (x==3) →⟨if (x==3), x==3⟩
Expr	⟨Value,Value,Value,OP⟩	x + y →⟨x + y, x, y, +⟩
UExpr	⟨Value,Value,OP⟩	!x →⟨!x, x, !⟩
Conlit	⟨Value⟩	All Constants, eg ⟨1⟩
Varlit	⟨Value⟩	All Variable literals, eg ⟨x⟩
CallSites	⟨Value,Call⟩	Relation between call sites and values
MustDef	⟨Node,Value⟩	At x = 3; ⟨x = 3,x⟩

depending on what path through the program's control flow graph was taken, the aliasing relationship depends on this path.

As with traditional dataflow analyses [1], the approach taken in Rosser is to divide relationships into 'must' and 'may' forms. For example, MustUse(x) @ n, indicates that for all execution paths at node n, x is used in the computation that occurs at node n. If MayUse(x) @ n, then there exists an execution path such that, at node n, x is used in a computation. The situation is symmetric for MayDef and MustDef. TRANS specifications, however, do not use these conditional variants of the predicates and must be refined accordingly by RosserC.

In order to be a sound refinement of the predicates in TRANS it is necessary for the may/must variants to conservatively approximate their behaviour. That is to say, they must never enable an optimisation that would otherwise be disabled. In order to determine whether the predicate would enable incorrect optimisation we use the concept of *polarity*. The polarity of a predicate is positive if there is an even number of negations preceeding the predicate, and negative otherwise. If a predicate has a positive polarity then nodes where it holds true are being added to the possible points of optimisation. The converse also holds true. Since the **must** variant of a predicate holds true at a subset of nodes where the predicate holds true we refine predicates with a positive polarity to their **must** variants. The **may** variant of a predicate holds true at a superset of nodes where its predicate holds true, so we refine predicates with a negative polarity to the **may** variant.

This approach to refining use/def predicates means that specifications written in the TRANS language are portable over both languages that allow and disallow aliasing. This has the added advantage of facilitating prototyping of optimisations in simple contexts (for example against Local primitives, which are pass by value) and then be able to apply them in more complicated situations. This underlies one of the design principles of Rosser: to move the burden of compiler development away from the optimisation specification and into the framework.

Table 3. Temporal Logic refinements

Before	After
AG p	¬ E (true U ¬ p)
A (p U q)	¬ (E (¬ q U (¬ p ∧ ¬ q)] ∨ EG ¬ q))
AX p	¬ EX ¬ p

3.4   Refinement and Type-Checking

The CTL formulae of a specification are initially refined to a smaller set of connectives in order to simplify the output phases.

Rewrite rules are refined to a pattern matching component, which becomes part of the side condition, and a **TRANS** action. In the case of dead code elimination, this is the *replace* action, which swaps an existing node bound to a meta-variable, inserting an IR element generated from variable bindings in its place.

RosserC also performs type checking. The goal is to statically identify the types of all the meta variables within the **TRANS** specification. This is beneficial for two reasons. Firstly the output code is statically typed, and so type checking **TRANS** formulae helps generate object code. Secondly it is helpful in order to reduce the number of accidental or transcription errors within **TRANS** formulae. If a meta-variable has to bind to a structure of one type in a certain place within the specification and a different type in another part, then it is clearly not a well-formed **TRANS** specification. Consider the hypothetical specification:

$$n : x := e \Rightarrow \text{skip } \textit{if } \text{conlit}(n)$$

This specification fails type checking because the metavariable n has to be a node in its use on the left hand side, and a constant literal if it is an argument to `conlit`.

Fig. 3 shows the effect of refinement on the specification of dead code elimination shown in Fig. 1. Here the pattern matching has become part of the side condition and the use/def predicates have been refined.

> *replace* n with skip
> if
>   stmt(x := e) @ n ∧ ¬ EX (E (¬ maydef (x) U mustuse (x) ∧ ¬ node(n))) @ n

Fig. 3. Refined specification of dead code elimination

3.5   Code Generation

The RosserC compiler outputs `Jedd` code, where for each optimisation a corresponding class is generated. The side condition is compiled into a method called `condition`, whose return type is a relation, with an attribute for each metavariable within the specification, its only parameter being the method to be optimised. A transformation is applied through method `transformation`, which in

```
1         <e ,n ,x ,x1 :N6>  x2  =  1B;
2         x2  =  x2{x1}  ><  meth.Nodes{n};
3         <e ,n ,x>  x3  =  meth.Assign ;
4         x2  =  x2{e ,n ,x}  ><  x3{e ,n ,x};
5         x2 &= (x1 => x1 ,x1 => n)((n => )(x2));
6         <e ,n ,x>  x4  =  (x1 => )(x2);
```

Fig. 4. Compilation of stmt(x := e) @ n

```
1         <e ,n ,x ,x6 :N7>  x7  =  1B;
2         x7  =  x7{x6 ,x}  ><  meth.MustUse{n ,x};
3         <e ,n ,x ,x6 :N8>  x8  =  1B;
4         x8 &= (x6 => x6 ,x6 => n)((n => )(x8));
5         x8  =   1B  −  x8;
6         x8  =  x7 &  x8;
```

Fig. 5. Compilation of mustuse(x) ∧ ¬ node(n)

turn calls the condition method and then iterates over all the values within the resulting valuation set. Generating the condition method body proceeds by recursion of the structure of the now refined TRANS side conditions.

Fig. 4 shows the compiled pattern matching for stmt(x := e) @ n from the specification of dead code elimination. First, a temporary attribute x1 is introduced into the valuation to designate the current node. This can be seen in the type of the variable x2 on line 1. Line 2 restricts this attribute to nodes. In lines 3 and 4 the variables e, n and x are restricted to the right hand side, result variable and node of assignments, respectively. Lines 5 and 6 show the temporary node being equated to n and then projected away.

The Jedd code shown in Fig. 5 illustrates predicates being compiled. Line 2 shows the restriction of mustuse to a local finite domain. In line 4 the temporary attribute x6, that fulfils the same purpose as x1 in the previous example is unified with the attribute n. Lines 3 and 4 calculate the set of valuations where the current node is n. Line 5 implements the ¬ operator, calculating valuations where the current node isn't n. Finally we take the intersection of the subcomponents, in order to satisfy the ∧ in the example. Note that literals after colons, for example N6, refer to physical domains that are used by the BDD implementation. The first letter is the same as the corresponding logical domain, for example N refers to Node. Since there may be multiple physical domains for each logical domain they are numbered.

The code generation algorithm used in Rosser generates standard imperative code, using Jedd as its object language. The return type of the condition method is a relation, containing one attribute that corresponds to a TRANS metavariable in the original specification. At every stage, intermediate variables that are generated are typed as the same type as the return type. When generating conditions for node conditions, a temporal part of the condition, there is additionally an attribute that represents the current node of the specification.

```
cs true          = [res = 1B]
cs False         = [res = 0B]
cs conlit(v)     = [t1 = 1B, res = t1{v} >< Conlit{c}]
cs varlit(v)     = [t1 = 1B, res = t1{v} >< Varlit{v}]
cs ¬ φ           = cs φ @ [res = 1B - pred]
cs φ @ n         = cs φ @ [res = (at =>) pred{n,at}
                       <> pred{at,n}]
cs φ ∧ ψ         = cs φ @ cs ψ @ [res = pred1 & pred2]
cs φ ∨ ψ         = cs φ @ cs ψ @ [res = pred1 | pred2]


ct true          = [res = 1B]
ct False         = [res = 0B]
ct node(n)       = [t1=1B, res=t1{n,at} >< t1{at,n}]
ct stmt(p)       = cp p at
ct ¬ φ           = ct φ @ [res = 1B - pred]
ct EX[e] φ       = ct φ @ [t1 = Edges{et}
                       >< new{et => e}{et}, res =
                       (to=>at) pred{at} <> t1{from} ]
ct EX φ          = ct φ @ [t1 = (et=>)Edges,
                       res = (to=>at) pred{at} <> t1{from} ]
ct E[ φ U ψ ]    = ct φ @ ct ψ @ until pred1 pred2
ct φ ∧ ψ         = ct φ @ ct ψ @ [res = pred1 & pred2]
ct φ ∨ ψ         = ct φ @ ct ψ @ [res = pred1 | pred2]
```
where the until function is defined as:

```
until pred1 pred2 = [ t1 = (et=>) Edges,
                      acc = pred2,
                      do { prev = acc;
                           t2 = (from=>) pred1{at} <> t1{to};
                           acc |= pred2 & t2
                         } while(prev != acc),
                      res = acc  ]
```

Fig. 6. Side Condition compilation

Fig. 6 describes how side conditions are compiled. The function *cs* compiles side conditions, whilst *ct* compiles the sub-expressions within side conditions that have some temporal aspect. There are a few common attributes about the way different components within the side condition introduce new temporary variables. Basic predicates, such as node(n), create new temporaries. TRANS unary operators, such as ¬, depend on the result of their inner expression, stored in a single temporary, referred to in the definition as pred, while binary operators, such as ∧ depend on two temporaries, pred1 and pred2. All expressions store the result of their component of the model checking in a variable, referred to as res in the definition. Variables called t1, t2 etc. refer to temporary variables within the object code of inner components. In the generated code, all these variables have disjoint names to each other, however, this is abstracted from the following section for reasons of readability. The function cp emits code to pattern match an expression with a sequence of nodes. Its first parameter is the pattern

```
 1 while (  _it . hasNext () ) {
 2    Object [] _val = ( Object []) _it . next ();
 3    try {
 4       Unit _x = _f . SkipPattern ();
 5       units . swapWith ((( Unit ) _val [1]) , _x );
 6       ObjNumberer . patch ((( Unit ) _val [1]) , _x );
 7    } catch ( Throwable t ) {
 8       System . err . println ( t );
 9    }
10 }
```

Fig. 7. Jedd code for the *replace* action

to match, and the second is the node to match it at. This is also ommitted from the presentation for reasons of brevity. The definition provides a mapping from TRANS IR to a list of Jedd instructions.

3.6 Action Code Generation

Fig. 7 gives the example action for code elimination, x := e => skip. In the code _it is the name of the iterator for the results set of the analysis. Line 1 shows the loop condition over this set. Line 2 shows that each element of this set is represented by an array of elements. Line 4 constructs the replacement skip instruction. Line 5 replaces the old instruction with the skip inside of Jimple. Line 6 replaces it within *Dimple* by renumbering the elements. Note that _f is a factory class for new Pattern instances.

The replacement becomes inherently simple due to the way pattern matching is refined into the side condition. Additionally to rewriting, Rosser supports the insertion and deletion of new nodes and edges. These are all implemented similarly, iterating over the elements of the finite set of valuations and replacing each element. By renumbering elements of the underlying domain that are being rewritten in simple cases such as this, rewrite rules don't need to alter the structure of the CFG at all, and thus the CFG doesn't need to be recalculated.

3.7 Interactive and Batch Mode

The RosserF runtime framework can be operated in one of two main modes: interactive or batch. The interactive mode is designed to allow the user to develop new optimisation specifications, while batch mode is a traditional compiler process that applies a list of optimisations sequentially. The interactive mode has been developed on the principle that the development of new ideas is informed by experiment. Building on this principle, interactive mode allows one to develop a specific method to apply to the program being optimised.

The interactive mode provides a *conditional* sub-view and a *transformational* sub-view. The *conditional* view provides the user with a view of the control flow graph of the selected method. The user can then enter a side condition, with which to model check the program. This then generates a set of valuations for the given program, and a visual representation of the valuations on the control flow graph. The *transformational* view allows the user to apply complete TRANS transformations to the selected method and visually see the results, in the form of before and after control flow graphs.

The ability to allow the user to test out the effectiveness of different compiler optimisations improves the productivity of developing an effective optimisation strategy. The approach of specifying optimisations by way of a domain specific language enables the user of the system to more easily apply an optimisation, than one could with a hand-written optimisation.

4   Performance Analysis

Since this approach to generating compiler optimisations involves generating compiler code indirectly from a specification, it raises questions about its practical applicability. We compare Rosser with hand-written optimisations in the mature Soot framework [17], which is arguably a very high standard against which the performance of generated optimisations can be measured.

We use the Scimark scientific computing benchmark [14] to compare the performance of optimisation phases. The performances are compared in terms of *effectiveness* (the extent to which the performance of the program being optimised is improved) and *efficiency* (how long it takes to apply a transformation to a program). The benchmarking was all performed on a 2Ghz Core 2 Duo with 2GB of RAM.

The performance of three optimisations is compared: lazy code motion, common subexpression elimination and dead code elimination. In both frameworks these optimisations are applied in this order. We chose only to compare these three optimisations since they are all commonly known compiler optimisations, and are used extensively in most compilers and therefore have a large effect on performance of compilers. We have experimented with more complex optimisations as well.

4.1   Effectiveness

The two sides of Fig. 8 show the running times of the Scimark 2.0 benchmark on two different virtual machines. The three columns for each program show runtimes without any static optimisation, optimised by Soot, and optimised by Rosser, respectively. Since the SUN JVM already incorporates many of the optimisations that are being applied, the speedup generated by Rosser is 13.5%, comparable to Soot which improves performance by 14.5%. Since the implementation demonstrates that this approach to optimisation works, rather than comparing the relative merits of ahead of time and runtime optimisation, this isn't a convincing argument against our approach to optimiser generation, as the performance of Rosser is comparable to the hand-written Soot optimisations for this benchmark. In both cases the program with best improvement is the SOR benchmark, and in both cases it is the lazy code motion optimisation that makes the impact, since the other two optimisations are performed by the SUN JVM

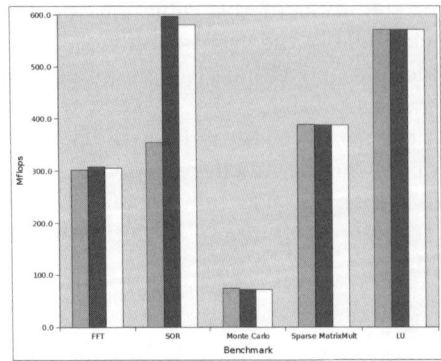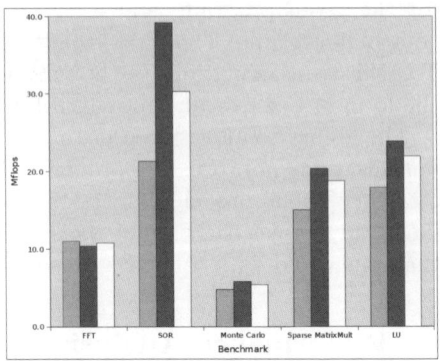

Fig. 8. Scimark 2.0 on SUN "Hotspot" JVM 1.6 and SableVM 1.13

anyway. The numbers on SableVM are more flattering to both Soot and Rosser, due to the more simplistic optimisations performed by the SableVM. Here Rosser improves performance by an average of 25%, while Soot achieves 42%. Again our generated optimisations perform slightly worse than hand-written optimisations, but offer a similar overall level of effectiveness. The Soot implementation of lazy code motion performs critical edge splitting before applying its optimisation, while Rosser doesn't. This might explain the difference in effectiveness.

4.2 Efficiency

The Soot system applied its optimisations to Scimark in 15 seconds, while Rosser took approximately 270 seconds. This does not seem very encouraging, but more detailed analysis revealed that two methods in Scimark were responsible for large amount of time used by Rosser. For the other 131 methods, the Rosser system only took 30 seconds, and the corresponding Soot time was 14 seconds. The two problematic methods weren't the largest within Scimark, and the nature of their pathology is currently unknown, and is being investigated. In most experiments the Rosser optimiser was about 2× slower than the hand-written Soot optimiser. Overall, a slowdown of a factor of two seems a reasonable price to pay considering the other benefits of the approach.

5 Related Work

Dataflow analysis has long been employed within the compiler optimisation community to iteratively compute the nodes within a program at which optimisations can be soundly applied [1,13]. Model checking is a technique in which a decision is made as to whether a given model satisfies some specification. David Schmidt and Bernhard Steffen recognised that there is a strong link between these two research areas. Equations for dataflow analyses have been shown to be expressible in Modal-Mu Calculus [15], and dataflow analysis algorithms have been generated from modal logics [16]. This approach is implemented in DFA & OPT-Metaframe [6], a toolkit designed to aid compiler construction by generating analyses and transformations from specifications. Transformations within this system are implemented imperatively, rather than using declarative style rewrite rules, however, the temporal logic specification is converted into a model checker and then optimised. In our case, we found CTL to be sufficient to model the side conditions of transformations.

Rewrite rules with temporal conditions have also been used in the Cobalt system [9] which focuses on automated provability and also provides executable specifications, achieved through temporal conditions common to many dataflow analysis approaches. This allows the basic inductive form of the correctness theorem to be proved once and for all, given sufficient optimisation specific conditions are met. The optimisation specific proof obligations can be discharged automatically, using an automatic theorem prover. The specific nature of Cobalt's temporal conditions, while facilitating automatic discharging of proof obligations, is limited compared to the flexibility provided in TRANS from supporting CTL side conditions, even if this may require more expensive model checking.

This is the main motivation for developing Rhodium [10], another domain specific language for developing compiler optimisations. Rhodium consists of local rules that manipulate dataflow facts. This is a significant departure in approach from TRANS , since it uses more traditional, data flow analysis based specifications rather than temporal side conditions.

The Temporal Transformation Logic (TTL) [5] also uses CTL, but emphasizes verification of the soundness of the transformations themselves. Accordingly, instead of approaching optimisation as rewriting, TTL has a set of transformational primitives, each representing a common element used within compiler optimisations, for example replacing an expression with a variable. Each of the transformational primitives has an associated soundness condition that, if satisfied, implies the soundness of the transformation. TTL is presented as a specification language for other compiler implementations; on the other hand, TRANS can be refined and executed as the optimisation stage of a compiler.

6   Conclusions

While programming language theorists and compiler design scholars have often proposed methods for improving trust in the optimisations applied during compilation, there is typically a gap in putting such methodologies in practice: the practitioner may devise more adventurous optimisations, which rely on a more subtle understanding of control flow for the justification of its correctness. The semantics of TRANS have been formalized within the Isabelle/HOL theorem prover, and a proof system is currently being developed to allow most of the proof obligations of verifying the soundness of new TRANS specifications to be discharged automatically.

The Rosser system described in this paper applies compiler optimisations specified formally to Java programs within standard program development environments: the optimisations are mechanically translated into running code, and applied to given object programs within the Soot environment using a simple model checker for matching side conditions of optimisations to object code.

There is of course a performance price to be paid by not programing the optimiser directly. We believe this cost is minimised by actually compiling the optimisations into Jedd rather than interpreting them, and the benefits of a declarative approach outweigh the performance cost, as sophisticated optimisations are often applied only when the code is ready for release—which is usually not a good time to find that the optimiser has introduced new bugs. The use of a formal notation has other benefits: it aids the interactive development of new optimisations and the explanation of the optimisations to third parties.

TRANS as described doesn't allow one to specify inter-procedural optimisations. Currently we are experimenting with using the inter-procedural control flow graph, with a slightly modified TRANS that matches against blocks in addition to nodes. We are also expanding the repertoire of intra-procedural optimisations, and also deal with the vexing issue of exception handling. The formal treatment of Java exceptions is an ongoing research exercise.

We have extended the work of David Lacey in several ways:

- an implementation that uses a widely used, real world, programming language by way of Java, rather than a small research prototype language.
- an algorithm that compiles, rather than interprets, TRANS specifications.
- a novel intermediate representation for programs, using BDDs.
- use of a domain specific language for output, showing how to minimise implementation effort.

A criticism that can be made to our approach is that it relies on the correctness of the translators for the domain specific languages. For example if either of the translations from Jedd to Java source or Java source to Java bytecode are incorrect, then the entire program translation/optimisation may introduce bugs, even if our specific tool doesn't introduce bugs.

Progress made by the language semantics community must be used in solving a very practical issue, namely the development of optimisation tools which do not introduce new errors into object code. The methodology presented here makes use of model-checking to enable the deployment of complex but potentially effective optimisations in a safe manner.

Acknowledgements

Richard Warburton is funded by the EPSRC under grant EP/DO32466/1 "Verification of the optimising phase of a compiler". We are grateful to the anonymous reviewers for their detailed and helpful suggestions.

References

1. Aho, A.V., Lam, M.S., Sethi, R., Ullman, J.D.: Compilers: Principles, Techniques, and Tools, 2nd edn. Pearson Education, London (2007)
2. Berndl, M., Lhoták, O., Qian, F., Hendren, L., Umanee, N.: Points-to analysis using BDDs. In: Proceedings of the ACM SIGPLAN 2003 Conference on Programming Language Design and Implementation, pp. 103–114. ACM Press, New York (2003)

3. Clarke, E.M., Emerson, E.A.: Design and synthesis of synchronization skeletons using branching-time temporal logic. In: Kozen, D. (ed.) Logic of Programs 1981. LNCS, vol. 131, pp. 52–71. Springer, Heidelberg (1982)
4. Kalvala, S., Warburton, R., Lacey, D.: Program transformations using temporal logic side conditions. Technical Report 439, Department of Computer Science, University of Warwick (2008)
5. Kanade, A., Sanyal, A., Khedker, U.: A PVS based framework for validating compiler optimizations. In: SEFM 2006: Proceedings of the Fourth IEEE International Conference on Software Engineering and Formal Methods, Washington, DC, USA, pp. 108–117. IEEE Computer Society Press, Los Alamitos (2006)
6. Klein, M., Knoop, D., Koschutzki, D., Steffen, B.: DFA & OPT-METAFrame: A toolkit for program analysis and optimization. In: Margaria, T., Steffen, B. (eds.) TACAS 1996. LNCS, vol. 1055, pp. 422–426. Springer, Heidelberg (1996)
7. Lacey, D.: Program Transformation using Temporal Logic Specifications. PhD thesis, Oxford University Computing Laboratory (2003)
8. Lacey, D., Jones, N.D., Wyk, E.V., Frederiksen, C.C.: Proving correctness of compiler optimizations by temporal logic. ACM SIGPLAN Notices 37(1), 283–294 (2002)
9. Lerner, S., Millstein, T., Chambers, C.: Automatically proving the correctness of compiler optimizations. In: Proceedings of the ACM SIGPLAN 2003 conference on Programming language design and implementation. ACM Press, New York (2003)
10. Lerner, S., Millstein, T., Rice, E., Chambers, C.: Automated soundness proofs for dataflow analyses and transformations via local rules. In: POPL 2005: Proceedings of the 32nd ACM SIGPLAN-SIGACT symposium on Principles of programming languages, pp. 364–377. ACM Press, New York (2005)
11. Lhoták, O., Hendren, L.: Jedd: A BDD-based relational extension of Java. In: Proceedings of the ACM SIGPLAN 2004 Conference on Programming Language Design and Implementation. ACM Press, New York (2004)
12. Lhoták, O., Hendren, L.: Context-sensitive points-to analysis: is it worth it? In: Mycroft, A., Zeller, A. (eds.) CC 2006. LNCS, vol. 3923, pp. 47–64. Springer, Heidelberg (2006)
13. Muchnick, S.: Advanced Compiler Design and Implementation. Morgan Kaufmann, San Francisco (1997)
14. Pozo, R., Miller, B.: Java Scimark 2.0. National Institute of Standard and Technology, http://math.nist.gov/scimark2/
15. Schmidt, D.A., Steffen, B.: Data-flow analysis as model checking of abstract interpretations. In: Levi, G. (ed.) SAS 1998. LNCS, vol. 1503. Springer, Heidelberg (1998)
16. Steffen, B.: Generating data flow analysis algorithms from modal specifications. Science of Computer Programming 21, 115–139 (1993)
17. Vallée-Rai, R., Gagnon, E., Hendren, L.J., Lam, P., Pominville, P., Sundaresan, V.: Optimizing Java bytecode using the Soot framework: Is it feasible? In: Watt, D.A. (ed.) CC 2000. LNCS, vol. 1781, pp. 18–34. Springer, Heidelberg (2000)
18. Vallée-Rai, R., Hendren, L., Sundaresan, V., Lam, P., Gagnon, E., Co, P.: Soot - a Java optimization framework. In: Proceedings of CASCON 1999, pp. 125–135 (1999)

A Framework for Exploring Optimization Properties

Min Zhao[1], Bruce R. Childers[2], and Mary Lou Soffa[3]

[1] Hewlett Packard
min.zhao@hp.com
[2] University of Pittsburgh
childers@cs.pitt.edu
[3] University of Virginia
soffa@cs.virginia.edu

Abstract. Important challenges for compiler optimization include determining what optimizations to apply, where to apply them and what is a good sequence in which to apply them. To address these challenges, an understanding of optimization properties is needed. We present a model-based framework, FOP, to determine how optimizations enable and disable one another. We combine the interaction and profitability properties to determine a "best" sequence for applying optimizations. FOP has three components: (1) a code model for the program, (2) optimization models that capture when optimizations are applicable and their actions, and (3) a resource model that expresses the hardware resources affected by optimizations. FOP determines interactions by comparing the create- and destroy-conditions of each optimization with the post conditions of other optimizations. We develop a technique with FOP to construct code-specific optimization sequences. Experimentally, we demonstrate that our approach achieves similarly good code quality as empirical techniques with less compile-time.

1 Introduction

The field of code optimization has been extremely successful over the past 40 years. Various reports from research and commercial projects indicate that the performance of software can be improved by 20% to 40% with aggressive optimization [1][2]. However, it has long been known that there are issues with the application of optimizations. First, optimizations may degrade performance in certain circumstances. For example, Briggs and Cooper reported improvements ranging from +49% to −12% for their algebraic re-association optimization [3]. Second, optimizations enable and disable other optimizations so the order of applying optimizations can have an impact on performance [1][18][21][10], which is known as the *phase ordering problem*. Finally, optimization configurations can impact the effectiveness of optimizations (e.g., how many times to unroll a loop or the tile size) [15][4][8]. These problems are compounded when different hardware platforms are considered. Due to these problems, optimizing compilers are not achieving their full potential. To systematically tackle these problems, we need to identify and study the properties of optimizations, especially those that target the application of optimizations. For example, to selectively

O. de Moor and M. Schwartzbach (Eds.): CC 2009, LNCS 5501, pp. 32–47, 2009.

apply only beneficial optimizations, we need to determine the impact of applying an optimization at a particular code point given the resources of the targeted platform (i.e., the *profitability property*). To efficiently determine a code-specific optimization sequence, we also need to detect the disabling and enabling interferences among optimizations (i.e., the *interaction property*) at code points.

There are two general approaches to exploring optimization properties. The first one uses formal techniques. The formal approach has been used to prove the soundness and correctness of optimizations [14][13][16]. Work also has been done to automatically generate the implementation of optimizations [20][21][9][12] from a formal specification. Another approach uses experimental techniques. That is, after performing optimizations, the properties are experimentally determined (e.g., the code is executed to evaluate performance for determining profitability). The empirical approach has been used to determine the correctness of an optimizer [6]. It has also been used to determine profitability and interactions for finding good optimization sequences and configurations [1][8][18][11]. A disadvantage of the experimental approach is its cost and scalability, as the execution of the program is required. It may take hours, or even days, to find a good optimization sequence for a complex program [10]. Ideally, we need a systematic way to address the application of optimizations, which is practical, effective and scalable [22].

Our approach is to develop a model-based framework that applies optimizations based on their properties which are automatically derived from models of the code, the optimizations themselves, and machine resources. These properties guide the compiler in the application of the optimizations. In prior work, we showed how to determine the profitability property from analytic models for code, optimizations and machine resources [23]. Using the models, the profitability of an optimization was determined to avoid the circumstances where an optimization can degrade performance.

This paper presents a **F**ramework for determining **O**ptimization **P**roperties, **FOP** and shows it can be used to determine the *interaction property*, caused by optimizations enabling and disabling other optimizations. We combine the interaction property with the previously studied profitability property to efficiently find a good code-specific optimization sequence. FOP includes code and optimization models. The code model, automatically constructed from the source, captures characteristics about the code related to the pre-conditions of an optimization. The optimization model, constructed by the optimizer engineer, captures the pre-conditions and actions (i.e., code changes) of optimizations. FOP also has a resource model but it is not needed to determine the interaction property.

We present an algorithm that derives the enabling and disabling interaction property for a set of optimizations. The key idea is to determine the **code changes** needed to meet the **pre-conditions** of an optimization, using the **post-conditions** of other optimizations. We also give a novel technique that automatically constructs code-specific optimization sequences using knowledge about the interaction and profitability properties at each code point. The sequences are used to guide the compiler in the actual application of optimizations.

We implemented FOP and used it to find code-specific sequences for a set of optimizations, including copy propagation(CPP), constant folding(CTF), dead code elimination(DCE), partial redundancy elimination(PRE), loop invariant code motion(LICM), global value numbering(GVN), branch elimination(BRE), branch chaining(BRC), and register allocation(RA). We compared our technique with a fixed-order approach and an empirical approach. The results show that our approach achieves better program performance than the fixed-order technique and determines similarly good sequences as the empirical approach with up to a 43 times reduction in compile-time. Our technique scales to large programs because it does not need to execute the program.

The contributions of this paper include: a formalization of optimization application and the interaction property; a framework to determine enabling and disabling interactions among optimizations; a technique to determine optimization order from the interaction and profitability properties; and, a study that demonstrates the usefulness of FOP in addressing the phase ordering problem.

2 Model-Driven Optimization

In this section, we formally define the interaction property. We start with basic definitions needed to express disabling and enabling conditions for an optimization. To apply an optimization, we must ensure that the semantics of a program are not changed by the optimization. Thus, a set of **pre-conditions** (both text and dependencies) is needed for an optimization to be applicable. When an optimization is applicable in some context, it can cause code conditions to change so that another optimization is **enabled** or **disabled**. We define how optimizations enable and disable one another. We begin with the definition of a Boolean operator ~ that returns true when the conditions D are met in a code segment C.

Def. 1: D ~ C if the code conditions D are true in code C; /~ is the negation of ~.
We express an optimization O as $[O^{Pre}, O^{Act}]$, where O^{Pre} represents the pre-conditions needed before the actions (i.e., code changes) O^{Act} are applied for semantic correctness. We express the application of an optimization as:

$$(C) [O^{Pre}, O^{Act}]_s <R> \Rightarrow (C') [O^{properties}]_s$$

where C is a code segment with a statement point, S, at which the optimization is applied. If $O^{Pre} \sim C$, the optimization is applicable. O^{Act} is applied in this case to C and C' is produced ($\Rightarrow$). R is the machine resources upon which the code segment is executed. $O^{properties}$ represents the different optimization properties that can be derived, such as interaction and profitability.

As can be seen, optimization properties depend on code context C, the optimization O and the machine resources R. We model each one of these components and use these models to analyze optimization properties; that is, $C_M \ O_M \ R_M \Rightarrow O^{properties}$ where C_M is the code model, O_M is an optimization model and R_M is the resource model (the subscript "M" refers to a model, rather than a specific optimization, code sequence or resource).

Instead of applying the optimizations, we use models to express the results of the optimizations and analyze the results to determine the properties. In addition, unlike actually applying optimizations, we do not apply a data flow algorithm after each optimization to detect data flow changes. We do this by analyzing the code model.

An example of our technique is shown in Figures 1 and 2. We give a brief discussion to motivate the definition of the interaction property. The example describes the determination of enabling interactions for copy propagation (CPP) and dead code elimination (DCE). A small source program is provided in Figure 1(a). From the source, FOP automatically generates the dependences needed for the code model as shown in Figure 1(b). A dependence is expressed as <S_i, S_j, type, dir, pos>. For example, there is a *flow* dependence between S_1 and S_2 which has equal direction for the first operand. Thus, the dependence is <S_1, S_2, flow, =, 1>. Figure 1 shows the optimization specification for DCE and CPP in (c) and (d).

We next define the enabling and disabling conditions for optimizations. Then, we present an efficient technique to compute the interaction property.

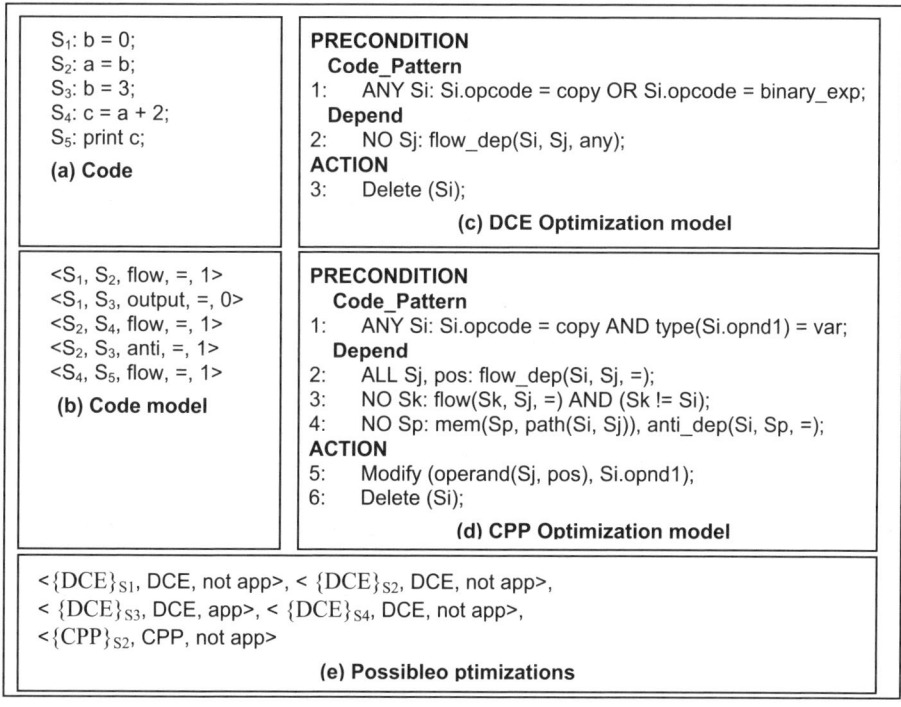

Fig. 1. An Example of Determining Interaction

Def. 2: Given a code segment, C, an optimization O_i **enables** an optimization O_k if the application of O_i creates the pre-conditions of O_k, expressed as:

$$O_i \text{ enables } O_k \text{ if } (C) \, [O_i^{Pre}, O_i^{Act}]_S \Rightarrow (C') \wedge [O_k^{Pre}] /\sim C \wedge [O_k^{Pre}] \sim C'$$

Def. 3: An optimization O_i **disables** O_k if the application of O_i destroys the pre-conditions of O_k:

$$O_i \text{ disables } O_k \text{ if } (C) \, [O_i^{Pre}, O_i^{Act}]_S \Rightarrow (C') \wedge [O_k^{Pre}] \sim C \wedge [O_k^{Pre}] /\sim C'$$

Intuitively, to determine the enabling and disabling interaction property between O_i and O_k, we need to analyze the **code changes** caused by applying O_i and the **code changes** that can **create** or **destroy** the **pre-condition** of O_k.

Def. 4: The **post-condition** of O, $[O^{Post-C}]_S$, is the set of the code changes, C_Δ, after applying O at statement S in code segment C. We use $\bullet$ to indicate the inclusion of the changes that are made to C by the optimization; that is, $C' = C \bullet C_\Delta$.

$$[O^{Post-C}]_S = \{ C_\Delta \mid (C)[O^{Act}]_S \Rightarrow C \bullet C_\Delta \}$$

We also define a set of code changes that are needed to create or destroy an opportunity for an optimization, O.

Def. 5: The **create-condition** of O, $\{[O^{Create-C}]_S\}$, is the set of code changes, C_Δ^i that make O applicable at statement S in code segment C.

$$\{[O^{Create-C}]_S\} = \{\{ C_\Delta^i \} \mid [O^{Pre}]_S /\sim C \wedge [O^{Pre}]_S \sim C \bullet C_\Delta^i \}$$

Def. 6: The **destroy-condition** of O, $\{[O^{Destroy-C}]_S\}$, is the set of code changes, C_Δ^i that make O not applicable at statement S in code segment C.

$$\{[O^{Destory-C}]_S\} = \{\{ C_\Delta^i \} \mid [O^{Pre}]_S \sim C \wedge [O^{Pre}]_S /\sim C \bullet C_\Delta^i \}$$

To detect enabling and disabling interactions, we compute the code changes that enable an optimization O_k by comparing the post-conditions of other optimizations, say O_i, against the create and destroy-conditions for O_k.

Theorem 1: An optimization O_i **enables** O_k if there exists a C_Δ^i in $\{[O_k^{Create-C}]_S\}$ such that $C_\Delta^i \subseteq [O_i^{Post-C}]_S$.

Proof: Straightforward, based on the Definitions 2 and 5.

Theorem 2: An optimization O_i **disables** O_k if exists a C_Δ^i in $\{[O_k^{Destroy-C}]_S\}$ such that $C_\Delta^i \subseteq [O_i^{Post-C}]_S$.

Proof: Based on Definitions 3 and 6.

We develop a new algorithm to determine the enabling and disabling interactions of optimizations at the per-statement level. For a statement in the program, the interaction algorithm determines how a set of optimizations interacts with one another. We now give a high-level overview of the interaction algorithm, which is discussed in detail in Section 3.3. The algorithm has three steps.

Step 1: For each $O \in O$ and each $S \in C$, compute the code changes needed to create or destroy an optimization opportunity.

Step 2: For each $O \in O$ and each $S \in C$, compute the post conditions after applying O at point S in C.

Step 3:   For each $O \in O$ and each $S \in C$, compare create- and destroy- conditions with post conditions of all optimizations to determine enabling and disabling properties.

Returning to Figures 1 and 2, when the interaction algorithm starts, it generates the specific post-, create-, and destroy- conditions for every possible optimization opportunity in the code. Figure 1e shows the possible optimizations. We show the details for two optimizations, $\{DCE\}_{S3}$ and $\{CPP\}_{S2,}$ in Figures 2(a) and (b).

$\{DCE\}_{S3}$ is a dead code elimination that operates on S_3 and is applicable. Thus, there is only one create- condition for $\{DCE\}_{S3}$ which is simply "true". There are three destroy-conditions for $\{DCE\}_{S3}$. The first one is deleting S_3. The second one is modifying S_3's operation. The third one is inserting a flow dependence that has S_3 as the source. The post-conditions for $\{DCE\}_{S3}$ show how it changes the code model, which includes deleting S_3, deleting the anti-dependence between S_2 and S_3 and deleting the output dependence between S_1 and S_3. Similarly, the create-, destroy- and post-conditions are generated for $\{CPP\}_{S2}$ from the CPP optimization model.

In the last step, the interaction algorithm compares the create- and destroy-conditions with the post-condition of other optimizations and determines the interactions. For example, there is only one condition needed for $\{CPP\}_{S2}$ to be applicable; i.e., <delete_dep, anti,S_2,S_3,=>. When the interaction algorithm checks $\{DCE\}_{S3}$'s post-conditions, it finds that $\{DCE\}_{S3}$ changes the dependency by deleting the anti-dependence between S_2 and S_3. This condition matches with the enabling expression of $\{CPP\}_{S2}$. Thus, $\{DCE\}_{S3}$ **enables** $\{CPP\}_{S2}$.

<{DCE}$_{S3}$, DCE, applicable>

  <Create-conditions, true>

  <Destroy-conditions, <delete S_3> ∨ <modify_opcode, S_3, ≠, copy/binary_arith>

    ∨ <insert_dep, flow, S_3, any, any> >

  <Postcondition, <delete S_3> ∧ <delete_dep, anti, S_2, S_3, =,>

  ∧ <delete_dep, output, S_1, S_3, =,>>

(a) Detailed conditions for {DCE}$_{s3}$

<{CPP}$_{S2}$, CPP, not applicable>

  <Create-conditions, <delete_dep,anti,S_2,S_3, =,>>

  <Destroy-conditions, <delete S_2>   ∨ <modify_opcode, S_2, ≠, copy>

  ∨ <modify_opnd, S_2, dst, ≠, var > ∨ <modify_opnd, S_2, opnd1, ≠, var>

  ∨ <delete_dep, flow, S_2, S_4, =,> ∨ <insert_dep, flow, S_2, any, =,>*

  ∨ <insert_dep, flow, any, S_4, =, any ≠ S_2>

  ∨ <insert_dep, anti, S_2, any, =, in_any_path(S_2, S_4)>>

  <Postcondition, <delete S_2>   ∧ <delete_dep, flow, S_1, S_2, =,>

    ∧ <modify_opnd, S_4, opnd1, S_2.opnd1> ∧ <delete_dep, flow, S_2, S_4, =,>

    ∧ <insert_dep, flow, S_1, S_4, =,>>

(b) Detailed conditions for {CPP}$_{s2}$

Fig. 2. Determining Interaction

3 FOP Components

To determine the enabling and disabling interactions, FOP uses models for both code and optimizations. The **code model** expresses the code context that is needed in determining the create-conditions, destroy-conditions and post-condition of an optimization. We use the control flow graph (CFG) as the basic code model and identify a distinguished code point, S, (i.e., statement) where an optimization may be applied. The general form of the statement is three-address code. We use dependencies to represent data flow information. A dependence is represented with the tuple $< S_s, S_d, type, dir, pos >$. There are four *types* of dependencies: flow, anti-, output, and control dependencies [5]. The *dir* element records the direction of the dependence, which can be forward, backward or equivalent, represented by <, >, or =, respectively. The direction is needed in loop optimizations. The *pos* element records the position of the operand dependence between S_s and S_d. An **optimization model** expresses the preconditions O^{Pre} and the actions O^{Act} of an optimization. We developed an optimization specification language, SpeLO, based on Gospel that specifies a class of scalar and loop optimizations [21]. SpeLO extends Gospel to a larger class of optimizations, including path-based ones (e.g., PRE). A compiler engineer uses SpeLO to describe the optimization model for FOP.

3.1 Optimization Models

3.1.1 SpeLO

The structure of a SpeLO specification is shown in Fig. 3. The PRECONDITION section specifies the conditions, O^{Pre}, under which the optimization is safe to apply. There are two parts in the pre-condition section: code patterns, $O^{Pattern}$ and dependencies, O^{Depend}.

```
OptName
PRECONDITION
    Code_Pattern
        [Quantifier ElementId: mem_list, element_format_list;]⁺
    Depend
        [Quantifier ElementId [, pos]: mem_list, condition_list;]*
ACTION
    [primitive_operation;]*
```

Fig. 3. The Format of a SpeLO Specification

Code Pattern. The code pattern gives the generic code structure that must be satisfied for the optimization to be applicable. The code pattern identifies program elements such as a statement or loop, which represent the distinguished code point where the optimization can be applied. If an element is a statement, then the code pattern expresses what statement operator and operands are needed for the optimization to be applicable. A quantifier includes **ANY** referring to any matching element, **ALL** referring to all matching elements, and **NO** indicating that there are no matching elements. *mem_list* specifies a set to which an element belongs, such as a path or a loop. Format expressions are used to give the specific format of the code element, *element_format_list*. Multiple expressions can be combined with "AND" and "OR". To standardize the format (without losing generality), SpeLO uses disjunctive normal form (DNF) to express the combination of multiple expressions.

Depend. The second part of the PRECONDITION section gives the generic control and data dependence relationships that must be satisfied for the optimization to be applicable. The *condition_list* consists of the relations combined by AND and OR operators in DNF. A relation can be a dependence relation in the form of *type_of_dependence* (*Ss*, *Sd*, *dir*). The dependence's type and direction are the same as in the code model. A position tag, *pos*, can also be given in a dependence relation to indicate the position of the dependence should be checked.

The ACTION section describes the modifications to the code or code properties (e.g., value number of a statement) that would result from applying the optimization. We decompose these effects into four primitive operations on the code: *move*, *add*, *delete* and *modify*. The semantics of the primitive operations are typical edit operations; they can be used to express the actions of optimizations [21].

3.1.2 Partial Redundancy Elimination (PRE) Optimization Model

Figure 4 gives the optimization model for PRE, a path-specific optimization. Line 1 shows that when a statement S_i is a binary expression, there is a possible PRE opportunity. All the same expressions S_j, executed on a path to S_i without a redefinition between them are found (lines 2-3). The definitions S_p of this statement are selected, where there is a path that does not include the collected same expressions (line 4). The immediate predecessors of the statement on the path that does not include the same expression are saved. These are insertion points where the computation should be added. At the same time, it is required that at these insertion points, the expression is anticipated, as shown on line 5. When applying PRE, the computation is added at the insertion points and before the same expressions S_j. The same expressions S_j and statement S_i are replaced with the assignment on lines 6-9.

```
PRECONDITION
  Code_Pattern
1:    ANY Si: Si.opcode = binary_exp;
2:    ALL Sj:  mem(path(Entry, Si)), Sj.opcode = Si.opcode
              AND Sj.opnd1= Si.opnd1 AND Sj.opnd2 = Si.opnd2;
  Depend
3:    NO Sk: anti_dep(Sj, Sk, =) AND flow_dep(Sk, Si, =);
4:    ALL Sp: flow_dep(Sp, Si, =) AND ¬ in_every_path(Sj, Sp, Si, save pred(Si))  AND
              ¬ in_any_path(pred(Si), Sj, Si) to Bq)
5:    NO Bl: mem(Bq), ¬post_dom(B(Si), Bl);
ACTION
6:    Add ((new_temp= Si.opnd1 Si.opcode Si.opnd2), Bq);
7:    Add (new_temp=Si.opnd1 Si.opcode Si.opnd2), Sj);
8:    Modify (Sj, (Sj.dst = new_temp));
9:    Modify (Si, (Si.dst = new temp));
```

Fig. 4. PRE Optimization Model

3.2 Interaction Algorithm

Given an optimization and a program point, the interaction algorithm determines the enabling and disabling interactions by comparing its post-condition with create- and destroy-conditions of other optimizations. The algorithm first considers every statement in the code segment and every optimization in a set of optimizations to determine the create-conditions and destroy-conditions for each optimization opportunity. In the second step, the algorithm generates the post-conditions for each optimization opportunity. In the last step, each optimization's create and destroy-conditions are compared with post-conditions of other optimizations to compute the enabling and disabling interaction.

3.2.1 Step 1: Generating Create- and Destroy-Conditions

For each optimization, O, and a code point, S, the interaction algorithm compares O^{Pre} with the create- and destroy-conditions for other optimizations. That is, for each $O \in O$ and each $S \in C$, we compute the create- and destroy-conditions using the pre-conditions and C: $(C)[O^{Pre}]_S \Rightarrow \{[O^{Create-C}]_S\}$ and $(C)[O^{Pre}]_S \Rightarrow \{[O^{Destroy-C}]_S\}$.

To find these code changes, the PRECONDITION of each optimization model is compared with the code model. The Code Pattern and Depend parts of the PRECONDITION section are consider separately; that is $[O^{Pre}] = [O^{Pattern} \wedge O^{Depend}]$. For example, consider the form, **A AND B OR D**, where A, B and D are basic expressions. The code pattern expression for CPP is

$$\text{Si.opcode = copy AND type (Si.opnd1) = var}$$

Thus, A is "Si.opcode = copy" and B is "type(Si.opnd1)=var". D is not given. For Depend, the second dependence expression of CPP is "flow(Sk, Sj, =) AND (Sk != Si)". In this case, A is "flow(Sk, Sj, =)" and B is "Sk != Si".

Code Pattern. When the code model (i.e., the state at code point S) is compared to the code pattern, two cases are possible. When the code *matches* Code Pattern, the create-conditions are true. Thus, step 1 of the interaction algorithm needs only to determine the destroy-conditions, $\{[O^{Destroy-C}]_S\}$. When the code does *not match* the pre-conditions, the destroy-conditions are true and the algorithm determines only create-conditions, $\{[O^{Create-C}]_S\}$.

Case 1: $[O^{Pattern}] \sim C$: The first case happens when the current statement S in C matches the code pattern. The destroy-conditions are generated. Suppose, the code pattern expression is A AND B OR D, the destroy-conditions are created as:

$$[O^{Destroy-Pattern-C}]_S = (\text{delete S}) \vee (\neg A \wedge \neg D) \vee (\neg B \wedge \neg D)$$

For example, the destroy-conditions for CPP_i are:

$$(\text{delete } S_{Stmtid}) \vee (\text{modify\_opnd, } S_{Stmtid}.\text{opcode} \neq \text{copy}) \vee$$
$$(\text{modify\_opcode, } \text{type}(S_{Stmtid}.\text{opnd1}) \neq \text{var})$$

Case 2: $[O^{Pattern}]_S /\sim C$: Another case occurs when the current statement S does not match the code pattern. The interaction algorithm generates the create-conditions, considering only the legal code changes that can be made by other optimizations. For example, constant folding requires that both operands are constant. Even if a statement has a variable operand, it is possible to perform constant folding when the statement's variable operand can be changed to a constant by other optimizations (e.g., constant propagation).

$$[O^{Create-Pattern-C}]_S = (\text{if } (A \wedge \neg B) \text{ insert B}) \vee \text{if } (\neg A \wedge B) \text{ insert A}) \vee (\text{if } (\neg D) \text{ insert D })$$

When it is impossible for any code change made by another optimization to match Code Pattern, an optimization opportunity is not created.

Depend. After determining create- and destroy-conditions for the code pattern, the create- and destroy-conditions are generated for the Depend specification. For each quantifier ANY, ALL and NO, there are two cases, corresponding to a match and no match between O^{Depend} and C. Again, assume the dependence rules are in the form of A AND B OR D.

Case 1: For the ALL quantifier, if there is a match $[O^{Depend}]_S \sim C$, then the create-condition is true and the destroy-conditions are generated as below. "Alldep" represents the All quantifier.

$$\{[O^{Destroy\text{-}alldep\text{-}C}]_S\} = (delete\ S1) \wedge...\wedge\ (delete\ Sn)\vee(insert\ A{\wedge}B)^* \vee (insert\ D)^*$$

$\{[O^{Destroy\text{-}alldep\text{-}C}]_S\}$ shows that if all of the matching statements are deleted, then the optimization opportunity is destroyed. It also includes insertion of a dependence that matches the dependence rule, (insert A $\wedge$ B)* or (insert D).

Case 2: For the ALL quantifier, when the code model does not match the dependence rule $[O^{Depend}]_S /\sim C$, the create-conditions are generated as:

$$\{[O^{Create\text{-}alldep\text{-}C}]_S\} = (insert\ A{\wedge}B)^* \vee (insert\ D)^*$$

Similarly, the interaction algorithm generates create and destroy-conditions for the ANY and NO quantifiers.

3.2.2 Step 2: Generating Post-conditions

The post-conditions of O are the code changes after applying the actions of O. In its second step, the interaction algorithm generates the post-conditions for each optimization opportunity according to the actions of the optimization.

Step 2: For each O in O and S, $(C)[O^{Act}]_S \Rightarrow (C) \bullet [O^{Post}]_S$

The primitive operations in the ACTION section specify the code modifications made by the optimization. The actions are decomposed into individual modifications during generation of the specific post-conditions.

Table 1. Generating Post-Conditions

Action	(Pattern) Code Modifications	(Depend) Dependence Modifications
Move	delete (S) insert (NewS, AfterS)	delete_dep (type, stat, S, dir) insert_dep (type, stat, NewS, dir) insert_dep (type, NewS, stat, dir)
Add	insert(S, AfterS)	insert_dep (type, S, stat, dir) insert_dep (type, stat, S, dir)
Delete	delete (S)	delete_dep (type, stat, S, dir)
Modify	modify_opnd(S, opnd, new_opnd)	delete_dep (type, stat, S, dir) where dep_position = opnd insert_dep (type, stat, S, dir) where dep_position= new_opnd insert_dep (type, S, stat, dir) where dep_position= new_opnd
	modify_opcode(S, new_opcode)	--

Table 1 shows how to generate post-conditions for each primitive action in the ACTION section. A row corresponds to an action, given in the first table column. The second and third columns give the changes to the code model. For example, the move operation deletes a statement from its original location and inserts a new one at a new location. When a statement is deleted, its dependences must also be deleted. When a new statement is inserted, dependences are inserted at the new location.

3.2.3 Step 3: Computing the Interactions

In this final step, the algorithm determines the interactions among optimizations by matching the create- and destroy-conditions of each optimization with the post-conditions of other optimizations.

Step 3: Compare conditions in $\{[O_k^{Destroy-C}]s\}$ and $\{[O_k^{Create-C}]s\}$ with $[O_i^{Post-C}]s$:

If there exists a C_Δ^i in $\{[O_k^{Destroy-C}]s\}$ such that $C_\Delta^i \subseteq [O_i^{Post-C}]s$ then O_i disables O_k

and if there exists a C_Δ^i in $\{[O_k^{Create-C}]s\}$ such that $C_\Delta^i \subseteq [O_i^{Post-C}]s$ then O_i enables O_k

The process for matching O_i's create- and destroy-conditions with the post-conditions is as follows. For each optimization opportunity, the algorithm tries to match the post-conditions of other optimizations. It finds the optimizations whose post-condition matches the condition. Next, it tries to match the set of optimizations whose post-conditions match conditions to enable/disable O_i together. The optimization whose post-conditions match condition C enables/disables O_i. The condition action (i.e., *delete, insert, delete_dep, insert_dep, modify_opnd,* or *modify_opcode*) and the object (e.g., statement or dependence) are compared. For example, if A is *<delete S_3>*, an optimization whose post-condition deletes S_3 matches A. If A is *<delete_dep, type, S_i, S_j, dir, other_condition>*, the post-condition has to match all parts of condition A. The post-condition has the same type of dependence between S_i and S_j, direction, and the other conditions are satisfied.

4 Optimization Ordering Using Properties

Typically, compilers apply optimizations in a predetermined order, perhaps guided by a compiler writer's expertise. In our approach, we use the profitability and interaction properties to determine the optimization order at the statement level.

Def. 7: The Profit of an optimization O, $O^{profit,}$ is the performance difference after applying O. Performance can be defined as execution time, dynamic instruction count or other metrics. Suppose (C) $[O^{Pre}, O^{Act}]_S <R> \rightarrow (C')[O^{profit}]$, then

$$O^{profit} = Performance\ (C', R) - Performance(C, R)$$

We determine optimization ordering based on properties, expressed as: O_i **before** O_j

If (O_i enables O_j) OR (O_j disables O_i)

OR (O_i, no interaction O_j AND Profit(O_i)) > Profit(O_j))

Fig. 5 shows our algorithm to determine phase ordering. A working set, app, tracks which optimizations to consider. A list, seq, holds the optimization sequence determined by the algorithm. app is initialized to all applicable optimizations and seq is initialized to the empty sequence. The algorithm iterates until the working set is empty (line 3). The algorithm evaluates the profit of optimizations in list, *Profit(O)*, on line 4. The profitability of an optimization is computed analytically [23]. The algorithm selects the optimization O_k with the largest *Profit* as the next optimization in the sequence. O_k is added to seq on line 6. On line 7, the algorithm updates app according to what optimizations are disabled and enabled by O_k. We require that when O_k along with other optimizations disables O_m and all the other optimizations are already in the sequence, then we remove O_m from app. For the enabling interaction, we also require that optimizations already in seq do not disable O_m, and then we can add O_m to app. We evaluate app until it is empty to achieve the sequence that maximizes the evaluation function.

Although we use a single optimization in the discussion, FOP can determine the properties for a series of optimizations, i.e., the combination of optimizations. In this case, $(C)[\,O_{i...k}^{Pre}, O_{i...k}^{Act}\,] <R> \Rightarrow (C')\,[\,O_{i...k}^{Properties}\,]$. The phase ordering among combinations of optimizations can also be determined using optimization properties.

```
1:  app = {all applicable optimization instances};
2:  seq = {};
3:  while (app ≠ empty) {
4:    Evaluate_Profit (list);
5:    select Oₖ that Profit(Oₖ) is the best;
6:    seq = seq + { Oₖ };
7:    app = app − { Oₖ }
8:    app = app − { Oₘ | Disable({Oₖ, ...}, Oₘ) ∧ {Oₖ, ...} ⊆ seq }
9:    app = app + { Oₘ | Enable({Oₖ, ...}, Oₘ) ∧ {Oₖ, ...} ⊆ seq
                       ∧ ¬∃ (Oₚ ∈ seq ∧ Disable(Oₚ, Oₘ))}
10:   app = app + { Oₘ₁Oₘ₂ | Enable({Oₖ, ...}, Oₘ₁Oₘ₂) ∧ {Oₖ, ...} ⊆ seq }; }
```

Fig. 5. Algorithm to determine a Good Optimization Sequence

5   Experiments

To evaluate FOP, we compared three approaches to applying optimizations: a fixed-order approach, an empirical approach that uses a genetic algorithm (GA) to search for effective optimization sequences [1] and our approach. We run experiments on an Intel Pentium IV 2.4GHz machine, with 512MB of memory and RedHat Linux.

We consider nine optimizations: CPP, CTF, DCE, PRE, LICM, GVN, BRC, BRE, and RA. The optimizations are incorporated into the MachSUIF optimizer [17] for the Intel IA-32 instruction set. The fixed-order sequence is "GVN, BRC, BRE, CPP, CTF, DCE, PRE, LICM, GVN, BRC, BRE, CPP, CTF, DCE, PRE, LICM, RA". The selection of the fixed order was based on a past study of interactions among these optimizations [21]. In all cases, register allocation is done as the last optimization.

The empirical approach (GA) has the same configuration as in [1]. We performed a search for each *function* in a program with 10 generations. Each generation had a population of 20 sequences. Every sequence had 16 optimization passes, picked from the possible optimizations. At each generation, the best 10% of the sequences survive without any change. The remaining part of the new generation is created with a

crossover operation, which is followed by character-by-character mutation (5% mutation rate). We tried more generations but there was no further improvement.

5.1 Compile-Time Comparison

The empirical approach both applies optimizations and executes the code to evaluate
profitability. For the SPEC benchmarks, the test inputs were used to execute the code.
FOP uses the interaction and the profitability properties to determine optimization
order. Table 2 shows the compile-time overhead of the approaches.

From the table, the compile-time for the fixed-order is small. It varies from 0.05 to
6.11 minutes. Because the empirical approach (GA) executes the application to determine profitability and to apply optimizations, and it recomputes the data flow to
detect interactions, its compile-time is large, varying from 5 minutes to 43.6 hours.
Each function is compiled for 200 sequences and evaluated by executing the code. Its
total compile-time is related to the compile-time and execution time for each function.
For example, there are 106 functions in *gzip*. The average compile-time for a function
is 0.8 seconds. The execution time for the test input is 2.4 seconds. Considering the
GA search time, it took 1181 minutes to find code-specific sequences for *gzip*.

With our approach, the compile-time is reduced: It varies from 0.7 to 82 minutes.
Our approach needs to determine the interaction property among optimizations and to
predict the profitability property. Its compile-time depends on the time to determine
the interaction property and the time to predict profitability. For example, in *mpeg* the
average compile-time to determine the interaction property is about 20 seconds and
the compile-time to determine profitability is about 6 seconds. Thus, it took 82.24
minutes for our approach to determine good optimization sequences for *mpeg*.

Table 2. Compile-time of Three Approaches (minutes)

Benchmarks	Fixed-order	Empirical	FOP
adpcm.rawcaudio	0.05	5.41	1.14
mpeg2.enc	1.92	726.67	82.24
bitcount	0.15	18.97	1.66
dijkstra.large	0.05	11.63	0.68
FFT	0.11	13.20	1.81
164.gzip	1.52	1180.67	53.82
175.vpr	6.11	1469.23	61.23
181.mcf	0.53	74.64	19.54
197.parser	5.4	976.34	49.23
256.bzip2	2.34	2618.79	58.68

5.2 Performance Comparison

We compared the performance of the three approaches, as shown in Fig. 6. The figure
shows the improvement of the empirical and the model-driven approaches over the
fixed-order approach. Performance is measured with dynamic instruction count.

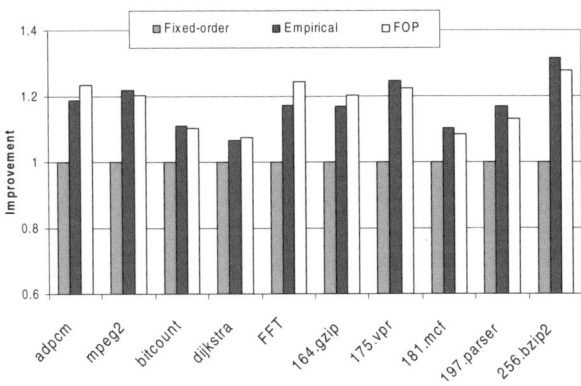

Fig. 6. Performance Comparison of Three Approaches

As the figure shows, the empirical and model-driven approaches improve performance more than the fixed-order approach. In *256.bzip2*, the improvement with the empirical and model-driven approaches over the fixed-order sequence is 32% and 28% respectively. In most cases, the model-driven approach has similar performance improvement as the empirical approach. However, the performance of the model-driven approach is better in a few cases. For example, in *adpcm*, the improvement is 19% with the empirical technique and 23% with our model-driven approach. This higher improvement happens because an optimization instance is not applied if it is predicted to be unprofitable.

In terms of memory, FOP uses 51KB to 723KB (average) to store data and control dependence information. The maximum memory requirements ranged from 106KB to 9815KB. On today's machines, this amount of memory is reasonable.

Our experiments show that optimization properties are useful in finding code-specific optimization sequences. Our techniques show it is practical to *analytically model optimizations and compute interactions to find a good code-specific order* in which to apply optimizations.

6   Related Work

Formal and empirical approaches have been used to determine the order to apply optimizations. Knuth and Bendix proposed a solution to express optimizations as a set of rewriting rules [9]. Their algorithm detects potential conflicts and resolves them by introducing new rewriting rules, derived from the existing set. However, the procedure is difficult to generalize. Whitfield and Soffa described a framework that enables the exploration, both analytically and experimentally, of properties of optimizations, including the interaction property [20], [21]. They proposed Gospel to express the pre-condition and post-conditions of optimizations. They studied the optimization interactions with proofs or examples. However, their approach can not automatically detect the interactions among optimizations based on code context.

Another approach uses heuristic-driven search algorithms to find a good optimization sequence. Almagor et al. performed a large experimental study on the space of optimization sequences [1]. Although their approach can produce efficient code, it can be slow. Kulkarni et al. proposed an interactive compilation system, VISTA, which used a genetic algorithm, performance information and user input to select an effective optimization sequence. They further proposed two approaches to improve search performance [7], [10], [11]. Triantifyllis et al. recognized the benefit of finding good optimization sequences [18], [19]. To limit compile-time, their system used a fixed set of optimization sequences and obtained the best result with the set. However, the selection of the sequences should be considered.

7   Conclusion

This paper presented a framework (FOP) which can automatically determine optimization properties. We use FOP to determine enabling and disabling interactions among optimizations without actually applying the optimizations. An application of FOP is to find a good code-specific order in which to apply optimizations. This paper presented an algorithm that constructs an effective optimization sequence using the interaction and profitability properties. We implemented FOP and experimentally found good code-specific orders. The results showed that we obtain sequences that have similar performance as an empirical approach with less compile-time. Our work demonstrates that an analytic approach can be used for optimization properties, which are useful in addressing phase ordering.

References

1. Almagor, L., Cooper, K., Grosul, A., Harvey, T., Reeves, S., Subramanian, D., Torczon, L., Waterman, T.: Finding Effective Compilation Sequences. In: Conf. On Languages, Compilers, and Tools for Embedded Systems (2004)
2. Bodík, R., Gupta, R., Soffa, M.L.: Complete removal of redundant expressions. SIGPLAN Not. 39(4) (April 2004)
3. Briggs, P., Cooper, K.D.: Effective Partial Redundancy Elimination. In: Conf. on Programming Language Design and Implementation (1994)
4. Coleman, S., McKinley, K.S.: Tile Size Selection Using Cache Organization and Data Layout. In: Conf. on Programming Language Design and Implementation (1995)
5. Ferrante, J., Ottenstein, K., Warren, J.: The program Dependence Graph and Its Use in Optimization. ACM Trans. on Programming Languages 9(3) (1987)
6. Jaramillo, C., Gupta, R., Soffa, M.L.: Comparison checking: An approach to avoid debugging of optimized code. In: Nierstrasz, O., Lemoine, M. (eds.) ESEC 1999 and ESEC-FSE 1999. LNCS, vol. 1687, p. 268. Springer, Heidelberg (1999)
7. Kulkarni, P., Hines, S., Hiser, J., Whalley, D., Davidson, J., Jones, D.: Fast Searches for Effective Optimization Phase Sequences. In: Conf. on Programming Language Design and Implementation (2004)
8. Kisuki, T., Knijnenburg, P.M.W., O'Boyle, M.F.P.: Combined Selection of Tile Size and Unroll Factors Using Iterative Compilation. In: Int'l. Conf. on Parallel Architectures and Compilation Techniques (2000)
9. Knuth, D.E., Bendix, P.B.: Simple word problems in universal algebras. In: Leech, J. (ed.) Computational problems in abstract algebra. Pergamon Press, Oxford (1970)
10. Kulkarni, P., Whalley, D.B., Tyson, G.S., Davidson, J.W.: Exhaustive Optimization Phase Order Space Exploration. In: Int'l. Symp. on Code Generation and Optimization (2006)

11. Kulkarni, P., Whalley, D.B., Tyson, G.S., Davidson, J.W.: Evaluating Heuristic Optimization Phase Order Search Algorithms. In: Int'l. Symp. on Code Generation and Optimization (2007)
12. Lacey, D.: Program Transformation using Temporal Logic Specifications. PhD dissertation, Univ. of Oxford (August 2003)
13. Lerner, S., Millstein, T., Chambers, C.: Automatically Proving the Correctness of compiler optimizations. In: Conf. on Programming Language Design and Implementation (2003)
14. Lacey, D., Jones, N., Wyk, E., Frederiksen, C.: Proving correctness of compiler optimizations by temporal logic. In: Symp. on Principles of Programming Languages (2002)
15. McKinley, K., Carr, S., Tseng, C.: Improving Data Locality with Loop Transformations. ACM Trans. on Programming Languages and Systems 18(4), 424–453 (1996)
16. Necula, G.C.: Translation validation for an optimizing compiler. In: Conf. on Programming Language Design and Implementation (2000)
17. Smith, M.D., Holloway, G.: An Introduction to Machine SUIF and Its Portable Libraries for Analysis and Optimization
18. Triantafyllis, S., Vachharajani, M., Vachharajani, N., August, D.I.: Compiler Optimization-space Exploration. In: Int'l. Symp. on Code Generation and Optimization (2003)
19. Triantafyllis, S., Vachharajani, M., August, D.I.: Compiler Optimization-space Exploration. Journal of Instruction-Level Parallelism (2005)
20. Whitfield, D., Soffa, M.L.: An Approach to Ordering optimizing transformations. In: Symp. on Principles and Practice of Parallel Programming (1990)
21. Whitfield, D., Soffa, M.L.: An Approach for Exploring Code Improving Transformations. ACM Trans. on Programming Languages and Systems 19(6), 1053–1084 (1997)
22. Yotov, K., Li, X., Ren, G., Cibulskis, M.: A Comparison of Empirical and Model-driven optimization. In: Conf. on Programming Language Design and Implementation (2003)
23. Zhao, M., Childers, B.R., Soffa, M.L.: A Model-based Framework: an Approach for Profit-driven Optimization. In: Int'l. Symp. on Code Generation and Optimization (2005)

Compile-Time Analysis and Specialization of Clocks in Concurrent Programs

Nalini Vasudevan[1], Olivier Tardieu[2], Julian Dolby[2], and Stephen A. Edwards[1]

[1] Department of Computer Science, Columbia University, New York, USA
{naliniv,sedwards}@cs.columbia.edu
[2] IBM T.J. Watson Research Center, New York, USA
{tardieu,dolby}@us.ibm.com

Abstract. Clocks are a mechanism for providing synchronization barriers in concurrent programming languages. They are usually implemented using primitive communication mechanisms and thus spare the programmer from reasoning about low-level implementation details such as remote procedure calls and error conditions.

Clocks provide flexibility, but programs often use them in specific ways that do not require their full implementation. In this paper, we describe a tool that mitigates the overhead of general-purpose clocks by statically analyzing how programs use them and choosing optimized implementations when available.

We tackle the clock implementation in the standard library of the X10 programming language—a parallel, distributed object-oriented language. We report our findings for a small set of analyses and benchmarks. Our tool only adds a few seconds to analysis time, making it practical to use as part of a compilation chain.

Keywords: Concurrency, Static Analysis, Synchronization, Clocks, X10, NuSMV.

1 Introduction

The correct coordination and synchronization of concurrent tasks is one of the major challenges of concurrent programming. Low-level primitives, such as locks or compare-and-swap, can lead to optimum performance but they are hard to use and error-prone. In this paper, we consider higher-level concurrency constructs that are supplied in libraries and provide the user a richer, less error-prone abstraction. The usual disadvantage of general-purpose libraries is their generality: their implementation includes code to handle all possible cases, which slows down the relatively few cases each program uses.

We present an optimization technique that greatly reduces the performance penalty of a general-purpose concurrency library. We statically analyze the use of clocks—a form of synchronization barriers—in the Java-derived X10 concurrent programming language [1,2] and use the results to safely substitute more specialized implementations of these standard library elements.

O. de Moor and M. Schwartzbach (Eds.): CC 2009, LNCS 5501, pp. 48–62, 2009.

A clock in X10 is a structured form of synchronization barrier useful for expressing patterns such as wavefront computations and software pipelines. Concurrent tasks registered on the same clock advance in lockstep.

Our static analysis technique models an X10 program as a finite automaton; we ignore data but consider the possibility of clocks being aliased. We pass this automaton to the NuSMV model checker [3], which reports erroneous usage of a clock and whether a particular clock follows certain idioms. If the clocks are used properly, we use the idiom information to restructure the program to use a more efficient implementation of each clock. The result is a faster program that behaves like one that uses the general-purpose library.

Our analysis flow has been designed to be flexible and amenable to supporting a growing variety of patterns. In the sequel, we focus on inexpensive queries that can be answered by treating programs as sequential. While analysis time is negligible, speedup is considerable and varies across benchmarks from a few percent to a 3× improvement in total execution time.

In summary, our contributions are

- a methodology for the analysis and specialization of clocked programs;
- a set of cost-effective clock transformations;
- a prototype implementation: a plug-in for the X10 v1.5 tool chain; and
- experimental results on some modest-size benchmarks.

After a brief overview of the X10 language in Section 2 and the clock library in Section 3, we describe our static analysis technique in Section 4 and how we use its results to optimize programs in Section 5. We present experimental evidence that our technique can improve the performance of X10 programs in Section 6. We discuss related work in Section 7 and conclude in Section 8.

2 The X10 Programming Language

X10 [1,2] is a parallel, distributed object-oriented language. To a Java-like sequential core it adds constructs for concurrency and distribution through the concepts of *activities* and *places*. An activity is a unit of work, like a thread in Java; a place is a logical entity that contains both activities and data objects.

The *async* construct creates activities; parent and child execute concurrently. The X10 program in Figure 1 uses clocks to recursively compute the first ten rows of Pascal's Triangle. The call of the method *row* on line 40 creates a new stream object, spawns an activity to produce the stream values, and finally returns the stream object to *main*. The rest of *main* executes in parallel with the spawned activity, printing the stream values as they are produced.

Spawned activities may only access final variables of enclosing activities, e.g.,

```
final int a = 3; int b = 4;
async { int x = a; // OK: a is a final
        int y = b; } // ERROR: b is not final
```

An X10 program runs in a fixed, platform-dependent set of places. The *main* method always runs in *place.FIRST_PLACE*; the programmer may specify where other activities run. Activities cannot migrate between places.

```
1   public class IntStream {
2     public final clock clk = clock.factory.clock(); // stream clock
3     private final int[] buf = new int[2]; // current and next stream values
4
5     public IntStream(final int v) {
6       buf[0] = v; // set initial stream value
7     }
8
9     public void put(final int v) {
10      clk.next(); // enter new clock phase
11      buf[(clk.phase()+1)%2] = v; // set next stream value
12      clk.resume(); // complete clock phase
13    }
14
15    public int get() {
16      clk.next(); // enter new clock phase
17      final int v = buf[clk.phase()%2]; // get current stream value
18      clk.resume(); // complete clock phase
19      return v;
20    } }
21
22  public class PascalsTriangle {
23    static IntStream row(final int n) {
24      final IntStream r = new IntStream(1); // start row with 1
25      async clocked(r.clk) { // spawn clocked task to compute row's values
26        if (n > 0) { // recursively compute previous row
27          final IntStream previous = row(n−1);
28          int v; int w = previous.get();
29          while (w != 0) {
30            v = w; w = previous.get();
31            r.put(v+w); // emit row's values
32          }
33        }
34        r.put(0); // end row with 0
35      }
36      return r;
37    }
38
39    public static void main(String[] args){
40      final IntStream r = row(10);
41      int w = r.get(); // print row excluding final 0
42      while (w != 0) { System.out.println(w); w = r.get(); }
43    } }
```

```
                              1
                            1   1
                          1   2   1
                        1   3   3   1
                      1   4   6   4   1
                    1   5   10  10  5   1
                  1   6   15  20  15  6   1
                1   7   21  35  35  21  7   1
              1   8   28  56  70  56  28  8   1
            1   9   36  84  126 126 84  36  9   1
          1   10  45  120 210 252 120 120 45  10  1
```

Fig. 1. A program to compute Pascal's Triangle in X10 using clocks

```
final IntStream s = new IntStream(4);
async (place.LAST_PLACE) { // spawn activity at place.LAST_PLACE
    // cannot call methods of s if LAST_PLACE != FIRST_PLACE
    final int i = 3;
    async (s) s.put(i); // spawn activity at the place of s; s is local => ok to deref
}
```

Activities that share a place share a common heap. While activities may hold references to remote objects, they can only access the fields and methods of a remote object by spawning an activity at the object's place.

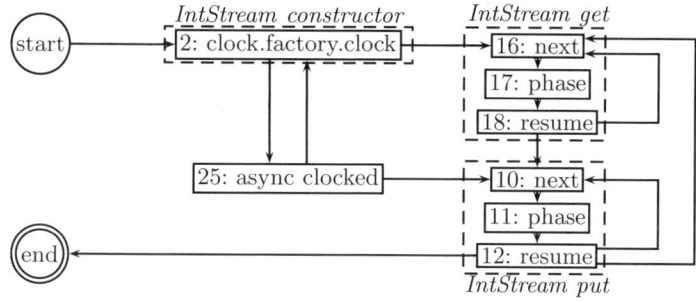

Fig. 2. The automaton model for the clock in the Pascal's Triangle example

X10 also introduces *value classes*, whose fields are all *final*. The fields and methods of an instance of a value class may be accessed remotely, unlike normal classes. Clocks are implemented as value classes.

X10 provides two primitive constructs for synchronization: *finish* and *when*. *finish p q* delays the execution of statement *q* until after statement *p* and all activities recursively spawned by *p* have completed. For example,

finish { **async** { **async** { System.out.print("Hello"); } } } System.out.println(" world");

prints "Hello world." The statement *when(e) p* suspends until the Boolean condition *e* becomes true, then executes *p* atomically, i.e., as if in one step during which all other activities in the same place are suspended.[1]

X10 also permits unconditional atomic blocks and methods, which are specified with the *atomic* keyword. For example,

atomic { **int** tmp = x; x = y; y = tmp; }

3   Clocks in X10

Clocks in X10 are a generalization of barriers. Unlike X10's *finish* construct, clocks permit activities to synchronize repeatedly. In contrast to *when* constructs, they provide a structured, distributed, and determinate form of coordination. While a complete discussion of X10's clocks is beyond the scope of this paper, the following sections will demonstrate that clocks are amenable to efficient and effective static analysis.

Figure 3 lists the main elements of the clock API. An activity must be registered with a clock to interact with it. Activities are registered in one of two ways: creating a clock with the *clock.factory.clock()* static method automatically registers the calling activity with the new clock. Also, an activity can register activities it spawns with the *async clocked* construct.

final clock clk = clock.factory.clock();
async clocked(clk) { A1; clk.next(); A2; clk.next(); A3 }
async clocked(clk) { B1; clk.next(); B2; }
async { C; }
M1; clk.resume(); M1_2; clk.next(); M2;

---

[1] X10 does not guarantee that *p* will execute if *e* holds only intermittently.

```
/* Create a new clock. Register the calling activity with this clock. */
final clock clk = clock.factory.clock();

/* Spawn an activity registered with clocks clk_1, ..., clk_n with body p. */
async clocked(clk_1, ..., clk_n) p

public interface clock {
        /* Notify this clock that the calling activity is done with whatever it intended
         * to do during this phase of the clock. Does not block. */
        void resume();

        /* Block until all activities registered with this clock are ready to enter the next
         * clock phase. Imply that calling activity is done with this phase of the clock. */
        void next();

        /* Return the phase index. Calling activity cannot be resumed on the clock. */
        int phase();

        /* Unregister the caller from this clock; release it from having to participate */
        void drop();
}
```

Fig. 3. The clock API

A clock synchronizes the execution of activities through phases. A registered activity can request the clock to enter a new phase with a call to *next*, which blocks the activity until all other registered activities are done with the current phase, i.e., have called *next* or *resume*. For instance, in the program above, action A1 must complete before action B2 can start. In other words, A1 and B1 belong to phase 1 of clock *clk*; A2 and B2 belong to phase 2. C, however, does not belong to an activity registered with *clk*; it may execute at any time.

The *resume* method provides slack to the scheduler.[2] An activity calls *resume* when it is done with the current clock phase but does not yet need to enter the next. Unlike *next*, *resume* does not block the activity, and the activity must still call *next* to enter the next phase. In the example above, while M1 must terminate before A2 can start and A1 must terminate before M2 can start, M1_2 may start before A1 completes and continue after A2 starts because of *resume*.

In Figure 1, the value at the pth column and nth row of this triangle ($0 \leq p \leq n$) is the number of possible unordered choices of p items among n. One task per row produces the stream of values for the row by summing the two entries from the row immediately above. Each stream uses a clock to enforce single-write-single-read interleaving, so each task registers with two clocks: its own and the clock for the row immediately above. The clocks ensure proper inter-row coordination.

The *phase* method returns the current phase index (counting from 1). Figure 1 demonstrates this and also how activities can register with multiple clocks (using recursion in this example).

Finally, activities can explicitly unregister from a clock by calling *drop*. Activities are implicitly unregistered from their clocks when they terminate.

---

[2] The *resume* method is typically used in activities registered with multiple clocks.

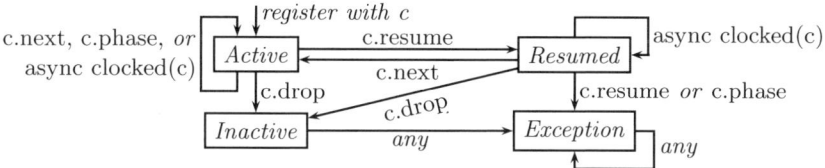

Fig. 4. The state of one activity with respect to clock c

The operations of an activity on a clock modify the state of this activity w.r.t. that clock. Figure 4 shows the behavior. The activity may be in one of four states: *Active, Resumed, Inactive,* or *Exception.* Transitions are labeled with clock-related operations: *async clocked, resume, next, phase,* and *drop.* For example, an activity moves from the *Active* state to *Resumed* if it calls *resume* on the clock. If it calls *resume* again, it moves to the *Exception* state. Any operation that leads to the *Exception* state throws the *ClockUseException* exception.

3.1 Clock Patterns

We now describe the four clock patterns we currently identify. We believe that our techniques can also be applied to find other patterns.

Our first pattern is concerned with exceptions: can an activity reach the exception state for a particular clock? The default clock implementation looks for transitions to this state and throws *ClockUseException* if they occur. Aside from the annoyance of runtime errors, runtime checks slow down the implementation. We want to avoid them if possible.

Our algorithm finds that the clocks are used properly in the program of Figure 1, e.g., no task erroneously attempts to use a clock it is not registered with. Therefore, it substitutes the default implementation with one that avoids the overhead of runtime checks for these error conditions.

We also want to know whether *resume* is ever called on a clock. This feature's implementation requires additional data structures and slows down all clock operations. We discuss this and other optimizations in Section 5.

Activities often use clocks to wait for sub-activities to terminate. Consider

```
final clock clk = clock.factory.clock();
async clocked (clk) A1;
async A2;
async clocked (clk) A3;
clk.next();
A4;
```

Here, if A1 and A2 do not interact with clock *clk*, *clk.next()* requires activities A1 and A3 to terminate before A4 starts executing and nothing else. In particular, A2 and A4 may execute in parallel. We want to detect sub-activities that are registered with the clock yet never request to enter a new clock phase.

Finally, the default clock implementation enables distributed activities to synchronize. If it turn out that all registered activities belong to the same place, a much faster clock implementation is possible. Our Pascal's Triangle program is a trivial example of this since all activities are spawned in the default place.

4   The Static Analyzer

In this section, we describe how we detect clock idioms. We start from the program's abstract syntax tree, compute its call graph, and run aliasing analysis on clocks. We then abstract data by replacing conditional statements with non-deterministic choice. From the control-flow graph of this abstract program, we extract one automaton per clock. This gives a conservative approximation of the sequences of operations that the program may apply to the clock.

To a model checker, we feed the automaton for the control-flow of the program along with an automaton model of the clock API and a series of temporal logic properties, one for each idiom of interest. For each property and each clock, the model checker either proves the property or returns a counterexample in the form of a path in the automaton that violates the property.

We use the T.J. Watson Libraries for Analysis (WALA) [4] for parsing, call- and control-flow-graph construction, and aliasing analysis. We have extended the Java frontend of WALA to accommodate X10 and extract from the AST the required automata in the form of input files for the NuSMV model checker [3].

We now describe the key technical steps in detail. We start with the construction of the automaton, then discuss the encoding of the clock API, the temporal properties, and finally aliasing.

4.1   Constructing the Automaton

Figure 2 shows the automaton we build for the clock *clk* in Figure 1. Each operation on *clk* in the text of the program becomes one state, which we label with the type of operation and its line number. Transitions arise from our abstraction of the program's control flow. We highlighted the fragments corresponding to the constructor and methods of the *IntStream* class.

methods. Each method body becomes a fragment of the automaton. Each call of a method adds a transition to and from its entry and exit nodes. For example, since *get* may be called twice in a row (lines 28 and 30), we added the edge from its exit node "18: resume" to its entry node "16: next." It may also be called after put, looping from line 31 back to line 30, so we added an edge from node "12: resume" to node "16: next."

conditionals. We ignore guards on conditionals and add arcs for both branches. For example, the *if* on line 26 runs immediately after the *async clocked* on line 25. The "then" branch of this *if* runs line 27, which starts with a call to *row* that starts by constructing an *IntStream* (line 24) whose constructor calls *clock.factory.clock()* (line 2). This gives the arc from node "25: async clocked" to "2: clock.factory.clock." The "else" branch is line 34, which calls *put*, which starts with a call to *next* (line 10). This gives the arc to "10: next."

async. Because we are not checking properties that depend on interactions among tasks, we can treat a spawned activity as just another path in the program. When execution reaches an *async* construct, we model it as either jumping directly to the task being spawned or skipping the child and continuing to execute the parent. This is illustrated in Figure 5.

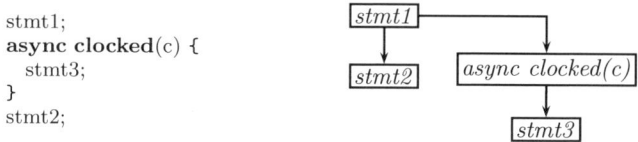

```
stmt1;
async clocked(c) {
  stmt3;
}
stmt2;
```

Fig. 5. Modeling *async* calls

In our Pascal's Triangle example, this means control may flow from the *IntStream* constructor exit point "2: clock.factory.clock" to the *async* construct "25: async clocked" or ignore the *async* and flow back via the *return* statement to the subsequent get method call in either *main* or *row*, i.e., node "16: next."

We give the NuSMV code for the automaton in an extended version of this paper [5].

We build one automaton for each call of *clock.factory.clock* in the source code, meaning our algorithm does not distinguish clocks instantiated from the same allocation site. So we construct only one automaton for our example, even though the program uses ten (very similar) clocks when it executes.

We have taken a concurrent program and transformed it into a sequential program with multiple paths. Thanks to this abstraction, we avoid state space explosion both in the automaton construction and in the model checker.

4.2 Handling Async Constructs with the Clock Model

Our model of clock state transitions—Figure 4—only considers a single activity, but X10 programs may have many. As explained in Section 4.1, we model *async* constructs with nondeterministic branches, so we have to extend the typestate automaton for the clock to do the same.

Figure 6 shows the additional transitions necessary for handling *async* actions. We consider two cases: when analyzing clock c and we encounter *async clocked(c)*, the new activity stays either *Active* or *Resumed*. By contrast, if we encounter an *async* not clocked on c, the new activity starts in the *Inactive* state (arcs labeled just *async*).

We give the NuSMV code for the complete automaton in the extended version of this paper [5].

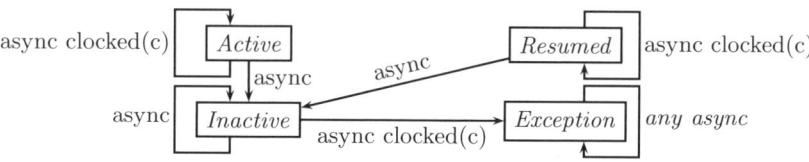

Fig. 6. Additional transitions in the clock state for modeling *async* operations

4.3 Specifying Clock Idioms

Once we have the automata modeling the program and clock state, it becomes easy to specify patterns for NuSMV as temporal logic formulas.

Three patterns are CTL reachability properties of the form

SPEC AG(!(target))

where *target* is either the *Exception* state, a *resume* operation, or an *async clocked(c)* node annotated with a place expression, that is, a remote activity creation. See the extended version of this paper [5] for details.

We check for the fourth pattern—whether spawned activities ever call *next* on the clock—by looking for control-flow paths that contain an *async clocked(c)* operation followed by a *c.next* operation. The LTL specification is

LTLSPEC G(c_next −> **H**(!async_clocked_c))

The extended version of this paper [5] gives the complete NuSMV input file for the Pascal's Triangle example.

4.4 Combining Clock Analysis with Aliasing Analysis

Clocks can be aliased just like any objects. Figure 7 shows an example of aliasing of clocks in X10. We create two clocks *c1* and *c2*. *x* can take the value of either *c1* or *c2* depending on the value of *n*.

We could abstract the program into two control paths, one that assumes $x = c1$ and one that assumes $x = c2$. However, this would produce a number of paths exponential in the number of aliases that have to be considered simultaneously.

Instead, we chose to bound the size of our program abstraction (at the expense of precision) as shown in the bottom three diagrams of Figure 7. We consider each clock operation on *x* in isolation and apply it non-deterministically to any of the possible targets of *x* as returned by WALA's aliasing engine.

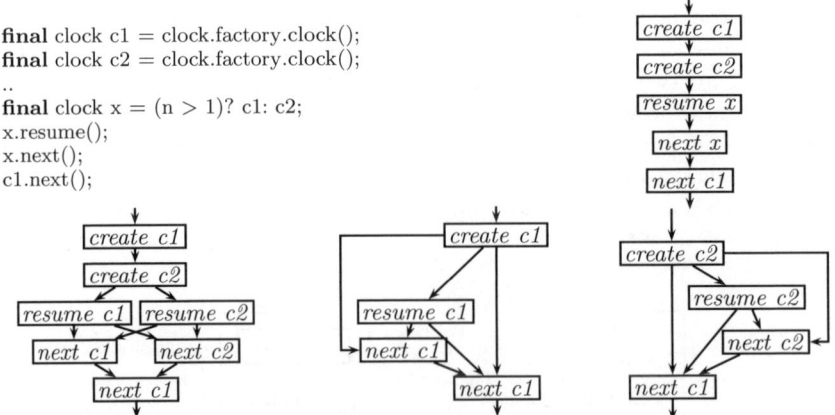

Fig. 7. *Top Left*: Aliasing clocks in X10, *Top Right*: the corresponding control flow graph, *Bottom Left*: our abstraction, *Bottom Center*: automaton for *c1*, *Bottom Right*: automaton for *c2*

```
final clock c1 =
    clock.factory.clock();
final clock c2 =
    clock.factory.clock();
..
final clock x = (n > 1)? c1: c2;
async clocked(x, c1) {
    x.next();
    c1.next();
}
c1.next();
```

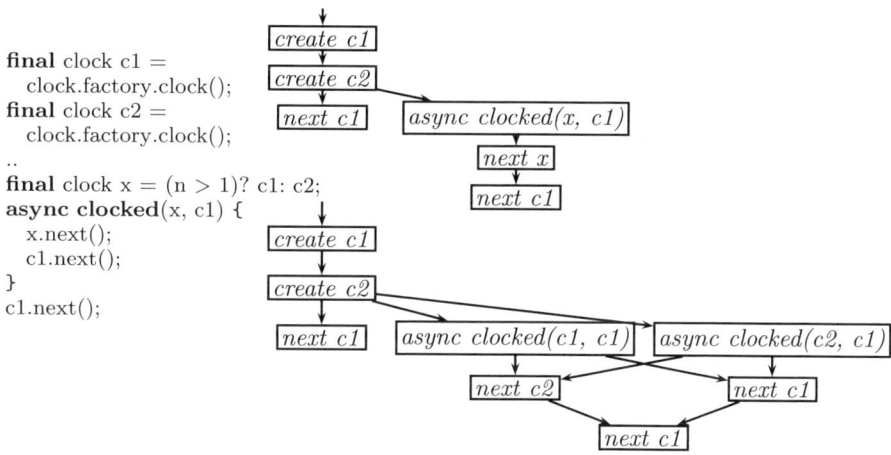

Fig. 8. Asyncs and Aliases

Figure 8 shows how we extend this idea to *async* constructs. Our tool reports that operations on clock *c1* cannot throw *ClockUseException*. However, it fails to establish the same for *c2* because our abstraction creates a false path—*next c2* following *async clocked(c1,c1)*.

5   The Code Optimizer

Results from our static analyzer drive a code optimizer that substitutes each instance of the clock class for a specialized version. We manually wrote an optimized version of the clock class for each clock pattern we encountered in our test cases; a complete tool would include more. Our specialized versions include a clock class that does not check for protocol violations (transitions to the *exception* state) and one that does not support *resume*.

There is one abstract clock base class that contains empty methods for all clock functions; each specialized implementation has different versions of these methods that uses X10 primitives to perform the actual synchronization. Our optimizer changes the code (actually the AST) to use the appropriate derived class for each clock, e.g., *c = clock.factory.clock()* would be replaced with *c = clock.factory.clockef()* if clock *c* is known to be exception-free.

The top of Figure 9 shows the general-purpose implementation of *next*. The *clock* value class contains the public clock methods; the internal *ClockState* maintains the state and synchronization variables of the clock. The *next* method first verifies that the activity is registered with the clock (and throws an exception otherwise), then calls the *select* function to wait on a *latch*: a data structure that indicates the phase. The *latch* is either *null* if *next()* was called from an *active()* state or holds a value if *next()* was called from a *resumed()* state. The *wait* function blocks and actually waits for the clock to change phase. The *check* method decrements the number of activities not yet resumed on the clock and advances the clock phase when all activities registered on the clock are resumed.

```
// The default implementation

class ClockState {                          value class clock {
  ..                                          ..
  atomic int check() {                        final ClockState state = new ClockState();
    int resumedPhase = currentPhase;          ..
    if (remainingActivities-- == 0) {         void select(nullable<future<int>> latch) {
      // set the number of activities           if (latch == null) {
      // expected to resume                       async (state) state.wait(state.check());
      remainingActivities =                     } else {
          registeredActivities;                   final int phase = latch.force();
      // advance to the next phase                async (state) state.wait(phase);
      currentPhase++;                           }
    }                                         }
    return resumedPhase;
  }                                           public void next() {
                                                if (!registered())
  void wait(final int resumedPhase) {             throw new ClockUseException();
    when(resumedPhase != currentPhase);       finish select(ClockPhases.put(this, null));
  } }                                         } }
```

```
// An exception–free implementation          // For when a clock is only in a single place

public void next() {                         void select(nullable<future<int>> latch) {
  finish                                        if (latch == null)
    select(ClockPhases.put(this, null));          state.wait(state.check());
}                                               else
                                                  state.wait(latch.force());
                                             }
// For when resume() is never used
                                             public void next() {
void select() {                                if (!registered())
  async (state) state.wait(state.check());       throw new ClockUseException();
}                                              select(ClockPhases.put(this, null));
                                             }
public void next() {
  if (!registered())
    throw new ClockUseException();
  finish select();
}
```

Fig. 9. Various implementations of *next* and related methods

A basic optimization: when we know the clock is used properly, we can eliminate the registration check in *next* and elsewhere. Figure 9 shows such an exception-free implementation.

Accommodating *resume* carries significant overhead, but if we know the *resume* functionality is never used, we can simplify the body of *select* as shown in Figure 9. We removed the now-unneeded *latch* object and can do something similar in other methods (not shown).

Figure 9 also shows a third optimization. Because clocked activities may be distributed among places, synchronization variables have to be updated by remote activities. When we know a clock is only used in a single place, we dispense with the *async* and *finish* constructs.

Table 1. Experimental Results

Example	Clocks	Lines	Result	Speed Up	Analysis Time Base	NuSMV
Linear Search	1	35	EF, NR, L	35.2%	33.5s	0.4s
Relaxation	1	55	EF, NR, L	87.6	6.7	0.3
All Reduction Barrier	1	65	EF, NR	1.5	27.2	0.1
Pascal's Triangle	1	60	EF, L	20.5	25.8	0.4
Prime Number Sieve	1	95	NR, L	213.9	34.7	0.4
N-Queens	1	155	EF, NR, ON, L	1.3	24.3	0.5
LU Factorization	1	210	EF, NR	5.7	20.6	0.9
MolDyn JGF Bench.	1	930	NR	2.3	35.1	0.5
Pipeline	2	55	Clock 1: EF, NR, L	31.4	7.5	0.5
			Clock 2: EF, NR, L			
Edmiston	2	205	Clock 1: NR, L	14.2	29.9	0.5
			Clock 2: NR, L			

EF: No ClockUseException, NR: No Resume, ON: Only the activity that created the clock calls *next* on it, L: Clocked used locally (in a single place)

6 Results

We applied our static analyzer to various programs, running it on a 3 GHz Pentium 4 machine with 1 GB RAM. Since we want to measure the overhead of the clock library, we purposely run our benchmarks on a single-core processor. Table 1 shows the results. For each example, we list its name, the number of clock definitions in the source code, its size (number of lines of code, including comments), what our analysis discovered about the clock(s), how much faster the executable for each example ran after we applied our optimizations, and finally the time required to analyze the example. (The *Base* column includes the time to read the source, build the IR, perform pointer analysis, build the automata, etc.; *NuSMV* indicates the time spent running the NuSMV model checker. Total time is their sum.)

The first example is a paced linear search algorithm. It consists of two tasks that search an array in parallel and use a clock to synchronize after every comparison. The Relaxation example, for each cell in an array, spawns one activity that repeatedly updates the cell value using the neighboring values. It uses a clock to force these activities to advance in lockstep. The All Reduction Barrier example is a variant on Relaxation that distributes the array across multiple places. Pascal's Triangle is the example of Figure 1. Our prime number sieve uses the Sieve of Eratosthenes. N-Queens is a brute-force tree search algorithm that uses a clock to mimic a join operation. LU Factorization decomposes a matrix in parallel using clocks. We also ported the MolDyn Java Grande Forum Benchmark [6] in X10 with clocks, the largest application on which we ran our tool. Pipeline has three stages; its buffers use two clocks for synchronization. Edmiston aligns substrings in parallel and uses two clocks for synchronization.

The Result column lists the properties satisfied by each example's clocks. For example, the N-Queens example cannot throw *ClockUseException*, does not call *resume*, and uses only locally created clocks. Our tool reports the JGF benchmark may throw exceptions and pass clocks around, although it also does not call *resume*. In truth, it does not throw exceptions, but our tool failed to establish this because of the approximations it uses. This reduced the speedup we could achieve, but does not affect correctness.

The Linear Search, Relaxation, Prime Number Sieve, and Pipeline examples use clocks frequently and locally, providing a substantial speedup opportunity. Although our analysis found N-Queens satisfies the same properties as these, we could improve it up only slightly because its clock is used rarely and only in one part of the computation. Switching to the local clock implementation provided the majority of the speedup we observed, but our 5% improvement on the already heavily optimized distributed LU Factorization example is significant.

Our tool analyzed each example in under a minute and the model checker took less than a second in each case. Most of the construction time is spent in call- and control-flow graph constructions and aliasing analysis, which are already done for other reasons, so the added cost of our tool is on the order of seconds, making it reasonable to include as part of normal compilation.

7   Related Work

Typestate analysis [7] tracks the states that an object goes through during the execution. Standard typestate analysis and concurrency analysis are disjoint. Our analysis can be viewed as a typestate analysis for concurrent programs. Clocks are shared, stateful objects. We therefore have to track the state of each clock from the point of view of each activity.

Model checking concurrent programs [8,3] is usually demanding because of the potential for exponentially large state spaces often due to having to consider different interleavings of concurrent operations. In contrast, our technique analyzes concurrent programs as if they were sequential—we consider spawned tasks to be additional execution paths in a sequential program—hence avoiding the explosion.

Concurrency models come in many varieties. Vasudevan et al. [9] showed that the state space explosion can also be avoided by carefully choosing the primitives of the concurrent programming language. Unfortunately, this restricts the flexibility of the language. Our work focuses on concurrency constructs similar to those advocated by Vasudevan et al., but features like resume and aliased clocks are absent from their proposal. We trade a more flexible concurrency model against the need for further approximation in modeling the programs.

Static analysis of concurrency depends greatly on the underlying model. Although X10 supports both message-passing-style and shared-memory-style concurrency (in the case of co-located activities), we focus exclusively on its message-passing aspects, as have others. Mercouroff [10] approximates the number of messages between tasks in CSP [11] programs. Reppy and Xiao [12] analyze communication patterns in CML. Like ours, their work aims at identifying patterns amenable to more efficient implementations. They attempt to approximate the number of pending send and receive operations on a channel. Our work is both more specific—it focuses on clocks—and more general: our tool can cope with any CTL or LTL formula about clock operations.

Reppy and Xiao use modular techniques; we consider an X10 program as a whole. A modular approach may improve out tool's scaling, but we have not explored this yet.

Analysis of X10 programs has also been considered. Agarwal et al. [13] describe a novel algorithm for may-happen-in-parallel analysis in X10 that focuses on atomic sections. Chandra et al. [14] introduce a dependent type system for the specification and inference of object locations. We could use the latter to decide whether activities and clocks belong to the same place.

8   Conclusions and Future Work

We presented a static analysis technique for clocks in the X10 programming language. The result allows us to specialize the implementation of each clock, which we found resulted in substantial speed improvements on certain benchmark programs. Our technique has the advantage of being able to analyze a concurrent language using techniques for sequential code.

We treat each clock separately and model subtasks as extra paths in the program, much like conditionals. We abstract away conditional predicates, which simplifies the structure at the cost of introducing false positives. However, our technique is safe: we revert to the unoptimized, general purpose clock implementation when we are unsure a particular property is satisfied. Adding counterexample guided abstraction refinement [15] could help.

We produce two automata for each clock: one models the X10 program; the other encodes the protocol (typestate) for the clock. We express the automata in a form suitable for the NuSMV model checker. Experimentally, we find NuSMV is able to check properties for modestly sized examples in seconds, which we believe makes it fast enough to be part of the usual compilation process.

In the future, we plan to check for properties such as deadlock, which would involve considering interleavings rather than just the sequential analysis we currently use. For this reason we started with a powerful model checker like NuSMV. We also want to investigate other applications, such as using clock information from our static analyzer to refine pointer analysis of X10 programs.

Our current approach analyzes each clock as a whole. We may be able to improve the granularity by analyzing the program on a statement-by-statement basis. This would enable optimizing a clock operation at a particular line number differently from the same operation at another line number if we know more about the context of one operation compared to the other.

References

1. Charles, P., Grothoff, C., Saraswat, V., Donawa, C., Kielstra, A., Ebcioglu, K., von Praun, C., Sarkar, V.: X10: an object-oriented approach to non-uniform cluster computing. SIGPLAN Not. 40(10), 519–538 (2005)
2. Saraswat, V.A., Sarkar, V., von Praun, C.: X10: concurrent programming for modern architectures. In: PPoPP 2007: Proceedings of the 12th ACM SIGPLAN symposium on Principles and practice of parallel programming, p. 271. ACM, New York (2007)
3. Cimatti, A., Clarke, E.M., Giunchiglia, E., Giunchiglia, F., Pistore, M., Roveri, M., Sebastiani, R., Tacchella, A.: NuSMV version 2: An OpenSource tool for symbolic model checking. In: Brinksma, E., Larsen, K.G. (eds.) CAV 2002. LNCS, vol. 2404, pp. 359–364. Springer, Heidelberg (2002)
4. IBM, et al.: T. j. watson libraries for analysis (2006), http://wala.sourceforge.net
5. Vasudevan, N., Tardieu, O., Dolby, J., Edwards, S.A.: Analysis of clocks in x10 programs (extended). Technical Report CUCS–052–08, Columbia University, Department of Computer Science, New York, USA (December 2008)
6. Smith, L.A., Bull, J.M., Obdržálek, J.: A parallel java grande benchmark suite. In: Supercomputing 2001: Proceedings of the 2001 ACM/IEEE conference on Supercomputing (CDROM), p. 8. ACM, New York (2001)
7. Strom, R.E., Yemini, S.: Typestate: A programming language concept for enhancing software reliability. IEEE Transactions on Software Engineering 12(1), 157–171 (1986)
8. Clarke, E.M., Emerson, E.A., Sistla, A.P.: Automatic verification of finite-state concurrent systems using temporal logic specifications. ACM Transactions on Programming Languages and Systems 8(2), 244–263 (1986)
9. Vasudevan, N., Edwards, S.A.: Static deadlock detection for the SHIM concurrent language. In: Proceedings of the International Conference on Formal Methods and Models for Codesign (MEMOCODE), Anaheim, California (June 2008)
10. Mercouroff, N.: An algorithm for analyzing communicating processes. In: Schmidt, D., Main, M.G., Melton, A.C., Mislove, M.W., Brookes, S.D. (eds.) MFPS 1991. LNCS, vol. 598, pp. 312–325. Springer, Heidelberg (1992)
11. Hoare, C.A.R.: Communicating Sequential Processes. Prentice-Hall, Upper Saddle River (1985)
12. Reppy, J., Xiao, Y.: Specialization of CML message-passing primitives. SIGPLAN Notices 42(1), 315–326 (2007)
13. Agarwal, S., Barik, R., Sarkar, V., Shyamasundar, R.K.: May-happen-in-parallel analysis of x10 programs. In: Proceedings of Principles and Practice of Parallel Programming (PPoPP), pp. 183–193. ACM, New York (2007)
14. Chandra, S., Saraswat, V., Sarkar, V., Bodik, R.: Type inference for locality analysis of distributed data structures. In: Proceedings of Principles and Practice of Parallel Programming (PPoPP), pp. 11–22. ACM, New York (2008)
15. Clarke, E.M., Grumberg, O., Jha, S., Lu, Y., Veith, H.: Counterexample-guided abstraction refinement. In: Emerson, E.A., Sistla, A.P. (eds.) CAV 2000. LNCS, vol. 1855, pp. 154–169. Springer, Heidelberg (2000)

Implementation and Use of Transactional Memory with Dynamic Separation

Martín Abadi[1,2], Andrew Birrell[1], Tim Harris[3],
Johnson Hsieh[1], and Michael Isard[1]

[1] Microsoft Research, Silicon Valley
[2] University of California, Santa Cruz
[3] Microsoft Research, Cambridge

Abstract. We introduce the design and implementation of dynamic separation (DS) as a programming discipline for using transactional memory. Our approach is based on the programmer indicating which objects can be updated in transactions, which can be updated outside transactions, and which are read-only. We introduce explicit operations that identify transitions between these modes of access. We show how to guarantee strong semantics for programs that use these DS operations correctly, even over an STM implementation that provides only weak atomicity. We describe a run-time checking tool (analogous to a data-race detector) that can test whether or not a program is using DS operations correctly. We also examine the use of DS in an asynchronous IO library.

1 Introduction

Recently there has been much work on implementing atomic blocks over transactional memory (TM [1]). This approach provides an alternative to using locks and condition variables for shared-memory concurrency. Much effort has focused on the language constructs that are exposed to the programmer [2,3,4,5] and the semantics that an implementation of these constructs must obey [6,7,8]. The interaction between program fragments running transactionally and those running concurrently in normal code has been found to be particularly subtle [6,9,7,5]. A problematic example is the "privatization" idiom [10,11,12,6,5]:

```
// Initially x==0, x_shared=true

        // Thread 1                             // Thread 2
T1.1:   atomic {                        T2.1:   atomic {
T1.2:     x_shared = false;             T2.2:     if (x_shared) {
T1.3:   }                               T2.3:       x ++;
T1.4:   // Access x non-transactionally: T2.4:     }
T1.5:   x = 100;                        T2.5:   }
```

A programmer might reason that Thread 1's update to x_shared at line T1.2 allows its subsequent update to x at T1.5 to be made as a normal non-transactional store. After these fragments have run, a programmer might expect that x==100 whichever order the atomic blocks ran in. However, implementations over software transactional memory (STM [13]) lead to other results, e.g., x==1 if the

O. de Moor and M. Schwartzbach (Eds.): CC 2009, LNCS 5501, pp. 63–77, 2009.

implementation of Thread 2's atomic block was still writing back a buffered update to x concurrently with Thread 1's non-transactional store at T1.5.

In this paper we describe the design and implementation of a technique called dynamic separation (DS) for controlling such interactions. With DS each object has a "protection mode" that says whether or not the object can be accessed transactionally, and the programmer explicitly indicates when this mode should be changed. In our privatization example, the programmer would add a statement at line T1.4 to change the protection mode of x.

DS provides more flexibility to the programmer than existing notions of static separation that require each piece of data to be accessed either only transactionally or only non-transactionally [6,2,7]. With static separation we could not have objects like x which change protection modes. At the same time, DS provides less flexibility to the programmer than violation-freedom [6], which allows objects like x to change protection modes implicitly. DS also provides less flexibility to the programmer than disciplines that offer strong atomicity [14,15,16].

In a companion paper we study DS and its relationship to other programming disciplines from a formal point of view [17]. In this paper we focus on the design and practical implementation of DS. Our technical report [18] provides further details.

We introduce DS in detail in Section 2. We define criteria for a program using DS to be "correctly synchronized". Informally, these criteria mean that the program never tries to access transactional data from outside a transaction, nor to access non-transactional data from inside a transaction. These criteria provide a contract between the programmer and the language implementor: if a program is correctly synchronized then the implementation of DS must run the program consistently with a simple interleaved model of execution in which complete transactions run as single atomic steps and the effects of program transformations or relaxed processor memory models are not visible. We call this the "strong semantics" [6].

Such a contract benefits programmers by insulating them from TM implementation details: correct programs run with strong semantics on all correct implementations. This guarantee is convenient in the short term, since it simplifies the task of learning to use transactional constructs. In the longer term it is important that programs be portable: that they run efficiently, with identical semantics, over a range of STM implementations, and that they continue to run with the same semantics, and without unnecessary overheads, once hardware transactional memory (HTM) becomes widely available. In addition, such a contract benefits the language implementor by providing a clear definition of which program transformations and implementation techniques are correct.

We discuss the application of DS to C# in Section 3, along with its implementation over an STM with in-place updates and optimistic concurrency control [19]. We sketch a correctness argument—in our companion paper we prove the correctness of a model based on our implementation [17].

In Section 4 we describe how we compile programs using DS in a debugging mode that dynamically checks whether or not a program is correctly synchronized from the point of view of a particular program run. The checking method gives no false alarms (i.e., no errors are reported for programs that are correctly synchronized), and no missing error reports (i.e., if there is no error report then the program executed with strong semantics in that run).

We evaluate the use of DS in a set of applications built over a concurrent IO library (Section 5). We wrote these applications in the AME programming model [3] where—in contrast with typical approaches that employ atomic blocks—the transactions are not block-structured, and the majority of execution occurs within transactions rather than outside them. We examine the extent to which DS may work in a "traditional" use of atomic blocks in Section 6.

We discuss related work in Section 7 and conclusions in Section 8.

2   Dynamic Separation

DS can be summarized as follows:

- We distinguish dynamically between transactional ("protected") data, non-transactional ("unprotected") data, and read-only data. By default, data allocated inside a transaction is created in "protected" mode and data allocated outside a transaction is created in "unprotected" mode.
- We provide explicit operations (protect/unprotect/share) to move data between these modes.
- For a program to be "correctly synchronized" it must use these operations so that it obeys two rules when run under strong semantics:
    Rule-1: The program accesses data only in the correct mode: read-only data may be read anywhere but not updated, protected data may be accessed freely inside transactions, and unprotected data may be accessed freely outside transactions.
    Rule-2: The DS operations to move data between these modes occur only outside transactions.

If a program obeys these rules then the language implementation is required to run it with strong semantics even if the underlying STM provides weaker guarantees. As an illustration, we return to the privatization example from the Introduction with an explicit unprotect operation added at line T1.4:

```
// Initially x==0, x_shared=true.
// Both variables are initially protected.

T1.1:  atomic { // A1              T2.1:  atomic { // A2
T1.2:    x_shared = false;        T2.2:    if (x_shared) {
T1.3:  }                          T2.3:      x ++;
T1.4:  unprotect(x);             T2.4:    }
T1.5:  x = 100;                   T2.5:  }
```

To show that the example is correctly synchronized we need to consider the different possible executions under strong semantics, and show that none of the conditions in Rule-1 and Rule-2 is violated.

Rule-2 is satisfied because the only DS operation, T1.4, occurs outside the atomic blocks. Rule-1 is satisfied with respect to the accesses to x_shared because that variable is initially protected, and is accessed only inside the atomic blocks. We must consider two cases to show that Rule-1 is also satisfied with respect to the accesses to x: (i) if A1 executes before A2 then A2 will see x_shared==false, so A2 will not attempt to access x; (ii) if A1 executes after A2 then A2 will access x when x is still protected. In either case, the accesses to x satisfy Rule-1.

Since the example is correctly synchronized, an implementation that supports DS must run it with strong semantics. To illustrate why this requirement may pose a problem, consider the execution of this example using an STM, such as Bartok-STM [19], that employs a combination of commit-time conflict detection and in-place updates. Suppose that A2 executes up to line T2.3, and A1 then executes in its entirety. The implementation will allow A1 to commit successfully, and will force A2 to roll back only at the point when it tries to commit. However, before A2 reaches that point, A2 will execute line T2.3 and will increment the value of x. The implementation of unprotect must ensure that T2.3 does not race with T1.5. Our implementation does this by causing an unprotect operation to block until conflicting transactions have finished rolling back. We present our implementation based on Bartok-STM in detail in Section 3.

Next, we resolve some subtleties in the details of DS, and discuss the rationale for the design (in particular the reasons for Rule-1 and Rule-2). Three principles motivate many of our design decisions:

1. The "fundamental property" [20]: The criteria for using DS correctly should be defined in terms of a program's execution under strong semantics. This makes programs portable across TM implementations.
2. Compatibility with normal memory accesses: We want to avoid needing to modify non-transactional memory accesses; we do not want to modify accesses from within the kernel, and we cannot add barriers to reads and writes performed by direct-memory-access (DMA) from devices.
3. Implementation flexibility and parallelism: We want to support a wide range of implementations—for example STMs which make in-place updates (e.g., [19,21]), STMs which defer updates until transactions commit (e.g., [11]) as well as HTMs and implementations based on lock inference. We want to avoid introducing contention between non-conflicting operations and to avoid adding costs to implementations with strong native guarantees (e.g., implementations based on lock inference should not have to dynamically track which objects are protected).

The semantics of DS requires several delicate design choices. For example, what if protect is called on a location that is already protected? Could DS operations be called anywhere (that is, could Rule-2 be eliminated)? What happens if data is accessed in the wrong way: should the access fail with an exception, or continue regardless? If such an access is implemented by a transaction, then should the transaction block, or be rolled-back and re-executed? What if code tries to write to read-only data?

Our goal of supporting DS over many different implementations provides a way of selecting between different options. Conversely, other decisions would be possible if we restricted attention to particular implementation techniques. Many design choices follow from considering two extreme kinds of TM:

- HTM with strong atomicity: We do not want to impose the overhead of tracking per-object protection states when the underlying TM provides strong atomicity. Hence we avoid design choices that require this information to be available at run-time: we cannot require DS operations to block or fail if called on the wrong kind of data. Similarly, we cannot require data accesses to block or fail if made on the wrong kind of data.
- STM implemented with in-place updates and optimistic concurrency control: Considering this particular kind of STM motivates the rule that DS operations cannot occur inside transactions. The following example, which does not obey Rule-2, illustrates this point:

```
// Initially b_shared=true, b_shared protected, b unprotected

atomic {                    atomic {
  // Atomic block A1          // Atomic block A2
  b_shared = false; // 3      if (!b_shared) { // 1
}                               protect(b); // 2
<update b>;  // 5               <update b>; // 4
                                unprotect(b);
                            } }
```

If we were to allow DS operations within atomic blocks then this example would be correctly synchronized (either A1 runs first, in which case A2 does not access b, or A2 runs first and A1 sees A2's updates). However, with optimistic concurrency control, the steps could execute in the order shown: A2 is doomed to roll back but, with lazy detection, the conflict has not yet been identified and the memory updates at 4 and 5 will race. It is insufficient to validate A2 as part of step 2 because the conflict does not occur until step 3. We therefore decide that DS operations cannot be invoked inside atomic blocks. Again, one could make other decisions if interest were restricted to particular implementation techniques. We return to this point in Section 6.

3   Implementing Dynamic Separation in C#

In this section, we discuss implementations of DS. First, we describe how we apply the idea of DS to the C# language (Section 3.1). Second, we describe how we extend the Bartok-STM implementation to support correctly synchronized programs with strong atomicity (Section 3.2).

3.1   Dynamic Separation in C#

Three general questions arise in applying dynamic separation to C#:

First, at what granularity do we associate protection status with data? We chose to dynamically associate a protection mode with each C# object. We considered alternatives: per-class settings would hinder code re-use (e.g., all Hashtable objects would have to be protected or all unprotected), and per-field settings would require repeated DS operations (e.g., on each element of an array, introducing similar asymptotic costs to marshaling the data by copying). We do not associate a protection mode with variables because they remain thread-local. We chose to statically declare the protection mode of static fields rather than letting them change mode dynamically. Our reasoning is that static fields often represent read-only state that is accessed by many threads in different protection modes: the field and the data reachable from it remain read-only. This engineering choice could readily be revisited.

The second design question is how to represent the DS operations. Rather than adding keywords we make the operations virtual methods on the `Object` superclass. By default these methods change the protection mode of the object itself. This lets the programmer override the methods to provide class-specific functionality (e.g., to change the protection mode of a whole object graph).

The final question is exactly which operations constitute "accesses" to data for the purpose of defining correct synchronization. Following our approach in Section 2 our design is motivated by considering a range of implementation techniques, and where problems or overheads would be incurred. This led us to the general principle that we police only accesses to the normal fields of objects (or, in the case of arrays, their elements); accesses to read-only information such as virtual method tables are permitted anywhere. Our technical report considers a number of language features in detail [18].

3.2   Implementation in Bartok-STM

Bartok-STM [19] uses weak atomicity with in-place updates and optimistic concurrency control. This combination of features has been found to perform well [21] and also to be particularly troublesome in terms of problems like privatization [6,5]. Therefore we focus in detail on it because we believe that this is the most challenging setting in which to implement DS correctly.

Background, Bartok-STM design. The STM associates meta-data with each heap object and, within transactions, adds operations to open each object before it is accessed—`OpenForRead` on objects about to be read and `OpenForUpdate` on objects about to be updated. The meta-data, called an object's "STM word", records a version number indicating how many times the object has been opened for update. This number is logged in `OpenForRead` and re-checked during transaction validation: a concurrent change indicates a conflict. The STM word also contains a flag indicating whether the object is currently "owned" by a transaction, i.e., open for update. This flag is used to enforce mutual exclusion between writers. An invalid transaction may continue to execute as a "zombie" before a conflict is detected [11]. The runtime system sandboxes failures such as null reference exceptions if they occur in this state. The runtime system also guarantees that zombie transactions will be detected and rolled back.

Representing protected objects dynamically. We modify the STM word to include a flag in place of one bit of the version number. If the flag is set then the object is protected. If the flag is clear then the object is either unprotected or read-only. (As we show, this implementation need not distinguish between these cases,

```
void DSOpenForUpdate(tm_mgr tx, object obj) {
  STMOpenForUpdate(tx, obj);
  if (!IsProtected(GetSTMWord(obj))) {
    if (STMIsValid(tx)) {
      // Valid and choosing to access an unprotected object
      throw new DynamicProtectionError(); // Fail (uncatchable)
    } else {
      // Choice to access object may be based on invalid state
      STMAbort(tx); // Roll back and re-execute
} } }
```

Fig. 1. Production implementation of open-for-update supporting DS

although our checking tool in Section 4 must.) The flag is initialized along with the rest of the object's header when an object is allocated and then modified only by the implementations of protect/unprotect/share.

Correctness argument. Our companion paper [17] contains a correctness theorem in the context of the AME calculus. Here we include a brief informal sketch of the main points. The modified STM implementation maintains an invariant that transactions update only objects whose protection flags are set. This means that zombie transactions will not trample on read-only or unprotected objects. So, if the program is correctly synchronized, such transactions' updates will not be seen by non-transactional code.

We maintain this invariant by (i) modifying the function OpenForUpdate so that it provides access only to protected objects, (ii) ensuring that unprotect and share (which revoke write access from protected code) block until there is no concurrent transaction with the object open for update (note that since DS operations can be used only outside transactions, this does not provide a way to create deadlock between transactions), and (iii) our restriction that DS operations occur only in unprotected code rather than during the execution of a (possibly invalid) transaction.

Our treatment of objects that are read (but not updated) is more subtle: we do not need to check whether or not they are protected. The reason is that we aim to guarantee strong semantics only for correctly synchronized programs: if a program is correctly synchronized, and a transaction running in it is still valid, then it will read only from protected and read-only objects. Conversely, if the transaction is not valid, then the invalidity will be detected in the normal way. In either case, we meet the requirement to run correctly synchronized programs with strong semantics.

Pseudo-code. Figure 1 shows DSOpenForUpdate in pseudo-code. (We use a DS prefix on functions provided by the new run-time with DS, and an STM prefix on the underlying functions provided by the existing STM.) The implementation starts by opening the object for update, leaving the protection bit unchanged. Then, before the transaction can update the object, it examines the protection bit. If the object is protected then the transaction proceeds as usual. Otherwise, if the object is not protected, then the transaction is validated. If it is valid then the program is not correctly synchronized: it is about to access an unprotected

```
void DSUnprotect(tm_mgr tx, object obj) {
  while (true) {
    w = GetSTMWord(obj);
    if (!IsProtected(w)) {
      break; // Already unprotected/readonly: done
    } else if (IsOwned(w)) {
      continue; // Wait until object not open for update
    } else {
      new_w = CreateSTMWord(w.GetVersion(),
                            NOT_PROTECTED, NOT_OWNED);
      if (CASSTMWord(obj, w, new_w)) {
        break; // Installed new STM word; done
} } } }
```

Fig. 2. Production implementation of `DSUnprotect`

object transactionally so the program fails with an error. If the transaction is invalid then the transaction is aborted and re-executed.

We extend the STM interface with operations that correspond to `protect`, `unprotect`, and `share`. We show `unprotect` in pseudo-code in Figure 2. This implementation is a loop which repeats until either (i) it observes that the object is already unprotected (either before the call, or by a concurrent `unprotect`), or (ii) it succeeds in making the object unprotected. In the second case, execution cannot proceed until the object is not owned by any transaction (`IsOwned` returns false) to preserve the invariant that protected code updates only protected objects. (Even in a correctly synchronized program, a zombie transaction may still have a previously protected object open for update: we must wait for such transactions to drain from the system.)

The implementation of `share` is identical to that of `unprotect` because the STM does not need to distinguish read-only objects from unprotected ones. The implementation of `protect` is symmetric to that of `unprotect` with the negation removed on `!IsProtected`, the STM word being created with a `PROTECTED` flag rather than `NOT_PROTECTED`, and the test of `IsOwned` being redundant.

4   Dynamically Checking Correct Usage

We extended the Bartok compiler with a debug mode that provides dynamic checks of whether or not a program run is correctly synchronized. This mode works much like dynamic race detectors. Our goal is to report errors without any false alarms, without missing error reports, and with all execution before the error being correct under strong semantics.

We do not place any dynamic checks on accesses to local variables since stacks are thread-local in C#. We handle accesses to static fields during compilation: the compiler generates two versions of each method, one for use inside transactions, and another for use outside. We compile correct-mode accesses as usual and incorrect-mode accesses to code that will report an error if it is executed.

Object accesses are handled by checking protection information in the object's STM word. Unlike in the production implementation we must distinguish between unprotected data and read-only data, in order to report errors where unprotected code attempts to update putatively read-only data. We make this distinction by reserving a further bit from the STM word. (We still have 27 bits of version number space and mechanisms to recover from overflow [19].)

We must distinguish four sources of memory accesses:

1. Transactional code: At runtime we must report an error if either (i) a valid transaction opens an unprotected or read-only object for writing, or (ii) a valid transaction sees an unprotected object in its read set.
2. Non-transactional code: We must check the object's protection mode atomically with the data access: otherwise, in an incorrectly synchronized program, a concurrent thread may protect the data and access it transactionally, letting us see a non-committed transaction's write without reporting an error. We deal with this difficulty in a similar way to Shpeisman et al. [14]: we expand each non-transactional access into a series of steps that accesses the STM word along with the data location. In effect we treat the access as a small transaction.
3. Runtime system (RTS) code: The GC and other pieces of the RTS are implemented in C# and compiled along with the application. The RTS performs its own concurrency control—e.g., using locks to protect free-lists in the memory allocator, or ensuring that all application threads are stopped before the GC traverses the heap. We must not report errors from such accesses made by RTS code. We therefore introduce a new source-code attribute `RTSRoot` to identify entry points to the RTS. Such methods are compiled without access-mode checks along, recursively, with any code they call. The RTS does not call into application code, so the resulting duplication is limited to a small number of system classes (e.g., `System.UIntPtr` whose instances represent pointer-sized integers).
4. Native code: In correctly synchronized programs an object passed to native code must have been pinned in unprotected code. We test that (i) an object is unprotected when it is pinned, and (ii) an object being protected is not pinned.

5   Evaluation

We have used the implementation described in Section 3 to study the effectiveness of DS. We evaluate DS within the AME programming model [3]. In this setting, all code runs inside a transaction by default and non-transactional code is explicitly delimited by the programmer. In Section 6 we briefly discuss how DS might be used in a traditional TM programming model with atomic blocks.

The performance of a program with DS depends on several factors: the immediate cost of the DS operations, the overhead that supporting them adds to the TM, and any costs incurred in structuring the program to use DS.

Using Bartok-STM, the fast-path of the DS operations is a single read then compare-and-swap (CAS) on the object's STM word. If the CAS fails then the slow path distinguishes the different cases as in the pseudo-code of Figure 2. DS operations block only if the object is open-for-update by a transaction (which, in a correctly synchronized program, must be a zombie transaction). This delay is the same as for a non-transactional access in typical software implementations of strong atomicity [14,15,16]. Supporting DS adds no overhead to the fast-path of the existing STM operations: the check of whether or not an object is protected is combined with an existing test of whether or not it is open for update.

These performance characteristics would change slightly for an STM with deferred updates: the DS operations would never need to wait for transactions to roll back, though they might still block while a transaction is committing. Again, these costs resemble those of a non-transactional access in Shpeisman *et al.*'s design. With hardware support for strong atomicity the DS operations would be no-ops and, of course, no changes would be needed to the TM implementation.

A more subtle question is how performance is affected by structuring a program to be correctly synchronized under DS. There are both positive and negative effects. In comparison with static separation, DS may allow marshaling code to be removed. In comparison with violation-freedom or a single-global-lock discipline, DS requires the DS operations themselves, of course, and also that the program be structured so that the DS operations are called appropriately. Moreover, while the DS operations add a cost, the underlying implementations of more permissive models limit scalability by introducing synchronization between non-conflicting transactions [8] and preclude the use of in-place updates [6].

We examined the performance of two applications built over an IO library used with the AME programming model [3]. Most of the code in these applications executes transactionally, with brief calls out into normal code to perform IO requests that have been enqueued by a transaction. Buffers are transferred between these modes by using DS operations. We describe the design and implementation of the IO library more thoroughly in our technical report [18].

The first application, `FileTest`, is a micro-benchmark which copies a file on disk using asynchronous IO requests. We build two versions: "dummy" in which the underlying IOs are not sent to the kernel, and "real" in which they are. The dummy version makes this loop CPU-bound, highlighting the overhead added by the DS operations. The second application, `WebProxy`, is a caching web proxy which interacts with multiple concurrent clients and web servers, maintaining an on-disk page cache. We load the web proxy with 1..4 concurrent client requests. In each case we use sufficiently large files that the execution time is readily measurable. We use an otherwise-unloaded machine with dual 4-core processors and plentiful memory. Both applications are quite simple, and our experiments can be interpreted mostly as a sanity check that our implementation does not introduce any unexpected overhead.

Figure 3 shows the results. We compare five different implementations. "Baseline" uses the underlying STM with DS disabled. We normalise against its performance. "Baseline + DS" is our implementation of DS. "Run-time checking" is the implementation described in Section 4. `WebProxy` performs and scales identically to a (more complicated) alternative built using traditional synchronization.

As expected, the overhead of "Baseline + DS" over "Baseline" is less than 1%, even in the CPU-bound program. However, the "Baseline" is not a correct

	FileTest (dummy)	FileTest (real)	WebProxy (1)	WebProxy (2)	WebProxy (3)	WebProxy (4)
Baseline	1.00	1.00	1.00	1.11	1.27	1.49
Baseline + DS	1.00	1.00	1.00	1.11	1.27	1.49
Serialized	1.41	1.27	1.00	1.11	1.27	1.49
Serialized + DS	1.42	1.27	1.00	1.11	1.27	1.49
Run-time checking	1.01	1.02	1.00	1.11	1.27	1.49

Fig. 3. Performance of test applications—execution time, normalised against "baseline" and, for `WebProxy`, a 1-client workload

implementation because it may allow undetected conflicts between transactional and non-transactional accesses in correctly synchronized programs. To confirm that this did not distort results (for example, if such race conditions delayed the baseline execution), we built an alternative "Serialized" implementation that serializes transactions with a global lock wrapped around the baseline STM implementation. This implementation correctly supports DS with the operations compiled as no-ops. In "Serialized + DS", we add the normal DS implementation.

Finally, we studied an alternative implementation of the IO library built to maintain static separation between transactional and non-transactional data. Prior to developing DS this was the only correct programmer-centric programming model we had identified for writing programs with Bartok-STM. Static separation requires data to be marshaled between access modes. Even with the IO-intensive AME applications we are using, this made the total execution time over 10 times longer than "Baseline + DS".

6   Using Dynamic Separation with Atomic Blocks

We designed the DS operations alongside the AME programming model [3]. There are several differences between AME and typical proposals to extend mainstream languages with atomic blocks. First, in the AME model, a program consists almost entirely of atomic sections. These are punctuated by "unprotected" code blocks which finish the ongoing atomic section, execute non-transactionally, and then start a new atomic section. Consequently the atomic sections are not necessarily block-structured. The second difference is that unprotected blocks are primarily intended for use in low-level libraries (such as the IO library of the examples in Section 5). They typically occur at the interface between code written in C# and native code, and include low-level operations like pinning objects in memory so that the GC does not move or reclaim them. In this context it seems reasonable to add other explicit operations, like those for DS.

To what extent is DS an appropriate discipline for programming with block-structured transactions in a mainstream language? We previously showed that such a language can be encoded in AME [6], so the theory carries over. The question is whether DS forms a palatable programming model.

One seemingly attractive feature of programming with atomic blocks is the notion that arbitrary sections of code may be placed in atomic blocks, so long as the program is correctly synchronized. This feature would not hold under our DS design, since changes in an object's protection mode may not occur inside atomic blocks (Rule-2 of Section 2). Consequently, any code that uses DS operations may be executed only non-transactionally, and programmers must be aware of whether or not functions that they call might use DS operations internally.

However, we speculate that programs in which data changes between transactional and non-transactional accesses will need to be carefully written anyway, in order to avoid race conditions. It may not be unreasonable, therefore, to imagine that programmers will already need to be aware of whether or not a given function call will attempt to change the access mode of a given piece of data.

If Rule-2 were to prove problematic, we believe it would be possible to permit DS operations to occur anywhere in a program, at the loss of some implementation flexibility. In particular, given the last example from Section 2, we believe that this change would restrict DS to STMs that make deferred updates or that detect conflicts eagerly.

7   Related Work

Adve and Hill pioneered the approach of requiring correctly synchronized programs to run with sequential consistency, and the use of a programmer-centric definition of which programs are correctly synchronized [22]. Hill subsequently argued that hardware should provide sequential consistency [23]. However, the design of a language's memory model must consider not only the properties of hardware but also program transformations made by compilers. Spear *et al.* [5] and Abadi *et al.* [6] concurrently identified the link between Adve and Hill's work and languages implemented over TM with weak atomicity.

Many papers have examined semantics and corresponding programming disciplines for the use of TM:

Strong programming disciplines.   Shpeisman *et al.* showed how to guarantee strong atomicity over an STM that natively provides weak atomicity [14]. Subsequent work has improved on the performance of such implementations [15,16]. Lev and Maessen introduced the idea of compiling non-transactional memory accesses to include a run-time check of whether the data being accessed is visible to transactions [24]. If so, the data is accessed using the TM. Their design tracks data's visibility at run-time, marking objects as transactional when they are made reachable via an existing transactional object. None of these approaches meets our goal of allowing implementations with weak atomicity in which the kernel or DMA transfers can access program data directly.

Violation-freedom.   Violation-freedom [6] formalizes the notion that the same data should not be accessed transactionally and non-transactionally at the same time. Running violation-free programs with strong semantics seems to conflict with our goal of implementation flexibility: it can preclude STM implementations with optimistic concurrency control and in-place updates [6].

Single-Global-Lock Atomicity (SGLA). Menon *et al.* [8] defined a "single-global-lock atomicity" semantics for transactions in Java. SGLA relates the behavior of a program with atomic blocks to one where those blocks are replaced by synchronized regions on a process-wide lock. The transactional program is correctly synchronized if the resulting lock-based program is correctly synchronized under the Java memory model. Supporting SGLA (like assuming violation-freedom) does not meet our goal of implementation flexibility. Known implementations of SGLA involve either pessimistic read locks or synchronization between non-conflicting transactions.

Transactional fences. Dice and Shavit identified the need for an operation to "quiesce" a transactionally accessed object before it is deallocated after a transaction [10]. This operation ensures that the STM implementation has finished all accesses to the object before, for example, the page holding it might be returned to the operating system. Wang *et al.*'s implementation of atomic blocks for C [12] uses a similar form of quiescence to ensure that code running after a transaction sees updates made by preceding transactions. Wang *et al.*'s implementation maintains a shared list of active transactions that is updated when transactions start or commit. These updates require synchronization with all concurrent transactions, rather than just those accessing a specific object. Spear *et al.* designed several techniques to implement privatization idioms correctly, including explicit "transactional fences" and "validation fences" [5]. A thread calling a transactional fence is blocked until any concurrent transactions have committed. A validation fence is similar, except that a thread may proceed once concurrent transactions have been validated. Unlike SGLA and violation-freedom, supporting these fences seems compatible with a wide range of TM implementations that allow non-conflicting transactions to run without synchronization between their implementations.

Static separation. Under static separation disciplines, each piece of data is accessed either only transactionally or only non-transactionally. Several definitions of static separation have been considered, typically implemented via type systems ([6,2,7]). While static separation is appealing in functional languages like Haskell [2], it is less palatable in imperative languages where most data comprises mutable shared objects. Data has to be marshaled between different access modes by copying. Moreover, if static separation is expressed through a type system, then simple versions of static separation can impede code re-use (much like all simple type systems). DS allows data to change access modes without being copied. Our implementation of DS aids code re-use by checking dynamically that data is accessed in the correct mode, rather than using a simple type system.

8   Conclusion

We believe that DS has several appealing properties. It can be used over a wide range of TM implementations. It does not introduce synchronization between non-conflicting transactions, and it allows unprotected data to be accessed freely by system calls and DMA transfers. When used with HTMs or with lock inference, it avoids imposing a runtime overhead for protection flags. Finally, DS is based on a simple, precise definition for correct synchronization which may serve as the foundation for further formal reasoning and for static checking.

Acknowledgements. We are grateful to the anonymous reviewers, and to Katie Coons, Rebecca Isaacs, Yossi Levanoni, Jean-Philippe Martin, Mark Moir, and Katherine Moore for helpful discussions and comments.

References

1. Herlihy, M., Moss, J.E.B.: Transactional memory: Architectural support for lock-free data structures. In: ISCA 1993, 20th International Symposium on Computer Architecture, pp. 289–301 (May 1993)
2. Harris, T., Marlow, S., Peyton Jones, S., Herlihy, M.: Composable memory transactions. In: PPoPP 2005, 10th ACM SIGPLAN Symposium on Principles and Practice of Parallel Programming, pp. 48–60 (June 2005)
3. Isard, M., Birrell, A.: Automatic mutual exclusion. In: HotOS 2007, 11th Workshop on Hot Topics in Operating Systems (May 2007)
4. Smaragdakis, Y., Kay, A., Behrends, R., Young, M.: Transactions with isolation and cooperation. In: OOPSLA 2007, 22nd ACM SIGPLAN Conference on Object Oriented Programming Systems and Applications (October 2007)
5. Spear, M.F., Marathe, V.J., Dalessandro, L., Scott, M.L.: Privatization techniques for software transactional memory. Technical Report 915, CS Dept, U. Rochester (February 2007)
6. Abadi, M., Birrell, A., Harris, T., Isard, M.: Semantics of transactional memory and automatic mutual exclusion. In: POPL 2008, 35th ACM SIGPLAN-SIGACT Symposium on Principles of Programming Languages, pp. 63–74 (2008)
7. Moore, K.F., Grossman, D.: High-level small-step operational semantics for transactions. In: POPL 2008, 35th ACM SIGPLAN-SIGACT Symposium on Principles of Programming Languages, pp. 51–62 (January 2008)
8. Menon, V., Balensiefer, S., Shpeisman, T., Adl-Tabatabai, A.R., Hudson, R.L., Saha, B., Welc, A.: Practical weak-atomicity semantics for Java STM. In: SPAA 2008, 20th Symposium on Parallelism in Algorithms and Architectures, pp. 314–325 (June 2008)
9. Blundell, C., Lewis, E.C., Martin, M.M.K.: Deconstructing transactional semantics: The subtleties of atomicity. In: WDDD 2005, 4th Workshop on Duplicating, Deconstructing and Debunking, pp. 48–55 (June 2005)
10. Dice, D., Shavit, N.: What really makes transactions faster? In: TRANSACT 2006, 1st ACM SIGPLAN Workshop on Languages, Compilers, and Hardware Support for Transactional Computing (June 2006)
11. Dice, D., Shalev, O., Shavit, N.: Transactional locking II. In: DISC 2006, 20th International Symposium on Distributed Computing, pp. 194–208 (September 2006)
12. Wang, C., Chen, W.Y., Wu, Y., Saha, B., Adl-Tabatabai, A.R.: Code generation and optimization for transactional memory constructs in an unmanaged language. In: CGO 2007, International Symposium on Code Generation and Optimization, pp. 34–48 (March 2007)

13. Shavit, N., Touitou, D.: Software transactional memory. In: Proc. 14th Annual ACM Symposium on Principles of Distributed Computing, pp. 204–213 (August 1995)

14. Shpeisman, T., Menon, V., Adl-Tabatabai, A.R., Balensiefer, S., Grossman, D., Hudson, R.L., Moore, K.F., Saha, B.: Enforcing isolation and ordering in STM. In: PLDI 2007, ACM SIGPLAN Conference on Programming Language Design and Implementation, pp. 78–88 (June 2007)

15. Schneider, F.T., Menon, V., Shpeisman, T., Adl-Tabatabai, A.R.: Dynamic optimization for efficient strong atomicity. In: OOPSLA 2008, 23rd ACM SIGPLAN Conference on Object Oriented Programming Systems Languages and Applications, pp. 181–194 (October 2008)

16. Abadi, M., Harris, T., Mehrara, M.: Transactional memory with strong atomicity using off-the-shelf memory protection hardware. In: PPoPP 2009, 14th ACM SIGPLAN Symposium on Principles and Practice of Parallel Programming (February 2009)

17. Abadi, M., Harris, T., Moore, K.F.: A model of dynamic separation for transactional memory. In: CONCUR 2008, 19th International Conference on Concurrency Theory, pp. 6–20 (August 2008)

18. Abadi, M., Birrell, A., Harris, T., Hsieh, J., Isard, M.: Dynamic separation for transactional memory. Technical Report MSR-TR-2008-43 (March 2008)

19. Harris, T., Plesko, M., Shinnar, A., Tarditi, D.: Optimizing memory transactions. In: PLDI 2006, ACM SIGPLAN Conference on Programming Language Design and Implementation, pp. 14–25 (June 2006)

20. Saraswat, V.A., Jagadeesan, R., Michael, M., von Praun, C.: A theory of memory models. In: PPoPP 2007, 12th ACM SIGPLAN Symposium on Principles and Practice of Parallel Programming, pp. 161–172 (March 2007)

21. Saha, B., Adl-Tabatabai, A.R., Hudson, R.L., Minh, C.C., Hertzberg, B.: McRT-STM: a high performance software transactional memory system for a multi-core runtime. In: PPoPP 2006, 11th ACM SIGPLAN Symposium on Principles and Practice of Parallel Programming, pp. 187–197 (March 2006)

22. Adve, S.V., Hill, M.D.: Weak ordering – a new definition. ACM SIGARCH Comput. Archit. News 18(3a), 2–14 (1990)

23. Hill, M.D.: Multiprocessors should support simple memory-consistency models. Computer 31(8), 28–34 (1998)

24. Lev, Y., Maessen, J.W.: Towards a safer interaction with transactional memory by tracking object visibility. In: SCOOL 2005, Workshop on Synchronization and Concurrency in Object-Oriented Languages (October 2005)

Exploiting Speculative TLP in Recursive Programs by Dynamic Thread Prediction

Lin Gao[1], Lian Li[1], Jingling Xue[1], and Tin-Fook Ngai[2]

[1] University of New South Wales, Sydney, Australia
[2] Microprocessor Technology Lab, Intel

Abstract. Speculative parallelisation represents a promising solution to speed up sequential programs that are hard to parallelise otherwise. Prior research has focused mainly on parallelising loops. Recursive procedures, which are also frequently used in real-world applications, have attracted much less attention. Moreover, the parallel threads in prior work are statically predicted and spawned. In this paper, we introduce a new compiler technique, called *Speculative Parallelisation of Recursive Procedures* (SPRP), to exploit speculative TLP (thread-level parallelism) in recursive procedures. SPRP combines a dynamic thread-spawning policy and a live-in prediction mechanism in a single helper thread that executes a distilled version of a procedure on a dedicated core. It serves to predict both the invocation order of recursive calls and their live-ins in concert and dispatches these calls to the other cores in a multicore system for parallel execution. To our knowledge, SPRP is the first compiler technique to speculatively parallelise recursive procedures this way. Compared with existing static thread prediction techniques, dynamic thread prediction reduces the number of useless threads spawned, and consequently, misspeculation overhead incurred. Our preliminary results demonstrate that this technique can speedup certain recursive benchmarks that are difficult to parallelise otherwise.

1 Introduction

Parallelisation of sequential programs has been an on-going research area. Prior work has focused mainly on loops. Recursive procedures, which are also frequently used in real-world applications, have attracted much less attention.

When call sites in a recursive procedure are data-independent (as in many divide-and-conquer algorithms), techniques for their automatic parallelisation exist [20, 22, 10, 24, 21]. Such techniques have demonstrated performance advantages in achieving task-level parallelism among independent calls in regular programs and even irregular programs when they are either augmented with dependence-related programmer annotations or written in a certain programming style, e.g., component-based programming. Also, parallel programming languages such as those discussed in [5, 4] allow a concise specification of parallel algorithms on irregular data; but they rely entirely on the domain-expert programmer to expose the parallelism by identifying the tasks that can safely be executed in parallel. However, when dependence analysis is inconclusive and user/programmer involvements are unavailable, the potential presence of dependences will limit parallelism to be exploited.

O. de Moor and M. Schwartzbach (Eds.): CC 2009, LNCS 5501, pp. 78–93, 2009.

Speculative multithreading (SpMT) processors [15, 18, 19, 1, 13, 9] enable the compiler to apply speculative parallelisation to optimistically create parallel threads for a sequential program without having to prove they are independent. The basic idea is to speculate on the absence of certain data/control dependences to expose more speculative TLP (thread-level parallelism) at the cost of small misspeculation penalties [30, 23, 3, 17, 27, 11, 18, 1, 26, 8, 25, 29]. So far research efforts have been largely devoted to extracting speculative TLP from loops. A few attempts have been made to speculatively parallelise whole programs [12, 15, 23, 3, 11, 6, 1]; but they are not designed to maximally exploit speculative TLP in recursive procedures. Moreover, parallel threads in all these existing approaches are either statically predicted and spawned or automatically extracted by hardware at procedures, loops or cache line boundaries.

Static (thread) prediction can be quite effective in parallelising loops because the execution order of loop iterations is statically predictable (except the last one, which needs to be control-speculated). However, this compile-time decision becomes less effective when applied to recursive procedures. The data structure operated on by a recursive procedure can vary from input to input and can also change dynamically during program execution. Therefore, when the dynamic call graph of a recursive procedure is speculated, the invocation order of recursive call instances becomes nondeterministic and the potential presence of speculation failures can severely limit parallelism to be exploited.

In this paper, we present a new compiler technique, called *Speculative Parallelisation of Recursive Procedures* (SPRP), to speculatively parallelise recursive procedures for SpMT architectures. We restrict ourselves to those irregular programs that cannot be parallelised effectively by existing techniques. Furthermore, we are particularly interested in those where recursive calls are control-dependent on some runtime values so that only a portion of their underlying data structures, which may also change at run time, may be traversed. As a result, the invocation order of recursive calls is non-trivial to predict accurately, even at run time.

For a given recursive procedure, SPRP will transform it into a helper thread running on a dedicated core and a group of worker threads running on the other cores in a SpMT multicore system. The helper thread, which is a smaller, faster version distilled from the original procedure, serves to predict both the invocation order of recursive calls made and their live-in values as well as to dynamically schedule these calls to run as parallel worker threads. The helper thread is not constrained by correctness. Thus, its predictions are validated whenever a worker thread has run to completion. When a prediction goes wrong, a recovery mechanism introduced in this paper will bring the helper thread back to the point where new predictions (for the future recursive calls) will be made. Due to dynamic thread prediction and thread spawning, SPRP is capable of exploiting more TLP in recursive procedures that is otherwise difficult to exploit in other ways as validated in our experiments.

We have evaluated SPRP using four representative irregular recursive procedures using a cycle-accurate simulator. Our preliminary results are encouraging. An average region speedup of 1.29 for recursive procedures and an average program speedup of 1.21 have been achieved by our technique on four cores. It is important to emphasise that such programs may have to be left to run sequentially on one single core otherwise (unless they are manually parallelised by domain experts). So this work demonstrates the significant performance potential achievable by automatic parallelisation of hard-to-parallelise recursive procedures, providing insights on further research in this area.

The rest of this paper is organised as follows. Section 2 reviews the related work. Section 3 introduces the basic idea behind SPRP by a motivating example. Section 4 discusses how to construct the helper thread for a recursive procedure. Section 5 describes our recovery mechanism. Section 6 presents and analyses our experimental results. Section 7 concludes the paper with some future work.

2   Related Work

Helper threads [28, 14, 7, 31, 16] have been used to speculatively execute a code region to reduce the latency of its expensive instructions. In these research efforts, a helper thread typically serves the purposes of data prefetching or branch predictions or both. In this work, the helper threads used in SPRP are required to predict quite accurately both the order of recursive calls and their live-ins in order to reduce the misspeculation overhead incurred and thus improve the overall parallelism achieved.

MSSP [32] runs a distilled version of a given program on a master processor to predict the live-ins for tasks running on slave processors. Our helper threads and worker threads used in SPRP are conceptually similar to the master and slave threads in MSSP but are specifically developed to parallelise recursive procedures. MSSP skips recursive procedures when constructing distilled programs. In contrast, a helper thread used in SPRP works not only as a producer for spawning worker threads to execute recursive calls but also as a predictor for pre-computing the live-ins for worker threads.

Some compilation techniques for SpMT architectures [12, 2, 23, 3, 27, 11, 18, 15] allow threads to be formed at arbitrary control flow edges. In [12], threads are formed at loop or procedure boundaries using actual profile-run execution times. PD (Program Demultiplexing) [2] attempts to execute different procedures in a program in parallel as long as their inputs are speculatively available. The Mitosis compiler [23] encodes a P-slice – a piece of code to predict thread live-in values (similar to a distilled program in MSSP and a helper thread in SPRP) – into a speculative thread. Unlike [12, 2], thread partitioning in Mitosis is not restricted to loop or procedure boundaries. However, what differs SPRP from all these previous techniques is that SPRP embraces dynamic thread prediction while all these earlier techniques resort to static thread prediction. Furthermore, if these earlier techniques are applied to parallelise a recursive procedure, the invocation order of recursive calls and their required live-in values have to be predicted separately. Therefore, speculative TLP attainable by these techniques seems to be limited for procedures with multiple recursive call sites.

Some researchers have also proposed microarchitecture enhancements to automatically extract threads from sequential programs at run time. Capsule [20] automatically parallelises component-based programs through frequent hardware resource probing. Thread creation is by means of self-replication, and in addition, threads are allowed to commit in any order. Hence, Capsule is applicable only to certain applications that can be componentised. Instead of program structures, Atlas [6] only considers memory access instructions when partitioning threads. DMT [1] creates threads at procedure and loop boundaries. A speculative thread is always spawned at the return address of a

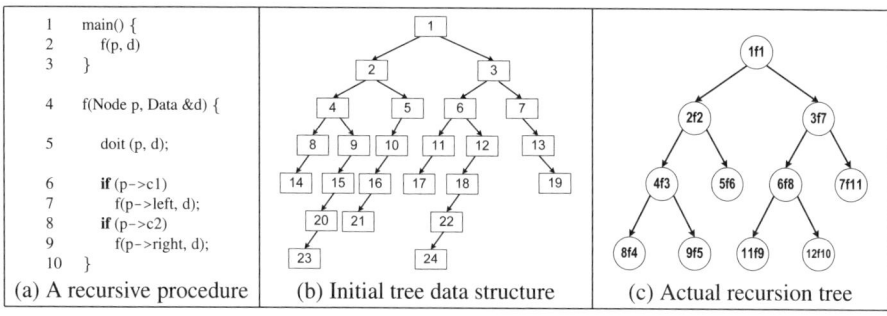

Fig. 1. A recursive procedure illustrated for some particular input

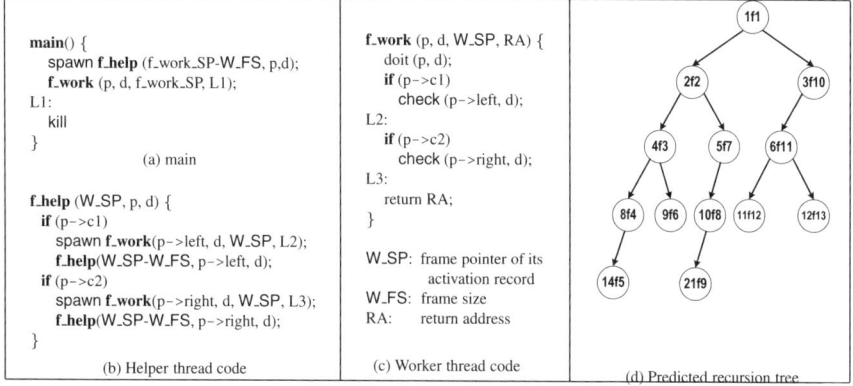

Fig. 2. Speculative parallelisation of the example in Figure 1 by the SPRP approach

call site. When DMT is applied to a recursive procedure, a speculative thread may be spawned to execute a recursive call too early to have its live-ins predicted accurately and its relevant dependences speculated successfully. This is because the spawner may later create many less speculated threads to execute some recursive calls that would have been executed earlier when the procedure were executed sequentially.

Techniques on automatic parallelisation of recursive procedures [22, 10, 24, 21] exploit task-level parallelism (i.e., coarse-grain parallelism) in embarrassingly parallel recursive calls. In [10], data speculation is said to be supported but for all benchmark applications used in their experiments, recursive calls are always independent. Irregular recursive procedures are allowed in [22] provided that all multiple recursive calls are independent and marked as such by (dependence-related) programmer annotations.

3   The SPRP Approach

Consider an irregular procedure given in Figure 1(a) with two recursive call sites. To make this example concrete, let us assume that the data structure operated on is a tree. The tree initially looks like what is shown in Figure 1(b) but may grow and shrink at run time. Whenever a tree node is visited, the core computations abstracted by doit(p, d) in line 5 are performed. This statement accesses two live-ins p, a pointer to a tree node, and d, some global data. Inside doit(p, d), all objects pointed to by p directly or indirectly and d may be modified. Therefore, in any recursive call, d in lines 7 and 9 may have different values since it may be modified in the first call made in line 7. The two call sites in lines 7 and 9 are control-dependent on p. Hence, two successive call invocations may be control-dependent or data-dependent. Figure 1(c) gives the dynamic call graph, known as the *recursion tree*, for some input. Note that not all tree nodes in Figure 1(b) may be visited. Each node in the recursion tree represents a recursive call invocation. The two children of a parent node are the two calls invoked directly inside the parent. The notation xfi shown inside a call node indicates that xfi is the i-th recursive call applied to the tree node x in the data structure. (This tree node may be one created at run time!) Sequential execution imposes a total ordering of all dynamic call invocations.

Figure 2 shows the parallelised code for the example. The *helper thread* running on a dedicated core, say, core 0, serves to predict the recursion tree and the live-ins for each recursive call and to dispatch these calls to run as worker threads on the remaining cores (numbered from 1) in parallel. The helper thread is a sequential program running in its own address space with its own runtime stack. All parallel worker threads run in a shared address space by sharing a common runtime stack (starting from f_work_SP). The meanings for W_SP, W_FS and RA are defined in Figure 2(c) and referred to later.

The execution starts from main (Figure 2(a)), which is spawned as the first worker thread to execute on a core. First, the spawn instruction is executed so that the helper thread (Figure 2(b)) is spawned to execute on its dedicated core. Second, the call f_work(p, d, f_work_SP, L1) (Figure 2(c)) is made to start the recursion. This first worker thread is the *head* thread. In speculative execution, the head thread is the only non-speculative worker thread that is allowed to commit. All other currently active worker threads are speculative. Each active worker thread represents the execution of a recursive call and thus runs in an activation record described in Section 5. Figure 2(d) depicts the recursion tree predicted by the helper thread (if being allowed to run alone to completion). However, the predicted recursion tree at run time may not be like this since it will adapt itself according to the validation outcomes from worker threads.

Figure 3 illustrates our approach by giving a snapshot of all key activities involved during program execution. In Figures 3(a) and (b), the head thread $1f1$ has committed and validated that the next call $2f2$ predicted by the helper thread is correct. So $2f2$ becomes the new head thread. Let us look at how roll-back is performed when a misspeculated call is detected as illustrated in Figures 3(c) – (e). In Figure 3(c), the speculative worker thread $8f4$ is validating if the execution of the next call predicted for $8f4$ is correct or not. The answer is negative since the next node to be visited should be node 9 rather than 14 as shown in Figure 1(c). So $14f5$ is squashed and the helper thread is instructed to roll back its state to spawn the next recursive call, $9f6$ (Figure 2(d)).

3.1   Helper Thread

In the helper thread given in Figure 2(b), the instructions abstracted by doit(p, d) happen to be all pruned according to our construction algorithm described in Section 4. The helper thread dynamically schedules worker threads by simulating the execution

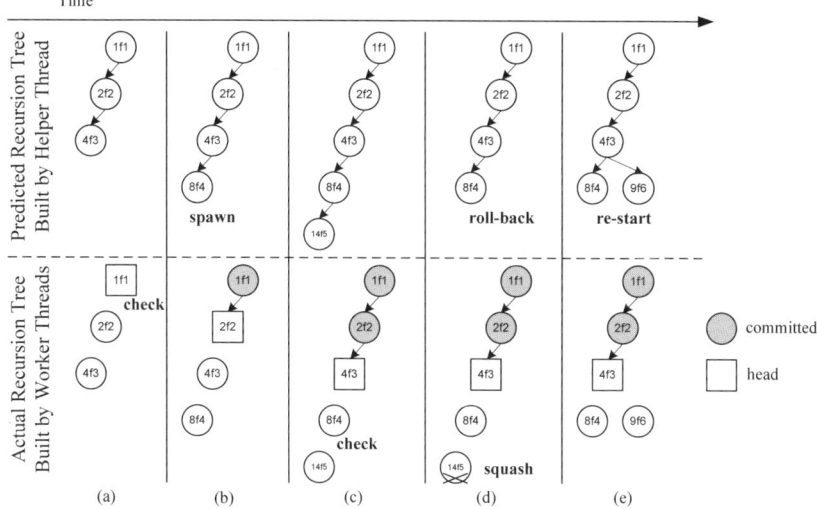

Fig. 3. An illustration of SPRP. An arrow linking two calls represents their caller-callee relation. For the helper thread, all calls are part of its predicted recursion tree. For worker threads, the recursion tree is dynamically constructed consisting of committed threads and the head thread.

of the given recursive procedure: it spawns a new worker thread by executing a **spawn** instruction whenever it reaches a call site. The helper thread is stalled if there is no free core for a new worker thread and resumed when a free core becomes available. For each predicted call, the predicted live-ins, the corresponding stack pointer and the return address for the call must be communicated to its executing worker thread. These data are passed as the arguments to f_work.

3.2 Boundaries or Lifetimes of Worker Threads

The actual execution of a procedure is done by worker threads. Every call invocation has a unique activation record. A worker thread T is executed in its own activation record if it represents a non-leaf call. For a leaf call, T initially executes in its own activation record and later in some of its callers. Let $T.SP$ be the stack pointer associated with the (current) activation record of T. Let Thread_List be the list of all committed and currently active worker threads in increasing order of their spawn times. Thread_List is the preorder traversal of the currently predicted recursion tree. All currently active worker threads are ordered from least to most speculative in Thread_List. The caller of an active worker thread T, denoted Caller(T), is the last thread T' preceding T in Thread_List such that $T.SP = T'.SP - \text{W\_FS}$. This means that the call executed by T would be made directly in the call executed by T' (during sequential execution).

The *boundary* or *lifetime* of a worker thread T is defined as follows. When executing f_work, T starts at its first instruction and terminates at either the first check that it *dynamically* executes or the kill instruction in main. There are three cases:

1. If p->c1 evaluates to true, T terminates at the first check.
2. If p->c1 evaluates to false and p->c2 to true, T terminates at the second check.

3. When both guards are false, T represents a leaf call. By executing the "return RA" instruction in f_work, T will continue to execute at the return address RA with the activation record of Caller(T) being set as its current activation record. The execution of the code of Caller(T) may cause T to reach the second check (where we are back to the second case) or the return RA instruction in Caller(T) (where we are back to the third case again) in f_work. As a result, a sequence of return instructions executed by T will take it to either a check or a kill instruction.

   To understand conceptually where a leaf call terminates, let $\mathcal{RA}(\text{Caller}^m(T))$ be the return address RA in the activation record of Caller$^m(T)$ at which T will continue its execution, where Caller$^m(T)$ stands for m applications of the function Caller to T. Let Caller$^*(T)$ be Caller$^n(T)$ for some unique $n \geqslant 1$ such that $\mathcal{RA}(\text{Caller}^n(T))$ is either L1 (Figure 2(a)) or L2 (Figure 2(c)), and p->c2 evaluates to true when $\mathcal{RA}(\text{Caller}^n(T)) = $ L2. If $\mathcal{RA}(\text{Caller}^*(T)) = $ L1, the dynamic last instruction of T is kill. If $\mathcal{RA}(\text{Caller}^*(T)) = $ L2, the dynamic last instruction of T is the second check to be executed in the activation record of Caller$^*(T)$. Consider Figures 3(c) – (e), where $8f4$ is assumed to be a leaf call. Then Caller$^*(8f4) = $ Caller($8f4$) $ = 4f3$ and $\mathcal{RA}(4f3) = $ L2. So $8f4$ will terminate after it has executed the second check in the activation record of $4f3$.

3.3   Validations of Predicted Calls

Consider when a worker thread T has reached its dynamically last instruction. There are two cases. In one case, the last instruction is the kill instruction. If T is speculative, then T is stalled. If T is the head thread, then the execution of the recursive procedure has completed successfully. So the helper thread is killed. In the other case, the last instruction of T is a check instruction. T will search for the *successor worker thread* of T, denoted Succ_Call(T), that is responsible for executing the next call to be made after T at the check call site in T during sequential execution. Succ_Call(T) is the first thread T' following T in Thread_List such that $T.SP = T'.SP + $ W_FS and the live-outs of T are identical to the predicted live-ins used by T'.

   If Succ_Call(T) is found, all threads between T and Succ_Call(T) in Thread_List are squashed. If T is speculative, T is stalled. Otherwise, T is the head thread. Thus, the results of the validated T' are committed and T' becomes the new head thread. If Succ_Call(T) is not found, all more speculative threads than T in Thread_List are squashed. A recovery mechanism introduced in Section 5 is used to steer the helper thread back to the right track so that the successor call can be spawned at the check call site. If T is the last thread in Thread_List, T is stalled until either T is squashed or a more speculative thread T' than T is spawned (so that the validation at T can be performed). Let us consider Figures 3(c) – (e) again under the assumption that $T = 8f4$ as shown in Figure 3(c) is a leaf call. Thus, Caller$^*(8f4) = $ Caller($8f4$) $ = 4f3$. By the time when $8f4$ reaches the second check instruction in the activation record of $4f3$, we have $8f4.SP = 4f3.SP$ and Thread_List $= \{1f1, 2f2, 4f3, 8f4, 14f5\}$. Since $14f5$ is the only worker thread following $8f4$ and $8f4.SP = 4f3.SP = (w - 160) \neq 14f5.SP + $ W_FS $= (w - 320) + 80$ as shown in Figure 5(a), the validation performed will fail. In fact, the next node to be visited

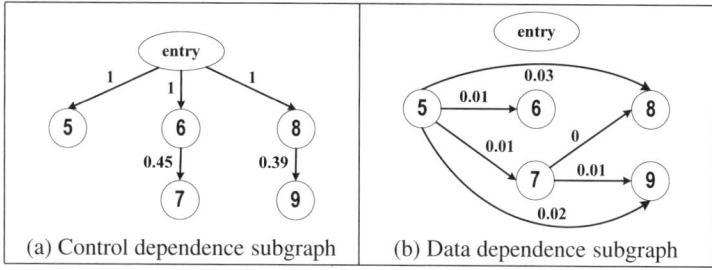

(a) Control dependence subgraph   (b) Data dependence subgraph

Fig. 4. Program dependence graph (PDG) of the procedure in Figure 1

should be node 9 rather than 14 as is clear in Figure 1(c). Thus, $14f5$ is squashed and the helper thread is re-directed to spawn $9f6$ (Figure 2(d)).

3.4 Memory Dependence Speculations

Misspeculated memory dependences are handled in the normal manner [23,27]. A misspeculation is raised if a worker thread writes into a memory location where a more speculative worker thread has already read from the same location. The misspeculated worker thread is squashed and re-started. All worker threads that depend on the misspeculated worker thread are also re-started.

4   Construction of Helper Threads

The accuracy and the size of the helper thread affect the amount of speculative parallelism SPRP can achieve but not the correctness of the SPRP execution.

The *Program Dependence Graph* (PDG) of a recursive procedure is used to construct its helper thread. In the data dependence subgraph of PDG, only true or flow data dependences are included. Each edge $x \rightarrow y$ in PDG is labelled with a probability value $p_{x \rightarrow y}$ in $[0, 1]$. If $x \rightarrow y$, is a data dependence, then $p_{x \rightarrow y}$ means that for every N writes at x, only pN reads will access the same memory/register location at y during program execution. If $x \rightarrow y$ is a control dependence, then $p_{x \rightarrow y}$ means that for every N execution of x, only pN will reach y. Figure 4 gives the PDG of the recursive procedure in Figure 1. A node is numbered using the line number of its corresponding statement.

Let $\mathcal{H}$ be the set of instructions forming the helper thread. $\mathcal{H}$ is initialised with the set of nodes in PDG that correspond to all the recursive call instructions. Next, for every node u in PDG, we add u to $\mathcal{H}$ if $\exists v \in \mathcal{H}$ such that (1) edge $u \rightarrow v$ is in PDG, and (2) $p_{u \rightarrow v} \geqslant D$, where D is relatively large, if $u \rightarrow v$ is in the data dependence subgraph and $p_{u \rightarrow v} \leqslant C$, where C is relatively small, if $u \rightarrow v$ is in the control dependence subgraph. Here, D and C are some tunable parameters. The intention is to ignore infrequently occurring data dependences and frequently occurring control dependences. The instructions in PDG are included in $\mathcal{H}$ iteratively until a pre-defined size limit has been reached or no more nodes can be added.

The values of D, C and the helper thread size are likely to be application-dependent. Our experience gained in this work is that data dependences tend to be bi-modal while

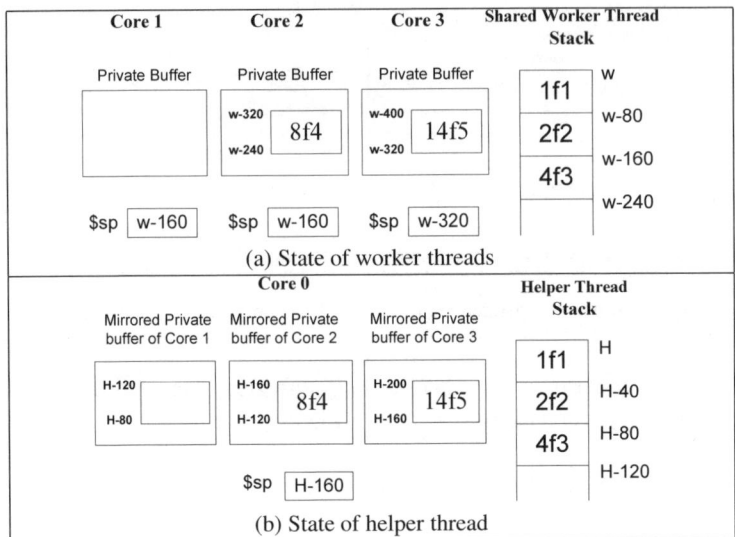

Fig. 5. Machine state when a misspeculation is detected as illustrated in Figure 3(c)

control dependences tend to be tri-modal. These parameters can be tuned by profiling and program analysis. In our experiments, $D \geqslant 0.8$ and $C \leqslant 0.6$ are reasonable.

In our example, let us assume $D = 0.8$ and $C = 0.6$. There are two call sites. So $\mathcal{H} = \{7, 9\}$ initially. Note that $6 \rightarrow 7$ is a control dependence. So node 6 is added to $\mathcal{H}$ since $p_{6 \rightarrow 7} < 0.6$. Node 8 is included in $\mathcal{H}$ for the same reason. The probabilities of of all data dependences are small. Finally, $\mathcal{H} = \{6, 7, 8, 9\}$. This leads to the corresponding helper thread as depicted in Figure 2(b).

5   Misprediction Recovery

This section describes our recovery mechanism developed to support the SPRP scheme using the motivating example with respect to Figure 3. As explained in Section 3.3, a misprediction is raised in Figure 3(c). SPRP will then roll back the states for the execution of both the helper thread and worker threads. Suppose that $4f3$, $8f4$ and $14f5$ run on cores 1, 2 and 3, respectively. (The helper thread runs on core 0.)

5.1   Recovering the State of Worker Threads

Figure 5(a) depicts the state of the worker threads at the time when a misprediction is detected. The activation records of all past and current head threads have already been committed to the shared runtime stack. The activation records of all speculative ones are buffered in on-chip memory. Let us assume that the frame size of an activation record is $W\_FS = 80$. In the example, the activation records of $1f1$ and $2f2$ have been committed to the shared stack. The activation records of $8f4$ and $14f5$ are buffered since both are speculative. The activation record of the head thread $4f3$ is on the shared stack. As a leaf call, $8f4$ branches to L2 to execute in the activation record of $\text{Caller}^*(8f4) = 4f3$

Table 1. SpMT multicore system simulated

Parameter	Value
Fetch, Issue, Commit	bandwidth 4, out-of-order issue
L1 I-Cache	16KB, 4-way, 1 cycle (hit)
L1 D-Cache	16KB, 4-way, 3 cycles (hit)
L2 Cache (Unified)	1MB, 4-way, 12 cycles (hit), 80 cycles (miss)
Local Register File	1 cycle
Spawn Overhead	5 cycles
Commit Overhead	5 cycles
Validation Overhead	15 cycles

where a misprediction is detected. Hence, $SP on core 2 is pointing to the activation record of $4f3$. The mispredicted thread $14f5$ is squashed (Figure 3(d)) and its buffered data discarded. The helper thread is then informed to spawn $9f6$ according to the current state of $8f4$ (Figure 3(e)), as described below.

5.2 Recovering the State of Helper Thread

As shown in Figure 5(b), the sequential execution of the helper thread is made to mirror the parallel execution of worker threads. For every worker thread running on a core, the execution results for the corresponding call invocation (including its activation record) made in the helper thread are buffered in the mirrored private buffer for the core on core 0. Whenever a private buffer on a core is committed, discarded or released, the mirrored private buffer is also committed, discarded or released in sync. Hence, the roll-back activities performed by both the helper thread and worker threads are synchronised. In general, the helper thread is smaller than a worker thread. For illustration purposes, we assume the frame size of an activation record for each recursive call to f_help made in the helper thread (Figure 2(b)) is 40 (bytes). Recall that when a misprediction is detected by the worker thread $8f4$ running on core 2, $8f4$ is pointing to the second check of f_work, causing $14f5$ running on core 3 to be squashed. Correspondingly, (1) the mirrored private buffer of core 3 is discarded, (2) the most up-to-date live-ins for the successor call after $8f4$, which is $9f6$, are passed to the mirrored private buffer of core 2, (3) $SP on core 0 is rolled back to the activation record corresponding to that of $4f3$ that $SP on core 2 is pointing to, and finally, (4) the execution of the helper thread is rolled back to point to the second spawn instruction in f_help. Therefore, the helper thread will be restarted to spawn a worker thread $9f6$ with the most up-to-date live-ins.

6   Experimental Results

To evaluate SPRP, a preliminary implementation of SPRP is built on top of GCC 4.1.1 with programmer annotations indicating which recursive procedures are to be parallelised. All benchmarks are compiled under the optimisation level "-O2". The generated code is simulated using a detailed execution-driven microarchitectural simulator built on top of SimpleScalar. The simulator models an SpMT quad-core system. Table 1 provides the main architectural parameters, which are similar to those used in the recent work [23,8]. Each core is capable of executing the Alpha ISA. One core is dedicated to the helper thread while the other three cores are used to execute worker threads.

Table 2. Benchmarks

Benchmark	I-size	Fan-out	W-size	H-size	H-size/W-size	#Live-ins
Bh	256	1...8	131	29	0.22	7
Bisort	8192	2	57	27	0.47	5
Knapsack	15	2	447	24	0.05	6
Queens	9	1..9	2887	68	0.02	8

In Section 6.1, we describe the benchmarks used. In Section 6.2, we present and discuss the performance speedups achieved by SPRP. The speedups on a quad-core system may not be huge but they are close to the ideal ones attainable. Otherwise, these hard-to-parallelise may have to be either run sequentially on one single core or manually parallelised by domain experts in a case-by-case basis. In Section 6.3, we compare SPRP with two existing compiler techniques to demonstrate further the performance stability and scalability of SPRP when dealing with the same program with varying inputs and dynamically changing runtime data structures.

6.1 Benchmarks

Four benchmarks are used in our experiments: Bh (Barnes-Hut) and Bisort are taken from the Olden benchmark suite and Knapsack and Queens are from the Cilk benchmark suite. These benchmarks represent a wide spectrum of application domains. Bh solves the N-body problem using hierarchical methods on a tree. Bisort implements a recursive bitonic sorting algorithm on a tree. Knapsack is a combinatorial optimisation algorithm that solves a one-dimensional backpack problem using branch-and-bound on an array. Queens is modified from Cilk to find all solutions to the N-queens problem on an array.

To evaluate the performance of SPRP, we parallelise only recursive procedures, although selected benchmarks may have more parallelism if other program structures such as loops are also used to form threads. Table 2 provides some statistics about the four benchmarks. The input size (I-size) for each benchmark is listed in Column 2. The fan-out in Column 3 represents the range for the number of child calls invoked directly in each parent call in the recursion tree of a recursive procedure. The fan-outs of all four benchmarks are larger than 1. Therefore, these four benchmarks allow us to evaluate the accuracy of our helper threads in predicting the invocation order of recursive calls made in these benchmarks. In Column 4, W-size represents the average number of instructions executed for all committed worker threads in a benchmark (i.e., all recursive calls made in the sequential execution of the benchmark). In Column 5, H-size is the average number of instructions executed by the helper thread between two successive spawn instructions for a benchmark. Thus, the ratio H-size/W-size listed in Column 6 indicates how much faster the helper thread spawns recursive calls than if a direct execution of the original procedure would do. The lower the ratio, the faster. The ratios are very low for Knapsack and Queens. As for Bh and Bisort, the sizes of their worker threads are small. It seems to be difficult to reduce the ratios any further.

In the last column, the number of live-ins for a procedure is given. This is the size of data to be passed to a spawned thread. A maximum of 8 live-ins has been observed in the four benchmarks, indicating that a latency of 5 cycles for spawn overhead is adequate in our experiments, as previously demonstrated in [23, 8].

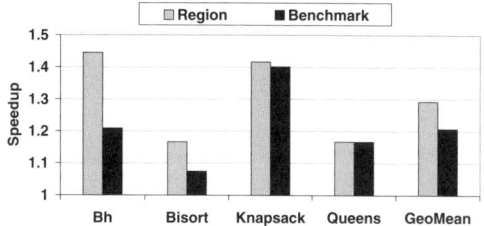

Fig. 6. Speedups of SPRP over sequential execution

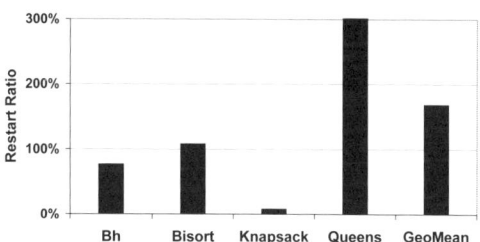

Fig. 7. Restart ratios of SPRP

6.2   Performance and Analysis

It is important to understand the performance improvements achieved by SPRP in the context that the recursive procedures selected and used in our experiments are very difficult to parallelise by existing methods. The parallelisation-inhibiting factors are that (1) there is more than one dynamic call site (as in all four benchmarks), (2) call sites are guarded by non-trivial expressions (as in Bh, Knapsack and Queens), (3) there are memory dependences among recursive calls (as in all four benchmarks), (4) the underlying data structure may dynamically change at run time (as in Bisort) and (5) only part of the underlying data structure is traversed (as in Bh, Knapsack and Queens).

Figure 6 gives the speedups of SPRP over sequential execution. The region speedups (for recursive procedures only) range from 1.16 to 1.45 with an average of 1.29. The program speedups are close to the region speedups for Knapsack and Queens. But this is not true Bh and Bisortsince the recursive procedures parallelised represent only 55% and 46% of their total execution times, respectively.

Let us now analyse the performance results achieved by SPRP. First of all, SPRP can achieve a good degree of speculative TLP in our benchmarks. The average number of active worker threads per cycle for Bh, Bisort, Knapsack and Queens are 2.51, 2.14, 1.79 and 2.19, respectively. Whether this amount of speculative thread-level parallelism can translate into performance gains or not depends on how often speculated work threads succeed and how precise the predictions made by helper threads are.

Figure 7 shows the restart ratios for all four benchmarks. The *restart ratio* for a benchmark represents the number of restarted threads over the number of committed threads. A call that is restarted n times will be counted to have been restarted n times. The restart ratio of a benchmark is a rough approximation of the impact of misspeculations on performance. For example, Queens has the highest restart ratio, which is caused

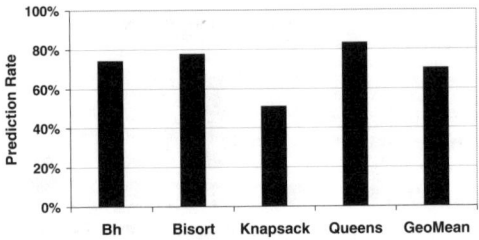

Fig. 8. Prediction rates of SPRP for correctly executed recursive calls

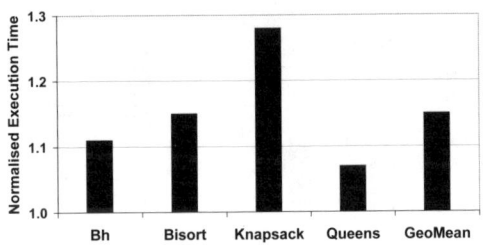

Fig. 9. Normalised execution times of SPRP with respect to ideal execution

by excessive misspeculations of memory dependences as discussed in Section 3.4. In the parallelised recursive procedure of Queens, every call invocation may depend on the earlier calls made – they may not be the immediate predecessors, since every call uses the passed-in array a and may also update one element of a as well as pass a to the ensuing call invocation. Hence, the performance improvement for Queens is limited.

Figure 8 gives the prediction rate, i.e., success rate at which the recursive calls have been correctly predicted by the helper thread for each benchmark. When constructing the helper thread for a recursive procedure, a trade-off between the prediction rate and the exposed speculative TLP has to be made. For example, Knapsack has the smallest prediction rate since most branches used to prune the searching space are not included in the helper thread. Hence, Knapsack has a very small H-size/W-size ratio as shown in Table 2 indicating a large portion of speculative TLP has been exposed by SPRP. Any further improvement on its prediction rate requires extra time-consuming computations to be included in the helper thread, resulting in a significant decrease of the exposed speculative TLP. Similarly, any further improvement on the prediction rate for Bh requires the entire subroutine subdivp to be included in the helper thread. As a result, very little speculative TLP could be exposed. On the other hand, as shown in Table 2, the H-size/W-size ratio of Bisort is the largest due to the strong memory dependences among the recursive calls since the underlying tree structure used by Bisort may be modified at run time. Any further reduction of its H-size/W-size ratio leads to a significant drop of its prediction rate, resulting in a performance slowdown. If we increase its H-size/W-size ratio to obtain a better prediction rate, the helper thread will be too large to expose any speculative TLP in the benchmark.

Figure 9 shows the performance gap between SPRP and what can be achieved during an ideal program execution (the H-size/W-size ratio during the ideal execution is

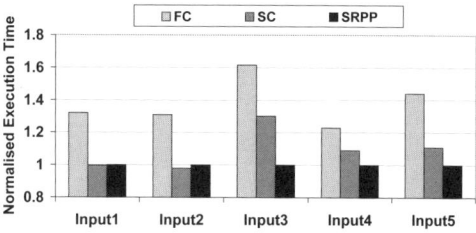

Fig. 10. Normalised execution times of FC, SC and SRPP with respect to SPRP

negligible and the helper thread always makes precise prediction). On average, the execution time of SPRP is only 14% longer than the ideal execution. Hence, SPRP is potentially effective in parallelising these irregular recursive procedures.

6.3   Dynamic Prediction and Static Prediction

Due to space limit, we use Knapsack to demonstrate the performance advantages of SPRP over two static thread prediction and spawning schemes used for parallelising recursive procedures, SC and FC. In *subroutine-continuation (SC)* spawning scheme [12,15,27,1], a speculative thread is always spawned at the return address of a recursive call site. In another scheme referred to as *First Call (FC)* in this paper, only the calls made at the first call site are control-speculated to be always invoked. Note that unlike SPRP, both FC and SC predict live-ins separately. By using a helper thread to predict both the recursion tree and live-ins required by each predicted recursive call, SPRP outperforms SC and FC almost always when different input data are used.

Figure 10 compares SPRP with SC and FC in terms of five different inputs. The search space of Knapsack is a binary tree. We have carefully selected these inputs so that five representative recursion trees are used at run time. The recursion trees exercised by Input1, Input2, Input3, Input4 and Input5 are a complete binary tree, a right-biased tree (the left child of every tree node is a leaf), a left-biased tree (the right child of every tree node is a leaf), a random tree (with its nodes randomly distributed) and a left-and-right-biased tree (a combination of a left-biased subtree and a right-biased subtree), respectively. FC is the worst performer in all cases, because it always sequentialises all leaf nodes that contain some computations. SC performs only slightly better than SPRP for Input2 (i.e., the right-biased tree) and similarly as SPRP for Input 1 (i.e., a complete binary tree). In the other three cases, SPRP significantly outperforms SC. SC is very sensitive to the shapes of recursion trees. When the underlying recursion trees are left-biased, a large number of threads created in SC are later squashed to release cores for less speculative threads.

By comparing with static thread prediction, SPRP can more precisely predict the order in which recursive calls are made and thus expose more parallelism.

7   Conclusion

We have presented a new compiler technique for speculatively parallelising irregular recursive procedures that are difficult to parallelise traditionally. These recursive procedures may sometimes be parallelised manually by domain experts in a case-by-case basis. However, the potential presence of some dependences in a program will cause even the expert programmers to be conservative, limiting the parallelism to be exploited. This works aims to make a case that these hard-to-parallelise recursive procedures can be potentially parallelised automatically. Our preliminary results using four representative benchmarks are very encouraging. Our approach is general since it can handle recursive procedures with code blocks appearing both before and after a call site by spawning threads using a combination of preorder, inorder and postorder traversals.

There are a number of interesting research issues we will pursue in the future. One is to develop good heuristics to construct faster helper threads with good prediction accuracies. Another way to improve the prediction accuracies of helper threads is to allow the helper thread to access more up to date memory variables. This means that some tradeoffs must be made between the efficiency and accuracy of a helper thread.

Acknowledgement

This work is supported the Australian Research Council Grant (DP0881330) and the UNSW Engineering-International Research Collaboration Grant (PS16380).

References

1. Akkary, H., Driscoll, M.A.: A dynamic multithreading processor. In: MICRO-31, pp. 226–236 (1998)
2. Balakrishnan, S., Sohi, G.S.: Program demultiplexing: Data-flow based speculative parallelization of methods in sequential programs. In: ISCA 2006 (2006)
3. Bhowmik, A., Franklin, M.: A general compiler framework for speculative multithreaded processors. IEEE Trans. Parallel Distrib. Syst. 15(8), 713–724 (2004)
4. Blelloch, G.E., Hardwick, J.C., Sipelstein, J., Zagha, M., Chatterjee, S.: Implementation of a portable nested data-parallel language. In: J. Parallel Distrib. Comput., pp. 4–14 (1994)
5. Blumofe, R.D., Joerg, C.F., Kuszmaul, B.C., Leiserson, C.E., Randall, K.H., Zhou, Y.L.: Cilk: an efficient multithreaded runtime system. In: PPoPP 1995 (1995)
6. Codrescu, L., Wills, D.S.: On dynamic speculative thread partitioning and the mem-slicing algorithm. In: Malyshkin, V.E. (ed.) PaCT 1999. LNCS, vol. 1662. Springer, Heidelberg (1999)
7. Collins, J.D., Wang, H., Tullsen, D.M., Hughes, C., Lee, Y.F., Lavery, D., Shen, J.P.: Speculative precomputation: long-range prefetching of delinquent loads. In: ISCA 2001, pp. 14–25 (2001)
8. Du, Z.H., Lim, C.C., Li, X.F., Yang, C., Zhao, Q., Ngai, T.F.: A cost-driven compilation framework for speculative parallelization of sequential programs. In: PLDI 2004 (2004)
9. Franklin, M.: The Multiscalar Architecture. PhD thesis, The University of Wisconsin at Madison (1993)
10. Gupta, M., Mukhopadhyay, S., Sinha, N.: Automatic parallelization of recursive procedures. International Journal of Parallel Programming 28(6), 537–562 (2000)
11. Johnson, T.A., Eigenmann, R., Vijaykumar, T.N.: Min-cut program decomposition for thread-level speculation. In: PLDI 2004 (2004)
12. Johnson, T.A., Eigenmann, R., Vijaykumar, T.N.: Speculative thread decomposition through empirical optimization. In: PPoPP 2007, pp. 205–214 (2007)

13. Krishnan, V., Torrellas, J.: Hardware and software support for speculative execution of sequential binaries on a chip-multiprocessor. In: ICS 1998, pp. 85–92. ACM Press, New York (1998)
14. Liao, S.W., Wang, P.H., Wang, H., Hoflehner, G., Lavery, D., Shen, J.P.: Post-pass binary adaptation for software-based speculative precomputation. In: PLDI 2002, pp. 117–128 (2002)
15. Liu, W., Tuck, J., Ceze, L., Ahn, W., Strauss, K., Renau, J., Torrellas, J.: Posh: a tls compiler that exploits program structure. In: PPoPP 2006, pp. 158–167 (2006)
16. Luk, C.K.: Tolerating memory latency through software-controlled pre-execution in simultaneous multithreading processors. In: ISCA 2001, pp. 40–51 (2001)
17. Marcuello, P., Gonzalez, A.: A quantitative assessment of thread-level speculation techniques. In: IPPS 2000 (2000)
18. Ohsawa, T., Takagi, M., Kawahara, S., Matsushita, S.: Pinot: Speculative multi-threading processor architecture exploiting parallelism over a wide range of granularities. In: MICRO-38 (2005)
19. Oplinger, J., Heine, D., Lam, M.: In search of speculative thread-level parallelism. In: Malyshkin, V.E. (ed.) PaCT 1999. LNCS, vol. 1662. Springer, Heidelberg (1999)
20. Palatin, P., Lhuillier, Y., Temam, O.: Capsule: Hardware-assisted parallel execution of component-based programs. In: MICRO-39, pp. 247–258 (2006)
21. Piper, A.J.: Object-oriented Divide-and-conquer for Parallel Processing. PhD thesis, University of Cambridge (July 1994)
22. Prechelt, L., Hänßgen, S.U.: Efficient parallel execution of irregular recursive programs. IEEE Transactions on Parallel and Distributed Systems (2002)
23. Quinones, C.G., Madrile, C., Sanchez, J., Marcuello, P., Gonzalez, A., Tullsen, D.M.: Mitosis compiler: An infrastructure for speculative threading based on pre-computation slices. In: PLDI 2005 (2005)
24. Rugina, R., Rinard, M.C.: Automatic parallelization of divide and conquer algorithms. In: PPoPP 1999, pp. 72–83 (1999)
25. Tsai, J.Y., Yew, P.C.: The superthreaded architecture: Thread pipelining with run-time data dependence checking and control speculation. In: Malyshkin, V.E. (ed.) PaCT 1999. LNCS, vol. 1662, pp. 35–46. Springer, Heidelberg (1999)
26. Vachharajani, N., Rangan, R., Raman, E., Bridges, M.J., Ottoni, G., August, D.I.: Speculative decoupled software pipelining. In: PaCT 2007, pp. 49–59 (2007)
27. Vijaykumar, T.N.: Compiling for the Multiscalar Architecture. PhD thesis, The University of Wisconsin at Madison (1998)
28. Wang, P.H., Collins, J.D., Wang, H., Kim, D., Greene, B., Chan, K.M., Yunus, A.B., Sych, T., Moore, S.F., Shen, J.P.: Helper threads via virtual multithreading on an experimental Itanium 2 processor-based platform. In: ASPLOS-XI 2004 (2004)
29. Wang, S., Dai, X., Yellajyosula, K.S., Zhai, A., Yew, P.-C.: Loop selection for thread-level speculation. In: Ayguadé, E., Baumgartner, G., Ramanujam, J., Sadayappan, P. (eds.) LCPC 2005. LNCS, vol. 4339, pp. 289–303. Springer, Heidelberg (2006)
30. Zhong, H.T., Mehrara, M., Lieberman, S., Mahlke, S.: Uncovering hidden loop level parallelism in sequential applications. In: HPCA 2008 (2008)
31. Zilles, C., Sohi, G.: Execution-based prediction using speculative slices. In: ISCA 2001, pp. 2–13 (2001)
32. Zilles, C., Sohi, G.: Master/slave speculative parallelization. In: MICRO-35 (2002)

Live Debugging of Distributed Systems

Darren Dao[1], Jeannie Albrecht[2], Charles Killian[3], and Amin Vahdat[1]

[1] University of California, San Diego, La Jolla, CA
[2] Williams College, Williamstown, MA
[3] Purdue University, West Lafayette, IN

Abstract. Debugging distributed systems is challenging. Although incremental debugging during development finds some bugs, developers are rarely able to fully test their systems under realistic operating conditions prior to deployment. While deploying a system exposes it to realistic conditions, debugging requires the developer to: (i) detect a bug, (ii) gather the system state necessary for diagnosis, and (iii) sift through the gathered state to determine a root cause. In this paper, we present MaceODB, a tool to assist programmers with debugging deployed distributed systems. Programmers define a set of runtime properties for their system, which MaceODB checks for violations during execution. Once MaceODB detects a violation, it provides the programmer with the information to determine its root cause. We have been able to diagnose several non-trivial bugs in existing mature distributed systems using MaceODB; we discuss two of these bugs in this paper. Benchmarks indicate that the approach has low overhead and is suitable for *in situ* debugging of deployed systems.

1 Introduction

Debugging a distributed system is challenging because its operation depends not only on its internal functions and state, but also on the functions and state of the set of nodes it runs on and the network linking them. At any point in time, correctness depends on a combination of past and present system, node, and network states. Replicating the vast array of possible states and exposing a distributed system to them prior to deployment is not feasible. As a result, many bugs only manifest during deployment, when the "perfect storm" of state transitions trigger them.

Despite recent advancements, most developers still debug distributed systems in an ad hoc fashion by inserting custom print statements to generate output logs, which they parse for errors after an execution ends. Ad hoc approaches require developers to know what to print and what to expect *a priori*, which limits their usefulness for finding unexpected bugs. Existing advanced debugging techniques, while useful, have drawbacks when used for debugging deployed systems. Model checkers force the programmer to define a specification of the system, and then systematically explore a system's state space for violations of the specification. However, the exploration does not capture the vast and complex set of node and network states that impact a deployed system. Replay-based tools, which enable offline analysis of systems, do not detect bugs at runtime, while log-based analysis tools, which systematically process output logs for errors, impose the high overhead of generating and storing log data.

An ideal tool for debugging deployed distributed systems has the following characteristics.

O. de Moor and M. Schwartzbach (Eds.): CC 2009, LNCS 5501, pp. 94–108, 2009.

- **Easy to Use.** The tool should hide low-level implementation details from the developer so it is easy to understand, as well as automate common tasks to minimize its impact on the standard development process.
- **Powerful.** The tool should be powerful and flexible enough to assist programmers in finding a wide variety of bugs in different distributed systems.
- **Low Overhead.** Since many bugs do not manifest until deployment, the tool must operate on deployed systems. Low overhead is essential for using on a deployed system without degrading its performance.

We designed and built MaceODB, an online debugging tool for the Mace [1] language, to satisfy these characteristics. Using MaceODB, we were able to find non-trivial bugs in existing mature distributed systems using only a small amount of additional information provided by the developer. Our performance evaluation shows that MaceODB has little impact on the performance of the systems under test.

The rest of this paper is organized as follows. Sections 2 and 3 detail the design and implementation of MaceODB. Section 4 reports on our experiences using MaceODB and Section 5 reports on its performance. Finally, we review related work in Section 6 and conclude in Section 7.

2   Design of MaceODB

Mace [1] is a C++ language extension and source-to-source compiler that translates a concise, but expressive, distributed system specification into a C++ implementation. Mace overcomes the limitations of low-level languages by providing a unified framework for networking and event handling, and the limitations of high-level languages by allowing programmers to write program components in a controlled and structured manner. Imposing structure and restrictions on application development allows Mace to support high-level debugging techniques, including efficient model checking and causal-path analysis [2]. The limitation of the Mace model checker is its inability to debug live systems: MaceODB addresses this limitation.

MaceODB is an extension to the Mace compiler that adds new instructions for translating developer-defined system properties into code that checks for property violations at runtime. To use MaceODB, the programmer adds liveness and safety properties to their Mace application (see Figure 1). After specifying a set of properties, the Mace compiler generates the application's C++ implementation from its specification. The compiler invokes MaceODB to parse the developer-defined properties and adds additional code that checks for property violations at runtime. During execution, the property-checking logic automatically reports violations back to the programmer.

2.1   Properties

MaceODB extends Mace by allowing programmers to define properties for their distributed systems. These properties are predicates that must hold true for some subset of the participating nodes in the system. (Note that predicates are always "const" functions, and thus cannot have side-effects on the state of the nodes.) MaceODB currently supports two types of properties: safety properties and liveness properties.

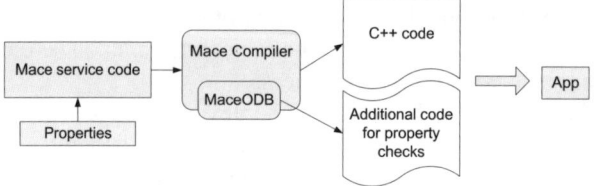

Fig. 1. Overview of MaceODB

Safety properties. Safety properties are predicates that should always be true. These properties assert that the program will never enter an unacceptable state [3]. Formally, they can be expressed as statements of the form *always p*, where *p* is predicate that must be evaluated to true at all times. For example, suppose we build a peer-to-peer file transfer system that constructs an overlay tree. An important safety property of this system is that there should never be any loops in the underlying topology. When defining safety properties, programmers must know exactly what violations to look for and define unacceptable states in advance.

Liveness properties. Liveness properties are predicates that should eventually be true [3]. For example, in a peer-to-peer file transfer system, all participants should eventually enter the joined state to be part of the overlay tree. Note that liveness properties, unlike safety properties, apply to an entire program's execution rather than individual states. As a result, liveness properties are more difficult than safety properties to evaluate for violations. The benefit of using liveness properties is that they more naturally align with the way developers reason about the state of a system. Defining high-level liveness properties is easier for a developer since they correspond more directly to design specifications defined by the developer.

2.2 Specifying Properties

The most effective way to specify safety and liveness properties is to analyze the correct system behavior under steady-state operation. After identifying the desirable behavior, the programmer writes liveness properties to verify that the desired behavior is upheld throughout an execution. If any liveness violations occur, the programmer can leverage insight from the violations to specify additional safety properties. Although safety properties are more difficult to define *a priori*, these properties contain more specific checks to help narrow down the bugs causing liveness violations. For example, consider a bug in which a certain timer becomes unscheduled and causes a liveness property to fail. After detecting this liveness violation, the programmer adds an additional safety property to ensure that the timer is always scheduled.

To write the safety and liveness properties, programmers use the Mace compiler's grammar. A simplified version of the grammar is in Figure 2. We have used this grammar to write safety and liveness properties for several existing Mace applications and services (see Table 1). We found that most properties permit concise specifications consisting of a few lines of code. For example, consider the property "AllJoined" in Table 1. "AllJoined" is an example of a liveness property of the Mace RandTree service, which is a simple distributed application that constructs a random overlay tree. The purpose of

Property $->$ GrandBExpression
GrandBExpression $->$ (BExpression Join) BExpression
JoinExpression $->$ or | and | xor | implies | iff
BExpression $->$ Equation | BinaryBExpression | Quantification
Equation $->$ NonBExpression Equality NonBExpression
BinaryBExpression $->$ ElementSetExpression | SetSetExpression
Equality $->$ == | != | >= | <= | > | <
NonBExpression $->$ Variable NonBExpressionOp Variable
NonBExpressionOp $->$ + | −
ElementSetExpression $->$ Variable SetOp Variable
SetOp $->$ in | not_in
SetSetExpression $->$ Variable SetComparisons Variable
SetComparisons $->$ subset | propertysubset | eq
Quantification $->$ Quantifier Id Variable : GrandBExpression
Quantifier $->$ forall | exists | for{Number}

Fig. 2. Simplified grammar for writing MaceODB safety and liveness properties

"AllJoined" is to check that all participating nodes eventually enter the `joined` state that signals a valid connection to the overlay. In this case, we express the property in a single line of code.

Now consider the "Timer" property in Table 1. In "Timer," `recovery` is a timer object defined by the RandTree developer (see Section 4.1). The timer object has a `nextScheduled()` method that returns the next time the recovery process will execute; the purpose of the property is to verify that once each system participant completes the `init` state it executes the `recovery` timer. The `recovery` timer ensures that subsequent failures trigger the recovery process.

2.3   Centralized Property Evaluation in MaceODB

Our initial design of MaceODB uses a centralized approach for evaluating the properties at runtime. The design uses a central server that is responsible for evaluating all the properties across the entire system (see Figure 3). The design consists of two components: the Data Exporter module and the Property Checking module. The Data Exporter module operates on each node in the system, extracts data that describes the execution's current state, and forwards the timestamped data to the central server. The central server then uses the Property Checking module to evaluate the data's liveness and safety properties. Upon receiving data from each Data Exporter module, the central server invokes the Property Checking module to perform the property evaluation, and generates a report of property violations.

To understand the Data Exporter and Property Checking modules, consider the Pastry [4] (a typical Distributed Hash Table) property "LeftRight" in Table 1. This property compares the size of `myleafset` to the size of `myleft` plus the size of `myright`. The data of interest is `myleafset.size()`, `myleft.size()`, and

Table 1. Examples of properties that are used in Mace applications (Pastry, Chord, RandTree)

Name	Property
LeftRight (Pastry)	*Test that size of leafset = sum of left and right set size.* ```\forall n \in \nodes : { n.myright.size() + n.myleft.size() = n.myleafset.size() };```
KeyMatch (Pastry)	*Test the consistency of the key of the node to the right.* ```\forall n \in \nodes : { n.getNextHop(n.range.second, -1).range.first = n.range.second };```
PredNotNull (Chord)	*Test that predecessor pointer is eventually not null.* ```\forall n \in \nodes : \not n.predecessor.getId().isNullAddress();```
Timer (RandTree)	*Test that either the node state is init or recovery timer is scheduled.* ```\forall n \in \nodes : { (n.state = init) \or (n.recovery.nextScheduled() != 0) };```
AllJoined (RandTree)	*Test that eventually all the nodes will join the system.* ```\forall n \in \nodes : n.state = joined;```

`myright.size()`; the Data Exporter module extracts these attributes from each participating node and sends them to the central server. The Property Checking process consists of iterating through the data and evaluating whether `myleafset.size()` is equal to `myleft.size() + myright.size()`; if they are not equal, the evaluation process returns false, indicating a property violation.

Our performance evaluation shows that the centralized approach is sufficient for most properties. However, some properties require each participating node to send large amounts of data to the central server, creating a bottleneck that slows down the property evaluation process and reduces overall system performance. We include optimizations to reduce the data sent using a binary diff tool [5] to compare the differences between snapshots of forwarded data. The optimization significantly reduces the bandwidth, although the central server remains a bottleneck for sufficiently large systems (*i.e.*, more than 100 nodes) due to the memory and processor time required to process diffs.

2.4   Decentralized Property Evaluation in MaceODB

In this section we describe a decentralized design for MaceODB to address problems with the centralized design. The decentralized design also uses the Data Exporter and

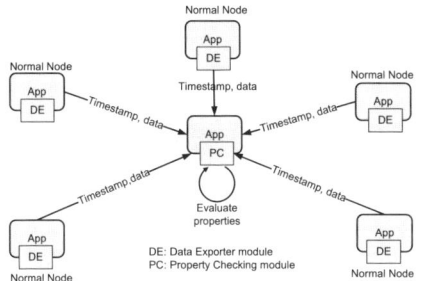

Fig. 3. MaceODB centralized design

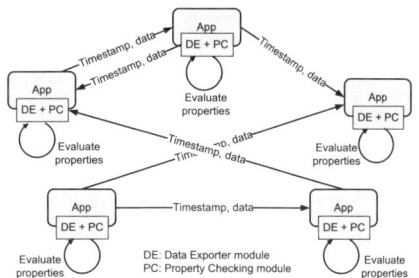

Fig. 4. MaceODB decentralized design

Property Checking modules. However, unlike the centralized approach, the Property Checking module is now present in all system nodes (see Figure 4), requiring each node to be responsible for evaluating their individual properties. The design eliminates the central server bottleneck, and eliminates the single point of failure. Additionally, we use a membership service to address network and node failures.

In decentralized MaceODB, we represent properties as dataflow graphs. Figure 5 shows an example of this representation for the "LeftRight" property described in Table 1. Dataflow graphs consist of three main components: the leaves, the vertices, and the arcs. The leaves correspond to the data used to evaluate properties, which come from the local node performing the evaluation or from the Data Exporter modules on other nodes. The vertices represent the operations that evaluate the properties. Together, these operations form the basis for the Property Checking module. The arcs represent the input/output flows, and describe the dependencies between the operations.

At runtime, each node generates instances of these graphs for each timestamp, and evaluates vertices of the graphs as soon as upstream inputs are available. The Property Checking module processes each vertex and evaluates vertices that are ready, and evaluates vertices of different timestamps simultaneously in a pipelined fashion. Exploiting the property-level parallelism demonstrates a key benefit of representing properties as dataflow graphs. The representation separates the data, operations, and input/output dependencies into independent blocks that are evaluated simultaneously in parallel.

Note that, in both the centralized and decentralized approach, the Data Exporter and the Property Checking modules are automatically generated by MaceODB. Developers do not write any additional code—only properties—and MaceODB generates all the low-level code for exporting state data and evaluating properties.

2.5 Globally Consistent Snapshots

For both centralized and decentralized designs, many MaceODB properties must be evaluated across all participating nodes. In order to evaluate these properties, we need a consistent snapshot of the state of the entire system. To support this, we added a logical clock [6] to the Mace language. Each node in the system maintains its own logical clock that starts at 0, and increases every time there is an event transition. Each time a node sends a message, it attaches its logical clock to the message. Upon receiving

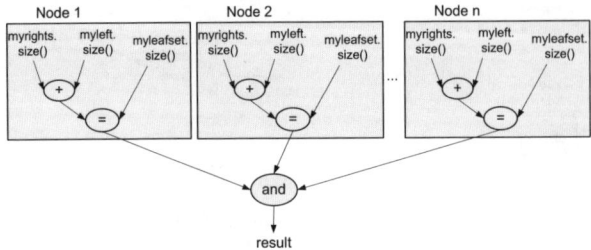

Fig. 5. Example of using a dataflow graph to represent the Pastry LeftRight property

the message, the receiving node updates its logical clock to be the maximum of its local logical clock and the clock attached in the message, establishing the happens-before relationship. Using this mechanism, MaceODB associates each node's data with a global timestamp, thus providing a globally consistent snapshot.

3 Implementation of MaceODB

This section discusses the centralized and decentralized implementations of MaceODB.

3.1 Centralized Implementation

The two key components of the centralized approach are the central Property Checking module and the distributed Data Exporter module. We now describe how MaceODB constructs these modules in detail.

Data Exporter Module. As described in Section 2.3, the Data Exporter module is responsible for sending data from participating nodes back to the central server for property evaluation. Thus, an important task in building the Data Exporter module is determining what data to send. In the simplest implementation, MaceODB uses the grammar specification in Figure 2 to parse through each property, and identify all the variables associated with that property. Each variable's value corresponds to the data sent to the central server. While this works well for most properties, there are edge cases that are inefficient or that the approach fails to cover.

First, consider how the simple implementation is inefficient. For the "Timer" property in Table 1, MaceODB identifies the following variables as exported data: `n.state`, `init`, `n.recovery.nextSchedule()`, and 0. Exporting this set of variables is inefficient since they are either constants or variables that come from the same node. As a result, it is possible to evaluate "Timer" without exporting any data. Therefore, instead of sending data to the central server, each node evaluates the property *locally*, and forwards only the result. The optimization reduces the data transmitted to the server. "LeftRight," "Timer," "PredNotNull," and "AllJoined" are all examples of local properties.

The simple implementation fails to work for properties that include methods with parameters that require data from other nodes. In this case, MaceODB requires each node to export the results from executing the method calls to the central server. Unfortunately, the nodes are not capable of completing the method calls independently, since they require data from peers. To solve this problem, each node sends its local state to the central server. The server then deserializes the state and constructs dummy objects for each node. Using these dummy objects, the server simulates method calls using the appropriate parameter inputs.

After determining the data to send, the next phase in building the Data Exporter module is to generate the actual code for sending the data. We leverage functionality provided directly by Mace's `Message` class, which allows programmers to write code for sending messages between peers.

Property Checking Module. The central server uses the Property Checking module to evaluate properties and alert the programmer of property violations. The module's primary task is to evaluate each property by parsing and breaking them into smaller expressions as specified by the grammar in Figure 2. These expressions correspond directly to the operations required in order to evaluate the properties. For example, consider again the "Timer" property in Table 1. When MaceODB parses that property, it identifies the following expressions/operations:

- Equation Expression #1 - Compares `n.state` and `init`.
- Equation Expression #2 - Compares `n.recovery.nextScheduled()` and `0`.
- Join Expression - Performs a logical OR operation on the results of #1 and #2.
- Quantification Expression - Performs a `forall` loop operation.

After identifying the above expressions, MaceODB generates a C++ method for each expression. Together, these methods form the complete Property Checking and Data Exporter modules that run on the central server.

3.2 Decentralized Implementation

The decentralized implementation also includes Property Checking and Data Exporter modules, but the implementations are different due to the distributed design. This section discusses the key differences in the construction of these modules.

Data Exporter Module. In the decentralized implementation, each node uses its own Data Exporter module to exchange data with other nodes. MaceODB generates two classes to accomplish this in the decentralized approach: `RequestMessage` and `ReplyMessage`. These classes extend the Mace `Message` class. As their names imply, the `RequestMessage` class is used for requesting data, and the `ReplyMessage` class is used for returning the result.

To understand the approach, consider the "KeyMatch" property in Table 1. The property has an equality operation that compares `range.first` and `range.second`. The `range.second` input comes from the node executing the operation. The `range.first` input comes from the node specified by the result of `n.getNextHop(n.range.second, -1)`. Until that input is available, it is impossible to execute the equality operation. As a result, the executing node uses the Data Exporter module to request the needed input. It sends a `RequestMessage` to node X, where X is the return value from calling `getNextHop(n.range.second, -1)`. When node X receives the request message, it replies with a `ReplyMessage`, which contains the requested data `range.first`. Upon receiving `ReplyMessage`, the original node extracts the returned data, and uses it as input in the equality operation.

Property Checking Module. The Property Checking module in decentralized MaceODB consists of operations that provide instructions for evaluating properties. In terms of the dataflow graph representation, these operations correspond to the vertices of the graphs. To generate code for the vertices, MaceODB parses the properties and identifies all operations required to check the properties. For each operation found, MaceODB then generates a C++ class to represent it. Note the difference from the centralized approach, where we generate methods instead of classes. Using classes is a more flexible and object-oriented technique for constructing dataflow graphs. With classes, we can set up the vertices as objects whose member variables contain data inputs for the operations, and whose methods are the operations themselves.

At runtime, instances of these classes are created and stored in a queue. In a separate method, we iterate through the queue, and evaluate any operations that are ready for execution. In terms of the dataflow graph, this corresponds to the process of traversing the graph and evaluating any vertices that are ready. This process is done on a per-node basis, thus allowing the properties to be evaluated in a distributed and parallel manner.

4   Experiences Using MaceODB

We have used MaceODB to test a variety of systems implemented in Mace, including RandTree, Pastry [4], Chord [7], Scribe [8], SplitStream [9] and Paxos [10]. Most of these systems are mature, stable, and have been tested extensively in the past. However, using MaceODB we were still able to find non-trivial bugs in RandTree and Chord.

4.1   RandTree

RandTree implements a random overlay tree that is resilient to node failures and network partitions. It serves as a backbone for a number of high level applications such as Bullet [11] and RanSub [12]. An important liveness property that RandTree must hold is that there should be only one overlay tree that includes all participating nodes. In case of network and node failures, this property does not always hold. To address this issue, a recovery timer was added that periodically checks to see if there was a network partition, and invokes the recovery process as needed. Using "Timer" in Table 1, we were able to find a bug where the recovery timer was not scheduled correctly. When running RandTree with MaceODB enabled, the property "Timer" evaluated to false, which indicated that for some nodes, the state was not `init` and the recovery timer was not set. Using that knowledge, we went back to the source code for RandTree and checked where the recovery timer was scheduled. Figure 6 shows an excerpt of the code that contains the bug.

The most obvious problem with the code shown in Figure 6 is that `recovery.reschedule(TIMEOUT)` never gets called if `peers` is empty. To fix the bug, we moved that statement out of the else block. Thus the recovery timer is always scheduled whenever a node joins the overlay network. An interesting note is that this same property was used previously in the Mace model checker, and yet, the model checker failed to catch the bug. This failure is caused by the way the system was set up for the model checking. The programmers set it up in such a way that whenever a

```
joinOverlay(const NodeSet& peerSet, registration_uid_t rid) {
    if (peers.empty()) {
        state = joined;
        ...
    }
    else {
        state = joining;
        ...
        recovery.reschedule(TIMEOUT);
    }
}
```

Fig. 6. RandTree bug found using MaceODB

node joins the system, it always joins together with another peer. Hence, when the code above is executed, `peers.empty()` will always return false, causing the execution flow to go directly to the else block and the recovery timer to be scheduled. This is an example of the limitations of using model checking: the checking is done in a specialized environment, which can be quite different from the environment in which the real system is deployed. This demonstrates the value of having a tool such as MaceODB that allows the checks to be done in real time and on real, live systems.

4.2 Chord

Chord is a P2P distributed lookup protocol that supports a single operation of mapping keys to nodes [7]. Using Chord, the participating nodes create a ring topology. Each node in this ring has pointers to its successor and predecessor nodes in the ring. To join the ring, a new node obtains its predecessor and successor from another node. Then, to insert itself into the ring, it tells the successor node to update its predecessor pointers. Finally, there is a stabilize process that runs to ensure that global successor and predecessor pointers are consistent and correct.

The predecessor pointers are used in the lookup and stabilize process in Chord, and it is important that they are updated correctly even in the presence of node churn and failures. To test our implementation of Chord, we use the "PredNotNull" liveness property (see Table 1) to check that eventually, all the predecessor pointers are not null. This minimal check ensures that in case of node failures, the predecessor pointers will eventually point to other valid nodes. Using this property, we set up an experiment where we simulate node failures. We observed that in a system of n nodes, if $n-1$ nodes go down, the predecessor pointer of the one remaining node will become null. It will eventually fix itself if the failed nodes recover. However, if they remain down indefinitely, the predecessor pointer will remain null for the rest of the program execution. The correct behavior is that the remaining node should have updated its predecessor pointer to be itself. Fortunately, this bug is quite trivial due to the rarity under which there is a failure of $n-1$ nodes. Nevertheless, this is a good demonstration of the effectiveness of MaceODB in finding rare bugs.

Table 2. Impact on goodput when using MaceODB

		Impact on Goodput	
Services	Number of Nodes	Centralized Approach	Decentralized Approach
RandTree	25 nodes	0.01%	0.05%
	50 nodes	1.68%	2.53%
	75 nodes	1.40%	2.29%
	100 nodes	1.58%	3.53%
ScribeMS	25 nodes	0.07%	0.33%
	50 nodes	8.35%	6.77%
	75 nodes	13.83%	7.16%
	100 nodes	20.17%	7.01%
SplitStream	25 nodes	0.93%	0.84%
	50 nodes	1.01%	1.07%
	75 nodes	2.19%	1.57%
	100 nodes	6.78%	2.55%

5   Performance Evaluation

To evaluate MaceODB's performance, we performed a macro-benchmark that measures its overhead. Our results show that MaceODB is lightweight, and incurs minimal overhead on systems. Additionally, we performed a micro-benchmark to quantify the time to evaluate different types of properties.

5.1   MaceODB Overhead

In this section we analyze the impact that MaceODB incurs on Macedon, a data streaming application that can be run on top of any multicast or unicast service. For our experiments, we run Macedon on top of RandTree, Scribe, and SplitStream. For each of these services, we run Macedon with and without MaceODB, and compare the differences in goodput, memory usage, and CPU usage.

We ran our experiments on several different network topologies that range from small systems of 25 clients to larger systems of 100 clients. These clients are emulated on 17 physical machines with the ModelNet network emulator [13]. Each physical machine has a dual-core Xeon 2.8 MHz processor with 2GB of RAM. The emulated topologies consist of an INET network with 5000 total nodes. The emulated clients have bandwidths ranging from 6,000–10,000 Kbps, and latencies ranging from 2–40 ms.

Goodput and Scalability. To evaluate goodput, we measured the number of packets Macedon sent and received for a specific timeframe (5 minutes). We then calculated the impact that MaceODB incurs on the system's goodput (useful throughput) by plotting the ratio of the loss in goodput when using MaceODB to the goodput of the system when run without MaceODB. We present the results in Table 2. Based on these results, we see that MaceODB performs well for systems with 50 nodes or less. For these systems, the impact in most cases is less than 7%. The results are quite different in larger systems. Using the centralized design, the performance is poor when running on Scribe and SplitStream. The impact on the goodput is as high as 13.8% for systems of 75 nodes

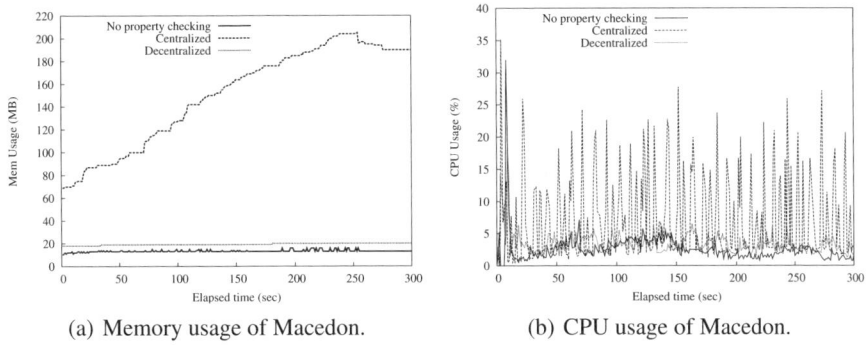

(a) Memory usage of Macedon.   (b) CPU usage of Macedon.

Fig. 7. Memory and CPU usage of Macedon with and without MaceODB

and up to 20.17% for systems of 100 nodes. This poor performance is not a surprise for us, since we know the centralized approach is not scalable. The performance of the decentralized design is much better. Its impact on the goodput is approximately 7% or less. More importantly, the results also indicate that as we increase the size of the system, the impact on performance increases very slowly. This trend allows us to believe that the decentralized approach of MaceODB is scalable for large systems.

Memory Usage. Besides measuring the goodput, we also measured memory and CPU usage. Figure 7(a) shows the results of memory usage during the 5 minute Macedon experiments. Without MaceODB, Macedon used approximately 18 MB of RAM. Using this as the base value, we compared it against the memory usage of Macedon when it was run with MaceODB enabled. Our results show that depending on how we evaluated the properties, the impact on memory usage was quite different. With the decentralized design, the memory usage was around 20 MB, which is slightly higher than the base value, but still acceptable. In the centralized design, the memory usage on the central server is significantly higher. Even with a special memory cleanup mechanism enabled, the central server still used as much as 200 MB of memory. The reason for such high memory usage is because the central server is responsible for storing all the data that is forwarded from the other nodes. This data is stored in memory and cannot be deleted until it forms a complete snapshot of the whole system. At that point, the central server evaluates the properties using the newly created snapshot and removes the old data.

CPU Usage. Figure 7(b) shows the CPU usage during the 5 minute Macedon experiments. Without MaceODB, the CPU usage fluctuates around 2–3%. With decentralized MaceODB, the CPU usage is only slightly higher. On the other hand, with the centralized approach, the property evaluation process is quite CPU-intensive. During the 5 minute run, there were spikes in the CPU usage that were as high as 28%. This further confirms the fact that the centralized approach is not scalable.

Summary. Overall, the macro-benchmark provides us with two important implications. First, the centralized approach is not scalable. When running on large systems, this approach causes a noticeable drop in goodput, and significant overhead in memory and CPU usage. Second, the decentralized approach is scalable and efficient for systems of at least 100 nodes. The impact on goodput is only 7% or less, and the memory/CPU overhead is quite low. We expect similar performance for larger systems. In conclusion, the decentralized approach allows us to satisfy our requirement of making MaceODB lightweight, thus allowing it to be left running on deployed systems without having a significant impact on the system's performance.

5.2   Evaluating Different Types of Properties

Next we measured the time required to evaluate different types of properties in decentralized MaceODB. The goal was to identify properties that are expensive to evaluate. Similar to the macro-benchmark, we ran our experiments on ModelNet, and this time we ran 100 instances of Macedon on top of RandTree and Pastry. We modified Macedon to log the time before and after each property evaluation. The experiments were then run for 5 minutes. At the end of each run, we processed the logs, and calculated the average time for each property evaluation. The average times were as follows: LeftRight/Pastry 79 μs, KeyMatch/Pastry 210 ms, Timer/RandTree 60 μs.

These results show that the cost of evaluation varies greatly among the properties. To understand the reason behind this variance, consider how the properties are evaluated. The properties with the shortest times are the ones that can be evaluated locally. These properties contain operations that do not require any data inputs from other nodes. Examples of such properties are "LeftRight" and "Timer." With this type of property, the cost of evaluation is a function of how fast the CPU can process each operation. For our particular setup, this value is approximately 70 microseconds on average.

Now consider properties that are more expensive to evaluate, such as "KeyMatch." Expensive properties contain operations that require data from other nodes. For these properties, the cost of evaluation is a function of how fast the operations can be executed and how fast the data can be transferred. Typically, the latter is the dominant factor, so that the speed of evaluating the properties depends directly on the bandwidth and latency of the network on which the system is deployed. For our particular network topology, the time it takes to send a ping message from one node to another is approximately 80–100 ms. The round trip time for sending and receiving a message is then 160–200 ms. This value aligns with our results since the cost of evaluating "KeyMatch" is slightly more than 200 ms.

6   Related Work

There are several related techniques for debugging distributed systems. We group these techniques into four categories: model checking, replay-based checking, log analysis, and on-line debuggers.

Model Checking. Prior work has proposed model checking as a mechanism for debugging distributed systems [2]. With model checking, the programmer defines system specifications, and uses the model checker to systematically explore the state-space of the system while checking for specification violations. The approach is a powerful debugging tool since it is possible to traverse large state-spaces in small timeframes, allowing the programmer to discover difficult-to-find bugs. However, the checking process is typically done in a controlled and virtualized environment that does not accurately reflect the deployment environment. MaceODB addresses the limitation and is able to detect bugs that appear during deployment.

Replay-based Checking. Much research has gone into replay-based checking where the programmer has the ability to replay a program while replicating its order and environment. A notable example of replay-based checking is *liblog* [14], which addresses large distributed systems. Liblog logs the execution of deployed application processes, and allows programmers to replay them deterministically. The benefit of using *liblog* or any replay tool is the ability to consistently reproduce bugs from previous executions. While the capability enables offline analysis, its weakness lies in the high cost of logging and replaying an entire execution, especially for large systems. However, MaceODB and replay tools are complementary. A programmer may use MaceODB to detect runtime bugs, and then use replay-based checking for offline analysis.

Log Analysis. Many systems focus on parsing through logs to perform postmortem analysis. A notable example of this methodology is Pip [15]. With Pip, programmers specify expectations about a system's structure, timing, and other properties. At runtime, Pip logs the actual behavior. Pip then provides the programmer with the capability to query the logs and a visual interface for exploring the expected and unexpected behavior. The main problem with Pip, and many other log-based analysis tools, is the high overhead incurred by logging the data.

Other On-line Debuggers. MaceODB is similar in spirit to D^3S [16]. Both share the ideas of using predicates and representing predicates using dataflow graphs. MaceODB differs from D^3S in the way predicates are written. D^3S predicates are written in a mixture of C++ and a scripting language, requiring programmers to specify the stages and the input/output dependencies. MaceODB predicates are written in the Mace language, and the compiler generates the C++ code to represent the stages and dependencies. As a result, MaceODB is easier to use. However, in some cases MaceODB is less efficient than D^3S since MaceODB has the potential to send more data than what is necessary. CrystalBall [17] is a concurrently developed extension of MaceMC [2] with similar goals as MaceODB. Both perform property checking of live running distributed systems. CrystalBall focuses on looking forward during execution, where MaceODB focuses on minimizing overhead and the distribution of property checking.

7   Conclusions

Debugging distributed systems is a challenging task. In this paper we present MaceODB, a tool that makes the task easier by providing programmers with the ability to perform online property checking for services written in Mace. MaceODB is easy to use, yet flexible and powerful enough to catch several non-trivial bugs in the existing Mace services. Our results show that MaceODB tolerates node and network failures inherent to distributed systems, and has low overhead, which makes it possible to use on live systems without significant performance degradation.

References

1. Killian, C.E., Anderson, J.W., Braud, R., Jhala, R., Vahdat, A.M.: Mace: Language Support for Building Distributed Systems. In: Proceedings of the ACM SIGPLAN Conference on Programming Language Design and Implementation (PLDI) (2007)
2. Killian, C.E., Anderson, J.W., Jhala, R., Vahdat, A.: Life, Death, and the Critical Transition: Finding Liveness Bugs in Systems Code. In: Proceedings of the ACM/USENIX Symposium on Networked Systems Design and Implementation (NSDI) (2007)
3. Kindler, E.: Safety and Liveness Properties: A Survey. Bulletin of the European Association for Theoretical Computer Science 53 (1994)
4. Rowstron, A., Druschel, P.: Pastry: Scalable, decentralized object location, and routing for large-scale peer-to-peer systems. In: Guerraoui, R. (ed.) Middleware 2001. LNCS, vol. 2218, p. 329. Springer, Heidelberg (2001)
5. Percival, C.: Naive Differences of Executable Code (2003)
6. Lamport, L.: Time, Clocks, and the Ordering of Events in a Distributed System. Communications of the ACM 21(7) (1978)
7. Stoica, I., Morris, R., Liben-Nowell, D., Karger, D.R., Kaashoek, M.F., Dabek, F., Balakrishnan, H.: Chord: A Scalable Peer-to-Peer Lookup Protocol for Internet Applications. IEEE/ACM Transactions on Networking 11(1) (2003)
8. Rowstron, A.I.T., Kermarrec, A.-M., Castro, M., Druschel, P.: SCRIBE: The Design of a Large-Scale Event Notification Infrastructure. In: Networked Group Communication (2001)
9. Castro, M., Druschel, P., Kermarrec, A.-M., Nandi, A., Rowstron, A., Singh, A.: SplitStream: High-Bandwidth Multicast in Cooperative Environments. In: Proceedings of the ACM Symposium on Operating Systems Principles (SOSP) (2003)
10. Lamport: The Part-Time Parliament. ACM Transactions on Computer Systems 16 (1998)
11. Kostić, D., Rodriguez, A., Albrecht, J., Vahdat, A.: Bullet: High Bandwidth Data Dissemination Using an Overlay Mesh. In: Proceedings of the ACM Symposium on Operating Systems Principles (SOSP) (2003)
12. Kostić, D., Rodriguez, A., Albrecht, J., Bhirud, A., Vahdat, A.: Using Random Subsets to Build Scalable Network Services. In: Proceedings of the USENIX Symposium on Internet Technologies and Systems (USITS) (2003)
13. Vahdat, A., Yocum, K., Walsh, K., Mahadevan, P., Kostić, D., Chase, J., Becker, D.: Scalability and Accuracy in a Large-scale Network Emulator. In: Proceedings of the ACM/USENIX Symposium on Operating System Design and Implementation (OSDI) (2002)
14. Geels, D., Altekar, G., Maniatis, P., Roscoe, T., Stoica, I.: Friday: Global Comprehension for Distributed Replay. In: Proceedings of the ACM/USENIX Symposium on Networked Systems Design and Implementation (NSDI) (2007)
15. Reynolds, P., Killian, C.E., Wiener, J.L., Mogul, J.C., Shah, M.A., Vahdat, A.: Pip: Detecting the Unexpected in Distributed Systems. In: Proceedings of the ACM/USENIX Symposium on Networked Systems Design and Implementation (NSDI) (2006)
16. Liu, X., Guo, Z., Wang, X., Chen, F., Lian, X., Tang, J., Wu, M., Kaashoek, M.F., Zhang, Z.: D^3S: Debugging Deployed Distributed Systems. In: Proceedings of the ACM/USENIX Symposium on Networked Systems Design and Implementation (NSDI) (2008)
17. Yabandeh, M., Knežević, N., Kostić, D., Kuncak, V.: CrystalBall: Predicting and Preventing Inconsistencies in Deployed Distributed Systems. Technical report, School of Computer and Communication Sciences, EPFL, Switzerland (2008)

Parsing C/C++ Code without Pre-processing

Yoann Padioleau

University of Illinois, Urbana Champaign

Abstract. It is difficult to develop style-preserving source-to-source transformation engines for C and C++. The main reason is not the complexity of those languages, but the use of the C pre-processor (`cpp`), especially ifdefs and macros. This has for example hindered the development of refactoring tools for C and C++.

In this paper we propose to combine multiple techniques and heuristics to parse C/C++ source files as-is, while still having only a few modifications to the original grammars of C and C++. We rely on the fact that in most C and C++ software, programmers follow a limited number of conventions on the use of cpp which makes it possible to disambiguate different situations by just looking at the context, names, or indentation of cpp constructs.

We have implemented a parser, Yacfe, based on these techniques and evaluated it on 16 large open source projects. Yacfe can on average parse 96% of those projects correctly. As a side effect, we also found mistakes in code that was not compiled because it was protected by particular ifdefs, but that was still analyzed by Yacfe. Using Yacfe on new projects may require adapting some of our techniques. We found that as conventions and idioms are shared by many projects, the adaptation time is on average less than 2 hours for a new project.

1 Introduction

The C pre-processor [19], `cpp`, is heavily used by C programmers. Using clever macros, programmers can overcome some of the limitations of C by introducing new features such as iterators, or can perform some metaprogramming, or can factorize any kind of source code text. This possibility to easily extend C is one of the reasons C is still a popular language even 35 years after its creation. As Stroustrup said "without the C preprocessor, C itself ... would have been stillborn" [23]. In fact, cpp is even used in programs written in modern languages such as Haskell [28] or λProlog. This freedom has nevertheless its price: it makes it hard to parse C source code as-is, which in turn makes it hard to perform style-preserving source-to-source transformations such as refactorings [9] on C source code.

The combination of C and cpp leads to the union of two languages that are easy to parse separately but very hard to parse together as the grammar of such union could be very large, contain many ambiguities, and be very different from the original C grammar. For instance, the sequence X (Y); could represent a

O. de Moor and M. Schwartzbach (Eds.): CC 2009, LNCS 5501, pp. 109–125, 2009.
© Springer-Verlag Berlin Heidelberg 2009

simple function call or a macro X corresponding to a declaration which happens to be followed by a variable Y surrounded by extra parenthesis.

Static analysis tools and compilers avoid those problems by simply first calling cpp on the source file and then analyze the pre-processed file that now contains only C constructs. Tools such as CIL [16] (C Intermediate Language) also work on a representation of the code that does not directly match the C language but makes the analysis simpler. This is appropriate when the goal is to find bugs or to generate code that no programmer will have to read or modify. However, for style-preserving source-to-source transformations, using this approach would mean working on a version of the file that is very different from its original form, which would make it very hard among other things to back-propagate the transformation to the original file.

Fortunately, what would be hard to parse and disambiguate for a tool would also be hard to parse and disambiguate for a human. Thus, many programmers follow conventions on the use of cpp such as the case sensitivity of macros, their indentation, or the context in which macros can be used (Section 2.3). Programmers can then visually rely on these conventions to easily recognize cpp usages. We thus propose to leverage such implicit information to parse C/C++ code, like humans do.

The challenges for this work are:

– Grammar engineering. The ANSI C and C++ grammars are already complex and large. Adding new constructions may lead to numerous conflicts. Resolving these conflicts may require significant changes in the grammar.
– The variety of cpp idioms. As macros can be used for many different purposes, we need general techniques to recognize those different usages, as well as extensible techniques that can be easily adapted to new software.

In this paper we make the following contributions:

– We have designed general techniques to recognize cpp idioms without adding any ambiguity in the ANSI C and C++ grammars. The main ideas are the notion of *fresh* tokens (transforming Yacc in some sense into a LALR(k) tool), the use of generic *views* to easily specify complex code pattern heuristics, and the use of a configuration file containing macro definitions and heuristic hints that can be used as a last resort.
– We have implemented a parser, Yacfe, that can parse most C/C++ code as is, by extending the C/C++ grammars and by writing heuristics that make use of contextual information, names, and indentation.
– We have evaluated Yacfe on large open source projects and shown that our heuristic-based approach is effective for most C/C++ projects and covers most uses of cpp.

The rest of the paper is organized as follows. Section 2 describes background on the parsing problems engendered by cpp. Section 3 then presents our extensions to the C/C++ grammars to handle cpp constructs and our heuristics that makes it possible to add the previous grammar rules without introducing any shift/reduce or reduce/reduce conflict. Section 4 describes briefly how to use our framework to perform a basic style-preserving program transformation. Section 5 describes the evaluation of Yacfe on large open source software. We finally discuss related work in Section 6 and conclude in Section 7.

2   Background

In the following, we use the term *ambiguity* when grammar rules authorize the same sequence of tokens to be parsed in more than one way. We use the term *conflict* when the ambiguity is only caused by the limitations of the LALR(1) parsing, as implemented by parser generators such as Yacc [11].

The main constructs and usages of cpp are:

- `#include`, mostly for header file inclusion.
- `#ifdef`, for conditional compilation and header file inclusion guards.
- `#define`, to define macros, with or without parameters; in the latter case the macros are often used to describe symbolic constants.

cpp directives can be used anywhere in a C file. Extending the C grammar to handle all possible usages of cpp directives would require extending rules to handle each possibility. The standard solution is instead to expand cpp directives before parsing.

2.1   #include

In practice, `#include` directives are mostly used at the start of a file, at the toplevel, and on very few occasions inside structure definitions. It is thus easy to extend the C grammar and the abstract syntax tree (AST) to handle just those cases. Moreover, as the `#include` token is different from any other C tokens, such extension does not introduce any parsing conflict.

2.2   #ifdef

In practice, `ifdef`s are mostly used either as inclusion guards at the very beginning and end of a file, or to support conditional compilation of sequence of statements, or to support function signature alternatives. It is also possible by extending the C grammar to handle this limited set of idioms. The following excerpts show one of these idioms and the grammar extension that supports it:

```
#ifdef MODULE
int init_module (int x)
#else
int init_foo (int x)
#endif
{
```

function_def ::= *dspec declarator* { *compound* }
             | `#ifdef` *dspec declarator* `#else` *dspec declarator* `#endif` { *compound* }

The problematic ifdefs are those that are used to support certain kinds of alternatives for expression or statement code as in the following:

```
    x = (1 +
#ifdef FOO
            2)
#else
            3)
#endif
    ;
#ifndef _WIN32
    if (is_unix)
      fd = socket(PF_UNIX, SOCK_STREAM, 0);
    else
#endif
      fd = socket(PF_INET, SOCK_STREAM, 0);
```

In the first case, the #else can break the structure of the expression at any place, leading to two branches with only partial expressions. It is thus not sufficient as in the previous extension to add a rule such as:

$$expr ::= \dots$$
$$\qquad | \quad \text{\#ifdef } expr \text{ \#else } expr \text{ \#endif}$$

Fortunately, these situations are rare as such code would also be difficult for the programmer to understand. One of our heuristics detects some of those situations by checking if the parenthesis or braces are closed in both branches; if not we currently treat as a comment the else branch and suggest to the user that he should perhaps rewrite the code. We found only 116 code sites in the 16 software we analyzed that trigger this heuristic.

In the second case, the #endif breaks the condition statement; the first branch is a partial statement with a trailing else. In such situations one of our heuristic treats instead the cpp directive itself as a comment, which allows to parse correctly the full statement. We currently treat 7.5% of the ifdef directives as comments and are working to lower this number by handling more ifdef idioms.

2.3   #define and Macro Uses

Dealing with the definition of macros and their uses is more complex. Figure 1 presents various uses of macros representing common idioms used by programmers. Even if most macro uses look like function calls or variable accesses as in (a), in which case they can be parsed by the original C grammar, this is still not the case for many of them. For (b) only switch/for/while/if can have a brace or statement after their closing parenthesis, for (c) and (d) it would require at least a trailing ';' to make the construction look like a regular statement or declaration, for (d) what looks like a function call in fact mixes types and expressions as arguments and is, when expanded, a declaration, for (e) what starts as a function declaration has a multiplication as an argument if we do not have more contextual information about 'UINT', for (f) there are too many identifiers in the prototype, for (g) it would require first to extend the grammar to recognize macro definitions, and to deal with the \ escape, but the body of this macro is only a partial statement as it lacks a trailing ';', and finally for (h), < is a binary

```#define MAX(a,b) \```
 ``` ((a)<(b)?(b):(a))```
 ```#define LIMIT 3```
 	
 ```int x = MAX(foo(1),10);```
 ```int y = LIMIT;```
 (a) mimicking functions or constants
	```list_for_each(l,e) {```
	 ``` printf("%s", e->name);```
	 ```}```
	
	 (b) iterator

```BEGIN_LOCK```
 ``` if(x != NULL)```
 ```   printf("%s", x->name);```
 ```END_LOCK```
 	
 (c) statement macro
	```DECL_LIST(x, int, 0);```
	 ```struct x {```
	 ``` ACPI_COMMON_FIELDS```
	 ``` int x;```
	 ```}```
	 (d) toplevel and structure macros

```#include <foo.h>```
 ```int f(UINT * y);```
 ```int foo() {```
 ``` return z * y;```
 ```}```
 (e) #include hiding typedefs
	```BZ_EXTERN```
	 ```void __init foo(int x);```
	
	 (f) attributes and qualifiers

```#define DEBUG(A) do \```
 ``` { printf("ERROR:", A); } \```
 ``` while(0)```
 ```DEBUG(1);```
 (g) #define partial statement
	```__P(int, foo, (int x, int y))```
	 ```{ ... }```
	 ```ASSERTCMP(x, <, b);```
	
	 (h) miscellaneous macros

Fig. 1. A few cpp idioms

operator that requires two operands and cannot be passed as an argument, and the `__P` macro does not really look like anything close to a C construction.

Extending the C grammar to handle most of those previous examples would lead to parsing conflicts and ambiguities. For instance, we could try to extend the grammar to deal with the iterator (Figure 1(b)) by adding the grammar rule on line 3:

```
1        statement ::= expr ;
2                    |  for ( [expr] ; [expr] ; [expr] ) statement
3                    |  id ( expr (, expr)* ) statement
4                    |  ...
5             expr ::= ...
6       arith_expr ::= ...
7     logical_expr ::= ...
8   primary_expr ::= id
9                    |  int
10                   |  string
11                   |  ...
```

Unfortunately this will generate a LALR(1) shift/reduce conflict. Indeed, having analyzed the identifier, seeing an open parenthesis the algorithm can not determine if it is the start of a function call (which requires to reduce to primary_expr), or the beginning of a foreach statement (which requires a shift in the statement rule). To be able to decide requires looking ahead at more tokens; in the previous case to know what token is after the closing parenthesis. One could avoid this conflict by reorganizing the grammar so that the reduce action can be delayed, but as the identifier corresponding to the function call in primary_expr (line 8) is deeply nested in the grammar, this would involve a substantial change to the original grammar. Another solution would be to have a more tolerant grammar where invalid constructions would be filtered out in a post-parsing phase. One could then add the rule at line 3 and later check that the leading *expr* can only have the form of a function call:

```
1 statement ::= expr ;
2          |   for ( [expr] ; [expr] ; [expr] ) statement
3          |   expr statement
4          |   ...
```

Unfortunately this will generate ambiguities, as the simple 1+1; statement could be parsed either as a single statement or as the expression 1 followed by the +1; statement, as + can be used both as an unary and binary operator.

Similar things happen for the other idioms. For instance, adding a rule to allow single identifiers to be used as statements or declarations leads to numerous ambiguities as the sequence X (1); could be either a function call or a macro statement X followed later by an expression surrounded by extra parenthesis. Moreover, one grammar extension can also make it harder to add further extensions. For instance, the naive iterator and macro statement extensions each generate numerous conflicts; when combined together they generate a number of conflicts that is superior to the sum of the previous conflicts. There is no guarantee that even if one refactors the grammar to avoid one conflict, this refactoring could be kept as one may have to undo or completely change it to make it possible to support another extension.

Note that for most of the idioms in Figure 1, even if one is not familiar with those idioms, it is quite easy for a human to disambiguate them. Indeed, the name, the presence of visual hints such as newlines or the lack of white-space between tokens, and the context surrounding the construct all contribute to make the meaning clear.

3   The Yacfe Engine

In this section we explain our different techniques to handle cpp, which are (1) our way to extend the C/C++ grammars, (2) a heuristic pre-parsing phase that makes the previous grammar extensions possible without introducing parsing conflicts, and (3) a configuration file that allows users to give additional hints to our heuristics.

3.1   Grammar Extensions and Ambiguities

Tokens such as identifiers can play many different roles. Our solution to this problem is mainly to avoid it by replacing widely used tokens such as identifiers with *fresh* tokens that can not generate any conflict with the existing rules. We re-classify tokens in a phase run between lexing and parsing. For instance, for the iterator extension we re-classify some identifier tokens as "iterator" tokens. Then, we can write grammar rules mentioning iterator tokens instead of identifier tokens. A LALR parser can then even with a look-ahead of 1, seeing an identifier decides which rule to use by inspecting the class of the token: a normal identifier, an iterator identifier, a macro statement identifier, etc. What we essentially do is to mimic what programming language designers do when they extend a language: adding new keywords to avoid ambiguities with previous constructions. Here are examples of some of our extensions to the C and C++ grammars that rely on these fresh tokens:

$$
\begin{aligned}
1 \quad & statement ::= \ldots \\
2 \quad & \mid \; \text{for (} [expr] \text{ ; } [expr] \text{ ; } [expr] \text{) } statement \\
3 \quad & \mid \; \text{id}^{\text{MacroIterator}} (\; expr \; (\text{, } expr)^{*} \;) \; statement \\
4 \quad & \mid \; \text{id}^{\text{MacroStatement}} \\
5 \quad primary\_expr ::= & \; \text{id} \\
6 \quad & \mid \; \text{int} \\
7 \quad & \mid \; \text{string} \\
8 \quad & \mid \; \text{id}^{\text{MacroString}} \; string^{*} \\
9 \quad & \mid \; \ldots \\
10 \quad declaration ::= & \; dspec \text{ ;} \\
11 \quad & \mid \; \text{id}^{\text{MacroDecl}} (\; expr\_or\_type \; (\text{, } expr\_or\_type)^{*} \;) \text{ ;} \\
12 \quad define\_body ::= & \; statement \\
13 \quad & \mid \; expr \\
14 \quad & \mid \; \{^{\text{BraceInit}} \; initializer \; (\text{, } initializer)^{*} \; \} \\
15 \quad & \mid \; \ldots \\
16 \quad init\_decl ::= & \; declarator \\
17 \quad & \mid \; declarator = initializer \\
18 \quad & \mid \; declarator \; (^{\text{ParenConstructorC++}} \; expr \; (\text{, } expr)^{*} \;) \\
19 \quad template\_id ::= & \; \text{id}^{\text{Template}} <^{\text{InfTplt}} \; type\_or\_expr \; (\text{, } type\_or\_expr)^{*} >^{\text{SupTplt}}
\end{aligned}
$$

Re-classifying some tokens requires recognizing some code patterns, which in turn requires a form of parsing. As we will explain in the next section, our heuristics need only simple forms of parsing. We thus use two layers of parsing where the final sophisticated parser relies on the job done using the simpler parser of the previous layer.

We also had to extend the C grammar to deal with C extensions that are often used by open source software such as the extensions implemented by gcc [22] (embedded assembly, case range, attributes, etc). We currently have added 65 new grammar rules on top of the original 195 C rules, to handle the cpp directives and common macro idioms, as well as 59 rules to handle gcc extensions. Note that we almost didn't modify the rules from the original grammar; we didn't have to reorganize the existing rules while adding the new rules because each extension was local, thanks to the fresh tokens. We only had to slightly refactor the original compound rule because of interactions with ifdefs constructs.

3.2 Heuristics and Views

Some heuristics are needed to detect specific tokens that must be re-classified. These interesting tokens are often identifiers, corresponding to different cpp macro idioms, but they can also be specific ifdef tokens or even some open parenthesis tokens. Our heuristics look at the context of those tokens, the structure of their names, or their indentation. Some of these heuristics may need to access to a large context of the token such as a large sequence of tokens after (look-ahead) or even before the specific token. Even if some programming languages such as ML provide powerful pattern-matching capabilities over lists and algebraic data-types (ADTs), it is not easy to write some of our heuristics working on such token lists. For instance, for the foreach heuristic, we may want informally to look at code patterns like `.*each.* (...) {`, but this can only be incompletely translated in ML (in the OCaml [12] syntax) as:

```
match token_list with
| Id(s)::TSym("(")::TSym(")")::TSym("{")::_
| Id(s)::TSym("(")::_::TSym(")")::TSym("{")::_
| Id(s)::TSym("(")::_::_::TSym(")")::TSym("{")::_
| ...
    when s =~ ".*each.*" ->
```

Moreover, even if we could use a form of generalized regular expression over ADTs (as in XDuce or Prolog-III), such regular expressions would not cope with the problem of possible nesting of parenthesized expressions.

To solve this problem we propose the notion of *view* over these tokens that offers an additional layer on top of the list of tokens, to group them into different classes. Views make it possible to use the traditional pattern-matching features of languages such as ML to easily express complex code patterns. This idea was proposed by Wadler in [27] but required originally to extend the programming language. In our case, we do not need to extend ML; we have implemented views using ordinary functions and references (to make it possible to modify elements in the views), looking at views as an idiom instead of a programming language feature. For the iterator example, a parenthesized view adds a tree layer over the list of tokens allowing the previous heuristic to be expressed as:

```
match paren_view  token_list with
| Leaf(Id(s) as t1)::ParenNode(_)::Leaf(TSym("{"))::_
    when s =~ ".*each.*" ->
      reclassify t1 TMacroIterator
```

This heuristic looks for a token identifier, followed by a parenthesized term (containing possibly some nested parenthesized terms), followed by an open brace, and re-classify the leading identifier as an iterator identifier if it contains the word "each". This heuristic will thus reclassify the `list_for_each` identifier in Figure 1(b) but not the `MAX` identifier in Figure 1(a) as the closing parenthesis of the `MAX` parameters is not followed by an open brace.

We have currently implemented 5 views: the parenthesized view, braceized view, ifdef view, line view, and combined line and parenthesized view. These views group tokens in different manners and cover most of our needs. The preceding heuristic is in fact incomplete as it could incorrectly reclassify function names in function definitions such as `int each(int i) { ...`. The current heuristic thus for instance also checks that the identifier is indented, is not at the toplevel, and is not preceded by any other token on its line, using the line view and contextual information from the braceized view. The heuristic also allows for more words than "each" to be part of the identifier (e.g. "loop").

Here is another heuristic using the combined line and parenthesized view.

```
(* ex: BEGIN_LOCK(X,Y)   without  trailing  ';' *)
match lineparen_view   token_list with
| Line ([NoL(Id(s) as tok1);ParenthisedL(_)])
  ::Line(tok2::_)
  ::_
  when indent_of tok1 <= indent_of tok2 &&
       is_upper_case s ->
    reclassify tok1 TMacroStatementParams
```

The code for our heuristics and view constructions currently consists of 2300 lines of OCaml code. An important part of this code is dedicated to the detection of typedefs or type-macro identifiers as in Figure 1(e). An alternative would be to write a dedicated analysis to gather all the typedef declarations from header files in order to build a symbol table for typedef identifiers. Nevertheless, it would require to know where are located those header files (usually specified in makefiles with the `-I` cpp flag) and to have access to those files. For the code of multi-platform applications, this is not always convenient or possible. For instance, one may not have access to the Windows system header files on a Unix machine. We thus opted to try to infer typedefs using heuristics and parse code even with partial information on types.

3.3   Configuration File and Extensibility

Even if the heuristics we have written using the previous views capture many conventions, there are still software or specific programmers using slightly different conventions. For these cases, it would be too demanding to ask to the users of Yacfe to modify the code of Yacfe to add new heuristics. Moreover, those heuristics might be valid only for a set of macros and generate false positives when applied globally. Therefore, to offer an easy way to partially extend Yacfe, we propose to use an external configuration file where the user can manually specify the *class* of specific but recurring macros that cause the above heuristics to originally fail. We have reused the syntax of cpp for the format of this file but Yacfe recognizes special keywords used in the body of macros as hints. Here is an excerpt of the configuration file for the Linux kernel:

```
#define change_hops YACFE_MACRO_ITERATOR
#define DBG         YACFE_MACRO_STATEMENT
#define KERN_EMERG  YACFE_MACRO_STRING
#define DESC_ALIGN  YACFE_MACRO_DECL
```

This file can also be used as a last resort as a way to partially call cpp for difficult macros, such as the one in Figure 1(h), by adding for instance this definition:

```
#define __P(returnt, name, params)  returnt name params
```

In this last case, the resulting expansion is marked specially in the AST so that even if a tool using Yacfe can match over such expansion, such tool will be warned if it wants to transform those expansions.

To assist the user in creating those configuration files, Yacfe remembers, while attempting to parse for the first time the different files of a software, the identifiers in the line before and on the same line than a parsing error. Yacfe then returns to the user the 10 most recurring identifiers and displays each time one example of a parsing error containing the identifier. This helps to quickly find and define the recurring difficult macros.

3.4   Other Techniques

To faithfully represent the original program, we also had to keep extra tokens in the AST which are normally abstracted away, such as extra parenthesis as in (1+((2))). We thus have more a concrete syntax tree (CST) than an AST.

We have also implemented an error recovery scheme so that a parsing error in one function does not hinder the parsing of the rest of the file. In case of a parsing error, Yacfe first displays the line where the error occured and the content of the file around that line. Yacfe then skips the set of tokens before the next function (using heuristics to detect the start of the next function), and returns a special AST error element, indicating the parsing error, containing all the tokens that were skipped (this is useful to compute the statistics of Section 5). Finally, Yacfe re-run the parser for the remaining tokens, for the next function.

Surprisingly, extending Yacfe to handle C++ was not as hard as we imagined. It took us about 2 weeks to parse more than 90% of the source code of Mozilla and MySQL. Parsing C++ is known to be difficult due to the complexity of the language and the numerous ambiguities and LALR(1) conflicts in its official grammar. These ambiguities require contextual information or post-processing semantic analysis to be resolved, as described in the annotated C++ reference manual [5]. Nevertheless, by applying the same techniques we used to disambiguate cpp idioms, we were able by introducing new fresh tokens and their associated heuristics to parse most C++ code, while using the original C++ grammar almost as-is.

4   Using Yacfe

Parsing is only one component of a program transformation system, but a crucial one. Yacfe offers other services such as type-checking, visitors, AST manipulations, and style-preserving unparsing. This last functionality was relatively easy to implement because of the way we originally parse the source code. The description of those features is outside the scope of this paper and Figure 2 illustrates

```
(* X == 0 -> X == NULL when X is a pointer *)
open Ast_c
let main =
  let ast = Parse_c.parse_c_and_cpp Sys.argv.(1) in
  Type_annoter_c.annotate_program ast;
  Visitor_c.visit_program {
    Visitor_c.kexpression = (fun k exp ->
      (match Ast_c.unwrap exp with
      | Binary(e1, Logical (Eq), Constant(Int("0"))) as e2) ->
          (match Type_c.type_of_expr e1 with
          | Pointer _ ->
              let idzero = Ast_c.get_tokens_ref1 e2 in
              Ast_c.modify_token (fun s -> "NULL") idzero;
          | _ -> ()
          )
      | _ -> k exp
      );
    );
  } ast;
  let tmpfile = "/tmp/modified.c" in
  Unparse_c.unparse ast tmpfile
```

Fig. 2. A simple style-preserving program transformation using Yacfe API in OCaml

just a simple example of program transformation using the Yacfe framework (in the OCaml [12] syntax). The transformation consists in replacing every occurrences of '0' by the NULL macro in expressions involving relational comparisons on pointers.

Note that as the pointer expression can be an arbitrary expression, including complex computations inside parenthesis, and as the transformation also requires semantic (type) information, it would be hard with lexical tools such as sed to correctly perform even this simple transformation. Moreover, as many macros expand to '0', working on the pre-processed code, like most tools do, could lead to many false positives.

C frontends such as CIL [16] also offer visitor services and program transformation abilities, but they output source code that is very different from the original code as they operate after preprocessing. C refactoring tools such as Xref [25] can not perform the transformation shown in Figure 2 as it is not part of their limited set of supported refactorings. Xref supports the renaming of simple macros but performs incorrectly for instance the renaming of an iterator macro.

5   Evaluation

In this section we evaluate the applicability of our techniques by testing if Yacfe can parse the code of popular software. All experiments were made on an Intel

Table 1. Yacfe parsing results and statistics on 16 large open source projects

Software	Languages	Age (Years)	Type	LOC (kilo)	skipped (%)	correct (%)
Linux	C	17	Kernel	8050k	1.33	98.96
Mozilla	C/C++	14	Browser	5073k	3.05	95.58
Mysql	C/C++	13	Database	1306k	1.82	93.23
Qemu	C	5	Emulator	434k	3.30	97.00
emacs	C/Lisp	31	Editor/OS	395k	4.30	96.14
git	C	3	VCS	94k	0.03	99.91
sparse	C	5	C frontend	26k	0.69	99.41
gcc	C	31	Compiler	1421k	1.45	97.39
Quake III	C	9	Game	311k	2.15	96.09
openssh	C	9	Network	82k	0.69	99.16
pidgin	C	9	Communication	426k	1.48	99.35
kdeedu	C++	7	Education	315k	1.19	95.22
glibc	C	30	Base Library	773k	3.95	92.37
libstdc++	C++	10	Base Library	438k	3.43	55.22
sdl	C	10	Game Library	201k	3.05	95.83
gtk	C	10	GUI Library	737k	0.75	98.20

Core 2 at 1.86GHz with 2Go of RAM and a 160Go SATA disk. Table 1 presents the parsing results of Yacfe on different types of software (kernel, browser, compiler, game, etc).

Yacfe can parse on average correctly 96% of the code. The percentage is in number of lines. By parsing correctly we mean returning successfully AST elements that are not the AST error element mentionned in Section 3.4. The AST elements may still contain mistakes as we may have bugs in our parser. In fact, we had such bugs in the past and for instance, because of a typo, we generated in the AST the same tree for expressions involving the < and > operators. But, as we have now used extensively the Yacfe framework for more than a year, to perform program transformations on Linux drivers [17], we found such typos and are now confident that the returned ASTs actually match the source correctly, at least for the C parser (we have not yet tested extensively our C++ parser).

The skipped column represents the percentage of lines that are either (1) completely skipped by Yacfe, for instance for code in branches containing partial statements as explained in Section 2.2 or in `#if` 0 branches, or (2) partially skipped, for instance when a line contains a problematic macro mentioned in the configuration file which must be expanded.

For each piece of software, it took us on average less than 2 hours to write the configuration file containing on average 56 hints or definitions of recurring problematic macros. The average time to parse a file is about 0.03s. Analyzing the whole Linux kernel with Yacfe takes 12 minutes, whereas compiling it with gcc (with the maximal number of features and drivers) takes 56 minutes.

Note that even if Yacfe does not parse correctly 100% of the code, it still analyzes in general more code than gcc which processes only certain ifdefs. On an Intel machine with all the features 'on', gcc compiles only 54% of the Linux kernel C files, as the code of other architectures is not considered. Moreover, using static analysis tools such as Splint [7] requires also a setup time. For instance, configuring Splint to analyze one Linux kernel driver took us more than 2 hours as Splint can work only after preprocessing which requires among other things to find the appropriate cpp options (more than 40 -D and -I flags), spread in Makefiles or specific to gcc, to also pass to Splint. This is not needed with Yacfe. Bug detection tools can thus have false positives, for code inside certain ifdefs, as they don't analyze the whole original source code.

The remaining errors are due to features not yet handled by our parser such as embedded assembly for Windows, Objective C code specific to MacOS, the gcc vector extension, or cpp idioms and macro body definitions not yet handled by our heuristics or grammar or configuration files. Among those errors, we also found true errors in certain ifdef branches which had probably not been compiled for a long time. Some Yacfe parsing errors were also raised because the indentation of macros was not correct, which prevents our heuristics to work (often because tools like indent are not aware of cpp constructs and wrongly indented the code). We found 31 such mistakes in the Linux kernel, and have submitted patches that have now been accepted and are part of the latest kernel. We also found 1 or 2 mistakes in Qemu, Openssh, Pidgin, and Mozilla.

Table 1 also shows that the younger the software, the easier it is for Yacfe to parse it. This is probably because the pitfalls of cpp are now widely known and thus programmers are more conservative in their use of cpp.

Yacfe can still not parse most of the C++ code in the C++ standard GNU library as this code use advanced C++ features and macros not yet handled by our heuristics and grammar. In fact the code is also arguably very hard to disambiguate for a human.

6   Related Work

Ernst et al. [6] presented an extensive study on the usage of cpp in 26 open source software, representing a total of 1.4 millions lines of code. They relied on the PcP3 [3] tool to compute various statistics. PcP3 is a framework for pre-processor aware code analysis where the code is still pre-processed but by an embedded cpp in which the user can write Perl functions invoked when certain cpp constructs are recognized. While this approach using hooks might be enough to statically analyze code, for instance to find cpp-related bugs, PcP3 offers no support for program transformation as the code is still in the end preprocessed.

Based on the above study, Brewer et al. [14] proposed a new pre-processor language for C, Astec, which can express many cpp idioms while being more amenable to program analysis. They also presented a tool to assist users in migrating code from cpp to Astec. They tested their approach on 3 small software and a small subset of Linux.

Past works to parse C code as-is have focused mainly on ifdefs [2,10]. Baxter et al. [2] proposed an extended C grammar, AST, and symbol table dealing with ifdef directives, similar to what we presented briefly in Section 2.2. They also impose constraints on where such directives can be placed, mainly at boundaries between statements or declarations. Garrido et al. [10] extended this approach to deal with directives not placed on clean boundaries, for instance between partial expressions as in the example in Section 2.2. They proposed the notion of pseudo-pre-processing where some code preceding ifdefs of partial statements or expressions are internally distributed in both branches, to complete them, but marked specially in the AST to make it still possible to back propagate modifications on the original code. They tested their approach on 2 small software. We found, on the code we analyzed, that more than 90% of the ifdefs are placed at clean boundaries as it makes the code more readable. Some programmers have also argued that some use of ifdefs are considered harmful [20].

Few works have focused on macros, which we found in practice more problematic than ifdefs regarding parsing. Livadas et al. [13] proposed another pre-processor, Ghinzu, allowing to track and map code location in the expanded code to the original code. Baxter et al. [4] briefly described the handling of cpp in their commercial program transformation system framework DMS. As in PcP3 they implemented their own pre-processor called between the lexing and parsing, but use it only when necessary. They retain some cpp macros uses in the AST when possible and fall-down to their embedded pre-processor by expanding some macros in case of parsing errors.

Baxter et al. [4] as well as McPeak et al. [15] have argued for the use of Generalized LR[24] parsing (GLR, or parallel LR) instead of LALR(1) as in Yacc, especially to deal with the C++ language, independently of the pre-processing problem. Using a GLR tool does not reduce the number of conflicts in a grammar, as GLR is still a LR-based technique. But, instead of favoring one choice, for instance shift over reduce, as in Yacc, GLR tries both possibilities and returns a set of parse trees. In some cases many parsing branches eventually reach a dead-end and only one parse tree is returned. The shift/reduce conflict introduced when adding the iterator construct in the grammar in Section 2.3 is thus irrelevant when using a GLR parser. In other cases, many parsing branches could succeed and GLR thus postpones the disambiguation problem to a post-parsing phase. Using more semantic information the programmer must then decide which of those parse trees are invalid. In this paper we opted instead to disambiguate a priori using views and heuristics, as lexical information such as name or indentation are more relevant than semantic information to disambiguate cpp idioms. Moreover, by using fresh tokens we can have a grammar without almost any LR conflicts whereas using GLR without our fresh tokens would lead for our C grammar to many conflicts and no static guarantees that all ambiguities are resolved by the post-parsing phase. The C++ grammar written by McPeak thus contains 138 conflicts, and does not handle any cpp constructs. Our C and C++ grammars, which also handle cpp constructs, contain respectively 1 and 6 shift/reduce conflicts, including the classic dangling else conflict, and were all resolved by adding precedence directives in the grammar.

To solve some of the C++ conflicts, Willink [29] has heavily rewritten the original C++ grammar, for instance to better deal with templates, which use the < and > symbols already used for relation comparisons in expressions. Nevertheless, as opposed to the original grammar which provides a useful readable specification of the language, the modified grammar of Willink is hard to read and breaks the conceptual structure of the original grammar. It is also a superset of the language and requires a post-processing analysis to generate the final AST and solve ambiguities.

There are two dedicated refactoring tools for C/C++ listed on the refactoring website [8], including Xref [26], and some IDEs such as Eclipse have some support for C/C++. Nevertheless, they support only a limited set of refactorings, which in turn represent only a small part of the program-transformation spectrum. They do not offer any general mechanism to deal with cpp. Instead, Xref uses a classical C front-end, EDG [1], which like PCP3 implements its own cpp preprocessor. It provides opportunities to track cpp uses, but not to transform them.

Spinnelis [21] focused on the rename-entity refactoring that existing refactoring tools may implement only partially as they can miss some code sites (false negatives). This is because cpp macros can concatenate identifiers with the # cpp operator, generating identifiers that may not be visible directly in the original source code. Spinnelis thus proposed techniques to statically track those concatenations. We instead extended the AST and the grammar to accept such concatenation constructs and postpone those analysis to transformation engines working on our extended AST.

No previous work tried to leverage the implicit information programmers use to disambiguate cpp usages, or to represent cpp idioms directly in the AST. They thus all work on program representations that do not directly reflect the original code. Most of the previous work have also been applied only to small software.

7   Conclusion

In this paper we have presented Yacfe, a parser for C/C++ that can represent most cpp constructs directly in the AST. This is made possible by adding new grammar rules, recognizing cpp idioms, without introducing any conflict and ambiguity in the original C and C++ grammars by using fresh tokens. Those fresh tokens are generated by heuristics that leverage the name, context, and indentation of cpp constructs.

We have used Yacfe in the past as part of a project to evolve Linux device drivers [17] in which the correct parsing of most code helped automate most of the work. We have also used it as part of a source code comment study [18] where the maintenance of cpp constructs in the AST was necessary. We hope Yacfe can be useful to other researchers in situations that require manipulating source code as-is, such as for refactoring, when evolving APIs, when offering a migration path from legacy code to modern languages, or to find bugs at the cpp-level for instance on the incorrect use of macros.

Availability

The source code of Yacfe as well as the data used for this paper are available on our web page: http://opera.cs.uiuc.edu/~pad/yacfe/.

Acknowledgments

Thanks are due to Julia Lawall and Lin Tan for comments on earlier drafts of this paper, to the anonymous reviewers for suggesting the idea to assist the user in creating the configuration file, and to YuanYuan Zhou to let me spend time on this paper. This work was carried out in part at the EMN. This work was supported in part by the Agence Nationale de la Recherche (France) and by the NSF under grant CNS 06 15372.

References

1. EDG C++ frontend. Edison Design Group, www.edg.com
2. Aversano, L., Penta, M.D., Baxter, I.D.: Handling preprocessor-conditioned declarations. In: International Workshop on Source Code Analysis and Manipulation (2002)
3. Badros, G.J., Notkin, D.: A framework for preprocessor-aware C source code analyses. Software, Practice and Experience (2000)
4. Baxter, I.D., Pidgeon, C., Mehlich, M.: DMS: Program transformations for practical scalable software evolution. In: ICSE (2004)
5. Ellis, M.A., Stroustrup, B.: The Annotated C++ Reference Manual. Addison-Wesley, Reading (1990)
6. Ernst, M.D., Badros, G.J., Notkin, D., Member, S.: An empirical analysis of C preprocessor use. IEEE Transactions on Software Engineering (2002)
7. Evans, D.: Splint (2007), http://www.splint.org/
8. Fowler, M.: Refactoring tools, http://www.refactoring.com/tools.html
9. Fowler, M.: Refactoring: Improving the Design of Existing Code. Addison-Wesley, Reading (1999)
10. Garrido, A., Johnson, R.: Analyzing multiple configurations of a C program. In: ICSM (2005)
11. Johnson, S.C.: Yacc: Yet another compiler-compiler. Tech. rep, Unix Programmer's Manual Vol 2b (1979)
12. Leroy, X.: Ocaml, http://caml.inria.fr/ocaml/
13. Livadas, P.E., Small, D.T.: Understanding code containing preprocessor constructs. In: IEEE Workshop on Program Comprehension (1994)
14. McCloskey, B., Brewer, E.: ASTEC: a new approach to refactoring C. In: FSE (2005)
15. McPeak, S., Necula, G.C.: Elkhound: A fast, practical GLR parser generator. In: Duesterwald, E. (ed.) CC 2004. LNCS, vol. 2985, pp. 73–88. Springer, Heidelberg (2004)
16. Necula, G.C., McPeak, S., Rahul, S.P., Weimer, W.: CIL: Intermediate language and tools for analysis and transformation of C programs. In: Horspool, R.N. (ed.) CC 2002. LNCS, vol. 2304, p. 213. Springer, Heidelberg (2002)

17. Padioleau, Y., Lawall, J.L., Hansen, R.R., Muller, G.: Documenting and automating collateral evolutions in Linux device drivers. In: EuroSys (2008)
18. Padioleau, Y., Tan, L., Zhou, Y.: Listening to programmers: Taxonomies and characteristics of comments in operating system code. In: ICSE (2009)
19. Ritchie, D.M., Kernighan, B.: The C Programming Language. Prentice-Hall, Englewood Cliffs (1988)
20. Spencer, H.: #ifdef considered harmful, or portability experience with C News. In: USENIX Summer (1992)
21. Spinellis, D.: Global analysis and transformations in preprocessed languages. IEEE Transactions on Software Engineering (2003)
22. Stallman, R. M. Using GCC. GNU Press, GNU C extensions (2003),
    http://gcc.gnu.org/onlinedocs/gcc/index.html#toc_C-Extensions
23. Stroustrup, B.: The Design and Evolution of C++. Addison-Wesley, Reading (1994)
24. Tomita, M.: An efficient context-free parsing algorithm for natural languages. In: IJCAI (1985)
25. Vittek, M.: Xrefactory for C/C++, http://xref-tech.com/xrefactory/main.html
26. Vittek, M.: Refactoring browser with preprocessor. In: Conference on Software Maintenance And Reengineering (2003)
27. Wadler, P.: Views: A way for pattern matching to cohabit with data abstraction. In: POPL (1987)
28. Wansbrough, K.: Macros and preprocessing in Haskell (1999),
    http://www.cl.cam.ac.uk/~kw217/research/misc/hspp-hw99.ps.gz
29. Willink, E.D., Vyacheslav, Muchnick, B.: Fog: A meta-compiler for C++ patterns. Tech. rep. (1998)

Faster Scannerless GLR Parsing

Giorgios Economopoulos, Paul Klint, and Jurgen Vinju

Centrum voor Wiskunde en Informatica (CWI), Kruislaan 413, 1098 SJ Amsterdam,
The Netherlands

Abstract. Analysis and renovation of large software portfolios requires syntax analysis of multiple, usually embedded, languages and this is beyond the capabilities of many standard parsing techniques. The traditional separation between lexer and parser falls short due to the limitations of tokenization based on regular expressions when handling multiple lexical grammars. In such cases scannerless parsing provides a viable solution. It uses the power of context-free grammars to be able to deal with a wide variety of issues in parsing lexical syntax. However, it comes at the price of less efficiency. The structure of tokens is obtained using a more powerful but more time and memory intensive parsing algorithm. Scannerless grammars are also more non-deterministic than their tokenized counterparts, increasing the burden on the parsing algorithm even further.

In this paper we investigate the application of the Right-Nulled Generalized LR parsing algorithm (RNGLR) to scannerless parsing. We adapt the Scannerless Generalized LR parsing and filtering algorithm (SGLR) to implement the optimizations of RNGLR. We present an updated parsing and filtering algorithm, called SRNGLR, and analyze its performance in comparison to SGLR on ambiguous grammars for the programming languages C, Java, Python, SASL, and C++. Measurements show that SRNGLR is on average 33% faster than SGLR, but is 95% faster on the highly ambiguous SASL grammar. For the mainstream languages C, C++, Java and Python the average speedup is 16%.

1   Introduction

For the precise analysis and transformation of source code we first need to parse the source code and construct a syntax tree. Application areas like reverse engineering, web engineering and model driven engineering specifically deal with many different languages, dialects and embeddings of languages into other languages. We are interested in the construction of parsing technology that can service such diversity; to allow a language engineer to experiment with and efficiently implement parsers for real and complex language constellations.

A parser is a tool, defined for a specific grammar, that constructs a syntactic representation (usually in the form of a parse tree) of an input string and determines if the string is syntactically correct or not. Parsing often includes a scanning phase which first splits the input string into a list of words or tokens. This list is then further analyzed using a more powerful parsing algorithm. This

O. de Moor and M. Schwartzbach (Eds.): CC 2009, LNCS 5501, pp. 126–141, 2009.

scanning/parsing dichotomy is not always appropriate, especially when parsing legacy languages or embedded languages. Scanners are often too simplistic to be able to deal with the actual syntax of a language and they prohibit modular implementation of parsers. Scannerless parsing [16,17,25] is a technique that avoids such issues that would be introduced by having a separate scanner [5]. Intuitively, a scannerless parser uses the power of context-free grammars instead of regular expressions to tokenize an input string.

The following Fortran statement is a notorious example of scanning issues [1]: $\boxed{\texttt{DO 5 I = 1.25}}$. It is not until the decimal point that it becomes clear that we are dealing here with an assignment to the variable DO5I.[1] However, in the slightly different statement: $\boxed{\texttt{DO 5 I = 1,25}}$, DO is a keyword and the statement as a whole is a loop construct. This example highlights that tokenization using regular expressions, without a parsing context, can easily be non-deterministic and even ambiguous. In order to restrict the number of possibilities, scanners usually apply several implicit rules like, e.g., *Prefer Longest Match*, *Prefer Keywords*, *Prefer First Applicable Rule*. The downside of such disambiguation is that the scanner commits itself to one choice of tokens and blocks other interpretations of the input by the parser. A scannerless parser with enough lookahead does not have this problem.

Another example is the embedding of Java code in AspectJ definitions and *vice versa*. If a scanner is needed for the combination of the two languages, you may end up with reserving the new AspectJ keywords from the Java code. However, existing Java code may easily contain such identifiers, resulting in parsing errors for code that was initially parsed correctly. One approach that could avoid this problem would be to use two separate scanners: one that is active while parsing pure AspectJ code and another that is active while parsing pure Java code. Once again, the parsing context would be used to decide which scanner is used in the tokenization. This problem does not exist when using a scannerless parser [6].

In a classical scanner/parser approach the scanner makes many decisions regarding tokenization. In a scannerless parser these decisions are postponed and have to be made by the parser. Consequently, scannerless parsers generally have to deal with more non-determinism than before, so the deterministic LR parsing algorithms can no longer be used. However, it turns out that the non-determinism introduced by the removal of the scanner can be gracefully handled by Generalized LR (GLR) parsing algorithms [20,14,15].

The advantages of a one phase scannerless parser over a traditional two phase scanner and parser may not be immediately obvious. The following list highlights the main benefits of scannerless parsing:

- Computational power: lexical ambiguity is a non-issue and full definition of lexical syntax for real languages is possible.
- Modularity: languages with incompatible lexical syntaxes can be combined seemlessly.
- Scope: to generate parsers for more languages, including ambiguous, embedded and legacy languages.

---

[1] Recall that Fortran treats spaces as insignificant, also inside identifiers.

- Simplicity: no hard-wired communication between scanning and parsing.
- Declarativeness: no side-effects and no implicit lexical disambiguation rules necessary.

So, on the one hand a language engineer can more easily experiment with and implement more complex and more diverse languages using a parser generator that is based on Scannerless GLR parsing. On the other hand there is a cost. Although it does not have a scanning phase, scannerless parsing is a lot more expensive than its two-staged counterpart. The structure of tokens is now retrieved with a more time and memory intensive parsing algorithm. A collection of grammar rules that recognizes one token type, like an identifier could easily have 6 rules, including recursive ones. Parsing one character could therefore involve several GLR stack operations, searching for applicable reductions and executing reductions. Consider an average token length of 8 characters and an average number of stack operations of 4 per character, a scannerless parser would do $4 * 8 = 32$ times more work per token than a parser that reads a pre-tokenized string. Furthermore, a scannerless parser has to consider all whitespace and comment tokens. An average program consists of more than 50% whitespace which again multiplies the work by two, raising the difference between the two methods to a factor of 64. Moreover, scannerless grammars are more non-deterministic than their tokenized counterparts, increasing the burden on the parsing algorithm even more.

Fortunately, it has been shown [5] that scannerless parsers are fast enough to be applied to real programming languages. In this paper we investigate the implementation of the Scannerless GLR (SGLR) parser provided with SDF [25,5]. It makes scannerless parsing feasible by rigorously limiting the non-determinism that is introduced by scannerless parsing using disambiguation filters. It is and has been used to parse many different kinds of legacy programming languages and their dialects, experimental domain specific languages and all kinds of embeddings of languages into other languages. The parse trees that SGLR produces are used by a variety of tools including compilers, static checkers, architecture reconstruction tools, source-to-source transformers, refactoring, and editors in IDEs.

As SDF is applied to more and more diverse languages, such as scripting and embedded web scripting languages, and in an increasing number of contexts such as in plugins for the Eclipse IDE, the cost of scannerless parsing has become more of a burden. That is our motivation to investigate algorithmic changes to SGLR that would improve its efficiency. Note that the efficiency of SGLR is defined by the efficiency of the intertwined parsing and filtering algorithms.

We have succeeded in replacing the embedded parsing algorithm in SGLR—based on Farshi's version of GLR [14]—with the faster Right-Nulled GLR algorithm [18,9]. RNGLR is a recent derivative of Tomita's GLR algorithm that, intuitively, limits the cost of non-determinism in GLR parsers. We therefore investigated how much the RNGLR algorithm would mitigate the cost of scannerless parsing, which introduces more non-determinism. The previously published results on RNGLR can not be extrapolated directly to SGLR because of (A) the missing scanner, which may change trade-offs between stack traversal and stack construction and (B) the fact that SGLR is not a parsing algorithm *per se*, but rather a parsing and filtering algorithm.The benefit of RNGLR may easily be insignificant compared to the overhead of scannerless parsing and the additional costs of filtering.

In this paper we show that a Scannerless Right-Nulled GLR parser and filter is actually significantly faster on real applications than traditional SGLR. The amalgamated algorithm, called SRNGLR, requires adaptations in parse table generation, parsing and filtering, and post-parse filtering stages of SGLR. In Section 2 we analyze and compare the run-time efficiency of SGLR and the new SRNGLR algorithm. In Sections 3 and 4 we explain what the differences between SGLR and SRNGLR are. We conclude the paper with a discussion in Section 6.

2   Benchmarking SRNGLR

In Sections 3 and 4 we will delve into the technical details of our parsing algorithms. Before doing so, we first present our experimental results. We have compared the SGLR and SRNGLR algorithms using grammars for an extended version of ANSI-C—dubbed C'—, C++, Java, Python, SASL and Γ_1—a small grammar that triggers interesting behaviour in both algorithms. Table 1 describes the grammars and input strings used. Table 2 provides statistics on the sizes of the grammars. We conducted the experiments on a 2.13GHz Intel Dual Core with 2GB of memory, running Linux 2.6.20.

SGLR and SRNGLR are comprised of three different stages: parse table generation, parsing and post-parse filtering. We focus on the efficiency of the latter two, since parse table generation is a one-time cost. We are not interested in the runtime of recognition without tree construction. Note that between the two algorithms the parsing as well as the filtering changes and that these influence each other. Filters may prevent the need to parse more and changes in the parsing algorithm may change the order and shape of the (intermediate) parse forests that are filtered. Efficiency measurements are also heavily influenced by the shapes of the grammars used as we will see later on.

The SRNGLR version of the parser was tested first to output the same parse forests that SGLR does, modulo order of trees in ambiguity clusters.

Table 3 and Figure 1 show the arithmetic mean time of five runs and Table 4 provides statistics on the amount of work that is done. GLR parsers use a Graph Structured Stack (GSS). The edges of this graph are visited to find reductions and new nodes and edges are created when parts of the graph can be reduced or the next input character can be shifted. Each reduction also leads to the construction of a new parse tree node and sometimes a new ambiguity cluster. An ambiguity cluster encapsulates different ambiguous trees for the same substring. For both algorithms we count the number of GSS edge visits, GSS node creations, edge and node visits for garbage collection, and parse tree node and ambiguity cluster visits for post-parse filtering. Note that garbage collection of the GSS is an important factor in the memory and run-time efficiency of GLR.

Table 1. Grammars and input strings used

Name	Grammar description	Input size (chars/lines)	Input description
C'	ANSI-C plus ambiguous exception handling extension	32M/1M	Code for an embedded system
C++	Approaches ISO standard, with GNU extensions	2.6M/111K	Small class that includes much of the STL
Java	Grammar from [6] that implements Java 5.0	0.5M/18k	Implementation of The Meta-Environment [3]
Python	Derived from the reference manual [24], ambiguous due to missing off-side rule[2]implementation	7k/201	spawn.py from Python distribution
SASL	Taken from [22], ambiguous due to missing off-side rule implementation	2.5k+/114+	Standard prelude, concatenated to increasing sizes
Γ_1	$S ::= SSS \mid SS \mid a$; triggers worst-case behaviour [9]	1–50/1	Strings of a's of increasing length

Table 2. Grammar statistics showing nullable non-terminals (NNT), nullable productions (NP), right-nullable productions (RNP), SLR(1) states, shifts and gotos, reductions and reductions with dynamic lookahead restriction (LA Reductions)

	NNT	NP	RNP	States	Shifts+Gotos	Reductions SGLR	SRNGLR	LA Reductions SGLR	SRNGLR
C'	71	93	94	182k	37k	18k	23k	5.9k	6.3k
C++	90	112	102	112k	18k	19k	19k	1.5k	1.5k
Java	81	112	116	67k	9.7k	5.9k	6.0k	1.0k	1.1k
Python	56	74	85	22k	3.4k	1.7k	1.9k	0	0
SASL	16	21	22	4.5k	0.9k	0.5k	0.6k	0	0
Γ_1	0	0	0	13	30	13	15	0	0

For this benchmark, SRNGLR is on average 33% faster than SGLR with a smallest speedup of 9.8% for C and a largest speedup of 95% for SASL. Apparently the speedup is highly dependent on the specific grammar. If we disregard SASL the improvement is still 20% on average and if we also disregard Γ_1^{50} the average drops to a still respectable 16% improvement for the mainstream languages C, C++, Java and Python. The results show that SRNGLR parsing speed is higher (up to 95%) for grammars that are highly ambiguous such as SASL. SRNGLR also performs better on less ambiguous grammars such as Java (14% faster). The *parsing time* is always faster, and in most cases the *filtering time* is also slightly faster for SRNGLR but not significantly so.

The edge visit statistics (Table 4 and Figure 3) explain the cause of the improved parsing time. Especially for ambiguous grammars the SGLR algorithm

---

[2] The off-side rule was not implemented because SDF does not have a declarative disambiguation construct that can expresses its semantics. It can be implemented in ASF as a post-parse traversal, but has no effect on the timings described here.

Table 3. Speed (characters/second), Parse time (seconds) , Filter time (seconds), Total time (seconds) and Speedup (%) of SGLR (S) and SRNGLR (SRN). $k = 10^3$.

	C'		C++		Java		Python		SASL^{80}		$\Gamma_1{}^{50}$	
	S	SRN	S	SRN	S	SRN	S	SRN	S	SRN	S	SRN
Speed (chars/sec.)	385k	443k	121k	175k	404k	467k	178	904	78	1k	4.7	24
Parse time (sec.)	84.2	73.2	21.5	14.9	2.1	1.8	39.2	7.7	4.8k	202.2	10.8	2.1
Filter time (sec.)	102.9	95.5	5.7	5.6	0.8	0.7	327.3	298.8	1.6	1.6	7.7	9.5
Total time (sec.)	187.2	168.8	27.3	20.6	2.9	2.5	366.5	306.5	4.8k	203.9	18.5	11.6
Speedup (%)		9.8		24.5		13.8		16.4		95		37.6

Table 4. Workload data. Edges traversed searching reductions (ET), edges traversed searching existing edge (ES), GSS nodes created (NC), GSS edges created (EC), edges traversed for garbage collection (GC), ambiguity nodes created while filtering (FAC), and parse tree nodes created while filtering (FNC). $k = 10^3$, $M = 10^6$, $B = 10^9$.

	C'		C++		Java		Python		SASL^{80}		Γ_1^{50}	
	S	SRN	S	SRN	S	SRN	S	SRN	S	SRN	S	SRN
ET	149M	44M	26M	6.6M	3.2M	0.9M	90M	3.4M	71B	165M	48M	0.7M
ES	81M	18M	145M	27M	5.0M	0.9M	1.8B	234M	16B	14B	28M	14M
NC	141M	143M	19M	20M	3.0M	3.0M	157k	157k	2.4M	2.4M	252	252
EC	154M	157M	30M	31M	3.5M	3.4M	962k	962k	44M	44M	3.9k	3.9k
GC	13M	13M	6.2M	6.8M	0.7M	0.6M	2.0M	2.0M	88M	88B	14k	14k
FAC	30k	30k	5.6k	5.6k	0	0	83k	83k	48k	48k	1.2k	2.1k
FNC	241M	241M	13M	13M	1.6M	1.6M	707M	707M	3.1M	3.1M	1.1M	1.3M

traverses many more GSS edges. According to the time measurements this is significant for real world applications of scannerless parsing.

Filtering time is improved in all but the Γ_1 case, although the improvement is not greater than 10%. The workload statistics show that about the same number of nodes are created during filtering. The differences are lost in the rounding of the numbers, except for the Γ_1 case which shows significantly more node creation at filtering time. This difference is caused by different amounts of sharing of ambiguity clusters between the two versions. The amount of sharing in ambiguity clusters during parsing, for both versions, depends on the arbitrary ordering of reduction steps. I.e. it is not relevant for our analysis.

Notice that the parse time versus filtering time ratio can be quite different between languages. This highly depends on the shape of the grammar. LR factored grammars have higher filtering times due to the many additional parse tree nodes for chain rules. The Python grammar is an example of such a grammar, while SASL was not factored and has a minimum number of non-terminals for its expression sub-language. Shorter grammars with less non-terminals have better filtering speed. We expect that by "unfactoring" the Python grammar a lot of speed may be gained.

Figure 2 depicts how SRNGLR improves parsing speed as the input length grows. For Γ_1 it is obvious that the gain is higher when the input gets larger.

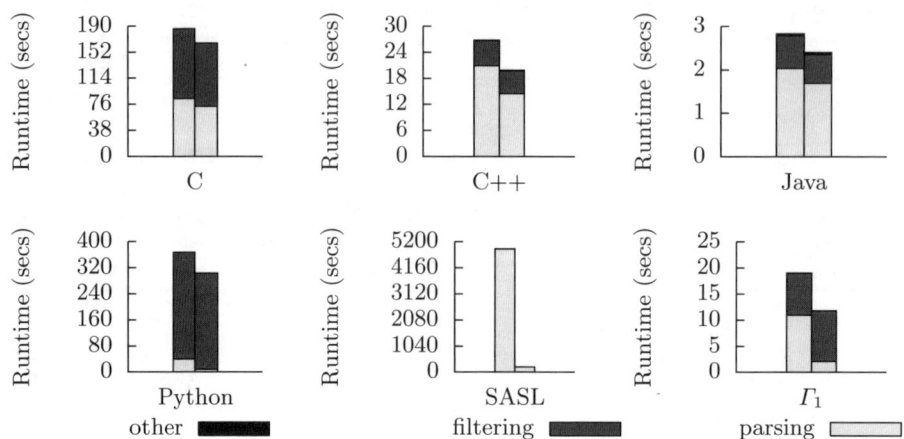

Fig. 1. Runtime comparison between SGLR (first col.) and SRNGLR (second col.). The *other* bar accounts for the time taken to read and process the input string and parse table.

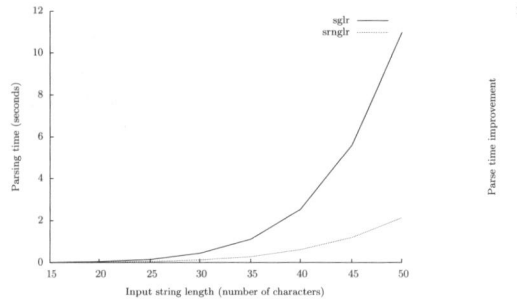

Fig. 2. Comparison of SGLR and SRNGLR parsing time for Γ_1

Fig. 3. Correlation between saving of edge traversals and parsing speedup

Note that although Γ_1 does not have any right-nullable productions (see Table 2) there is still a significant gain. The reason for this is that SRNGLR prevents work from being done for all grammars (see Section 3).

From these results we may conclude that SRNGLR clearly introduces a structural improvement that increases the applicability of scannerless GLR parsing to large programs written in highly ambiguous scripting languages such as Python and SASL. Also, we may conclude that it introduces a significant improvement for less ambiguous or non-ambiguous languages and that the shape of a grammar highly influences the filtering speed.

3   SGLR and RNGLR

In this section we outline the RNGLR and SGLR algorithms and highlight the main differences between them. There are four main differences between the SGLR and RNGLR algorithms:

- Different parse tables formats are used; SLR(1) [25] versus RN [9].
- SGLR does more traversals of the GSS during parsing than RNGLR.
- Different parse forest representations are used; maximally shared trees [23] versus SPPF's [15].
- SGLR implements disambiguation filters [5] whereas RNGLR does not.

The RNGLR algorithm combines adaptations in the parse table generation algorithm with simplifications in the parser run-time algorithm. It is based on Tomita's algorithm, called Generalized LR (GLR) [20]. GLR extends the LR parsing algorithm to work on all context-free grammars by replacing the stack of the LR parsing algorithm with a Graph Structured Stack (GSS). Using the GSS to explore different derivations in parallel, GLR can parse sentences for grammars with parse tables that contain LR conflicts rather efficiently. However, the GLR algorithm fails to terminate on certain grammars. Farshi's algorithm fixes the issue in a non-efficient manner, by introducing extra searching of the GSS [14]. This algorithm is the basis for SGLR. The RNGLR algorithm fixes the same issue in a more efficient manner.

RNGLR introduces a modified LR parse table: an RN table. RN tables are constructed in a similar way to canonical LR tables, but in addition to the standard reductions, reductions on right nullable rules are also included. A right nullable rule is a production rule of the form $A ::= \alpha\beta$ where $\beta \stackrel{*}{\Rightarrow} \varepsilon$[3]. By reducing the left part of the right nullable rule (α) early, the RNGLR algorithm avoids the problem that Tomita's algorithms suffered from and hence does not require Farshi's expensive correction. However, since the right nullable symbols of the rule (β) have not been reduced yet it is necessary to pre-construct the parse trees of those symbols. These nullable trees are called ε-trees and since they are constant for a given grammar, they can be constructed at parse table generation time and included in the RN parse table. The early RN reduction will construct a full derivation simply by including the pre-constructed trees.

It is well known that the number of parses of a sentence with an ambiguous grammar may grow exponentially with the size of the sentence [7]. To avoid exponential complexity, GLR-style algorithms build an efficient representation of all possible parse trees, using subtree sharing and local ambiguity packing. However, the SGLR and RNGLR algorithms construct parse trees in different ways and use slightly different representations. RNGLR essentially follows the approach described by Rekers – the creation and sharing of trees is handled directly by the parsing algorithm – but does not construct the most compact representation possible. The SGLR algorithm uses the ATerm library [23] to

---

[3] α, β are possibly empty lists of terminals and non-terminals, ϵ is the empty string and $\stackrel{*}{\Rightarrow}$ represents a derivation in zero or more steps

construct parse trees thereby taking advantage of the maximal sharing it implements. This approach has several consequences. The parsing algorithm can be simplified significantly by replacing all parse tree creation and manipulation code with calls to the ATerm library. Although the library takes care of all sharing, the creation of ambiguities and cycles requires extra work (see Section 4.1).

As previously mentioned, in addition to the different construction approaches, a slightly different representation of parse forests is used. RNGLR labels interior nodes using non-terminal symbols and uses packing nodes to represent ambiguities [18]. SGLR labels interior nodes with productions and represents ambiguous trees using ambiguity clusters labeled by non-terminal symbols. The reason that production rules are used to label the interior nodes of the forest is to implement some of the disambiguation filters that are discussed later in this section.

The SGLR algorithm. Is different from RNGLR mainly due to the filters that are targeted at solving lexical ambiguity. Its filters for priority and preference will be discussed as well. SGLR introduces the following four types of filters: follow restrictions, rejects, preferences and priorities. Each filter type targets a particular kind of ambiguity. Each filter is derived from a corresponding declarative disambiguation construct in the SDF grammar formalism [5]. Formally, each filter is a function that removes certain derivations from parse forests (sets of derivations). Practically, filters are implemented as early in the parsing architecture as possible, i.e. removing reductions from parse tables or terminating parallel stacks in the GSS.

Four filter types. We now briefly define the semantics of the four filter types for later reference. A *follow restriction* is intended to implement longest match and first match behaviour of lexical syntax. In the following example, the -/- operator defines a restriction on the non-terminal I. Its parse trees may not be followed immediately by any character in the class $[A\text{-}Za\text{-}z0\text{-}9\_]$, which effectively results in longest match behaviour for I:

$$I ::= [A\text{-}Za\text{-}z][A\text{-}Za\text{-}z0\text{-}9\_] * \qquad I \text{ -/- } [A\text{-}Za\text{-}z0\text{-}9\_] \qquad (3.1)$$

In general, given a follow restriction A -/- α where A is a non-terminal and α is a character class, any parse tree whose root is $A ::= \gamma$ will be filtered if its yield in the input string is immediately followed by any character in α. Multiple character follow restrictions, as in A -/- $\alpha_1.\alpha_2 \ldots \alpha_n$, generalize the concept. If each of the n characters beyond the yield of A, fit in their corresponding class α_i the tree with root A is filtered. Note that the follow restriction incorporates information from beyond the hierarchical context of the derivation for A, i.e. it is not context-free.

The *reject* filter is intended to implement reservation, i.e. keyword reservation. In the following example, the {reject} attribute defines that the keyword `public` is to be reserved from I:

$$I ::= [A\text{-}Za\text{-}z][A\text{-}Za\text{-}z0\text{-}9\_] * \qquad I ::= \text{``}public\text{''}\{\text{reject}\} \qquad (3.2)$$

In general, given a production $A ::= \gamma$ and a reject production $A ::= \delta\{\text{reject}\}$, all trees whose roots are labeled $A ::= \delta\{\text{reject}\}$ are filtered and any tree whose root is labeled $A ::= \gamma$ is filtered if its yield is in the language generated by δ. Reject filters give SGLR the ability to parse non-context-free languages such as $a^n b^n c^n$ [25].

The *preference* filter is intended to select one derivation from several alternative overlapping (ambiguous) derivations. The following example uses the $\{\text{prefer}\}$ attribute to define that in case of ambiguity the preferred tree should be the only one that is not filtered. The dual of $\{\text{prefer}\}$ is $\{\text{avoid}\}$.

$$I ::= [A\text{-}Za\text{-}z][A\text{-}Za\text{-}z0\text{-}9\_] * \qquad I ::= \text{``public''} \{\text{prefer}\} \qquad (3.3)$$

In general, given n productions $A ::= \gamma_1$ to $A ::= \gamma_n$ and a preferred production $A ::= \delta\{\text{prefer}\}$, any tree whose root is labeled by any of $A ::= \gamma_1$ to $A ::= \gamma_n$ will be filtered if its yield is in the language generated by δ. All trees whose roots are $A ::= \delta\{\text{prefer}\}$ remain. Dually, given an avoided production $A ::= \kappa\{\text{avoid}\}$ any tree whose root is $A ::= \kappa\{\text{avoid}\}$ is filtered when its yield is in one of the languages generated by γ_1 to γ_n. In this case, all trees with roots $A ::= \gamma_1$ to $A ::= \gamma_n$ remain. Consequently, the preference filter can not be used to recognize non-context-free languages.

The *priority* filter solves operator precedence and associativity. The following example uses priority and associativity:

$$E ::= E \text{``}\rightarrow\text{''} E\{\text{right}\} \qquad > \qquad E ::= E \text{``or''} E\{\text{left}\} \qquad (3.4)$$

The $>$ defines that no tree with the "$\rightarrow$" production at its root will have a child tree with the "or" at its root. This effectively gives the "$\rightarrow$" production higher precedence. The $\{\text{right}\}$ attribute defines that no tree with the "$\rightarrow$" production at its root may have a first child with the same production at its root. In general, we index the $>$ operator to identify for which argument a priority holds and map all priority and associativity declarations to sets of indexed priorities. Given an indexed priority declaration $A ::= \alpha B_i \beta >_i B_i ::= \delta$, where B_i is the ith symbol in $\alpha B_i \beta$, then any tree whose root is $A ::= \alpha B_i \beta$ with a subtree that has $B_i ::= \delta$ as its root at index i, is filtered. The priority filter is not known to extend the power of SGLR beyond recognizing context-free languages.

4 SRNGLR

We now discuss the amalgamated SRNGLR algorithm that combines the scannerless behaviour of SGLR with the faster parsing behaviour of RNGLR. Although the main difference between SRNGLR and SGLR is in the implementation of the filters at parse table generation time — all of SGLR's filters need to be applied to the static construction of SRNGLR's ϵ-trees — there are also some small changes in the parser run-time and post-parse filtering.

4.1   Construction of ε-Trees

The basic strategy is to first construct the complete ε-trees for each RN reduction in a straightforward way, and then apply filters to them. We collect all the productions for nullable non-terminals from the input grammar, and then for each non-terminal we produce all of its derivations, for the empty string, in a top-down recursive fashion. If there are alternative derivations, they are collected under an ambiguity node.

We use maximally shared ATerms [4] to represent parse trees. ATerms are directed acyclic graphs, which prohibits by definition the construction of cycles. However, since parse trees are not general graphs we may use the following trick. The second time a production is used while generating a nullable tree, a cycle is detected and, instead of looping, we create a cycle node. This special node stores the length of the cycle. From this representation a (visual) graph can be trivially reconstructed.

Note that this representation of cycles need not be minimal, since a part of the actual cycle may be unrolled and we detect cycles on twice visited productions, not non-terminals. The reason for checking on productions is that the priority filter is specific for productions, such that after filtering, cycles may still exist, but only through the use of specific productions.

4.2   Restrictions

We distinguish single character follow restrictions from multiple lookahead restrictions. The first are implemented completely statically, while the latter have a partial implementation at parse table generation time and a partial implementation during parsing.

Parse table generation. An RN reduction $A ::= \alpha \cdot \beta$ with nullable tree T_β in the parse table can be removed or limited to certain characters on the lookahead. When one of the non-terminals B in T_β has a follow restriction B -/- γ, T_β may have less ambiguity or be filtered completely when a character from γ is on the lookahead for reducing $A ::= \alpha \cdot \beta$. Since there may be multiple non-terminals in T_β, there may be multiple follow restrictions to be considered.

The implementation of follow restrictions starts when adding the RN reduction to the SLR(1) table. For each different kind of lookahead character (token), the nullable tree for T_β is filtered, yielding different instances of T_β for different lookaheads. While filtering we visit the nodes of T_β in a bottom-up fashion. At each node in the tree the given lookahead character is compared to the applicable follow restrictions. These are computed by aggregation. When visiting a node labelled $C ::= DE$, the restriction class for C is the union of the restriction classes of D and E. This means that C is only acceptable when both follow restrictions are satisfied. When visiting an ambiguity node with two children labeled F and G, the follow restrictions for this node are the intersections of the restrictions of F and G. This means that the ambiguity node is acceptable when either one of the follow restrictions is satisfied.

If the lookahead character is in the restricted set, the current node is filtered, if not the current node remains. The computed follow restrictions for the current node are then propagated up the tree. Note that this algorithm may lead to the complete removal of T_β, and the RN reduction for this lookahead will not be added. If T_β is only partially filtered, and no follow restriction applies for the non-terminal A of the RN reduction, the RN reduction is added to the table, including the filtered ϵ-tree.

Parser run-time. Multiple character follow restrictions cannot be filtered statically. They are collected and the RN-reductions are added and marked to be conditional as lookahead reductions in the parsetable. Both the testing of the follow restriction as well as the filtering of the ϵ-tree must be done at parse-time.

Before any lookahead RN-reduction is applied by the parsing algorithm, the ϵ-tree is filtered using the follow restrictions and the lookahead information from the input string. If the filtering removes the tree completely, the reduction is not performed. If it is not removed completely, the RN reduction is applied and a tree node is constructed with a partially filtered ϵ-tree.

4.3 Priorities

Parse table generation. The priority filters only require changes to be made to the parse table generation phase; the parser runtime and post parse filtering phases remain the same as SGLR. The priority filtering depends on the chosen representation of the ϵ-trees (see also Section 3); each node holds a production rule and cycles are unfolded once. Take for example $S ::= SS\{\text{left}\}|\epsilon$. The filtered ϵ-tree for this grammar should represent derivations where $S ::= SS$ can be nested on the left, but *not* on the right. The cyclic tree for S must be unfolded once to make one level of nesting explicit. Then the right-most derivations can be filtered. Such representation allows a straightforward filtering of all trees that violate priority constraints. Note that priorities may filter all of the ϵ-tree, resulting in the removal of the corresponding RN reduction.

4.4 Preferences

Parse table generation. The preference filter strongly resembles the priority filter. Preferences are simply applied to the ϵ-trees, resulting in smaller ϵ-trees. However, preferences can never lead to the complete removal of an ϵ-tree.

Post-parse filter. RN reductions labeled with $\{\text{prefer}\}$ or $\{\text{avoid}\}$ are processed in a post-parse filter in the same way as normal reductions were processed in SGLR.

4.5 Rejects

The implementation of the reject filter was changed in both SGLR and SRNGLR to improve the predictability and of its behaviour.

Parse table generation. If any nullable production is labeled with {reject}, then the empty language is not acceptable by that production's non-terminal. If such a production occurs in an ϵ-tree, we can statically filter according to the definition of rejects in Section 3. If no nullable derivation is left after filtering, we can also remove the entire RN reduction.

Parser run-time. Note that we have changed the original algorithm [25] for reject filtering at parser run-time for *both* SGLR and SRNGLR. The completeness and predictability of the filter have been improved. The simplest implementation of reject is to filter redundant trees in a post-parse filter, directly following the definition of its semantics given in Section 3. However, the goal of the implementation is to prohibit further processing on GSS stacks that can be rejected as early as possible. This can result in a large gain in efficiency, since it makes the parsing process more deterministic, i.e. there exist on average less parallel branches of the GSS during parsing.

The semantics of the reject filter is based on syntactic overlap, i.e. ambiguity (Section 3). So, the filter needs to detect ambiguity between a rejected production $A ::= \gamma \{\text{reject}\}$ and a normal production for $A ::= \delta$. The goal is to stop further processing reductions of A. For this to work, the ambiguity must be detected *before* further reductions on A are done. Such ordering of the scheduling of reductions was proposed by Visser [25]. However, there are certain grammars (especially those with nested, or nullable rejects) for which the ordering does not work and rejected trees do not get filtered correctly. Alternative implementations of Visser's algorithm have worked around these issues at the cost of filtering too many derivations.

We have implemented an efficient method that does not rely on the order that reductions get performed. The details of this reject implementation are:

- Edges created by a reduction of a rejected production are stored separately in GSS nodes. We prevent other reductions traversing the rejected edges, thereby preventing possible further reductions on many stacks.
- In GLR, edges collect ambiguous derivations, and if an edge becomes rejected because one of the alternatives is rejected, it stays rejected.
- Rejected derivations that escape are filtered in a post-parse tree walker. They may escape when an alternative, non-rejected, reduction creates an edge and this edge is traversed by a third reduction before the original edge becomes rejected by a production marked with {reject}.

Like the original, this algorithm filters many parallel stacks at run-time with the added benefit that it is more clearly correct. We argue that: (A) we do not filter trees that should not be filtered, (B) we do not depend on the completeness of the filtering during parse time, and (C) we do not try to order scheduling of reduce actions, which simplifies the implementation of SRNGLR significantly.

The Post-parse filter. This follows the definition of the semantics described in Section 3. To handle nested rejects correctly, the filter must be applied in a bottom-up fashion.

5   Related Work

The cost of general parsing as opposed to deterministic parsing or parsing with extended lookahead has been studied in many different ways. Our contribution is a continuation of the RNGLR algorithm applied in a different context.

Despite the fact that general context-free parsing is a mature field in Computer Science, its worst case complexity is still unknown. The algorithm with the best asymptotic time complexity to date is presented by Valiant [21]. However, because of the high constant overheads this approach is unlikely to be used in practice. There have been several attempts at speeding the run time of LR parsers that have focused on achieving speed ups by implementing the handle finding automaton (DFA) in low-level code (see [12]). A different approach to improving efficiency is presented in [2], the basic ethos of which is to reduce the reliance on the stack. Although this algorithm fails to terminate in certain cases, the RIGLR algorithm presented in [13] has been proven correct for all CFGs.

Two other general parsing algorithms that have been used in practice are the CYK [27] and Earley [8] algorithms. Both display cubic worst case complexity, although the CYK algorithm requires grammars to be transformed to Chomsky Normal Form before parsing. The BRNGLR [19] algorithm achieves cubic worst case complexity without needing to transform the grammar.

Saloman and Cormack [16] first used scannerless parsing to describe determinstic parsers of complete character level grammars. Another deterministic scannerless parsing technique that uses Parsing Expression Grammars instead of CFGs, is the Packrat [10] algorithm and its implementations [11]. It has been shown to be useful in parsing extensible languages. Another tool that has been used to generate scanners and parsers for extensible languages with embedded DSLs is Copper [26]. It uses an approach called context-aware scanning where the scanner uses contextual information from the parser to be more discriminating with the tokens it returns. This allows the parser to parse a larger class of languages than traditional LR parsers that use separate scanners.

6   Conclusions

We improved the speed of parsing and filtering for scannerless grammars significantly by applying the ideas of RNGLR to SGLR. The disambiguation filters that complement the parsing algorithm at all levels needed to be adapted and extended. Together the implementation of the filters and the RN tables make scannerless GLR parsing quite a bit faster. The application areas in software renovation and embedded language design are directly serviced by this. It allows experimentation with more ambiguous grammars, e.g. interesting embeddings of scripting languages, domain specific languages and legacy languages.

Acknowledgements. We are grateful to Arnold Lankamp for helping to implement the GSS garbage collection scheme for SRNGLR. The first author was partially supported by EPSRC grant EP/F052669/1.

References

1. Aho, A.V., Sethi, R., Ullman, J.D.: Compilers: Principles, Techniques and Tools. Addison-Wesley, Reading (1986)
2. Aycock, J., Horspool, R.N., Janousek, J., Melichar, B.: Even faster generalised LR parsing. Acta Inform. 37(9), 633–651 (2001)
3. van den Brand, M.G.J., van Deursen, A., Heering, J., de Jong, H.A., de Jonge, M., Kuipers, T., Klint, P., Moonen, L., Olivier, P.A., Scheerder, J., Vinju, J.J., Visser, E., Visser, J.: The ASF+SDF meta-environment: A component-based language development environment. In: Wilhelm, R. (ed.) CC 2001. LNCS, vol. 2027, pp. 365–370. Springer, Heidelberg (2001)
4. van den Brand, M.G.J., de Jong, H.A., Klint, P., Olivier, P.A.: Efficient Annotated Terms. Softw., Pract. Exper. 30(3), 259–291 (2000)
5. van den Brand, M.G.J., Scheerder, J., Vinju, J.J., Visser, E.: Disambiguation Filters for Scannerless Generalized LR Parsers. In: Horspool, R.N. (ed.) CC 2002. LNCS, vol. 2304, pp. 143–158. Springer, Heidelberg (2002)
6. Bravenboer, M., Tanter, É., Visser, E.: Declarative, formal, and extensible syntax definition for AspectJ. SIGPLAN Not. 41(10), 209–228 (2006)
7. Church, K., Patil, R.: Coping with syntactic ambiguity or how to put the block in the box on the table. American Journal of Computational Linguistics 8(3–4), 139–149 (1982)
8. Earley, J.: An efficient context-free algorithm. Comm. ACM 13(2), 94–102 (1970)
9. Economopoulos, G.R.: Generalised LR parsing algorithms. PhD thesis, Royal Holloway, University of London (August 2006)
10. Ford, B.: Parsing expression grammars: a recognition-based syntactic foundation. In: POPL 2004, pp. 111–122. ACM, New York (2004)
11. Grimm, R.: Better extensibility through modular syntax. In: PLDI 2006, pp. 38–51. ACM, New York (2006)
12. Horspool, R.N., Whitney, M.: Even faster LR parsing. Softw., Pract. Exper. 20(6), 515–535 (1990)
13. Johnstone, A., Scott, E.: Automatic recursion engineering of reduction incorporated parsers. Sci. Comp. Programming 68(2), 95–110 (2007)
14. Nozohoor-Farshi, R.: GLR parsing for ε-grammars. In: Tomita, M. (ed.) Generalized LR Parsing, ch. 5, pp. 61–75. Kluwer Academic Publishers, Netherlands (1991)
15. Rekers, J.: Parser Generation for Interactive Environments. PhD thesis, University of Amsterdam (1992)
16. Salomon, D.J., Cormack, G.V.: Scannerless NSLR(1) parsing of programming languages. SIGPLAN Not. 24(7), 170–178 (1989)
17. Salomon, D.J., Cormack, G.V.: The disambiguation and scannerless parsing of complete character-level grammars for programming languages. Technical Report 95/06, Dept. of Computer Science, University of Manitoba (1995)
18. Scott, E., Johnstone, A.: Right nulled GLR parsers. ACM Trans. Program. Lang. Syst. 28(4), 577–618 (2006)
19. Scott, E., Johnstone, A., Economopoulos, R.: BRNGLR: a cubic Tomita-style GLR parsing algorithm. Acta Inform. 44(6), 427–461 (2007)
20. Tomita, M.: Efficient Parsing for Natural Languages. A Fast Algorithm for Practical Systems. Kluwer Academic Publishers, Dordrecht (1985)
21. Valiant, L.G.: General context-free recognition in less than cubic time. J. Comput. System Sci. 10, 308–315 (1975)

22. van den Brand, M.G.J.: Pregmatic, a generator for incremental programming environments. PhD thesis, Katholieke Universiteit Nijmegen (1992)
23. van den Brand, M.G.J., de Jong, H.A., Klint, P., Olivier, P.A.: Efficient annotated terms. Softw., Pract. Exper. 30(3), 259–291 (2000)
24. van Rossum, G.: Python reference manual, `http://docs.python.org/ref/`
25. Visser, E.: Syntax Definition for Language Prototyping. PhD thesis, University of Amsterdam (1997)
26. Eric, R., Van Wyk, E.R., Schwerdfeger, A.C.: Context-aware scanning for parsing extensible languages. In: GPCE 2007, pp. 63–72. ACM Press, New York (2007)
27. Younger, D.H.: Recognition and parsing of context-free languages in time n^3. Inform. and control 10(2), 189–208 (1967)

Decorated Attribute Grammars:
Attribute Evaluation Meets Strategic Programming

Lennart C.L. Kats[1], Anthony M. Sloane[1,2], and Eelco Visser[1]

[1] Software Engineering Research Group, Delft University of Technology,
The Netherlands
L.C.L.Kats@tudelft.nl,visser@acm.org
[2] Department of Computing, Macquarie University,
Sydney, Australia
Anthony.Sloane@mq.edu.au

Abstract. Attribute grammars are a powerful specification formalism for tree-based computation, particularly for software language processing. Various extensions have been proposed to abstract over common patterns in attribute grammar specifications. These include various forms of copy rules to support non-local dependencies, collection attributes, and expressing dependencies that are evaluated to a fixed point. Rather than implementing extensions natively in an attribute evaluator, we propose *attribute decorators* that describe an abstract evaluation mechanism for attributes, making it possible to provide such extensions as part of a library of decorators. Inspired by strategic programming, decorators are specified using generic traversal operators. To demonstrate their effectiveness, we describe how to employ decorators in name, type, and flow analysis.

1 Introduction

Attribute grammars are a powerful formal specification notation for tree-based computation, particularly for software language processing [26], allowing for modular specifications of language extensions and analyses. At their most basic, they specify declarative *equations* indicating the functional relationships between *attributes* (or properties) of a tree node and other attributes of that node or adjacent parent and child nodes [19]. An *attribute evaluator* is responsible for scheduling a tree traversal to determine the values of attributes in a particular tree.

Attribute grammars are nowadays employed in a wide range of application domains and contexts. To extend their expressiveness for use in particular domains, and to abstract over commonly occurring patterns, basic attribute grammars have been extended in many ways, in particular supporting attribution patterns with non-local dependencies. For example, *remote attribution* constructs allow equations that refer to attributes of nodes arbitrarily far above or below the node for which they are defined [5,15]. *Chain attributes* express a dependence that is threaded in a left-to-right, depth-first fashion through a sub-tree that contains definitions of the chain value [15]. *Self rules* provide a local copy of subtrees, which may be adapted for tree transformations [2]. More generally, *collection attributes* enable the value of an attribute of one node to be determined

O. de Moor and M. Schwartzbach (Eds.): CC 2009, LNCS 5501, pp. 142–157, 2009.

at arbitrary other nodes [5,22]. A different kind of remote attribute is provided by *reference attribute grammars* that allow references directly to arbitrary non-local nodes and their attributes [12], allowing for attributes that look up a particular node or collection of nodes. Finally, some attribute grammar systems support equations with *circular dependencies* that are evaluated to a fixed point [4,23].

All of these extensions aim to raise the level of abstraction in specifications, by translation into basic attribute grammars or by using an extended evaluator. Unfortunately, each of these extensions has been designed and implemented separately and is hardwired into a particular attribute grammar system.Potential users may find that a particular system does not provide the set of demanded extensions. Adding new abstractions is non-trivial, since it requires modification of the attribute evaluation system itself.For example, it can sometimes be useful to thread attribute values from right-to-left (e.g., when computing backward slices or use-def relations between variables). In a system with only left-to-right chained attributes, this dependence must be encoded using basic attribute equations, despite the similarity of the abstractions.

In his OOPSLA'98 invited talk, "Growing a Language" [28], Guy Steele argued that "languages need to put the tools for language growth in the hands of the users," providing high-level language features that abstract over various extensions, rather than directly providing language features to solve specific problems. To this effect, we propose *attribute decorators* as a solution for the extensibility problem of attribute grammar specification languages. A decorator is a generic declarative description of the tree traversal or evaluation mechanism used to determine the value of an attribute. Decorators augment basic attribute equations with additional behavior, and can provide non-local dependencies or a form of search as required. For instance, a decorator can specify that the value of an attribute is to be sought at the parent node (and recursively higher in the tree) if it is not defined at the current node. Decorators can also enhance the usability of attribute equations for specific domains, separating the generic behavior from specific equations such as type checker constraints or data-flow equations, supported in other systems through specialized extensions.

In this paper, we present ASTER, a system for *decorated attribute grammars* (available from [1]). Decorators are powerful enough to specify all of the attribute grammar extensions listed above, avoiding the need to hardwire these into the system. A library of decorators suffices to cover common cases, while user-defined, domain-specific decorators can be used for specific applications and domains.

Decorators are inspired by *strategic programming*, where generic traversal strategies enable a separation between basic rewrite rules defining a tree transformation and the way in which they are applied to a tree [33,20,21]. In our case, local attribute equations define the core values of a tree computation, while decorators describe how those values are combined across the tree structure. The ASTER specification language is built as an extension of the Stratego strategic programming language [8]. We reuse the generic traversal operators of Stratego for the specification of decorators, and its pattern matching and building operations as the basis for attribute equations.

We begin this paper with background on attribute grammars and introducing our basic notations. Section 3 defines decorators, showing how they augment basic equations and capture common patterns. In Section 4 we present typical language engineering applications, demonstrating how decorators can be effectively applied in this area. We briefly outline our implementation in Section 5. Finally, we conclude with a comparison to related work and some pointers to future directions.

2   Attribute Grammars

As they were originally conceived, attribute grammars (AGs) specify dependencies between attributes of adjacent tree nodes [19]. Attributes are generally associated with context-free grammar productions. For example, consider a production X ::= Y Z. Attribute equations for this production can define attributes for symbols X, Y and Z. Attributes of X defined at this production are called *synthesized*, as they are defined in the context of X. They can be used to pass information upwards. Conversely, attributes of Y and Z defined in this context can be used to pass information downwards, and are called *inherited* attributes.

2.1   Pattern-Based Attribute Grammars

In this paper we adopt a notational variation on traditional AGs in which attribute equations are associated with tree or term patterns instead of grammar productions [10,6]. Trees can be denoted with prefix constructor *terms* such as Root(Fork(Leaf(1), Leaf(2))). Tree patterns for matching and construction are terms with variables (indicated in italics throughout this paper), e.g. Fork(t_1, t_2).

Basic attribute equations have the form

```
eq p: r.a := v
```

and define equations for a term that matches pattern p, where attribute a with a relation r to the pattern has value v. The relation r can be a subterm of p indicated by a variable or the term matched by the pattern itself, indicated by the keyword id.

As an example, consider the transformation known as Bird's *repmin* problem [3], which can be well expressed as an AG, as illustrated in Figure 1. In this transformation, a binary tree with integer values in its leaves is taken as the input, and a new tree with the same structure and its leaves replaced with the minimum leaf value is produced as the output. For example, the tree Root(Fork(Leaf(1),Leaf(2))) is transformed to Root(Fork(Leaf(1),Leaf(1))).

In the specification of Figure 1, the local minimum leaf value in a subtree is computed in the synthesized attribute min (lines 3, 8 and 12). At the top of the tree, the minimum for the whole tree is copied to the inherited global-min attribute (line 2), which is then copied down the tree to the leaves (lines 6 and 7). Finally, the replace attribute constructs a tree where each leaf value is replaced by the global minimum (lines 4, 9, 13).

Attribute equations are often defined in sets that share a common pattern, but may also be grouped to define a common attribute, which can make it easier to show the flow of information at a glance. Consider Figure 2, which is equivalent to the specification in Figure 1, but organizes the equations per attribute instead. Equations can be defined in separate modules, across different files, and are automatically assembled into a complete specification. Thus, language definitions can be factored per language construct and/or per attribute to support modular, extensible language definitions [13,31].

```
 1  eq Root(t):
 2     t.global-min  := t.min
 3     id.min        := t.min
 4     id.replace    := Root(t.replace)

 5  eq Fork(t₁,t₂):
 6     t₁.global-min := id.global-min
 7     t₂.global-min := id.global-min
 8     id.min      := <min> (t₁.min,t₂.min)
 9     id.replace  := Fork(t₁.replace,
10                            t₂.replace)

11  eq Leaf(v):
12     id.min      := v
13     id.replace  := Leaf(id.global-min)
```

Fig. 1. An attribute grammar specification for *repmin* in pattern major form

```
eq min:
   Root(t)      → t.min
   Fork(t₁,t₂)  → <min> (t₁.min,t₂.min)
   Leaf(v)      → v

eq global-min:
   Root(t).t      → id.min
   Fork(t₁,t₂).t₁  → id.global-min
   Fork(t₁,t₂).t₂  → id.global-min

eq replace:
   Root(t)      → Root(t.replace)
   Fork(t₁,t₂)  → Fork(t₁.replace,
                           t₂.replace)
   Leaf(v)      → Leaf(id.global-min)
```

Fig. 2. An attribute grammar specification for *repmin* in attribute major form

Using patterns helps separation of concerns when specifying a syntax and AG analyses. However, it can still be useful to use the concrete syntax of a language. ASTER supports this using the generic approach of *concrete object syntax embedding* as described in [32]. For example, instead of a pattern $While(e,s)$, we can use a concrete syntax pattern, which is typically enclosed in "semantic braces":

```
eq |[ while (e) s ]|:
   id.condition = e
```

Concrete syntax patterns are parsed at compile-time, and converted to their abstract syntax equivalents. Section 4 includes further examples of this technique.

2.2 Copy Rules

In theory, basic attribute equations with local dependencies are sufficient to specify all non-local dependencies. Non-local dependencies can be encoded by passing context information around using local inherited and synthesized attributes. In the repmin example, this pattern can be seen in the definition of the global minimum value, which is defined in the root of the tree. This information is passed down by means of so-called *copy rules*, equations whose only purpose is to copy a value from one node to another.

To accommodate for the oft-occurring pattern of copying values through the tree, many AG systems provide a way to *broadcast* values, eliminating the need for tedious and potentially error-prone specification of copy rules by hand. For example, the repmin example can be simplified using the `including` construct of the GAG and LIGA systems [15], which provide a shorthand for specifying copy rules. Using this construct, the copy rules in Figure 1, lines 6 and 7 could be removed and line 13 replaced by `id.replace := Leaf(including Root.global-min)`, specifying that the value is to be copied downward from the `Root` node.

3 Decorators

While constructs such as `including` provide notational advantages for some specifications, they cannot be used if the desired pattern of attribution does not precisely fit their definition. These notations are built into AG systems, and as such a developer is faced with an all-or-nothing situation: use a nice abstract notation if it fits exactly or fall back to writing verbose copy rules if there is no suitable shorthand. This section proposes attribute decorators as a more flexible alternative to building these shorthand abstractions into the AG system. Decorators can be defined to specify how attribute values are to be propagated through the tree. Common patterns such as including can be provided in a decorator library, while user-defined decorators can be written for other cases.

To define high-level attribute propagation patterns, we draw inspiration from strategic programming [33,20,21]. This technique allows the specification of traversal patterns in a generic fashion, independent of the structure of a particular tree, using a number of basic, generic traversal operations.

3.1 Basic Attribute Propagation Operations

Consider the specification of Figure 3. It specifies only the principal repmin equations, avoiding the copy rules. The flow of information is instead specified using decorators (at the top of the specification). For instance, global-min uses the down decorator, which specifies that values should be copied downwards. Before we elaborate on the decorators used in this example, let us first examine the unabbreviated set of equations and reduce them to a more generic form that uses elementary propagation operations. After this, we will show how these operations can be used in the specification of decorators.

Downward propagation of the global-min attribute, first defined at the root of the tree (as seen in Figure 3), was originally achieved by

```
eq Fork(t1,t2):
    t1.global-min  := id.global-min
    t2.global-min  := id.global-min
```

Another reading of this specification says that 'the global-min of any non-root term is the global-min of its parent.' Thus, if we can reflect over the tree structure to obtain the *parent* of a node, we can express this propagation as

```
eq Fork(t1,t2):
    id.global-min  := id.parent.global-min
eq Leaf(v):
    id.global-min  := id.parent.global-min
```

```
def down        global-min
def up          min
def rewrite-bu  replace

eq Root(t):
    t.global-min := id.min

eq Fork(t1,t2):
    id.min := <min> (t1.min,
                     t2.min)
eq Leaf(v):
    id.min      := v
    id.replace  :=
        Leaf(id.global-min)
```

Fig. 3. Repmin using decorators

This notation makes the relation to the parent node's attribute value explicit, rather than being than implied by the context. It forms the basis of specifying the downward propagation in a more generic way: id.parent.global-min could be used as the default definition of global-min, used for nodes where no other definition is given (here, all non-root nodes). This is essentially what the down decorator in Figure 3 does.

A different form of propagation of values was used in the replace attribute:

```
eq replace:
    Root(t)      →  Root(t.replace)
    Fork(t1,t2)  →  Fork(t1.replace, t2.replace)
```

Here we can recognize a (common) rewriting pattern where the node names remain unchanged and all children are replaced. We abstract over this using the all operator:

```
eq replace:
   Root(t)       →  all(id.replace)
   Fork(t₁,t₂)   →  all(id.replace)
```

all is one of the canonical *generic traversal operators* of strategic programming [33,20]. It applies a function to all children of a term. Other generic traversal operators include one, which applies a function to exactly one child, and some, which applies it to one or more children. In this case, we pass all a reference to the replace attribute. This reveals an essential property of attribute references in ASTER: they are *first-class citizens* that can be passed as the argument of a function in the form of a closure. The expression id.replace is a shorthand for a closure of the form $\lambda t \rightarrow (t.\texttt{replace})$. It can be applied to the current term in the context of an attribute equation or in a sequence of operations, or to a term t using the notation $<f> t$.

3.2 Attribute Propagation Using Decorators

We implement attribute definitions using functions that map terms to values. Parts of such a function are defined by attribute equations. Some attribute definitions form only a partial function, such as those in Figure 3. In that figure, copy rules are implicitly provided using decorators. Decorators are essentially higher-order functions: they are a special class of attributes that take another attribute definition (i.e., function) as their argument, forming a new definition with added functionality. This means that the declaration def down global-min and the accompanying equations for the global-min attribute effectively correspond to a direct (function) call to decorator down:

```
eq Root(t):
   t.global-min  := id.down(the original global-min equations, here t.min)
```

A basic decorator d decorating an attribute a is specified as follows:

```
decorator d(a) = s
```

The body s of a decorator is its evaluation strategy, based on the Stratego language [8]. It provides standard conditional and sequencing operations. Using *generic traversal operators*, the evaluation strategy can inspect the current subtree. These operators are agnostic of the particular syntax used, making decorator definitions reusable for different languages. In this paper, we introduce the notion of *parent references* as an additional generic traversal operator, in the form of the parent attribute. Furthermore, we provide a number of *generic tree access attributes* that are defined using these primitives, such as the prev-sibling and next-sibling attributes to get a node's siblings, and child(c) that gets the first child where a condition c applies. Finally, we introduce *reflective attributes* that provide information about the attribute being decorated. These include the defined attribute, to test if an attribute equation is defined for a given term, and the name and signature attributes to retrieve the attribute's name and signature.

To illustrate these operations, consider the definition of the down decorator, which defines downward propagation of values in the tree (see Figure 4). This decorator automatically copies values downwards if there is no attribute equation defined for a given node. It checks for this condition by means of the defined reflective attribute (1). In case there is a matching equation, it is simply evaluated (2). Otherwise, the decorator acts as a copy rule: it "copies" the value of the parent. For this it recursively continues

```
     decorator down(a) =                    decorator rewrite-bu(a) =
(1)  if a.defined then                         all(id.rewrite-bu(a))
(2)    a                                     ; if a.defined then
     else                                        a
(3)    id.parent.down(a)                     end
     end
                                            decorator down at-root(a) =
     decorator up(a) =                         if not(id.parent) then
     if a.defined then                            a
       a                                       else
     else                                        fail
       id.child(id.up(a))                     end
     end
```

Fig. 4. Basic decorator definitions

evaluation at the parent node (3). Conversely, the up decorator provides upward propagation of values. If there is no definition for a particular node, it inspects the child
nodes, eventually returning the first successful value of a descendant node's attribute
equation.

The `rewrite-bu` decorator provides bottom-up rewriting of trees, as we did with the
`replace` attribute. Using the `all` operator, it recursively applies all defined equations
for an attribute, starting at the bottom of the tree. Rewrites of this type produce a new
tree from an attribute, which in turn has attributes of its own, potentially allowing for
staged or repeated rewrites.

In the next section we provide some examples of more advanced decorators. At their
most elaborate, these may specify a pattern p, can be parameterized with functions $a*$
and values $v*$, and may themselves be decorated ($d*$):

```
decorator d* [p .] name (d [, a* ] [| v* ]) = s
```

Note in particular the vertical bar '|', used to distinguish function and value argu-
ments; in a call $f(|x)$, x is a value argument, in a call $f(x)$ it is a function. The
same convention, based on the Stratego notation, is supported for attributes. Furthermore, note that decorators can import other decorators $d*$. Such decorators are said to
be *stacked*, and provide opportunity for reuse. To illustrate this, consider the at-root
decorator of Figure 4. It evaluates attribute equations at the root of a tree, where the
current node has no parent. Using the down decorator, the result is propagated downwards. Effectively, applying this stacked decorator results in a function application of
the form id.down(id.at-root(a)). Stacking can also be achieved by declaring multiple decorators for an attribute. For example, we can add a "tracing" decorator to the
global-min attribute, logging all nodes traversed by the down decorator:

```
def down trace global-min
```

4   Applications

In this section we discuss a number of common idioms in AG specifications, and show
how attribute decorators can be used to encapsulate them. We focus on language processing, a common application area of AG systems. As a running example we use a
simple "while" language (see Figure 5). We demonstrate different language analysis
problems and how they can be dealt with using high-level decorators that are agnostic

Program	::=	*Function**	*Type*	::= *IntType* | ...
Function	::=	function *ID(Arg*) { Stm* }*	*IntType*	::= int
Stm	::=	{ *Stm** }	*Arg*	::= *ID : Type*
	|	if (*Expr*) *Stm* else *Stm*	*Expr*	::= *Int* | *Var* | *ID(Expr**)
	|	while (*Expr*) *Stm*		| *Expr* + *Expr* | *Expr* ∗ *Expr*
	|	var *ID* : *Type* | *ID* := *Expr*	*Int*	::= *INT*
	|	return *Expr*	*Var*	::= *ID*

Fig. 5. The "while" language used in our examples

of the object language. As such, they are reusable for more sophisticated languages and other applications.

4.1 Constraints and Error Reporting

A fundamental aspect of any language processing system is reporting errors and warnings. We define these as declarative *constraints* using conditional attribute equations. These equations specify a pattern and a conditional `where` clause that further restricts the condition under which they successfully apply:

```
eq error:
  |[ while (e) s ]| → "Condition must be of type Boolean"
  where not(e.type ⇒ BoolType)

  |[ e₁ + e₂ ]|      → "Operands be of type Int"
  where not(e₁.type ⇒ IntType ; e₂.type ⇒ IntType)
```

Each equation produces a single error message string if the subexpression types do not match `IntType` or `BoolType`. Rather than having them directly construct a list, we can collect all messages using the `collect-all` decorator (see Figure 6). It traverses the tree through recursion, producing a list of all nodes where the attribute succeeds. Note that this decorator does not test for *definedness* of the equations (using a.`defined`), but rather whether they can be successfully applied. Using `collect-all` with the `error` attribute, we can define a new `errors` attribute:

```
def collect-all errors :=
  id.error
```

This notation both declares the decorators and a default equation body, which refers to `error`.

```
decorator node.collect-all(a) =
  let results =
    node.children.map(id.collect-all(a))
  ; concat
in if <a> node then // add to results
     ![<a> node | <results>]
   else
     results
   end
end
```

Fig. 6. The `collect-all` decorator

To provide usable error messages, however, the error strings need further context information. We can define a new, application-specific decorator to add this information before they are collected, and use it to augment the `error` attribute:

```
decorator add-error-context(a) =
  <conc-strings> (a," at ",id.pp," in ",id.file,":",id.linenumber)

def add-error-context error
```

With this addition, the `errors` attribute now lists all errors, including a pretty-printed version of the offending construct (provided a pp attribute is defined), and its location in the source code (given a `file` and `linenumber` attribute).

4.2   Name and Type Analysis

Type analysis forms the basis of static error checking, and often also plays a role in code generation, e.g. for overloading resolution. Types of expressions typically depend on local operands, or are constant, making them well-suited for attribute equations. Moreover, an AG specification of a type analysis is highly modular, and may be defined across multiple files. Thus, let us proceed by defining a `type` attribute for all expressions in our language to perform this analysis:

```
eq type:
  Int(i)              →  IntType
  |[ e₁ + e₂ ]|       →  IntType where e1.type ⇒ IntType; e2.type ⇒ IntType
  Var(v)              →  id.lookup-local(|v).type
  |[ f(args) ]|       →  id.lookup-function(|f, args).type
```

Variable references and function calls require non-local *name analysis* to be typed. This can be done using parameterized *lookup attributes* that given a name (and any arguments), look up a declaration in the current scope [12]. In the example we reference the local `type` attribute of the retrieved node, but lookup attributes can be used to access arbitrary non-local attributes for use in various aspects of the system. The actual lookup mechanism is provided by means of reusable decorators: to do this for a particular language, it suffices to select an appropriate decorator and define the declaration sites and scoping constructs of the language. Our lookup attributes are defined as follows:

```
def lookup-ordered(id.is-scope) lookup-local(x) :=
  id.decl(|x)

def lookup-unordered(id.is-scope) lookup-function(|x, args) :=
  id.decl(|x, args)
```

Figure 7 shows the prerequisite `decl` and `is-scope` attribute definitions for the name analysis, specified as arguments of the above attributes. Again, these are highly declarative and each address a single aspect. Declaration sites are identified by the `decl` attribute, which is parameterized with an identifier name x and optionally a list of arguments. It only succeeds for matching declarations. All declarations also define a `type` attribute. Similarly, the `is-scope` attribute is used to identify scoping structures. Note in particular the equations of the "if" construct, which, for the purpose of this example, defines scopes for both arms, similar to try/catch in other languages.

Languages employ varying styles of scoping rules. In our language we have two kinds of scoping rules: C-like, *ordered* scoping rules, and Algol-like, *unordered* scoping rules. In many languages, local variables typically use the former, while functions typically use the latter. We define the `lookup-ordered` and `lookup-unordered` decorators to accommodate for these styles (see Figure 8). They traverse up the tree, inheriting the behavior of the `down` decorator, thus giving precedence to innermost scopes. Along this path, the `lookup-ordered` decorator visits the current node (1). If no declaration is found there (i.e., `fetch-decl` fails), the `<+` combinator specifies that it should proceed at (2), visiting any preceding siblings using the helper function `lookup-outside-scopes`. This function performs a local lookup for declarations in

```
eq |[ var x : t ]|:
  id.type      := t
  id.decl(|x) := id

eq |[ x : t ]|: // function parameters
  id.type      := t
  id.decl(|x) := id

eq |[ function f(params) : t stm ]|:
  id.type           := t
  id.decl(|f, args) := id where params.map(id.type).eq(|args.map(id.type))

eq is-scope:
  |[ function f(params) : t { stm* } ]|  →  id
  |[ if (e) s₁ else s₂ ]|.s₁  →  s₁
  |[ if (e) s₁ else s₂ ]|.s₂  →  s₂
  |[ while (e) s ]|              →  id
  |[ { s* } ]|                   →  id
```

Fig. 7. Attributes for name analysis and types of declarations

these nodes, respecting the scoping rules by avoiding traversal of scoping constructs (3). In contrast, lookup- unordered follows a straight path to the root of the tree, doing a search in encountered scopes (4).

4.3 Flow Analysis

Control-flow analysis forms the foundation of data-flow analysis, which is prerequisite to various compiler optimizations, refactorings, and static checks for bug patterns or security violations. A recent paper by Nilsson-Nyman et al. [25] demonstrated how AGs can be employed for modularly specifying such analyses, ensuring separation of concerns and reusability with different data-flow analyses.

We take an approach similar to that of the JastAdd project, using reference attributes [12] to declaratively define the control flow graph. Consider Figure 9, which defines a succ attribute, providing a reference to all successors of a statement. For instance, for the "if" statement, the successors are the "then" and "else" branches (1).

A helper attribute, succ-enclosing, determines the default successors based on the enclosing block. For sequences of statements, the successor is the next statement in the

```
    decorator down lookup-ordered(fetch-decl, is-scope) =
(1)  fetch-decl
(2)  <+ id.prev-sibling(lookup-outside-scopes(fetch-decl, is-scope))

    decorator down lookup-unordered(fetch-decl, is-scope) =
     (id.is-root <+ is-scope) // only look in scoping structures
(4)  ; lookup-in-scope(fetch-decl, is-scope)

    lookup-in-scope(fetch-decl, is-scope) =
     fetch-decl
     <+ id.child(lookup-outside-scopes(fetch-decl, is-scope)) // enter scope

    lookup-outside-scopes(fetch-decl, is-scope) =
     fetch-decl
(3)  <+ not(is-scope) // do not enter scope subtrees
     ; id.child(lookup-outside-scopes(fetch-decl, is-scope))
```

Fig. 8. Lookup attributes and decorators

sequence (2). The "while" statement overrides this behavior, by setting the successor of the enclosed block to itself (3). For any non-control flow statements, we specify succ-enclosing as the default successor succ (4), using the default decorator (5).

```
      def down succ-enclosing:
          Program(_)              → []
(2)     [s₁, s₂ | _].s₁          → [s₂]
(3)     |[ while (e) s ]|.s → [id]

(4) def default(id.succ-enclosing) succ:
          |[ { s; s* } ]|              → [s]
(1)     |[ if (e) s₁ else s₂ ]| → [s₁, s₂]
          |[ return e ]|              → []
          |[ while (e) s ]|
              → [s|s.succ-enclosing]

(5) decorator default(a, default) =
        if a then
          a
        else
          default
        end
```

Fig. 9. Specification of the control flow

The specification of the succ attribute allows for a natural, declarative way of specifying the forward control flow of a language. However, a number of data-flow analyses depend on the *predecessors* of a statement. To avoid specifying these by hand, it is possible to use *collection attributes* [5,22,4] to *derive* the reverse flow graph. Collection attributes introduce a *"contributes to"* clause, allowing nodes to contribute values to collections in other nodes. Using this technique, we can define the predecessor graph in a single equation, by contributing each statement to its successors:

```
def contributes-to(id.succ) stm:
    id.pred := stm
```

Figure 10 defines the contributes-to decorator. Note that for clarity, we use fragments of pseudocode in lieu of more advanced Stratego constructs. The complete, 20-line source is available from [1]. This decorator operates in two phases: the first time any collection attribute is evaluated, it enters the *survey phase* (1), where the complete tree is traversed, adding all contributing nodes to a list maintained for each node contributed to. This is done only once, rather than for every collection attribute retrieved. After this phase completes (2), referenced collections only require the application of any attribute equations associated with it (for pred, stm is returned). Note that all required book-keeping operations (i.e., storing contributions and whether the survey phase completed) are performed in the context of the current attribute: they are stored in tables associated with the attribute's unique signature and its argument values (i.e., id.signature).

The control flow graph, specified by the succ and pred attributes, forms the foundation of any data-flow analysis. As such a graph may have cycles in it, these analyses have the peculiar property that their equations may involve circular dependencies. This makes them unsuitable for traditional AGs. However, by extending the formalism with

```
     decorator contributes-to(a, targets) =
        if not(completed survey phase) then
(1)       mark survey phase complete
        ; id.root
        ; in a topdown fashion:
              for a node x, apply targets and add them to the list of contributions for x
        ; end
(2) ; apply a to the list of contributions for the current node
```

Fig. 10. The contributes-to decorator, contributing values to a list of nodes

circular attributes [23,4], it becomes possible to use declarative AG equations to specify such analyses [25]. Circular attribute equations can be solved by fixed point iteration, as long as their underlying data forms a lattice. We implemented this in a decorator that evaluates circular attributes. However, due to a lack of space to fully explain the rather intricate algorithm that underlies it (see [23,4]), we do not include it here, and refer the interested reader to the technical report that accompanies this paper [17].

5 Implementation

The ASTER language is built as an extension of the Stratego strategic programming language [8], which natively supports the canonical generic traversal operators. The ASTER compiler is implemented in standard Stratego, using only a (bootstrapped) AG specification for error reporting (using constraint rules similar to those in Section 4.1). It compiles AG specifications to regular Stratego programs through a series of normalization steps. The normalization process starts by grouping attribute equations together, forming separate strategies for each attribute and decorator. As illustrated in Section 3.2, attribute equations and decorators are implemented as functions with generic traversal operations (called *strategies* in strategic programming). Inherited attributes are defined at the parent of a node; therefore, their implementation uses the `parent` primitive. Attribute references and imported decorators are converted to strategy calls. For decorator calls, static reflective data is added for reflective attributes such as `signature`. Finally, a memoization mechanism is added to cache all attribute and decorator calls. In the technical report that accompanies this paper, we elaborate on these normalization steps, using the repmin specification as an example [17].

Using memoization, attributes are evaluated at most once, thus achieving optimal evaluation. Similar memoization-based dynamic evaluation has been used before in many other systems, e.g. by Jalili [14] and recently in JastAdd [13]. In ASTER, memoization can be selectively disabled and overridden with custom behavior using decorators. For example, we disable it for fixpoint evaluation of data-flow equations.

Our current, experimental implementation has not been tuned for performance. One constraining factor is currently the ATerm library used to represent trees, which forms an integral part of Stratego. It is optimized for a maximally shared representation of terms, where identical subtrees occupy the same space in memory [7]. This makes it less suitable for storing additional, dynamic information in tree nodes, in our case parent references (for `id.parent`) and memoized attribute values. We worked around this by annotating tree nodes with unique keys, and use these to store the added information in separate tables. In the future, we would like to adapt or replace the underlying implementation to better accommodate for this. Regardless, preliminary performance measurements indicate promising results. We compared our compiler against JastAdd [13], a mature AG system that uses an evaluation mechanism conceptually very similar to our own. We used the repmin program of Figure 1 as a test case. Over an average of fifty runs, JastAdd took 51 ms to replace all leaves in a large tree with 2^{16} leaves. Our system took 150 ms, or 180 ms for the version of Figure 3 where decorators are used in place of manual copy rules. Further testing confirms an unfortunate, but constant overhead of about a factor three in the base performance level, due to the expensive memoization and term initialization operations. Still, the results indicate a low overhead of the decorator mechanism. Furthermore, both our specifications, especially when using decorators, are more concise than the version implemented in JastAdd.

6 Related Work

The general principle behind attribute decorators shares similarities with the Decorator design pattern, which describes how to add functionality to objects at run-time [11]. Variations of this idea exist in languages such as Python, which features decorators for functions [27]. In our case, we augment basic attribute definitions with either propagation of values from other nodes or with higher-level behavior such as a circular evaluation scheme. This kind of augmentation is similar to code weaving used in many forms of aspect-oriented programming [18].

Although considerable research has been devoted to various special-purpose extensions of AGs (as illustrated in the preceding sections), rather less attention has been paid to extensibility of AG systems. Two systems that do aim at different degrees of extensibility are Silver [29] and first-class attribute grammars [24].

In first-class AGs, attribute equations are *first-class citizens*, allowing them to be combined and manipulated using the language itself. Using function combinators, basic basic up, down, and chain copy rules can be defined [24]. These combinators show similarities with decorators, although they are purely defined in terms of functional dependencies, and lack the reflective and traversal primitives that form the building blocks of decorators. The paper does not indicate that they could be used to implement more sophisticated forms of propagation and manipulation of equations, such as the collection and circularity decorators. Based on the Haskell type checker, first-class AGs prevent errors where the use of an attribute does not match its type. Errors due to cyclic dependencies or a mismatch between attribute equations and grammar productions are not reported. Our system is based on Stratego, which is largely untyped (but could be typed [21]). Further complicated by the use of parent node references, it currently does not provide a fully typed system, other than basic static pattern coverage checking.

Silver supports extension with automatic copy rules as well as more advanced features such as collection attributes in a relatively accessible manner [29]. Implemented in itself, the Silver language can be used to modularly implement such extensions. While adding extensions of this kind is made easier through facilities such as forwarding for local transformations [30] and higher-order attributes, it is hard to imagine a regular Silver user building such an extension. Moreover, it is difficult to encapsulate these extensions in a single application or library, as they must be integrated in the base AG system. In contrast, many decorators are light-weight so they can be developed quickly and easily as needed.

A system that particularly inspired our design has been JastAdd [13], which extends traditional AGs in a number of interesting ways.[1] JastAdd uses reference attributes [12], which we also use in a number of decorators. Its extensions include collection attributes [22] and circular computations [23]. These are built into the JastAdd implementation; there is no user-level mechanism to define similar extensions. As described

---

[1] For the purposes of this paper, we focus on the attribute grammar features of JastAdd, ignoring its support for rewriting trees during evaluation [9].

in Section 4, decorators can be used to define these same features at a higher level. Admittedly, we would not expect users to define relatively complex features like this very often, but building on the high-level framework provided by decorators is likely to be much easier than modifying the underlying implementation of an AG evaluation system. JastAdd is designed to be used in conjunction with hand-written code, particularly using visitors. As such, it provides a way to write traversals that interoperate with declarative attribution. In theory, this facility could be used to implement something similar to decorators, but this would require the addition of generic traversal on top of the Java implementation of trees, essentially duplicating the Stratego platform we use.

7 Conclusions and Future Work

We propose decorated attribute grammars as a formalism for application-level extensibility of AG systems. To this end, we have identified primitives for the specification of decorators to define abstract evaluation strategies for attributes. By means of a prototype implementation and by employing decorators in different language engineering applications, we demonstrated the feasibility of using decorators to implement common abstractions over basic attribute grammars. These can be provided in the form of a library, and may be extended with user-defined decorators, where decorator stacking can be applied to reuse existing definitions.

In the future, we would like to explore further applications of decorated attribute grammars, in particular in the domain of implementing domain-specific languages and modular language extensions. For this we want to build upon the rewriting capabilities of the Stratego transformation language, the foundation of ASTER. As such, we aim to take the best of both worlds; rewriting with Stratego and declarative analysis with attribute grammars.

Building on our past experience [16], another application area to which we want to apply ASTER is that of integrated development environments (IDEs). ASTER's performance is already sufficient to be usable, and its demand-driven evaluation further helps interactive application. As such, we would like to employ it as part of an IDE in the future, encapsulating logic for typical editor service components, incremental compilation concerns, and related patterns in decorators.

Acknowledgments. We would like to thank Nicolas Pierron for the discussions on attribute grammar systems and their implementation. This research was supported by NWO projects 638.001.610, *MoDSE: Model-Driven Software Evolution*, 612.063.512, *TFA: Transformations for Abstractions*, and 040.11.001, *Combining Attribute Grammars and Term Rewriting for Programming Abstractions*.

References

1. Aster project home page, http://strategoxt.org/Stratego/Aster
2. Baars, A., Swierstra, D., Löh, A.: UU AG System User Manual. Department of Computer Science, Utrecht University (September 2003)
3. Bird, R.: Using circular programs to eliminate multiple traversals of data. Acta Informatica 21(3), 239–250 (1984)

4. Boyland, J.: Descriptional Composition of Compiler Components. PhD thesis (1996)
5. Boyland, J.: Remote attribute grammars. Journal of the ACM (JACM) 52(4), 627–687 (2005)
6. Boyland, J., Graham, S.L.: Composing tree attributions. In: POPL 1994, pp. 375–388. ACM, New York (1994)
7. van den Brand, M.G.J., de Jong, H., Klint, P., Olivier, P.: Efficient annotated terms. Software, Practice & Experience 30(3), 259–291 (2000)
8. Bravenboer, M., Kalleberg, K.T., Vermaas, R., Visser, E.: Stratego/XT 0.17. A language and toolset for program transformation. Science of Computer Programming 72(1-2), 52–70 (2008)
9. Ekman, T., Hedin, G.: Rewritable reference attributed grammars. In: Odersky, M. (ed.) ECOOP 2004. LNCS, vol. 3086, pp. 144–169. Springer, Heidelberg (2004)
10. Farnum, C.: Pattern-based tree attribution. In: POPL 1992, pp. 211–222 (1992)
11. Gamma, E., Helm, R., Johnson, R., Vlissides, J.: Design patterns: elements of reusable object-oriented software. Addison-Wesley Professional, Reading (1995)
12. Hedin, G.: Reference attributed grammars. Informatica (Slovenia) 24(3), 301–317 (2000)
13. Hedin, G., Magnusson, E.: JastAdd – an aspect-oriented compiler construction system. Science of Computer Programming 47(1), 37–58 (2003)
14. Jalili, F.: A general linear time evaluator for attribute grammars. ACM SIGPLAN Notices 18(9), 35–44 (1983)
15. Kastens, U., Waite, W.M.: Modularity and reusability in attribute grammars. Acta Informatica 31(7), 601–627 (1994)
16. Kats, L.C.L., Kalleberg, K.T., Visser, E.: Generating editors for embedded languages. Integrating SGLR into IMP. In: LDTA 2008 (April 2008)
17. Kats, L.C.L., Sloane, A.M., Visser, E.: Decorated attribute grammars – Attribute evaluation meets strategic programming. Extended technical report TUD-SERG-2008-038a. Software Engineering Research Group, Delft University of Technology (2008), http://swerl.tudelft.nl/bin/view/Main/TechnicalReports#2008-038
18. Kiczales, G., et al.: Aspect-oriented programming. In: Aksit, M., Matsuoka, S. (eds.) ECOOP 1997. LNCS, vol. 1241, pp. 220–242. Springer, Heidelberg (1997)
19. Knuth, D.E.: Semantics of context-free languages. Math. Syst. Theory 2(2), 127–145 (1968)
20. Laemmel, R., Visser, E., Visser, J.: Strategic programming meets adaptive programming. In: Proceedings of Aspect-Oriented Software Development (AOSD 2003), Boston, USA, pp. 168–177. ACM Press, New York (2003)
21. Lämmel, R.: Typed generic traversal with term rewriting strategies. Journal of Logic and Algebraic Programming 54(1), 1–64 (2003)
22. Magnusson, E., Ekman, T., Hedin, G.: Extending attribute grammars with collection attributes – evaluation and applications. In: Proc. of the Int. Working Conference on Source Code Analysis and Manipulation, pp. 69–80 (2007)
23. Magnusson, E., Hedin, G.: Circular reference attributed grammars - their evaluation and applications. Science of Computer Programming 68(1), 21–37 (2007)
24. de Moor, O., Backhouse, K., Swierstra, S.: First-class attribute grammars. Informatica 24(3), 329–341 (2000)
25. Nilsson-Nyman, E., Ekman, T., Hedin, G., Magnusson, E.: Declarative intraprocedural flow analysis of Java source code. In: LDTA 2008 (2008)
26. Paakki, J.: Attribute grammar paradigms - a high-level methodology in language implementation. ACM Computing Surveys (CSUR) 27(2), 196–255 (1995)
27. van Rossum, G.: Python Reference Manual. iUniverse (2000)
28. Steele, G.: Growing a language. Higher Order Symb. Comp. 12(3), 221–236 (1999)
29. Van Wyk, E., Bodin, D., Gao, J., Krishnan, L.: Silver: an extensible attribute grammar system. In: LDTA 2007. ENTCS, vol. 203, pp. 103–116. Elsevier Science, Amsterdam (2008)

30. Van Wyk, E., de Moor, O., Backhouse, K., Kwiatkowski, P.: Forwarding in attribute grammars for modular language design. In: Horspool, R.N. (ed.) CC 2002. LNCS, vol. 2304, pp. 128–142. Springer, Heidelberg (2002)
31. Van Wyk, E., Krishnan, L., Bodin, D., Johnson, E.: Adding domain-specific and general purpose language features to Java with the Java language extender. In: Companion to OOPSLA 2006, pp. 728–729. ACM, New York (2006)
32. Visser, E.: Meta-programming with concrete object syntax. In: Batory, D., Consel, C., Taha, W. (eds.) GPCE 2002. LNCS, vol. 2487, pp. 299–315. Springer, Heidelberg (2002)
33. Visser, E., Benaissa, Z.-e.-A., Tolmach, A.: Building program optimizers with rewriting strategies. In: International Conference on Functional Programming (ICFP 1998), pp. 13–26. ACM, New York (1998)

SSA Elimination after Register Allocation

Fernando Magno Quintão Pereira and Jens Palsberg

UCLA
University of California, Los Angeles

Abstract. Compilers such as gcc use static-single-assignment (SSA) form as an intermediate representation and usually perform SSA elimination before register allocation. But the order could as well be the opposite: the recent approach of SSA-based register allocation performs SSA elimination after register allocation. SSA elimination before register allocation is straightforward and standard, while previously described approaches to SSA elimination after register allocation have shortcomings; in particular, they have problems with implementing copies between memory locations. We present *spill-free SSA elimination*, a simple and efficient algorithm for SSA elimination after register allocation that avoids increasing the number of spilled variables. We also present three optimizations of the core algorithm. Our experiments show that spill-free SSA elimination takes less than five percent of the total compilation time of a JIT compiler. Our optimizations reduce the number of memory accesses by more than 9% and improve the program execution time by more than 1.8%.

1 Introduction

Register allocation is the process of mapping a program that uses an unbounded number of *variables* to a program that uses a fixed number of *registers*, such that variables with overlapping live ranges are assigned different registers. If registers cannot accommodate all the variables that are live at some point in the program, some of these variables must be *spilled*, that is, stored in memory. Register allocation is one of the most important compiler optimizations and can improve the speed of compiled code by more than 250% [17].

Static Single Assignment (SSA) form is an intermediate representation that defines each variable at most once [9,24] and in which φ-functions express renaming of variables. φ-functions are normally not present in the instruction sets of actual computer architectures. Thus, compilers that use SSA form must eventually do SSA elimination, replacing each φ-function with copy and swap instructions [2,5,8,10,19]. Many industrial compilers use the SSA form as an intermediate representation, including gcc 4.0 [11], Sun's HotSpot JVM [29], IBM's Java Jikes RVM [30], and LLVM [15], and they all perform SSA elimination before register allocation. But the order could as well be the opposite: the recent approach of SSA-based register allocation [3,7,12,13,21] performs SSA elimination after register allocation. SSA-based register allocation has three main

O. de Moor and M. Schwartzbach (Eds.): CC 2009, LNCS 5501, pp. 158–173, 2009.

advantages: (1) the problem of finding the minimum number of registers that are needed for a program in SSA form has a polynomial-time solution, (2) a program in SSA form requires at most as many registers as the source program, and (3) register allocation can proceed in two separate phases, namely first spilling and then register assignment. The two-phase approach works because the number of registers needed for a program in SSA-form is equal to the maximum of the number of registers needed at any given program point. Thus, spilling reduces to the problem of ensuring that for each program point, the needed number of registers is no more than the total number of registers. The register assignment phase can then proceed without additional spills. The next figure illustrates the phases of SSA-based register allocation:

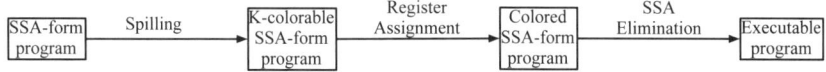

SSA elimination *before* register allocation is easier than *after* register allocation. The reason is that after register allocation, when some variables have been spilled to memory, SSA elimination may need to copy data from one memory location to another. The need for such copies is a problem for many computer architectures, including x86, that do not provide memory-to-memory copy or swap instructions. The problem is that at the point where it is necessary to transfer data from one memory location to another, all the registers may be in use! In this case, no register is available as a temporary location for performing a two-instruction sequence of a load followed by a store.

One solution to the memory-transfer problem would be to permanently reserve a register to implement memory-to-memory copies. We have evaluated that solution by reducing the number of available x86 integer registers from seven to six, and we observed an increase of 5.2% in the lines of spill code (load and store instructions) that LLVM [15] inserts in SPEC CPU 2000. Another solution would be to force the register allocator to assign the same register to all the variables that are part of a φ-function. In this case, each φ-function would be trivially implemented as a no-op; however, this form of aggressive coalescing might lead to sub-optimal registers assignments. For instance, Pereira and Palsberg [19, Fig.3] showed an example program where aggressive coalescing produces a minimal allocation with three registers, whereas the variables of the same program in SSA-form can be allocated in two registers.

Brisk [6, Ch.13] has presented a flexible solution that spills a variable on demand during SSA elimination, uses the newly vacant register to implement memory transfers, and later reloads the spilled variable when a register is available. We are unaware of any implementation of Brisk's approach, but have gauged its potential quality by counting the minimal number of basic blocks where spilling would have to happen during SSA elimination in LLVM, independent on the assignment of physical locations to variables. We found that for SPEC CPU 2000, memory-to-memory transfers are required for all benchmarks except 181.mcf - the smallest program in the set. We also found that the lines of spill code must increase by at least 0.2% for SPEC CPU 2000, and we speculate that an implementation of Brisk's algorithm would reveal a substantially higher number. However, in our view, the main problem with Brisk's approach is that its second spilling phase - during SSA-elimination - substantially complicates the design of a register allocator.

Our goal is to do better. We will present *spill-free SSA elimination*, a simple and efficient algorithm for SSA elimination after register allocation. Spill-free SSA elimination never needs an extra register, entirely eliminates the need for memory-to-memory transfers, and avoids increasing the number of spilled variables. The next figure summarizes the three approaches to SSA elimination.

	Accommodates optimal register assignment	Avoids spilling during SSA elimination
Spare register	No	Yes
On-demand spilling [6]	Yes	No
Spill-free SSA elimination	Yes	Yes

The starting point for our approach to SSA-based register allocation is *Conventional SSA (CSSA)-form* [28] rather than the SSA form from the original paper [9] (and text books [2]). CSSA form ensures that variables in the same φ-function do not interfere. We show how CSSA-form simplifies the task of replacing φ-functions with copy or swap instructions. As explained by Sreedhar *et al.* [28, p.196], and Briggs *et al.* [5, p.873], the original algorithm that converts a program into SSA form [9] already guarantees the CSSA property; however, compiler optimizations such as copy folding might produce interferences between variables related by φ-functions and thereby lose the CSSA property. Thus, our approach to SSA elimination requires us to convert the source program back into CSSA form before register allocation starts.

In this paper we make two assumptions. First, we assume that the CSSA-form program contains no *critical edges*. A critical edge is a control-flow edge from a basic block with multiple successors to a basic block with multiple predecessors. Algorithms for removing critical edges are standard [2]. Second, we assume that the target architecture provides us with a way to swap the contents of two registers. If swaps are not provided, then the problem of finding the minimal number of registers required by a program is NP-complete [4,20]. For integer registers, architectures such as x86 provide a swap instruction, while on other architectures one can implement a swap with a sequence of three xor instructions. In contrast, for floating point registers, most architectures provide neither direct swap instructions nor xor instructions, so instead compiler writers have to use one of the other approaches to SSA-elimination, e.g: separate a temporary register or perform spilling on demand.

We will present both a core algorithm for spill-free SSA elimination as well as three optimizations. We have implemented our SSA elimination framework in a puzzle-based register allocator [21]. Our experiments show that our approach to SSA elimination, including the conversion of source program into CSSA-form, takes less than five percent of the total compilation time of a JIT compiler.

Our optimizations reduce the number of memory accesses by more than 9% and improve the program execution time by more than 1.8%. Our SSA elimination framework works for any SSA-based register allocator such as [13], and it can also be used to insert the fixing code required by register allocators that follow the bin-packing model [14,21,26,31].

We will state three theorems with either just a proof sketch or no proof at all; the proofs can be found in Pereira's Ph.D. dissertation [18, Ch.5].

2   Example

We now present an example that assumes a target architecture with a single register r. Figure 1(a) shows a program in SSA form that contains six variables: a, a_1, a_2, b, b_1 and b_2. We use an abstract notation to represent instructions. For instance, the assignment $a_2 = b$ does not represent a move instruction, but just an instruction that defines variable a_2 and uses variable b. In the same way, $b_2 = \bullet$ is an instruction that defines b_2, and $\bullet = a$ is an instruction that uses a. Figure 1(b) shows the program after spilling and register assignment. A pair such as (b, r) indicates that variable b has been allocated to register r. Our example uses the disjoint memory addresses m, m_2 and m_b as locations for the spilled variables. Figure 1(c) shows the program after SSA elimination with on-demand spilling. Notice that in Figure 1(c), a φ-function has been replaced with four instructions that implement a copy from m_2 to m. The address m_b is used to temporarily hold the contents of r, while this register is used in the memory-to-memory transfer. The need for that copy happens at a program point where the only register r is occupied by b_2. So we must first spill r to m_b, then we can copy from m_2 to m via the register r, and finally we can load m_b back into r.

Now we go on to illustrate that spill-free SSA elimination can do better. Figure 1(d) shows the same program as in Figure 1(a), but this time in CSSA form, Figure 1(e) shows the program after spilling and register assignment, and Figure 1(f) shows the program after spill-free SSA elimination. Notice that in Figure 1(d), top right corner, CSSA makes a difference by requiring the extra instruction that copies from a_2 to a_3. This instruction splits the live range of a_2, what is necessary because variables a and a_2 interfere. We now do register allocation and assign each of a, a_1, and a_3 to the same memory location m because those variables do not interfere. In Figure 1(e), top right corner, the value of a_2 arrives in memory location m_2, and is then copied to memory location m via the register r. The point of the copy is to let both elements of the first row of the φ-matrix be represented in m, just like both elements of the second row of the φ-matrix are represented in r. We finally arrive at Figure 1(f) without any further spills.

3   CSSA Form and Spartan Parallel Copies

We now show that for programs in CSSA-form, the problem of replacing each φ-function with copy and swap instructions is significantly simpler than for

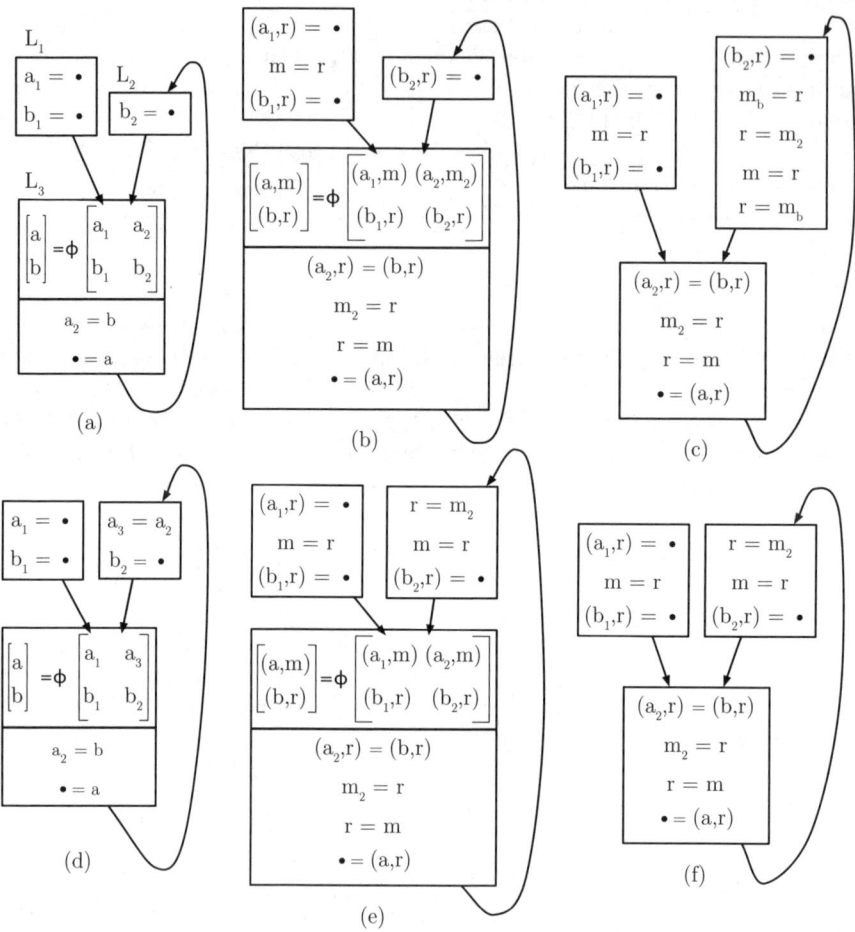

Fig. 1. Top: SSA-based register allocation and SSA elimination with on-demand spilling. Bottom: SSA-based register allocation and spill-free SSA elimination.

programs in SSA-form (Theorem 1). Along the way, we will define all the concepts and notations that we use.

SSA form uses φ-functions to express renaming of variables. We will describe the syntax and semantics of φ-functions using the matrix notation introduced by Hack et al. [13]. Figure 1 contains examples of φ-matrices. An assignment such as $V = \varphi M$, where V is a vector of length n, and M is an $n \times m$ matrix, represents n φ-functions and m *parallel copies* [16,27,32]. Each column in the φ-matrix corresponds to an incoming control-flow edge. A φ-function works as a multiplexer: it assigns to each element v_i of V an element v_{ij} of M, where j is determined by the actual control-flow edge taken during the program's execution. The parameters of a φ-function are evaluated simultaneously at the beginning of the basic block where the φ-function is defined [1]. For instance, the φ-matrix in

Figure 1 (a) represents the parallel copies $(a, b) := (a_1, b_1)$ and $(a, b) := (a_2, b_2)$. The first parallel copy is executed if control reaches L_3 from L_1, while the second is executed if control reaches L_3 from L_2.

Conventional Static Single Assignment (CSSA) form was first described by Sreedhar et al. [28] who used CSSA form to facilitate register coalescing. In order to define CSSA form, we first define an equivalence relation $\equiv$ over the set of variables used in a program. We define $\equiv$ to be the smallest equivalence relation such that for every set of φ-functions $V = \varphi M$, where V is a vector of length n with entries v_i, and M is an $n \times m$ matrix with entries v_{ij}, we have

$$\text{for each } i \in 1..n : v_i \equiv v_{i1} \equiv v_{i2} \equiv \ldots \equiv v_{im}.$$

Sreedhar et al. use φ-*congruence classes* to denote the equivalence classes of $\equiv$.

Definition 1. *A program is in CSSA form if and only if for every pair of variables v_1, v_2, we have that if $v_1 \equiv v_2$, then v_1 and v_2 do not interfere.*

Budimlic et al. [8] presented a fast algorithm for converting an SSA-form program to CSSA-form. A register allocator for a CSSA-form program can assign the same location to all the variables $v_i, v_{i1}, \ldots, v_{im}$, for each $i \in 1..n$, because none of those variables interfere. We say that register allocation is *frugal* if it uses at most *one* memory location together with any number of registers as locations for $v_i, v_{i1}, \ldots, v_{im}$, for each $i \in 1..n$.

The problem of doing SSA-elimination consists of implementing one parallel copy for each column in each φ-matrix. We can implement each parallel copy independently of the others. We will use the notation

$$(l_1, \ldots, l_n) := (l'_1, \ldots, l'_n)$$

for a single parallel copy, in which $l_i, l'_i, i \in 1..n$, range over $R \cup M$, where $R = \{r_1, r_2, \ldots, r_k\}$ is a set of registers, and $M = \{m_1, m_2, \ldots\}$ is a set of memory locations. We say that a parallel copy is *well defined* if all the locations on its left side are pairwise distinct. We will use ρ to denote a *store* that maps elements of $R \cup M$ to values. If ρ is a store in which $l'_1, \ldots, l'_n$ are defined, then the meaning of a parallel copy $(l_1, \ldots, l_n) = (l'_1, \ldots, l'_n)$ is $\rho[l_1 \leftarrow \rho(l'_1), \ldots l_n \leftarrow \rho(l'_n)]$.

We say that a well-defined parallel copy $(l_1, \ldots, l_n) = (l'_1, \ldots, l'_n)$ is *spartan* if

1. for all l'_a, l'_b, if $l'_a = l'_b$, then $a = b$; and,
2. for all l_a, l'_b such that l_a and l'_b are memory locations, we have $l_a = l'_b$ if and only if $a = b$.

Informally, condition (1) says that the locations on the right-hand side are pairwise distinct, and condition (2) says that a memory location appears on both sides of a parallel copy if and only if it appears at the same index.

Theorem 1. *After frugal register allocation, the φ-functions used in a program in CSSA-form can be implemented using spartan parallel copies.*

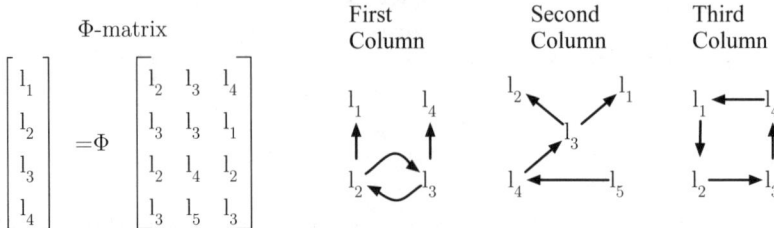

Fig. 2. A φ-matrix and its representation as three location transfer graphs

4   From Windmills to Cycles and Paths

We now show that a spartan parallel copy can be represented using a particularly simple form of graph that we call a spartan graph (Theorem 2).

We will represent each parallel copy by a *location transfer graph*.

Definition 2. Location Transfer Graph. *Given a well-defined parallel copy* $(l_1, \ldots, l_n) := (l'_1, \ldots, l'_n)$, *the corresponding location transfer graph* $G = (V, E)$ *is a directed graph where* $V = \{l_1, \ldots, l_n, l'_1, \ldots, l'_n\}$, *and* $E = \{(l'_a, l_a) \mid a \in 1..n\}$.

Figure 2 contains a φ-matrix and its representation as three location transfer graphs. The location transfer graphs that represent well-defined parallel copies form a family of graphs known as *windmills* [23]. This name is due to the shape of the graphs: each connected component has a central cycle from which sprout trees, like the blades of a windmill.

The location transfer graphs that represent spartan parallel copies form a family of graphs that is significantly smaller than windmills. We say that a location transfer graph G is *spartan* if

- the connected components of G are cycles and paths;
- if a connected component of G is a cycle, then either all its nodes are in R, or it is a self loop (m, m);
- if a connected component of G is a path, then only its first and/or last nodes can be in M; and
- if (m_1, m_2) is an edge in G, then $m_1 = m_2$.

Notice that the first and second graphs in Figure 2 are not spartan because they contain nodes with out-degree 2. In contrast, the third graph in Figure 2 is spartan as long as l_1, l_2, l_3, l_4 are registers because the graph is a cycle.

Theorem 2. *A spartan parallel copy has a spartan location transfer graph.*

Proof. It is straightforward to prove the following properties:

1. the in-degree of any node is at most 1;
2. the out-degree of any node is at most 1; and
3. if a node is a memory location m then:

(a) the sum of its out-degree and in-degree is at most 1, or
(b) G contains an edge (m, m).

The result is immediate from (1)–(3).   □

5   SSA Elimination

Our goal is to implement spartan parallel copies in the language Seq that contains just four types of instructions: register-to-register moves $r_1 := r_2$, loads $r := m$, stores $m := r$, and register swaps $r_1 \oplus r_2$. Notice that Seq does not contain instructions to swap or copy the contents of memory locations in one step. We use ι to range over instructions. A Seq program is a sequence I of instructions that modify a store ρ according to the following rules:

$$\frac{\langle \iota, \rho \rangle \to \rho'}{\langle \iota; I, \rho \rangle \to \langle I, \rho' \rangle}$$

$$\langle l_1 := l_2, \rho \rangle \to \rho[l_1 \leftarrow \rho(l_2)]$$

$$\langle r_1 \oplus r_2, \rho \rangle \to \rho[r_1 \leftarrow \rho(r_2), r_2 \leftarrow \rho(r_1)]$$

The problem of implementing a parallel copy can now be stated as follows.

IMPLEMENTATION OF A SPARTAN PARALLEL COPY
Instance: a spartan parallel copy $(l_1, \ldots, l_n) = (l'_1, \ldots, l'_n)$.
Problem: find a Seq program I such that for all stores ρ,

$$\langle I, \rho \rangle \to^* \rho[l_1 \leftarrow \rho(l'_1), \ldots l_n \leftarrow \rho(l'_n)].$$

Our algorithm **ImplementSpartan** uses a subroutine **ImplementComponent** that works on each connected component of a spartan location transfer graph and is entirely standard.

Algorithm 1. ImplementComponent: Input: G, Output: program I

Require: G is a cycle or a path
Ensure: I is a Seq program.
 1: **if** G is a path $(l_1, r_2), \ldots, (r_{n-2}, r_{n-1}), (r_{n-1}, l_n)$ **then**
 2:     $I = (l_n := r_{n-1}; r_{n-1} := r_{n-2}; \ldots; r_2 := l_1)$
 3: **else if** G is a cycle $(r_1, r_2), \ldots, (r_{n-1}, r_n), (r_n, r_1)$ **then**
 4:     $I = (r_n \oplus r_{n-1}; r_{n-1} \oplus r_{n-2}; \ldots; r_2 \oplus r_1)$
 5: **end if**

Theorem 3. *For a spartan location transfer graph G, **ImplementSpartan**(G) is a correct implementation of G.*

Once we have implemented each spartan parallel copy, all that remains to complete spill-free SSA elimination is to replace the φ-functions with the generated code. As illustrated in Figure 1, the generated code for a parallel copy must be inserted at the end of the basic block that leads to the parallel copy.

Algorithm 2. ImplementSpartan: Input: G, Output: program I

Require: G is a spartan location transfer graph.
Require: G has connected components $C_1, \ldots, C_m$.
Ensure: I is a Seq program.
  1: $I = \textbf{ImplementComponent}(C_1); \ldots; \textbf{ImplementComponent}(C_m);$

---

6   Optimizations

We will present three optimizations of the **ImplementSpartan** algorithm. Each optimization (1) has little impact on compilation time, (2) has a significant positive impact on the quality of the generated code, (3) can be implemented as constant-time checks, and (4) must be accompanied by a small change to the register allocator.

6.1   Store Hoisting

Each variable name is defined only once in an SSA-form program; therefore, the register allocator needs to insert only one store instruction per spilled variable. However, algorithm **ImplementSpartan** inserts a store instruction for each edge (r, m) in the location transfer graph. We can change **ImplementComponent** to avoid inserting store instructions:

  1: **if** G is a path $(l_1, r_2), \ldots, (r_{n-2}, r_{n-1}), (r_{n-1}, m)$ **then**
  2:     $I = (r_{n-1} := r_{n-2}; \ldots; r_2 := l_1)$
  3:     $\ldots$
  4: **end if**

For this to work, we must change the register allocator to insert a store instruction after the definition point of each spilled variable. On the average, store hoisting removes 12% of the store instructions in SPEC CPU 2000.

6.2   Load Lowering

Load lowering is the dual of store hoisting: it reduces the number of load and copy instructions inserted by the **ImplementSpartan** Algorithm. There are situations when it is advantageous to reload a variable right before it is used, instead of during the elimination of φ-functions. Load lowering is particularly useful in algorithms that follow the bin-packing model [14,21,26,31]. These allocators allow variables to reside in different registers at different program points, but they require some fixing code at the basic block boundaries. The insertion of fixing code obeys the same principles that rule the implementation of φ-functions in SSA-based register allocators. In Figure 3 we simulate the different locations of variable v by inserting mock φ-functions at the beginning of basic blocks L_2 and L_7, as pointed in Figure 3 (b). The fixing code will be naturally inserted when these φ-functions are eliminated. The load lowering optimization would replace the instructions used to implement the φ-functions, shown in Figure 3 (c), with a single load before the use of v at basic block L_7, as outlined in Figure 3 (d).

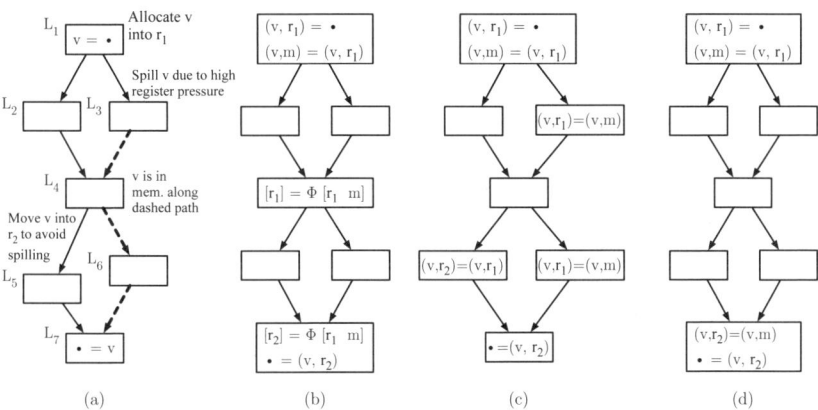

Fig. 3. (a) Example program (b) Program augmented with mock φ-functions. (c) SSA elimination without load-lowering. (d) Load-lowering in action.

Variables can be lowered according to the nesting depth of basic blocks in loops, or the static number of instructions that could be saved. The SSA elimination algorithm must remember, for each node l in the location transfer graph, which variable is allocated into l. During register allocation we mark all the variables v that would benefit from lowering, and we avoid inserting loads for locations that have been allocated to v. Instead, the register allocator must insert reloads before each use of v. These reloads may produce redundant memory transfers, which are eliminated by the memory coalescing pass described in Section 6.3. The updated elimination algorithm is outlined below:

1: **if** G is a path $(m, r_2), \dots, (r_{n-2}, r_{n-1}), (r_{n-1}, l_n)$ **then**
2:   **if** m is holding a variable marked to be lowered **then**
3:     $I = (l_n := r_{n-1}; r_{n-1} := r_{n-2}; \dots; r_3 := r_2)$
4:   **else**
5:     $I = (l_n := r_{n-1}; r_{n-1} := r_{n-2}; \dots; r_3 := r_2; r_2 := m)$
6:   **end if**
7:   $\dots$
8: **end if**

6.3   Memory Coalescing

A memory transfer is a sequence of instructions that copies a value from a memory location m_1 to another memory location m_2. The transfer is redundant if these locations are the same. The CSSA-form allows us to coalesce a common occurrence of redundant memory transfers. Consider, for instance, the code that the compiler would have to produce in case variables v_2 and v, in the figure below, are spilled. In order to send the value of v_2 to memory, the value of v would have to be loaded into a spare register r, and then the contents of r would have to be stored, as illustrated in figure (b). However, v and v_2 are mapped to the same memory location because they are φ-related. The store instruction can always be eliminated, as in figure (c). Furthermore, if the variable that is the target of the copy - v_2 in our example - is dead past the store instruction, then the whole memory transfer can be completely eliminated, as we show in figure (d) below. Notice that (d) is not a simple case of dead-code elimination, as the pair (v_2, m) might not be dead, e.g, variable v_2 might be reloaded from m at some future program point. However, the compiler can safely eliminate this store because the value of v, which equals the value of v_2, has already been stored in m by a frugal register allocator.

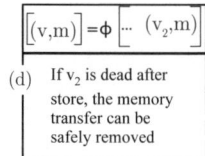

7   Experimental Results

The data presented in this section uses the SSA-based register allocator described by Pereira and Palsberg [21], which has the following characteristics:

- the register assignment phase occurs before the SSA-elimination phase;
- registers are assigned to variables in the order in which they are defined, as determined by a pre-order traversal of the dominator tree of the source program;
- variables related by move instructions are assigned the same register if they belong into the same φ-equivalence class whenever possible;
- two spilled variables are assigned the same memory address whenever they belong into the same φ-equivalence class;
- the allocator follows the bin-packing model, so it can change the register assigned to a variable to avoid spilling. Thus, the same variable may reach a join point in different locations. This situation is implemented via the mock φ-functions discussed in Section 6.2.
- SSA-elimination is performed by the Algorithm **ImplementSpartan** augmented with code to handle register aliasing, plus load-lowering, store hoisting, and elimination of redundant memory transfers.

Our register allocator is implemented in the LLVM compiler framework [15], version 1.9. LLVM is the JIT compiler used in the openGL stack of Mac OS 10.5. Our tests are executed on a 32-bit x86 Intel(R) Xeon(TM), with a 3.06GHz cpu clock, 4GB of memory and 512KB L1 cache running Red Hat Linux 3.3.3-7. Our benchmarks are the C programs from SPEC CPU 2000.

Impact of our SSA Elimination Method Figure 4 summarizes static data obtained from the compilation of SPEC CPU 2000; we have ordered the benchmarks by size. Our SSA Elimination algorithm had to implement 197,568 location transfer graphs when compiling this benchmark suite. These LTGs contain

	gcc	pbk	gap	msa	vtx	twf	cfg	vpr	amp	prs	gzp	bz2	art	eqk	mcf
#ltg	72.6	40.3	22.1	15.6	15.8	6.8	7.7	4.5	4.0	5.2	.9	.73	.36	.27	.44
%sp	3.3	5.0	9.8	2.3	9.3	6.5	14.9	13.5	7.9	6.5	10.9	22.7	9.2	20.8	25.6
#edg	586.2	256.3	150.8	96.9	121.5	58.0	124.2	101.7	29.6	35.5	11.1	14.3	2.7	5.8	6.1
%mt	56.4	41.7	43.5	50.6	47.1	57.3	66.8	75.4	37.4	42.8	63.6	71.8	46.0	72.0	57.7

Fig. 4. #ltg: number of location transfer graphs (in thousands), %sp: percentage of LTG's that are potential spills, #edg: number of edges in all the LTG's (in thousands), %mt: percentage of the edges that are memory transfers

1,601,110 edges, out of which 855,414, or 53% are memory transfers. Due to the properties of spartan location transfer graphs, edges representing memory transfers are always loops, that is, an edge from a node m pointing to itself. Because our memory transfer edges have source and target pointing to the same address, the SSA Elimination algorithm does not have to insert any instruction to implement them. Potential spills could have happened in 11,802 location transfer graphs, or 6% of the total number of graphs, implying that, if we had used a spilling on demand approach instead of our SSA elimination framework, a second spilling phase would be necessary in all the benchmark programs. We mark as potential spills the location transfer graphs that contain memory transfers, and in which the register pressure is maximum, that is, all the physical registers are used in the right side of the parallel copy.

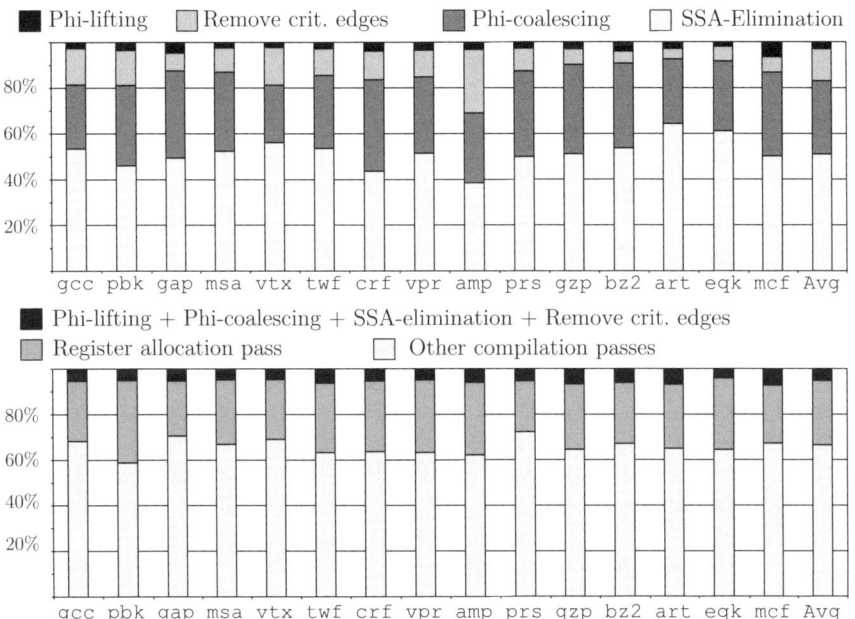

Fig. 5. Execution time of different compilation passes

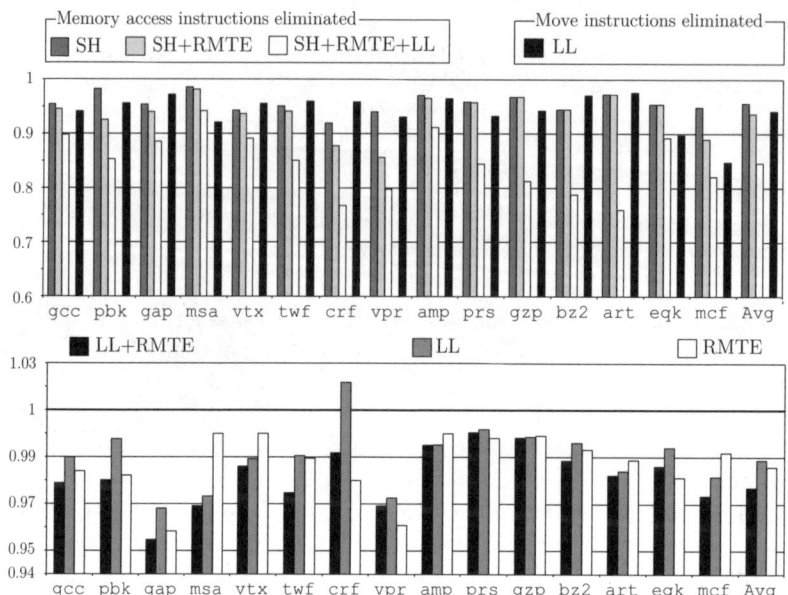

Fig. 6. Impact of Load Lowering (LL) and Redundant Memory Transfer Elimination (RMTE) on the code produced after SSA-elimination. (Up) Code size. (Down) Run-time.

Time Overhead of SSA-Elimination. The charts in Figure 5 show the time required by our compilation passes. Register allocation accounts for 28% of the total compilation time. This time is similar to the time required by the standard linear scan register allocator, as reported in previous work [22,25]. The passes related to SSA elimination account for about 4.8% of the total compilation time. These passes are: (i) phi-lifting, which splits the live ranges of all the variables that are part of φ-functions using "method I" due to Sreedhar *et al.* [28, pg.199]; (ii) a pass to remove critical edges; (iii) phi-coalescing, which reduces the number of copies inserted by phi-lifting using a variation of the algorithm proposed by Budimlic *et al* [8]; (iv) our spill-free SSA elimination pass. The amount of time taken by each of these passes is distributed as follows: (i) 0.2%, (ii) 0.5%, (iii) 1.6% and (iv) 2.5%. Our experiments show that converting a program from SSA to CSSA-form is a fast process. Passes (i) and (iii) take less than 2% of the total compilation time. The conversion algorithm described by Budimlic *et al* [8] is linear space and almost linear time in the number of variables in φ-functions.

Impact of the Optimizations. Figure 6 shows the static reduction of load, store and copy instructions due to the optimizations described in Section 6. The criterion used to determine if a variable should be lowered or not is the number of reloads that would be inserted for that variable versus the number of uses of the variable. Before running the SSA-elimination algorithm we count the number of reloads that would be inserted for each variable. The time taken to get this measure is negligible compared to the time to perform SSA-elimination: loads can only be the last edge of a spartan location transfer graph (Theorem 2). A variable is lowered if its spilling causes the allocator to insert more reloads than the number of uses of that variable in the source program. Store hoisting (SH) alone eliminates on average about 12% of the total number of stores in the target program, which represents slightly less than 5% of the lines of spill code inserted. By plugging in the elimination of redundant memory transfers (RMTE) we remove other 2.6% lines of spill code. Finally, load lowering (LL), on top of these other two optimizations, eliminates 7.8% more lines of spill code. Load lowering also removes 5% of the copy instructions from the target programs.

The chart in the bottom part of Figure 6 shows how the optimizations influence the run time of the benchmarks. On the average, they produce a speed up of 1.9%. Not all the programs benefit from load lowering. For instance, load lowering increases the run time of `186.crafty` in almost 2.5%. This happens because, for the sake of simplicity, we do not take into consideration the loop nesting depth of basic blocks when lowering loads. We speculate that more sophisticated criteria would produce more substantial performance gains. Yet, these optimizations are being applied on top of a very efficient register allocator, and they do not incur in any measurable penalty in terms of compilation time.

8   Conclusion

We have presented spill-free SSA elimination, a simple and efficient algorithm for SSA elimination after register allocation that avoids increasing the number of spilled variables. Our algorithm runs in polynomial time and accounts for a small portion of the total compilation time. Our approach to SSA elimination works for any SSA-based register allocator.

Acknowledgments. Fernando Pereira was sponsored by the Brazilian Ministry of Education under grant number 218603-9.

References

1. Appel, A.W.: SSA is functional programming. SIGPLAN Notices 33(4), 17–20 (1998)
2. Appel, A.W., Palsberg, J.: Modern Compiler Implementation in Java, 2nd edn. Cambridge University Press, Cambridge (2002)
3. Bouchez, F.: Allocation de registres et vidage en mémoire. Master's thesis, ENS Lyon (October 2005)
4. Bouchez, F., Darte, A., Guillon, C., Rastello, F.: Register allocation: What does the NP-completeness proof of chaitin et al. really prove? or revisiting register allocation: Why and how. In: 19th International Workshop on Languages and Compilers for Parallel Computing, pp. 283–298 (2006)
5. Briggs, P., Cooper, K.D., Harvey, T.J., Simpson, L.T.: Practical improvements to the construction and destruction of static single assignment form. Software Practice and Experience 28(8), 859–881 (1998)

6. Brisk, P.: Advances in Static Single Assignment Form and Register Allocation. PhD thesis, UCLA, University of California, Los Angeles (2006)
7. Brisk, P., Dabiri, F., Jafari, R., Sarrafzadeh, M.: Optimal register sharing for high-level synthesis of SSA form programs. IEEE Trans. on CAD of Integrated Circuits and Systems 25(5), 772–779 (2006)
8. Budimlic, Z., Cooper, K.D., Harvey, T.J., Kennedy, K., Oberg, T.S., Reeves, S.W.: Fast copy coalescing and live-range identification. In: PLDI, ACM SIGPLAN Conference on Programming Language Design and Implementation, pp. 25–32. ACM Press, New York (2002)
9. Cytron, R., Ferrante, J., Rosen, B.K., Wegman, M.N., Zadeck, F.K.: Efficiently computing static single assignment form and the control dependence graph. TOPLAS 13(4), 451–490 (1991)
10. de Ferriére, F., Guillon, C., Rastello, F.: Optimizing the translation out-of-SSA with renaming constraints. ST Journal of Research Processor Architecture and Compilation for Embedded Systems 1(2), 81–96 (2004)
11. Gough, B.J.: An Introduction to GCC, 1st edn. Network Theory Ltd. (2005)
12. Hack, S., Goos, G.: Copy coalescing by graph recoloring. In: PLDI, ACM SIGPLAN Conference on Programming Language Design and Implementation, pp. 227–237 (2008)
13. Hack, S., Grund, D., Goos, G.: Register allocation for programs in SSA-form. In: Mycroft, A., Zeller, A. (eds.) CC 2006. LNCS, vol. 3923, pp. 247–262. Springer, Heidelberg (2006)
14. Koes, D.R., Goldstein, S.C.: A global progressive register allocator. In: PLDI, ACM SIGPLAN Conference on Programming Language Design and Implementation, pp. 204–215 (2006)
15. Lattner, C., Adve, V.: LLVM: A compilation framework for lifelong program analysis & transformation. In: CGO, International Symposium on Code Generation and Optimization, pp. 75–88 (2004)
16. May, C.: The parallel assignment problem redefined. IEEE Trans. Software Eng. 15(6), 821–824 (1989)
17. Nandivada, V.K., Pereira, F., Palsberg, J.: A framework for end-to-end verification and evaluation of register allocators. In: Proceedings of SAS, International Static Analysis Symposium, Kongens Lyngby, Denmark, August 2007, pp. 153–169 (2007)
18. Pereira, F.M.Q.: Register Allocation by Puzzle Solving. PhD thesis, UCLA, University of California, Los Angeles (2008)
19. Pereira, F.M.Q., Palsberg, J.: Register allocation via coloring of chordal graphs. In: Yi, K. (ed.) APLAS 2005. LNCS, vol. 3780, pp. 315–329. Springer, Heidelberg (2005)
20. Pereira, F.M.Q., Palsberg, J.: Register allocation after classical SSA elimination is NP-complete. In: Aceto, L., Ingólfsdóttir, A. (eds.) FOSSACS 2006. LNCS, vol. 3921, pp. 79–93. Springer, Heidelberg (2006)
21. Pereira, F.M.Q., Palsberg, J.: Register allocation by puzzle solving. In: PLDI, ACM SIGPLAN Conference on Programming Language Design and Implementation, pp. 216–226 (2008)
22. Poletto, M., Sarkar, V.: Linear scan register allocation. Transactions on Programming Languages and Systems (TOPLAS) 21(5), 895–913 (1999)
23. Rideau, L., Serpette, B.P., Leroy, X.: Tilting at windmills with Coq: formal verification of a compilation algorithm for parallel moves (2008)
24. Rosen, B.K., Zadeck, F.K., Wegman, M.N.: Global value numbers and redundant computations. In: POPL, ACM SIGPLAN-SIGACT Symposium on Principles of Programming Languages, pp. 12–27. ACM Press, New York (1988)

25. Sagonas, K., Stenman, E.: Experimental evaluation and improvements to linear scan register allocation. Software, Practice and Experience 33, 1003–1034 (2003)
26. Sarkar, V., Barik, R.: Extended linear scan: An alternate foundation for global register allocation. In: Krishnamurthi, S., Odersky, M. (eds.) CC 2007. LNCS, vol. 4420, pp. 141–155. Springer, Heidelberg (2007)
27. Sethi, R.: Complete register allocation problems. In: STOC, 5th Annual ACM Symposium on Theory of Computing, pp. 182–195. ACM Press, New York (1973)
28. Sreedhar, V.C., Ju, R.D.-C., Gillies, D.M., Santhanam, V.: Translating out of static single assignment form. In: Cortesi, A., Filé, G. (eds.) SAS 1999. LNCS, vol. 1694, pp. 194–210. Springer, Heidelberg (1999)
29. JVM Team. The java HotSpot virtual machine. Technical Report Technical White Paper, Sun Microsystems (2006)
30. The Jikes Team. Jikes RVM home page (2007),
    http://jikesrvm.sourceforge.net/
31. Traub, O., Holloway, G.H., Smith, M.D.: Quality and speed in linear-scan register allocation. In: PLDI, ACM SIGPLAN Conference on Programming Language Design and Implementation, pp. 142–151 (1998)
32. Welch, P.H.: Parallel assignment revisited. Software Practice and Experience 13(12), 1175–1180 (1983)

Register Spilling and Live-Range Splitting for SSA-Form Programs

Matthias Braun[1] and Sebastian Hack[2]

[1] Institut für Programmstrukturen und Datenorganisation
Universität Karlsruhe (TH)
braun@ipd.info.uni-karlsruhe.de
[2] Computer Science Department
Saarland University
hack@cs.uni-sb.de

Abstract. Register allocation decides which parts of a variable's live range are held in registers and which in memory. The compiler inserts *spill code* to move the values of variables between registers and memory. Since fetching data from memory is much slower than reading directly from a register, careful spill code insertion is critical for the performance of the compiled program.

In this paper, we present a spilling algorithm for programs in SSA form. Our algorithm generalizes the well-known furthest-first algorithm, which is known to work well on straight-line code, to control-flow graphs.

We evaluate our technique by counting the *executed* spilling instructions in the CINT2000 benchmark on an x86 machine. The number of executed load (store) instructions was reduced by 54.5% (61.5%) compared to a state-of-the-art linear scan allocator and reduced by 58.2% (41.9%) compared to a standard graph-coloring allocator. The runtime of our algorithm is competitive with standard linear-scan allocators.

1 Introduction

The register allocation phase of a compiler maps the variables of a program to the registers of the processor. Usually, the register pressure (i.e. the number of simultaneously live variables at an instruction) in a program is much higher than the number of available registers. Thus, the compiler has to generate so-called spill code that moves the contents of the variables between memory and registers. Since accessing memory is much slower than accessing a register, the amount of executed spill code has to be minimized.

The key to good spill-code generation lies in splitting the live-range of a variable at the right places: Consider a loop with excessive register pressure and a variable that is defined before the loop and used afterwards. Ideally, a compiler would store (spill) the variable in front of the loop and load (reload) the variable after the loop. If the variable was reloaded inside the loop, the reload would be executed in each loop iteration. Another example is a variable that is used in a loop but has already been spilled before the loop. Reloading this variable directly

O. de Moor and M. Schwartzbach (Eds.): CC 2009, LNCS 5501, pp. 174–189, 2009.

before its use in the loop will cause memory traffic in each loop iteration. Thus, it is preferable to put the reload in front of the loop.

Register allocation is often formulated as a NP-hard problem. In such a setting, the actual register demand can exceed the maximum register of a program and become NP-hard to determine. Therefore, compilers allocate registers heuristically (e.g. using graph coloring [1,2] or linear scan [3,4,5]). If this heuristic runs out of registers, variables are spilled until enough registers have been freed and the heuristic can resume its work. In such a situation, the generation of spill code is driven by the failure of the allocation heuristic instead of the program's structure. In extreme cases [1,4], such a failure results in spilling the whole live range of a variable: Stores will be put after each definition and loads in front of each use, regardless of their location in the program.

Recent results show that if the program is in SSA form, its register demand equals its maximum register pressure (see [6,7,8]). This allows for decoupling spill code generation and register assignment: Once the maximum register pressure in the program is lowered to the number of available registers, registers can be assigned *optimally* using a linear-time algorithm that provably does not cause further spill code.

In this paper, we propose a program transformation that limits the maximum register pressure of an SSA-form program by inserting efficient spill code. Its main features are:

- It extends the well-known MIN algorithm [9], which has proven to be very successful [10] in straight-line code register allocation, to control-flow graphs.
- Our algorithm retains the SSA form. Hence, it is ideal for the use in SSA-based register allocation.
- It is effective. Our algorithm meets the requirements described above. It is sensitive to the structure of the program by splitting live-ranges around loops. Our experiments show a reduction of executed reload instructions by 54.5% (executed spills by 61.5%) compared to one of the most sophisticated live-range splitting algorithms available [5].
- It is efficient. Our algorithm consists of two passes: An enhanced liveness analysis and a single sweep over the program. Required analysis information is a loop tree and def-use chains; both are usually available during the backend phase of a modern compiler. Furthermore, we do not build large or complex data structures (such as an interference graph).

Structure of this paper. The next section recaps the MIN algorithm and its use in register allocation of straight-line code. In Section 3 we discuss, by way of examples, how the MIN algorithm can be generalized to code with branches. Section 4 presents our algorithm in detail. We evaluate our algorithm experimentally in Section 5. The last two sections discuss related work and conclude.

2   The Min Algorithm and Local Register Allocation

The original MIN algorithm was developed as a page replacement strategy in operating systems. Its basic idea is: If a memory page has to be removed to

Algorithm 1. The MIN algorithm

```
def limit(W, S, insn, m):                def minAlgorithm(block, W, S):
    sort(W, insn)                            for insn ∈ block.insnuctions:
    for v ∈ W[m:−1]:                             R ← insn.uses \ W
        if v ∉ S ∧ nextUse(insn,v) ≠ ∞:          for use ∈ R:
            add a spill for v before insn            W ← W ∪ {use}
        S ← S \ {v}                                  S ← S ∪ {use}
    W ← W[0:m]                                    limit(W, S, insn, k)
                                                 limit(W, S, insn.next,k−|insn.defs|)
                                                 W ← W ∪ {insn.defs}
                                                 add reloads for vars in R
                                                 in front of insn
```

---

swap in a new one, remove the page whose next use is farthest in the future. If the MIN algorithm knew the future and thus always knew whose page's use is farthest away, it would perform the minimum number of replacements (see van Roy [11] for a proof). The MIN algorithm has often been applied to straight-line register allocation and has shown to be very effective [10] in this setting.

Let us now review the MIN algorithm in the setting of register allocation for a single basic block. For the rest of this paper, we assume that the program is in SSA form. The *next-use distance* of a variable v at an instruction I is the number of instructions between I and the next use of v in the block. Especially I itself can be the next user, leading to distance 0. If there is no further use in the block, the distance is ∞.

The content of the register file is reflected in a set W containing the variables currently available in a register. Initially W is empty. We traverse the basic block from entry to exit, updating W according to the effects of each instruction. Assuming a conventional load/store architecture, each instruction

$$I : \underbrace{(y_1, \ldots, y_m)}_{\text{defs}_I} \leftarrow \tau(\underbrace{x_1, \ldots, x_n}_{\text{uses}_I})$$

requires that its operands x_i are available in registers and writes its results y_i to registers. At each program point, W must not contain more than k (the number of available registers) variables. Hence, the effects of an instruction I on W are as follows:

1. All variables in $\text{uses}_I \setminus W$ have to be reloaded in front of I. Thus, they have to be added to W. If W has not enough room, $|W| + |\text{uses}_I \setminus W| - k$ variables in W have to be spilled.
2. None of the variables in defs_I can be in W directly in front of I since all of these variables are dead there. Hence, we need $|\text{defs}_I|$ free registers. If there is not enough room in W to hold $|\text{defs}_I|$ variables, $|W| + |\text{defs}_I| - k$ variables have to evicted from W.

Algorithm 1 shows the MIN algorithm for straight-line code. minAlgorithm performs the steps 1 and 2 on each instruction of the block. limit takes the set W, sorts it according to the next-use distance from instr, and evicts all variables but the first m. Note carefully that for an instruction I we call limit twice. The first time, to make room for the operands and the second time to provide registers for the result variables of I. In the latter case, the next-use distance is measured from the instruction *behind* I because the uses of I do no longer matter when I writes its results.

Furthermore, minAlgorithm takes a *subset* S of W. Because the program is in SSA form, each variable has only one definition and thus needs to be spilled at most once. If a variable is evicted multiple times, a spill has to be placed only at the place of the first eviction. The set S records all variables in W for which a spill has already been inserted. Updating S is easy: Whenever a variable is reloaded, it must have been spilled before. Hence, we add it to S. When evicting variables from W, we only create spills for variables not in S whose next use is not ∞.

3   Overview

Guo et al. [10] empirically showed that the MIN algorithm gives very good results on straight-line code. The intuitive explanation for this is that evicting the variable with the furthest next use frees a register for the longest possible time. In this paper however, we are not only interested in spill-code generation for single basic blocks but for a whole control-flow graph (CFG).

To this end, let us first investigate how the straight-line version would perform on single *execution traces* of a CFG. Consider the CFG in Figure 3. The $\natural n$ sign denotes regions with high register pressure where at most n variables can live through in registers. Consider the following the execution traces of the CFG:

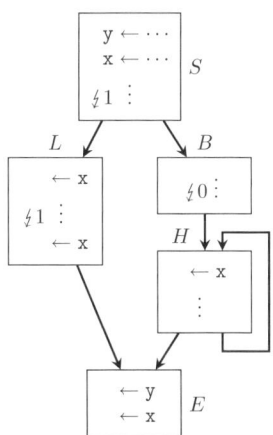

Fig. 1. Example CFG

1. S, L, E: The register pressure is critical at the end of S and either x or y have to be evicted from W. The farthest next use is the one of y in block E. Thus, y is evicted.

2. S, B, H, H, H, E: As in the previous example, y is evicted in S. The register pressure in B is so high that x has to be evicted from W. Thus, x is reloaded upon its first use in the first execution of H. The register pressure in H is uncritical. Hence, x can remain in a register for the second and third execution of the loop body H.

Let us go back to the static setting where we consider a CFG, not single traces. To develop an *effective* spilling algorithm, we have to place the spill and reload instructions in the CFG such that the straight-line MIN algorithm is emulated as good as possible *for every possible* trace. In principle, this can be achieved by applying the MIN algorithm to each block separately. However, reviewing the trace examples above, we have to consider each block in its context:

- When reaching the end of S, we have to decide whether x or y is evicted. In a naive per-block application of Algorithm 1 both, x and y have a next-use distance ∞ at the end of S because they have no further use in S. However, to choose y, as in example 1 above, we need a CFG-global next-use view: The earliest possible next use of x is closer than the one of y (blocks L and B in contrast to E).
- Algorithm 1 assumes that the register set W is empty at the entry of the block. This implies that every live-in variable is reloaded on its first use in the block.

  Considering both trace examples above, we observe that x is in registers at the end of L and H. Thus, it is also in registers at the entry of E. Consequently, applying the MIN algorithm to all predecessors of a block before applying it to the block itself, makes the state of the register set at their exits available. The initialization of W can then be chosen accordingly.
- Consider the second trace above: x was spilled in B. In the first execution of H it was reloaded and used from a register in the following two executions. However, we cannot have one version of H with the reload and one without! Placing a reload in H is not a good solution since this reload would be executed needlessly in every iteration except for the first. It is much better to place the reload in front of the loop at the exit of B. Therefore, we need to know that H is a loop head and initialize W with the variables used next in the loop. This has the effect of hoisting the reloads out of the loop.

4   A Min Algorithm for CFGs

The following outline summarizes the presented algorithm:

1. Compute liveness and global next uses (Section 4.1):
   We present a modification to the standard data-flow formulation of liveness analysis to compute CFG-global next-use values for each variable.
2. For each block B in *reverse post order* of the CFG:
   (a) Determine initialization W_B^{entry} of register set (Section 4.2):
       We compute a set of variables, which we assume to be in registers at the entry of the block.

   (b) Insert coupling code at the block entry (Section 4.3):
       Depending on the state of the register file at the exit of the predecessor of B, we add spill and/or reload code on B's incoming control-flow edges to ensure that all variables in W_B^{entry} are indeed in registers at the entry of B.

   (c) Perform MIN algorithm on B (Section 2)
3. Reconstruct SSA (Section 4.4):
   Inserting reloads for a variable creates multiple definitions for this variable. This clearly violates the static single assignment property. We describe, how SSA is reconstructed after spill/reload code insertion.

4.1   Global Next-Use Distances

The next-use distances beyond a single block are computed by augmenting a standard liveness analysis. Instead of computing live-in and live-out sets, we compute maps that associate variables with next-use distance; instead of unifying live sets at control-flow splits, we merge the maps by taking the minimum next-use distance per variable. This modelling actually entails liveness information: If the next-use distance of a variable is smaller than ∞, the variable is live, otherwise it is dead.

To reflect the dynamic behavior of the program, each control-flow edge (P, Q) is assigned a *length* $\ell_{P,Q}$. Edges leading out of loops are assigned a very high length M^1; all other edges have length 0. When computing the next-use distances, the length of the edges are added to the next-use distances of the variables that live over the edge. The effect is that the distances of uses behind loops are larger than the distances of all uses inside the loop.

Formalism. Let us now briefly discuss the next-use analysis formally. For an introduction to data-flow analysis, we refer to Nielson et al. [12]. Our domain is the set

$$\mathbb{D} = \mathbf{Var} \rightarrow \mathbb{N} \cup \{\infty\}$$

of maps from variables to natural numbers (augmented by a value ∞). The join of two maps $a, b \in \mathbb{D}$ is defined by taking the minimum of the variables' next-use distances:

$$a \sqcup b := \lambda v. \min\{a(v), b(v)\}$$

$\langle \mathbb{D}, \sqcup \rangle$ is a *join semi-lattice* that satisfies the *ascending chain condition*[2].

The transfer function f_B for a block B takes the next-use distances at the exit of the block and computes the next-use distance at the entry of the block. (Just like liveness analysis takes the set of live variables at the exit and computes the set of live variables at the entry.) There are two cases:

1. If a variable v has at least one use in B that is not preceded by the definition of v, the distance to v's next use is the length of the block ℓ_B[3] plus the distance $\nu_B(v)$ from the entry of the block to the first use of v in B that is not preceded by the definition of v.
2. If v has no such use in B, the distance from B's entry to v's next use is the sum of ℓ_B, the length $|B|$ of B, and the distance from B's exit to the next use of v.

---

[1] M has to be larger than the number of instructions on the longest path through the loop. Hence, in practice, a value like 100000 works nicely.

[2] The proof is straightforward and is omitted here for the sake of brevity.

[3] Using the standard formalization of data-flow analyses (see also [12]), we cannot incorporate information on control-flow edges in the transfer function. As we assume critical edges to be split, the length of an edge can be uniquely attributed to some block.

This yields

$$f_B(a) = \lambda v.\ \ell_B + \begin{cases} \nu_B(v) & \text{if } \nu_B(v) \neq \infty \\ |B| + a(v) & \text{otherwise} \end{cases}$$

Finally, the initial value $\imath$ of each block maps each variable to the distance of its first local use:

$$\imath_B := \lambda v.\ \infty$$

We chose $\sqcup$ as the minimum in order to ensure the convergence of the data-flow analysis. A more appropriate choice for the spilling problem would be to compute the next-use distance as a weighted sum of the successor's distances, using execution frequencies as weights. However this would violate the laws for a proper lattice join operation and the theoretical framework of data-flow analysis could no longer be used soundly. The practitioner however may just iterate the analysis long enough to obtain sufficiently precise information.

4.2   Initialization of the Register Set

For each block B we compute the set W_B^{entry} of variables, which we require to be in registers at the entry of B. As discussed in Section 3, the choice of W_B^{entry} is essential for the effectiveness of the algorithm. According to the examples of Section 3, W^{entry} is computed differently for loop headers and normal blocks.

Normal blocks. Let B be a non-loop-header block. As we process the nodes in reverse postorder, every predecessor of B has already been processed. Let W_P^{exit} denote the set W after the MIN algorithm has been applied to block P. Furthermore, let

$$all_B = \bigcap_{P \in pred(B)} W_P^{\text{exit}} \qquad some_B = \bigcup_{P \in pred(B)} W_P^{\text{exit}}$$

The variables in all_B are in registers on every incoming edge at B. Thus, we can assume them to be in registers at the entry of B. The variables in $some_B \setminus all_B$ are available in registers at some of the predecessors. They are sorted according to their next-use distance and put into the remaining slots of W_B^{entry}. initUsual in Algorithm 2 shows the pseudocode for computing W^{entry} of normal blocks.

Loop headers. Now, let B be a loop header. Consider some variable v that is live-in at and used in B. Furthermore, assume that v has been spilled in some block P outside B's loop, like variable x in Figure 2a. In this example, x $\notin W_P^{\text{exit}}$. If we determined W_B^{entry} by looking at the contents of W_P^{exit} (as we would do for normal blocks), x would not be contained in W_B^{entry}. This would cause the insertion of a reload of x inside the loop; something that has to be avoided at all costs. It is much better, to allocate x to W_B^{entry} so that the reload is put on the edge from P to B, as shown in Figure 2b.

But there are also variables that should not be put in W_B^{entry}: Consider Figure 2c. Variable x lives throughout the loop but is not used inside. Inside the loop, the register pressure is critical such that x cannot "survive" the loop in a register.

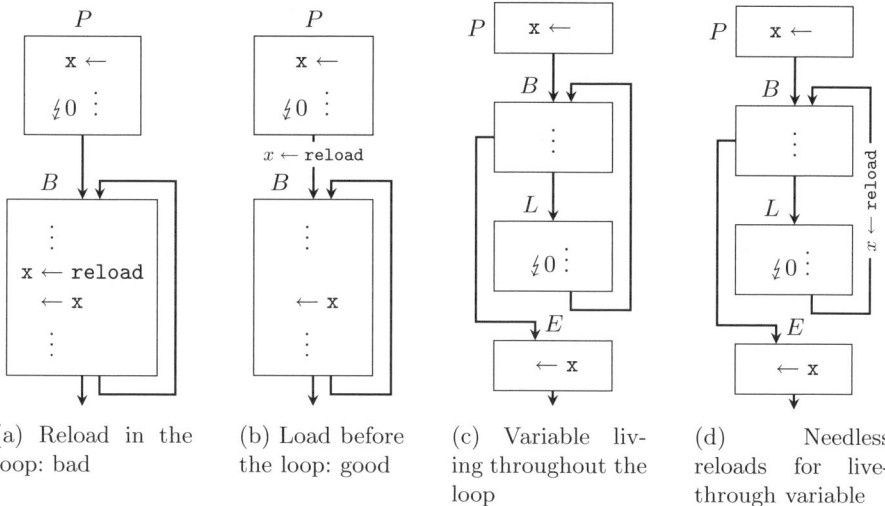

(a) Reload in the loop: bad

(b) Load before the loop: good

(c) Variable living throughout the loop

(d) Needless reloads for live-through variable

Fig. 2. Reloads in loops

By allocating x to W_B^{entry} we definitely require x to be in a register at the entry of B. Hence, a reload has to be put on the loop backedge (see Figure 2d). When determining W_S^{entry}, we already processed H. As the register pressure in H is uncritical, x is in W_S^{exit}. Thus, x is also included in W_S^{entry} and x can be used from a register. This reload is executed in every loop iteration. However, only in the last iteration that exits the loop, the reloaded value will be actually used (in block E). In this case, the reload should clearly be put at the entry of E.

So which variables should be put into W_B^{entry}? Following the discussion above and in Section 3, we ignore the predecessors of B. Let I_B be the set of variables that are live-in at B as well as defined by ϕ-functions in B. The candidates for W_B^{entry} are all variables in I_B used within B's loop $\mathcal{L}$. The variables are sorted according to their next-use distance and the first k are allocated to W_B^{entry}.

If there is room left in W_B^{entry}, we consider the set $T_B \subseteq I_B$ of variables that are not used in $\mathcal{L}$. The example Figure 2c shows that such a variable should only be assigned to W_B^{entry} if we are sure that the variable will survive the loop without being evicted. We determine how many variables of T_B can be kept in registers throughout $\mathcal{L}$ heuristically: Consider the *maximum register pressure* $p_\mathcal{L}$ of the loop. The difference $p_\mathcal{L} - |T_B| =: t$ gives an estimate on the register pressure caused by variables used *inside* the loop[4]. If t is smaller than k, we conclude that $k - t$ variables can survive the loop in registers. In this case, the remaining slots in W_B^{entry} are filled with at most $k - t$ variables from T_B.

The maximum loop register pressure $p_\mathcal{L}$ can easily be computed during the liveness analysis presented in the last subsection. As we have to traverse the

---

[4] If $\mathcal{L}$ is a single-exit loop or T_B only consists of variables defined outside $\mathcal{L}$ this estimation is exact, else it might be an under-approximation.

Algorithm 2. Initialization of W

```
def initLoopHeader(block):                    def initUsual(block):
    entry ← block.firstInstruction                freq ← map()
    loop ← loopOf(block)                          take ← ∅
    alive ← block.phis ∪ block.liveIn             cand ← ∅
    cand ← usedInLoop(loop, alive)                for pred in block.preds:
    liveThrough ← alive \ cand                        for var in pred.Wend:
    if |cand| < k:                                        freq[var] ← freq[var] + 1
        freeLoop ← k − loop.maxPressure                   cand ← cand ∪ {var}
                  + |liveThrough|                      if freq[var] = |block.preds|:
        sort(liveThrough, entry)                          cand ← cand \ {var}
        add ← liveThrough[0:freeLoop]                     take ← take ∪ {var}
    else:                                         entry ← block.firstInstruction
        sort(cand, entry)                         sort(cand, entry)
        cand ← cand[0:k]                          return take ∪ cand[0:k−|take|]
        add ← ∅
    return cand ∪ add
```

---

instructions of each block anyways, we can also keep track of the maximal register pressure inside each block. $p_{\mathcal{L}}$ is then simply computed by taking the maximum over the maximum register pressures of the blocks of $\mathcal{L}$.

4.3   Connecting a Block to Its Predecessors

When applying the MIN algorithm to a block B, we need to insert coupling code at B's borders. For example, a variable that we require to be in W_B^{entry} might not be in W_P^{exit} of some predecessor P. For this variable, a reload on the way from P to B has to be inserted.

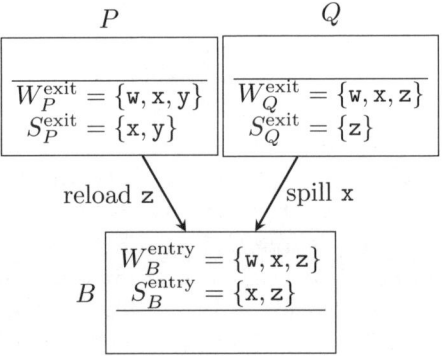

Additionally, we have to provide a sensible initialization S_B^{entry} for the set S that records which variables in W have already been spilled. The invariant for S is: v is in S at instruction I iff v was spilled on all paths from the CFG root to I. To avoid redundant spills, S_B^{entry} is set to all variables in W_B^{entry} that are spilled on some path to B:

Fig. 3. Coupling code at block borders

$$S_B^{\text{entry}} := \left[\bigcup_{P \in \text{pred}(B)} S_P^{\text{exit}} \right] \cap W_B^{\text{entry}}$$

The coupling code for a predecessor P of B has to be inserted as follows:

- All variables in $W_B^{entry} \setminus W_P^{exit}$ need to be reloaded on the edge from P to B.
- All variables in $(S_B^{entry} \setminus S_P^{exit}) \cap W_P^{exit}$ need to be spilled from P to B.

The example in Figure 4.3 shows a block B, its predecessors P and Q which have already been processed, and the inserted code for $W_B^{entry} = \{w, x, z\}$.

In the preceding paragraphs of this subsection, we assumed that all predecessors have already been processed. Let us now consider a loop header B and a predecessor P of B that has not yet been processed. Thus, S_P^{exit} and W_P^{exit} are not available. When processing B, we simply ignore P and add the corresponding spills and reloads as soon as P has been processed.

4.4   Retaining the SSA Form

In this section, we briefly discuss the interdependency of spill-code generation and the SSA form. Due to space limitations, we only give a brief overview; a more in-depth discussion can be found in [13]. Let us first consider the requirements on the input program and then sketch how SSA is retained during the algorithm.

Requirements on the input program. In a non-SSA-form program, each variable is assigned one spill slot (i.e. the memory location where the spilled values of that variables are written to and read from). In SSA form, we *need* to assign all variables of a ϕ-congruence class (cf. Sreedhar et al. [14]) the same spill slot. Else, spilled ϕ-functions result in memory copy instructions. To this end, we demand that each ϕ-congruence class is free of interference, i.e. the CFG is in *conventional* SSA form [14].

Producing SSA output. Inserting a reload for an SSA variable creates a second definition of that variable. Consider the example in Figure 4a. There are two definitions for x_0; the original one and the reload. Creating a new variable x_1 for the reload and renaming the following use, re-establishes the single assignment property. However, the use of x_0 at the lower block is then no longer correct: Coming from the left block, x_0 holds the right value, while coming from the right, the variable to use is x_1. Hence, we have to place a ϕ-function in the lower block that selects over x_0 and x_1 and defines a new variable x_2. Thus, spilling a variable can cause new ϕ-functions to be inserted.

All in all, we need to record all inserted reload operations per variable and *reconstruct* SSA for those variables. This can be achieved with an efficient algorithm by Sastry and Ju [15].

In short, the algorithm takes the original definition of a variable v, a set of new definitions of v (in our case the inserted reloads) and the list of uses of v. Then, for each use, the dominance tree is walked upwards. The first found definition is responsible for that use. When passing an iterated dominance frontier (see Cytron et al. [16]), the algorithm lazily inserts ϕ-functions and wires their operands to suitable definitions. As a side effect, dead definitions are never reached by this search process and can thus be eliminated.

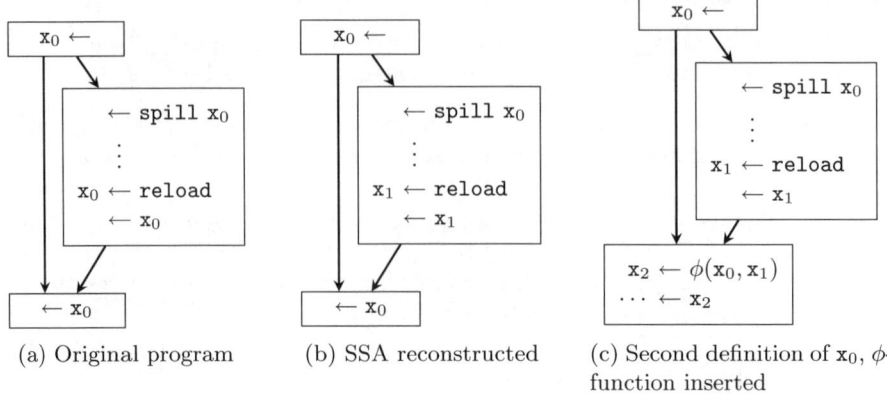

(a) Original program   (b) SSA reconstructed   (c) Second definition of x_0, ϕ-function inserted

Fig. 4. Adding a reload causes a ϕ-function to be created

5   Evaluation

Our experimental evaluation consists of two parts: First, we briefly discuss the compile-time behavior of our algorithm. Second, we assess the quality of the produced code.

Setup. We implemented the presented spilling algorithm in the libFIRM [17] compiler. This compiler produces code for the x86 architecture and features a completely SSA-based register allocator as presented in [13]. All measurements were conducted on the integer part CINT2000 of the CPU2000 benchmark [18]. The program 252.eon was not compiled because the used compiler is not able to process C++. The compile-time measurements were taken on a Core 2 Duo 2GHz PC with 2GB RAM running Linux with kernel version 2.6.22. All presented data only considers the 7 general-purpose registers of the x86. The low number of available registers emphasizes the importance of spill-code generation.

5.1   Runtime of the Algorithm

Figure 5 shows the time spent in the spilling phase in relation to the size of the compiled function. The granularity limit of the time values is 1ms resulting in discrete looking values. The linear regression is also drawn in the diagram to indicate that the time spent on spilling scales roughly linear with the number of instructions. The average throughput is 430 instructions per millisecond.

5.2   Code Quality

We compare our algorithm to the spill code generated by a standard Chait-in/Briggs [1,2] allocator (IFG) and the Wimmer & Mössenböck [5] variant of linear-scan implemented in LLVM version 2.3 [19]. Instead of re-implementing

Table 6. Ratio of spill and reload instructions compared to SSA spilling

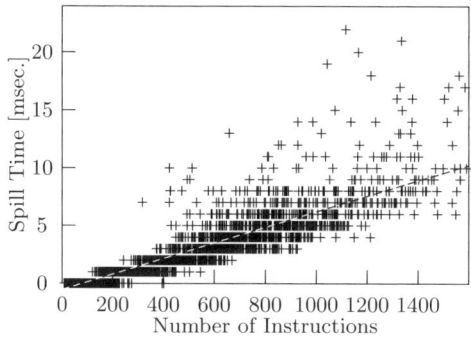

Fig. 5. Time spent on spilling

Bench.	IFG Spilling		Linear Scan	
	Spills	Rel.	Spills	Rel.
gzip	2.39	3.39	1.63	2.91
vpr	1.78	2.83	0.79	1.34
gcc	2.06	2.54	1.69	2.86
mcf	2.01	3.29	15.62	5.87
crafty	1.43	2.04	1.23	1.61
parser	1.54	1.92	1.17	1.38
perlbmk	0.93	1.28	0.77	1.22
gap	1.71	2.78	1.04	1.79
vortex	1.58	2.15	1.62	1.93
bzip2	2.01	2.21	1.83	2.05
twolf	1.53	1.85	1.21	1.25
Average	1.72	2.39	2.60	2.20

the linear-scan allocator in our framework, we decided to directly compare to the fine-tuned implementation within LLVM. Of course, comparing two different compilers is always problematic. However, the backend passes in LLVM and libFIRM are quite similar and LLVM's middle-end is usually more powerful than libFIRM's. We verified this by manual inspection of the code generated for some important inner loops.

To assess the quality of the produced code as general as possible, we count the executed spill and reload instructions of the benchmark programs. We deliberately do not compare runtimes of the produced code as they are biased by all sorts of microarchitectural effects like caching, out-of-order execution and the like. Those influences can greatly vary among different processor architectures and even different implementations of the same architecture. To count the reload and spill instructions, we modified the code generators of libFIRM and LLVM to

Table 7. Executed instructions (billions), percentage of spills and reloads

Benchmark	SSA Spilling			IFG Spilling			Linear Scan		
	Insns.	Spills	Reloads	Insns.	Spills	Reloads	Insns.	Spills	Reloads
164.gzip	329	4.2%	5.9%	374	9.0%	17.5%	347	6.6%	16.2%
175.vpr	196	5.2%	9.4%	223	8.2%	23.5%	176	4.6%	14.1%
176.gcc	158	3.9%	5.5%	171	7.4%	12.9%	172	6.1%	14.5%
181.mcf	51	0.5%	3.1%	53	1.0%	9.7%	60	7.0%	15.3%
186.crafty	208	6.7%	7.4%	219	9.1%	14.2%	198	8.7%	12.5%
197.parser	322	4.6%	7.6%	339	6.8%	13.9%	304	5.7%	11.1%
253.perlbmk	397	11.1%	9.8%	392	10.5%	12.7%	357	9.6%	13.3%
254.gap	252	3.7%	4.2%	263	6.1%	11.1%	215	4.5%	8.7%
255.vortex	321	5.0%	5.3%	341	7.4%	10.6%	340	7.6%	9.6%
256.bzip2	287	4.2%	6.8%	313	7.7%	13.8%	320	6.9%	12.5%
300.twolf	297	3.8%	5.7%	306	5.7%	10.2%	293	4.7%	7.2%
Average	256	4.82%	6.41%	272	7.16%	13.65%	253	6.53%	12.27%

add a special NOP instructions in front of each spill and reload. We then executed all benchmarks with the Valgrind [20] machine-code instrumentation tool and used a home-made plugin to count the marked spill and reload instructions.

The dynamic instruction counts (in billions) are shown in Table 7 along with the percentage of executed spill and reload instructions. Our algorithm is labeled "SSA Spilling". "IFG Spilling" is the graph-coloring spilling and "Linear Scan" shows the results of the code generated by LLVM. Table 7 shows that 3.5% to 20% of the executed instructions are spill and reload instructions. Hence, the spilling heuristic has a significant impact on code quality.

Table 6 shows the ratio of executed spill instructions compared to the results of our algorithm. Our algorithm produces better code than the IFG and the linear-scan algorithm in almost all of the cases. We constantly produce less executed reloads, sometimes even less than the half. On average, the linear-scan (IFG) approach performs 2.60 (1.72) times as many spills and 2.20 (2.39) times as many reloads.

6   Related Work

This paper's approach of separating register allocation from register assignment is in line with Proebsting and Fischer [21]. Their algorithm also globally allocates on top of local information. However, Proebsting and Fischer calculate for each use a probability that this use can be made from a register. This probability needs to be propagated through *all possible* paths to that use. Finally, whenever their algorithm decides to allocate a global variable to a register, the probabilities of all remaining variables need to be updated, which renders the algorithm quadratic in the number of (global) variables where we visit each variable only once.

Morgan [22] proposes to handle some of the spilling before main register allocation in order to improve spill code placement. He describes an algorithm that identifies variables that live throughout a loop but are not used inside it. These variables are spilled in front of and reloaded behind the loop. This improves the situation for a common class of variables but still leaves most spilling decisions to the register allocator. Our algorithm yields a program for which an SSA-based register allocator does not need to insert additional spill code. In our technique the complex analysis of Morgan is replaced by the CFG-global modelling of next-use distances, especially the length assignment loop-exiting edges.

Guo et. al. [10] apply the MIN algorithm as described in Section 2 to long basic blocks. They are able to considerably improve the runtime of their benchmarks compared to a standard MIPSPro or GCC compiler. However, their improvements are mostly visible in basic blocks with long live ranges resulting from extensive loop unrolling. Their good results lead us to investigate the applicability of the MIN algorithm in global register allocation.

Farach and Liberatore [23] prove that the spill-problem is NP-hard for basic blocks. They also prove that the MIN algorithm algorithm gives a $2C$-approximation to the local spilling problem. This supports the good experimental results by Guo et al.

The main motivation for this work were recent results in SSA-based register allocation (see [6,7,8]). If the maximum register pressure in the program is lowered to the number of available registers, a linear-time algorithm can assign the registers *optimally* without adding further spill code. Up to now, a good and fast heuristic to lower the register pressure was missing in this context.

Wimmer and Mössenböck [5] perform live-range splitting while allocating registers in a linear-scan allocator. In the tradition of linear-scan allocators, the CFG is flattend to linear code. In this setting, a list of use-points is constructed per variable. For points with high register pressure the variables with the furthest next-use (in the flattened code!) are spilled first. They present a technique for moving the split positions for spills and reloads to earlier points to move spills and reloads in front of loops. The linear order of the basic blocks however is too restrictive: At control-flow splits, blocks are forced into an arbitrary order which often unnecessarily prohibits hoisting spills or reloads. The original linear-scan allocator (Poletto & Sarkar [4]) introduced CFG flattening to deliver the best possible compile-time performance by avoiding any expensive analysis and additional passes.

To improve code quality, several extensions like Wimmer and Mössenböck [5], Traub et al.[3], and Sarkar & Barik [24] were developed over the years. They successively left the rapid linear-scan paradigm by adding liveness analysis, various other analyses, and fix-up passes. Many of these extensions implicitly rely on the CFG although all algorithms still use the flattened view. We demonstrated that flattening the CFG is not necessary for efficient high-quality spill-code generation.

7   Conclusions

We presented an efficient and effective approach to spill-code generation and live-range splitting. Unlike most existing techniques, our approach is not entangled with a register allocator: It is a program transformation that limits the register pressure of an arbitrary SSA-form program to a given number. While this is useful as a pre-spill phase in any compiler, our technique is predestined for the use in SSA-form register allocation: If a SSA-form program has a maximum register pressure of k, a SSA-based allocator can find an optimal register allocation without introducing further spills in linear time.

Our algorithm is most sensitive to the structure of the program: It carefully splits live ranges around loops to avoid reload instructions in loops where possible. Our evaluation on the CINT2000 benchmark suite shows that our approach reduced the number of executed reload instructions by 54.5% compared to the state-of-the-art linear-scan allocator and by 58.2% compared to a standard graph-coloring allocator. At the same time, the compile-time overhead is competitive with popular linear-scan allocators: We perform liveness analysis and one sweep over the program's CFG.

Acknowledgements

We thank Michael Beck, Alain Darte, Gerhard Goos, Daniel Grund, Christoph Mallon, Fabrice Rastello, Jan Reineke, and Christian Würdig for several insightful discussions. Furthermore, we thank the anonymous reviewers for their valuable comments.

References

1. Chaitin, G.J., Auslander, M.A., Chandra, A.K., Cocke, J., Hopkins, M.E., Markstein, P.W.: Register allocation via graph coloring. Journal of Computer Languages 6, 45–57 (1981)
2. Briggs, P., Cooper, K.D., Torczon, L.: Improvements to graph coloring register allocation. ACM Trans. Program. Lang. Syst. 16(3), 428–455 (1994)
3. Traub, O., Holloway, G., Smith, M.D.: Quality and speed in linear-scan register allocation. In: PLDI 1998: Proceedings of the Conference on Programming Language Design and Implementation, pp. 142–151. ACM Press, New York (1998)
4. Poletto, M., Sarkar, V.: Linear scan register allocation. ACM Trans. Program. Lang. Syst. 21(5), 895–913 (1999)
5. Wimmer, C., Mössenböck, H.: Optimized interval splitting in a linear scan register allocator. In: VEE 2005: Proceedings of the 1st international conference on Virtual execution environments, pp. 132–141. ACM, New York (2005)
6. Bouchez, F., Darte, A., Guillon, C., Rastello, F.: Register allocation: What does the NP-completeness proof of chaitin et al. Really prove? Or revisiting register allocation: Why and how. In: Almási, G.S., Caşcaval, C., Wu, P. (eds.) KSEM 2006. LNCS, vol. 4382, pp. 283–298. Springer, Heidelberg (2007)
7. Brisk, P., Dabiri, F., Jafari, R., Sarrafzadeh, M.: Optimal Register Sharing for High-Level Synthesis of SSA Form Programs. IEEE Trans. on CAD of Integrated Circuits and Systems 25(5), 772–779 (2006)
8. Hack, S., Grund, D., Goos, G.: Register allocation for programs in SSA-form. In: Mycroft, A., Zeller, A. (eds.) CC 2006. LNCS, vol. 3923, pp. 247–262. Springer, Heidelberg (2006)
9. Belady, L.A.: A study of replacement algorithms for a virtual-storage computer. IBM Systems Journal 5(2), 78–101 (1966)
10. Guo, J., Garzarn, M.J., Padua, D.: The power of beladys algorithm in register allocation for long basic blocks. In: The 16th International Workshop on Languages and Compilers for Parallel Computing (2003)
11. Roy, B.V.: A short proof of optimality for the min cache replacement algorithm. Inf. Process. Lett. 102(2-3), 72–73 (2007)
12. Nielson, F., Nielson, H.R., Hankin, C.: Principles of Program Analysis. Springer, Heidelberg (1999)
13. Hack, S.: Register Allocation for Programs in SSA Form. PhD thesis, Universität Karlsruhe (TH) (October 2007)
14. Sreedhar, V.C., Ju, R.D.C., Gillies, D.M., Santhanam, V.: Translating out of static single assignment form. In: Cortesi, A., Filé, G. (eds.) SAS 1999. LNCS, vol. 1694, pp. 194–210. Springer, Heidelberg (1999)
15. Sastry, A.V.S., Ju, R.D.C.: A new algorithm for scalar register promotion based on SSA form. In: PLDI 1998: Proceedings of the conference on Programming language design and implementation, pp. 15–25. ACM, New York (1998)

16. Cytron, R., Ferrante, J., Rosen, B.K., Wegman, M.N., Zadek, F.K.: Efficiently computing static single assignment form and the control dependence graph. Transactions on Programming Languages and Systems 13(4), 451–490 (1991)
17. Firm: The libFirm Compiler, http://www.libfirm.org
18. Standard Performance Evaluation Corporation: SPEC CPU2000 V1.3, http://www.spec.org/cpu2000/
19. LLVM: The LLVM Compiler Infrastructure, http://www.llvm.org
20. Valgrind: Valgrind Instrumentation Framework for Building Dynamic Analysis Tools, http://www.valgrind.org
21. Proebsting, T.A., Fischer, C.N.: Probabilistic register allocation. SIGPLAN Not. 27(7), 300–310 (1992)
22. Morgan, R.: Building an Optimizing Compiler. Digital Press (1998)
23. Farach, M., Liberatore, V.: On local register allocation. In: SODA 1998: Proceedings of the ninth annual symposium on Discrete algorithms, Philadelphia, PA, USA, Society for Industrial and Applied Mathematics, pp. 564–573 (1998)
24. Sarkar, V., Barik, R.: Extended linear scan: An alternate foundation for global register allocation. In: Krishnamurthi, S., Odersky, M. (eds.) CC 2007. LNCS, vol. 4420, pp. 141–155. Springer, Heidelberg (2007)

Loop-Aware Instruction Scheduling with Dynamic Contention Tracking for Tiled Dataflow Architectures

Muhammad Umar Farooq and Lizy K. John

Department of ECE,
The University of Texas at Austin
ufarooq@mail.utexas.edu, ljohn@ece.utexas.edu
http://www.ece.utexas.edu

Abstract. Increasing on-chip wire delay along with the distributed nature of processing elements, makes instruction scheduling for tiled dataflow architectures very crucial. Our analysis reveals that careful placement of frequently executed sections of applications, and dynamic resource contention tracking can significantly improve the performance of the application. The former reduces the operand network latency, while the latter reduces stalls due to contention for processing elements. We augment one of the most recent instruction scheduling algorithms —hierarchical instruction scheduling —to better exploit spatial locality between instructions within a loop, thereby reducing expensive communication overhead by 6.5% and increasing average IPC by 5.13%. Secondly, in the presence of conditional branches and variable latency memory instructions, estimating resource contention, at compile time, is not only complex but also imperfect. We suggest dynamic tracking of contending instructions, and their re-location, once a contention threshold is exceeded. Results showed that dynamic contention tracking reduced the average ALU conflicts by 23%, thereby improving the average IPC by 14.22%. Combined together, these augmentations improve the average IPC by 19.39% and over 30% for some benchmarks.

Keywords: tiled dataflow architectures, instruction scheduling, resource contention, operand network latency.

1 Introduction

Tiled architectures are gaining popularity as an alternative to monolithic processors, because of their simpler designs, and scalability. TRIPS [1], WaveScalar [13], RAW [14], and Smart-Memories [5] are examples of such architectures. Some examples of these architectures consist of processing elements (PEs), distributed across a grid, and connected through an on-chip network [1][13]. Their performance largely depends on the instruction scheduling. As opposed to monolithic processors, instruction scheduling for tiled architectures has two aspects: (1) temporal —decides when to fetch an instruction (2) spatial —decides where

O. de Moor and M. Schwartzbach (Eds.): CC 2009, LNCS 5501, pp. 190–203, 2009.

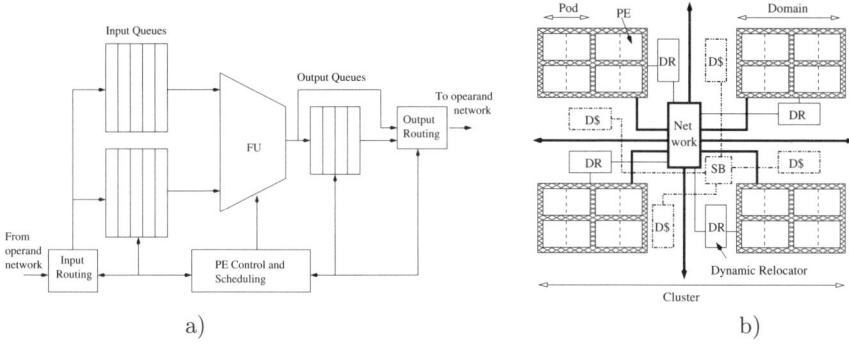

Fig. 1. a) Processing Element (PE)   b) WaveScalar Cluster

to execute an instruction. Scheduling for monolithic processors focuses on the temporal aspect of scheduling. However, for tiled architectures, scheduling also decides *where* an instruction should be executed in the grid. A good instruction scheduling can reduce operand network latency by placing dependent instructions on the same or adjacent tiles, while minimizing the contention for tile resources and maintaining high ILP. Previous attempts at solving resource contention problem for tiled architectures relied on profiling[4] or compile time heuristics[2]. In the presence of variable latency memory instructions, estimating at compile time, whether an instruction will contend with another instruction is impossible. For example, in case a load instruction misses in L1 cache, all its consumers will execute at a time that is different from their estimated firing time. The focus of this work is:

- to reduce operand network latency by careful placement of instructions within the loop.
- to minimize resource contention by dynamically tracking and re-locating contending instructions.

Our target architecture is WaveScalar [13]. In this architecture, the basic processing element (PE) is a 5-stage in-order pipeline. Two adjacent PEs form a pod, and communicate through a low-latency bypass network. Four pods make a domain, communicating over a fixed latency pipelined network. Four domains constitute a cluster, and communicate through a fixed-route network switch. Several clusters combine to form a grid. Inter-cluster communication is through a dynamically-routed packet network. Recently, a hierarchical instruction scheduling algorithm [6] has been proposed for the WaveScalar architecture, which partitions the application's dataflow graph into smaller groups, and assign these groups to PEs. We augmented hierarchical instruction scheduling algorithm to take into consideration the control flow information (i.e. loops) while partitioning the dataflow graph. We also explored addressing contention for execution resources dynamically by re-locating instructions that contend with other instructions within their PE past some pre-defined threshold.

We compared the performance of the augmented algorithm with the original algorithm on WaveScalar [13] simulator using benchmarks from EEMBC [11] benchmark suites.

In the next section, we will discuss the background, and the original hierarchical scheduling algorithm. Section 3 describes our augmentations to the original algorithm. Our evaluation methodology, and results are shown in section 4. Section 5 discusses related work. Section 6 concludes the paper.

2   Background

We begin this section by giving an overview of the target architecture for the scheduling techniques presented here. We will then explain the state of the art in instruction scheduling for this architecture which is the baseline for our comparisons.

2.1   WaveScalar Architecture

WaveScalar is a dataflow architecture. As in other dataflow architectures, a program is represented as a dataflow graph, and instruction dependencies are explicit [3][10][8][13]. There is no program counter, instructions are fetched and placed on the grid as they are required. There is no register file, the result produced by an instruction is directly communicated to all the consumers. In this architecture, instructions are grouped in blocks called *Waves*. Waves can be defined as acyclic dataflow graphs, for which each instruction executes at most once every time the wave is executed, and to which control can enter at a single point. On exit and re-entry to this acyclic dataflow graph, the wave number is increased. Waves are used to support memory models of imperative programming languages such as C. Each dynamic instruction is identified by a tag, which is the aggregate of its wave number and location on the grid. When an instruction has received all its input operands for a particular matching wave number, it fires, provided an ALU is available, and there is room to store the result in the output queue. The output is temporary stored in the output queue before it is communicated to the consumers.

Figure 1(b) shows the basic WaveScalar Microarchitecture. The substrate consists of replicated clusters connected through a dynamically routed packet network. Each cluster consists of four domains, communicating through a fixed-route network switch, which has a 4 cycle latency. Additionally, each cluster has a 32KB 4-way set associative L1 data cache, and a store buffer. Each domain is composed of eight PEs, grouped into pairs of two. Each pair is called a pod. Pods communicate through a fixed 1 cycle latency pipeline network. Adjacent pods form a half-domain, with 2 cycle communication latency. Within PE, instructions communicate through a bypass network. Each PE, shown in Figure 1(a), is a 5-stage in-order pipeline with a small instruction cache capable of holding 64 static instructions. Each PE has a 16 entry input queue, and an 8 entry output queue.

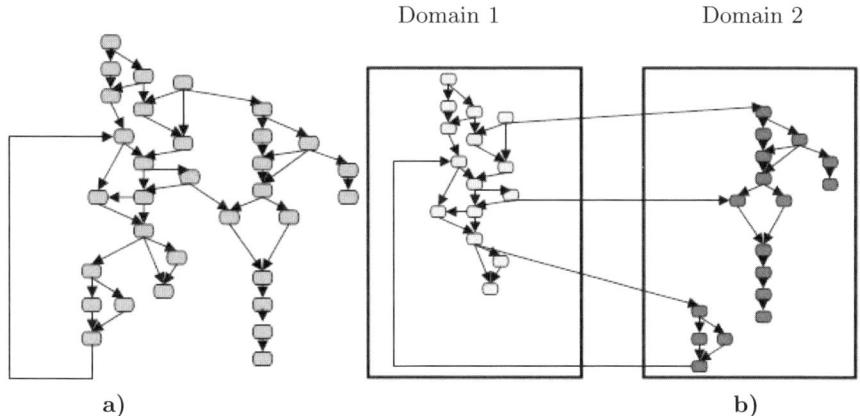

Fig. 2. a) Application Dataflow Graph   b)Coarse Grain Scheduling

Loading instructions onto the grid is done through co-operation of the microarchitecture and the runtime system. When an instruction produces a result for a consumer instruction not already on the grid, the runtime system is signalled [6]. The placement of the incoming instruction is decided using either a statically constructed table, or an online algorithm which creates a new mapping.

2.2   Hierarchical Instruction Scheduling Algorithm

Recently, a hierarchical instruction scheduling algorithm [6] has been proposed. It breaks the instruction scheduling problem into two phases – Coarse grain and Fine grain. Coarse grain phase assigns instructions to domains according to their execution order, while fine grain phase refines initial placement, and assigns instructions to the PEs. Coarse grain scheduling uses instruction execution order, obtained through profiling, to assign instructions to a domain, and when the domain is full, it moves to the next domain, thereby assigning all the instructions to some domain. Figure 2 shows an example of how an application dataflow graph shown in 2(a) is assigned to domains during coarse grain scheduling 2(b).

Once all the instructions are assigned to some domain, fine grain scheduling refines the assignments, and generates the final placement of instructions to the PEs. Fine grain scheduling has two passes. First pass forms groups of instructions within each domain according to the topology of the dataflow graph. It uses two parameters (a)*MaxDepth* - which controls how many dependent instructions are assigned to the same PE, (b) *MaxWidth* - which limits the amount of parallelism within each PE. A higher value of *MaxDepth* will reduce operand network latency since more dependent instruction will be assigned to the same PE. A higher value *MaxWidth* will increase the ALU contention as more parallel instructions will share the PE resources. In the second pass, fine grain scheduling assigns the groups formed in first pass to the processing elements. In doing so, this phase uses the parameter *DepDegree*. This parameter has a value between zero and

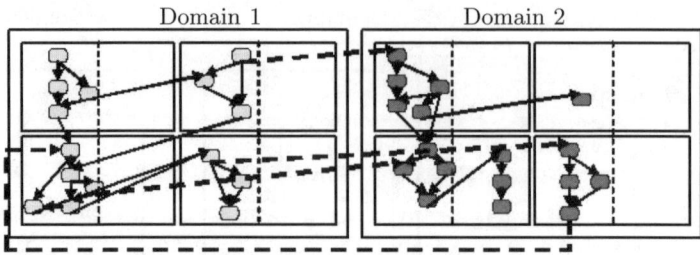

Fig. 3. Fine Grain Scheduling

one, and is used to control how much emphasis there is on inter-group operand dependencies in the choice of PE for a group. A value close to zero will assign dependent groups to the same PE. A value close to one will separate dependent groups by assigning them to different PEs. Figure 3 shows the final instruction placement after fine grain scheduling.

3   Enhanced Hierarchical Instruction Scheduling

This section will explain our augmentations to the baseline hierarchical instruction scheduling algorithm, namely loop-aware instruction scheduling, and dynamic tracking and re-location of contending instructions.

3.1   Loop Awareness

Loops are structures where a program spends most of its time. Careful placement of instructions within a loop can significantly improve the performance of the program by reducing long operand latencies. The baseline algorithm does not differentiate between sequential code within and outside loop constructs, when assigning instructions to domains. During the coarse grain scheduling, the baseline algorithm uses profiled execution order to assign instructions to domains. Once a domain is completely full (512 instructions for the current implementation), the algorithm moves to the next domain until all the instructions in the program are assigned to some domain in the grid. However, this sequential assignment of instructions to domain could result in a loop being split into two different domains (see Figure 2) thereby increasing the inter-domain traffic proportional to the execution frequency of the loop.

In our algorithm, a counter, S_{curr}, is maintained during the coarse grain placement phase. Every time an instruction is assigned to a domain, this counter is incremented. When the coarse grain placement algorithm encounters an instruction that is in a loop it checks the static size of the loop, S_{loop}. If S_{loop} is $<$ S_{max} - S_{curr}, where S_{max} is the maximum instructions that can fit in a domain, it continues the assignment to the current domain since the loop can completely fit in the current domain. If S_{loop} is $>$ S_{max}, implying that the loop can not completely fit in any domain it continues with the assignment to the current domain.

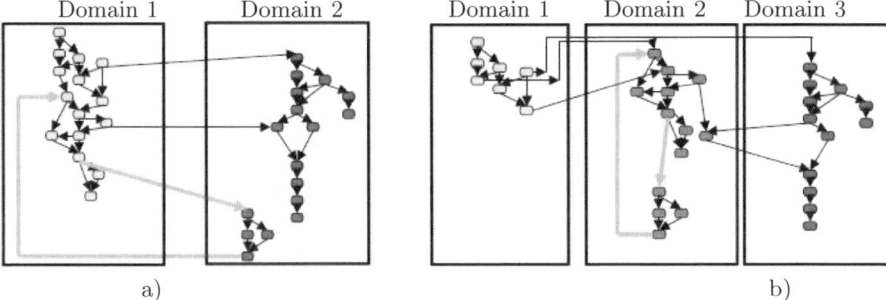

Fig. 4. a) Instruction placement using baseline algorithm. Note that, loop is split between domains. b)Loop-aware instruction placement. Avoids loop splitting by placing all loop instructions in a new domain.

However, if S_{max} - $S_{curr} < S_{loop} < S_{max}$, i.e. loop can not fit in current domain but can completely fit in a new domain, then the assignment to the current domain is stopped, and entire loop is assigned to a new domain. Doing so decreases the amount of inter-domain communication that would have taken place if the loop was divided between domains. Figure 4 shows a sample placement of a loop with the baseline instruction placement 4(a), and with loop-aware instruction placement 4(b).

3.2   Dynamic Contention Tracking

When more instructions become ready to execute in the same cycle than there are execution slots in the PE, we have resource contention problem. Reducing resource contention requires estimating the execution cycle of every instruction, and placing those instructions with same execution cycle into different PEs. One of the shortcomings of static instruction scheduling is its imperfect estimation of resource contention. For example, variable latency memory instructions make it impossible to statically identify firing time of instructions and their dependants. One can only estimate the firing time, but in case an estimation goes wrong (e.g. because of cache miss), firing time of dependent instructions will be different from their estimated time, and can cause contention with other instructions. Extensive research has been done to compute optimal schedule. Profiling is used in [4] to assign cache hit or miss latency to memory instructions. Load balancing heuristic is used in [2] to penalize instructions that can cause resource contention. To account for imperfect estimates, the algorithm leaves single cycle slack in either direction for the firing time. These attempts can, at best, produce an imperfect local (intra-block) contention estimate. When attempting to find a placement for the dataflow graph corresponding to an application on a grid, such estimates cannot be useful.

   We propose a dynamic contention tracking algorithm. Instructions are assigned to the processing element according to the static scheduling algorithm. A *contention counter* is associated with each instruction i, which is incremented whenever instruction i contends with other instructions in the processing element. When the *contention counter* for instruction i reaches the *contention threshold*, a re-location request for instruction i is generated. Implementation details of dynamic contention tracking algorithm are further explained in the next section.

To allow re-location within the same domain, processing elements are not filled to completion during initial instruction assignment. Re-location outside the initial domain is not considered, as it would increase the communication cost of the instruction with its producers and consumers, and could also result in a loop being split into different domains. For re-locating instruction i, the cost of placing instruction i is computed for all the PEs in that domain, including the original PE, using the algorithm shown in Figure 5. Instruction i is then assigned to the PE with the minimum cost. If no PE within the domain has cost less than the original PE, then instruction i is not re-located. After re-location, the *contention counter* for that instruction is reset. The cost consists of three components:

a) communication cost between producer of instruction i to instruction i.
b) contention cost of instruction i in PE.
c) communication cost between instruction i to its consumers.

Computing the (a) and (c) portions of the cost is straight forward as each instruction knows the locations of its producers and consumers. Computing contention cost involves finding whether an instruction i, if placed in PE p, will contend with the instructions already present in PE p. One simple approach for finding if two instructions will contend with each other is to check if they have the same producer. There are two problems with this approach. First, an instruction can have multiple producers for the same data, e.g. instructions in the merge block following a conditional branch. Second, instructions that do not have a common producer but can possibly fire at the same time are not considered. A second approach is to maintain a history of the last 'k' cycles in which each instruction became ready. If two instructions have high correlation in their ready times, they are likely to contend with each other, if they are in the same PE. For our experiments we use k=1. The instruction re-locator keeps a count of how many instructions from each PE became ready every cycle. When a re-location request is issued, this information is used to calculate contention cost of each PE being considered. Results showed that even with k=1, ALU contention is reduced significantly. We have assumed a 20 cycle penalty for finding the best PE for the contending instruction, and announcing its new location to its producers and consumers. This penalty is the same as the penalty of bringing an instruction on demand from L2. When an instruction, not already present on the grid, is brought from L2, all its producers and consumers are updated with the instruction's location on the grid. Some or all of the 20 cycle penalty can be hidden since instruction re-location process starts as soon as the instruction reaches its *contention threshold*. If the next message to this re-located instruction arrives after x cycles, then the actual penalty is (20 - x) cycles, (zero if x > 20).

Input: Contending Instruction i
Output: PEnew —new location of instruction i
 1: runningCost = infinity
 2: **for all** PEs p in Domain **do**
 3:   Cost(i, p) = inputLatency(Producer(i), i) +
     contentionCost(i, p) + outputLatency$(i,$ Consumers$(i))$
 4:   **if** Cost(i, p) < runningCost **then**
 5:     runningCost = Cost(i, p)
 6:     PEnew = p
 7:   **end if**
 8: **end for**

Fig. 5. Dynamic Contention Tracking Algorithm

3.3   Implementation of Dynamic Contention Tracking Algorithm

The dynamic contention tracking algorithm is implemented using a hardware structure called the *dynamic re-locator*, see Fig 1(b). This is a distributed structure with one re-locator per domain. The purpose of this re-locator is to calculate the best PE location for an instruction, whose contention counter exceeds the threshold. This new PE location should have the least value of cost function among the 8 PEs in that domain.

When an instruction surpasses the threshold, it sends a re-location request along with the PE location of its sources and sinks to the dynamic re-locator in its domain. Once the re-locator receives this information, computing the communication cost between a candidate PE and PEs containing the sources/sinks is not costly. This is just a matter of adding numbers based on the distance of the source and sink PEs. For computing the contention cost, the re-locator requires information regarding how many instructions became ready in each PE in the previous cycle. Every cycle, each PE (8 of them) sends this information to the local re-locator in their domain. Upon receiving a re-location request, these 8 stored values are observed by the re-locator to calculate the contention cost of each PE, which is incorporated into the overall cost function of each PE.

Another job of re-locator is to update the source and sink instructions with the new location of the re-located instruction. This will only be done when an instruction is re-located, and not every cycle. All the sources and sinks are informed in the same way they would know the place of an instruction being initially brought in from L2 [12]. Due to these similarities to an L1 miss, we have considered a 20 cycle penalty for the re-location, same as the penalty of accessing L2 cache.

4   Experimental Evaluation and Results

The hierarchical placement explained in section 2 is the baseline for our evaluation. We carefully implemented the recent hierarchical instruction placement

Table 1. Parameter settings for experimental evaluation

PEs per Domain	8(4 pods)
PE Input Queue	16 entries
PE Output Queue	8 entries
Instructions per PE	64
ALUs per PE	2
L1 Cache	32KB, 4-way set associative, 128B line, 4 accesses per cycle
L2 Cache	16MB, 4-way set associative, 1024B line, 20 cycle access
Network Latencies	
Within Pod	1 Cycle
Within Half Domain	2 Cycles
Within Domain	4 Cycles
Within Cluster	7 Cycles
Inter Cluster	7 + hop count

presented in [6] within the publicly available WaveScalar toolchain. Then following changes were made to help evaluate our enhancements to the hierarchical instruction scheduling.

a) We augmented the binary translator of WaveScalar, which is used to translate binaries from an Alpha compiler to WaveScalar binaries, to consider control flow information about the loops during the coarse grain scheduling phase.

b) We added to the simulator the dynamic contention tracking algorithm explained in Figure 5.

In order to show the effects of loop-awareness and dynamic contention tracking, we ran benchmarks from the EEMBC benchmark suite. Each benchmark ran for all the combinations of the parameters of the hierarchical instruction placement algorithm ($MaxDepth \in \{2, 4, 8, 12, 16, 32, 50, 64, 128\}$, $MaxWidth \in \{1, 2, 3, 4, 6, 10\}$, and $DepDegree \in \{.1, .5, .9\}$). For each of the aforementioned combinations each benchmark ran four times: 1) without loop optimization without contention tracking, 2) with loop optimization without contention tracking, 3) without loop optimization with contention tracking, 4) with loop optimization with contention tracking. For each benchmark we averaged the results for all the combinations of $MaxDepth$, $MaxWidth$ and $DepDegree$.

We setup three different experiments to see the effect of our approach on (a) intra-domain traffic (b) ALU contention and (c) IPC. Table 1 shows microarchitectural parameter settings used for the evaluation. Following subsections will discuss these experiments and their results.

4.1   Intra-domain Communication

Inter-domain communication latency is 7 cycles, compared to maximum 4 cycles within the domain. Reducing the inter-domain traffic can significantly improve

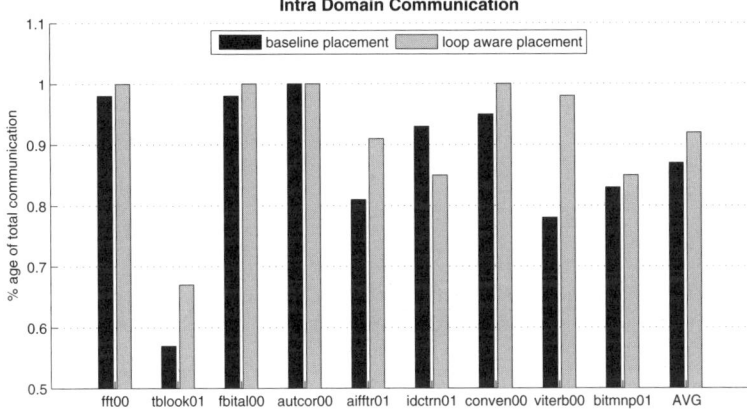

Fig. 6. Intra-domain communications: For each benchmark communication values shown are averaged for all 162 combinations of depth, width and depdegree

the performance. One way of reducing the inter-domain communication is to avoid splitting the loops of a program across multiple domains during instruction placement. This was the focus of our loop-awareness optimization. In order to evaluate the affect of this optimization on intra-domain and inter-domain communication, we measured these values with and without our loop awareness optimization. Experiments showed that by confining the loops to a domain, average intra-domain traffic increased by 6.5% and as high as 25.64% for some benchmarks (see Figure 6). 4 out of 10 benchmarks achieve 99.9+% intra-domain communication. Some of the benchmarks (e.g. idctrn01) however showed a decrease in the intra-domain traffic. This situation arises when a big loop with small iteration count is assigned a new domain by our algorithm, thereby separating the loop instructions from their parent instructions. Since the iteration count is small, assigning a new domain will not increase the intra-domain traffic, however it increases the inter-domain communication between the parent instructions in one domain and loop instructions in another. This situation can be avoided by profiling the loop and starting new domains for only those loops that execute enough times to justify paying the cost of separating the loop's instructions from its producer instructions and is the subject of future work.

4.2   ALU Contention

This experiment shows that dynamic re-location of contending instructions helps reduce ALU contention. Our experiment shows that dynamic contention tracking algorithm reduces average ALU contention by 23%(see Table 2). Total ALU contention with and without dynamic contention tracking algorithm, and the average number of instructions selected for re-location along with their re-location frequencies are shown in Table 2. We would also like to evaluate how accurate our heuristics for re-location of instructions are. Table 2 shows that 46.1% of

Table 2. ALU contention and frequency of instruction re-location during dynamic contention tracking

	Static Instr.		ALU conflicts		% of instructions that are moved			
	Total	Moved	before optimization	after optimization	1-5 times	6-10 times	11-20 times	above 21 times
fft00	15903	602	622365	549867	47.1	3.4	5.7	43.8
tblook01	15498	1198	791137	679818	49	22.7	6.9	20.9
fbital00	14774	383	1263916	883164	47.2	4.6	4.6	43.2
autcor00	14194	77	2823384	2179031	38.8	9	9	42.6
aifftr01	11856	1970	1698660	1286201	39.4	12.8	10.8	36.1
pntr01	16208	501	667252	580794	27.2	3.1	1.7	67
idctrn01	21412	3832	2054979	1618157	68.8	7.7	5.7	17
conven00	14677	363	2510123	1864493	40.4	2.4	4.9	51.4
viterb00	15278	627	938309	620596	58.8	12.3	5.1	22.4
bitmnp01	17437	1349	446836	303761	45.9	23.2	22	8
Average			**1381696**	**1056588**	**46.1**	**10.1**	**7.6**	**36.2**

instructions were moved less than 6 times during the execution of the program. An interesting observation from Table 2 is that most of the instructions are either moved less than 6 times or they are moved for more than 20. This is because during re-location an instruction either finds a PE in which it rarely contends with other instructions early, and stays there for a long period of time or it keeps bouncing back and forth between two PEs. The back and forth movement of instructions between two PEs can be related to the following scenario. A number of instructions start contending within a PE for execution resources. A subset of these instructions reaches the re-location threshold and is moved. The remainder of the contending instructions will also soon reach the threshold and will then look for a place to be re-located. During the re-location process, this second subset of instructions find the same PE that the first set had found due to the fact that the producer and consumer communication benefits of that PE outweigh its contention cost. This movement of instructions back and forth between two PEs is clearly not desirable. The trade off that exists here is between the threshold at which the re-location is initiated and the number of times we pay the price of re-location in order to separate contending groups. A small threshold has the advantage of separating contending groups quickly in order to acheive more parallelism while having to pay the price of re-location more often, whereas a large threshold pays the re-location price less but pays more in terms of contention while we wait for the threshold to be met. An appropriate threshold value can be decided upon with help from profiling and using a metric such as the number of iterations of loops in the program to guide the choice. This will set some sort of upper bound on the value of the threshold in order for there to be any use in re-locating instructions and benefiting from less contention in future iterations of the loop. A lower bound for the threshold value will involve the re-location cost. We experimentally found the threshold of 20 used in these experiments to be a sweet spot for the threshold.

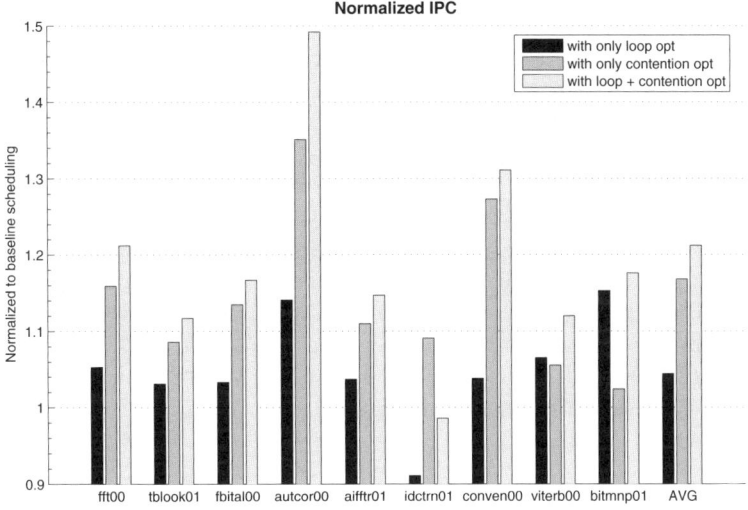

Fig. 7. IPC: For each benchmark IPC values shown are averaged for all 162 combinations of depth, width and depdegree

4.3   IPC

Increased intra-domain traffic as well as reduced ALU contention have significant positive impact on the IPC. Reducing the inter-domain communication through loop-awareness and ALU contention by dynamic contention tracking algorithm improves average IPC by 19.39% and over 30% for some benchmarks e.g., conven00 and autcor00. Figure 7 shows the individual and combined effect of our enhancements on IPC. Note that for benchmarks idctrn01, combined IPC decreases because of decrease in the intra-domain communication explained in Section 4.1. However for this benchmark increase in IPC due to reduction in ALU contention is still achieved although outweighed by the decrease in IPC due to decreased intra-domain communication.

5   Related Work

In this section we dicuss the most relevant work on algorithms designed for instruction scheduling which have a spatial component.

5.1   Spatial Path Scheduling Algorithm

One of the most recent instruction schedulers proposed for tiled dataflow architectures is the SPS algorithm presented for the EDGE architecture in [2]. The spatial path scheduling algorithm factors in previously fixed locations which it calls anchor points for each placement. An anchor point is an instruction whose placement is known because it accesses a known location such as the register file (if the architecture has one), a cache bank or other resources. As the placement for instructions is decided upon, the instructions that have been placed become new anchor points for the remainder of the instructions to be placed. The proposed approach uses simulated annealing to estimate the best results that are possible and uses heuristics to close the gap between the basic algorithm explained above and the results obtained via simulated annealing. To do so the basic algorithm is augmented with three heuristics: (1) local and global ALU and network link contention modeling, (2) global critical path estimates and (3) dependence chain path reservation. Using these heuristics the placement cost function is modified to account for the mentioned criteria. In [2] it is shown that with all the heuristics in place, the final scheduler improves over the basic SPS algorithm by 7%, and is within 5% of the annealed results. This method is not very suitable for a dataflow architecture such as WaveScalar because such an architecture does not have register files to use as anchor points at the beginning of the algorithm.

5.2   Instruction Scheduling for Clustered VLIW

A number of instruction scheduling algorithms have been proposed for clustered VLIW architectures [4][7][9]. Unified assign and schedule [7] is a general scheduling framework which is augmented with heuristics for the target architecture by the compiler writer. This work was compared to the baseline hierarchical fine grain algorithm in [1]. [9] predicts the inter-cluster communication cost of a loop, and uses an integer-optimization method to control loop unrolling and unroll-and-jam to limit the effects of inter-cluster data transfers. This method differs from our algorithm in the way information from loops is used since it does not address inter-cluster communication by taking loops into account in instruction scheduling. By addressing minimization of inter-domain communication through placement our algorithm does not need to restrict unrolling to limit this communication if a loop structure can fit in a domain of its own.

6   Conclusion

Loop-Awareness and dynamic contention tracking techniques were added to the hierarchical placement algorithm [6]. Loop-aware hierarchical instruction scheduling improves the performance of tiled architectures by considering control flow information, specifically loop information, when doing coarse grain instruction placement. This avoids splitting of loops into multiple domains thereby increasing average intra-domain communication by 6.5% and average IPC by 5.13% and as high as 15% for some benchmarks. Dynamic tracking and relocation of contending instructions resulted in an average 23% reduction in ALU conflicts thereby increasing average IPC by 14.22%. These two enhancements put together achieved an average IPC improvement of 19.39% and over 30% for some presented benchmarks.

References

1. Burger, D., Keckler, S.W., McKinley, K.S., Dahlin, M., John, L.K., Lin, C., Moore, C.R., Burrill, J., McDonald, R.G., Yoder, W., The TRIPS Team: Scaling to the End of Silicon with EDGE Architectures. Computer 37(7), 44–55 (2004)
2. Coons, K.E., Chen, X., Burger, D., McKinley, K.S., Kushwaha, S.K.: A Spatial Path Scheduling Algorithm For EDGE Architectures. In: ASPLOS-XII: Proceedings of the 12th international conference on Architectural support for programming languages and operating systems, pp. 129–140. ACM Press, New York (2006)
3. Dennis, J.B., Misunas, D.P.: A preliminary architecture for a basic data-flow processor. SIGARCH Comput. Archit. News 3(4), 126–132 (1974)
4. Gibert, E., Sanchez, J., Gonzalez, A.: Effective instruction scheduling techniques for an interleaved cache clustered VLIW processor. In: MICRO 35: Proceedings of the 35th annual ACM/IEEE international symposium on Microarchitecture, pp. 123–133. IEEE Computer Society Press, Los Alamitos (2002)
5. Mai, K., Paaske, T., Jayasena, N., Ho, R., Dally, W.J., Horowitz, M.: Smart Memories: A Modular Reconfigurable Architecture. In: ISCA 2000: Proceedings of the 27th annual international symposium on Computer architecture, pp. 161–171. ACM Press, New York (2000)
6. Mercaldi, M., Swanson, S., Petersen, A., Putnam, A., Schwerin, A., Oskin, M., Eggers, S.J.: Instruction scheduling for a tiled dataflow architecture. In: ASPLOS-XII: Proceedings of the 12th international conference on Architectural support for programming languages and operating systems, pp. 141–150. ACM Press, New York (2006)
7. Ozer, E., Banerjia, S., Conte, T.M.: Unified assign and schedule: A new approach to scheduling for clustered register file microarchitectures. In: MICRO 31: Proceedings of the 31st annual ACM/IEEE international symposium on Microarchitecture, pp. 308–315. IEEE Computer Society Press, Los Alamitos (1998)
8. Papadopoulos, G.M., Culler, D.E.: Monsoon: An explicit token-store architecture. In: ISCA 1998: 25 years of the international symposia on Computer architecture (selected papers), pp. 398–407. ACM Press, New York (1998)
9. Qian, Y., Carr, S., Sweany, P.H.: Optimizing Loop Performance For Clustered VLIW Architectures. In: PACT 2002: Proceedings of the 2002 International Conference on Parallel Architectures and Compilation Techniques, Washington, DC, USA, pp. 271–280. IEEE Computer Society Press, Los Alamitos (2002)
10. Sakai, S., Yamaguchi, y., Hiraki, K., Kodama, Y., Yuba, T.: An architecture of a dataflow single chip processor. In: ISCA 1989: Proceedings of the 16th annual international symposium on Computer architecture, pp. 46–53. ACM Press, New York (1989)
11. EEMBC Benchmark Scores, http://www.eembc.org
12. Swanson, S., Michelson, K., Schwerin, A., Oskin, M.: Dataflow: The Road Less Complex. In: WCED 2003: Proceedings of the 3rd Workshop on Complexity-Effective Design (2003)
13. Swanson, S., Michelson, K., Schwerin, A., Oskin, M.: WaveScalar. In: MICRO 36: Proceedings of the 36th annual IEEE/ACM International Symposium on Microarchitecture, Washington, DC, USA, p. 291. IEEE Computer Society Press, Los Alamitos (2003)
14. Waingold, E., Taylor, M., Sarkar, V., Lee, V., Lee, W., Kim, J., Frank, M., Finch, P., Devabhaktumi, S., Barua, R., Babb, J., Amarsinghe, S., Agarwal, A.: Baring it all to Software: The Raw Machine. Technical report, Cambridge, MA, USA (1997)

Scheduling Tasks to Maximize Usage of Aggregate Variables in Place

Samah Abu-Mahmeed[1], Cheryl McCosh[1], Zoran Budimlić[1], Ken Kennedy[1],
Kaushik Ravindran[2], Kevin Hogan[2], Paul Austin[2],
Steve Rogers[2], and Jacob Kornerup[2]

[1] Computer Science Department, Rice University, Houston, TX 77005
{samah,chom,zoran}@cs.rice.edu
[2] National Instruments, 11500 North MoPac Expressway, Austin, TX 78759
{kaushik.ravindran,kevin.hogan,paul.austin,steve.rogers,
jacob.kornerup}@ni.com

Abstract. Single-assignment languages with copy semantics have a very simple and approachable programming model. A naïve implementation of the copy semantics that copies the result of every computation to a new location, can result in poor performance. Whereas, an implementation that keeps the results in the same location, when possible, can achieve much higher performance.

In this paper, we present a greedy algorithm for in-place computation of aggregate (array and structure) variables. Our algorithm greedily picks the most profitable opportunities for in-place computation, then updates the scheduling and in-place constraints in the program graph. The algorithm runs in $O(T \log T + E_W V + V^2)$ time, where T is the number of in-placeness opportunities, E_W is the number of edges and V the number of computational nodes in a program graph.

We evaluate the performance of the code generated by the LabVIEW^{TM} compiler using our algorithm against the code that performs no in-place computation at all, resulting in significant application performance improvements. We also compare the performance of the code generated by our algorithm against the commercial LabVIEW compiler that uses an ad-hoc in-placeness strategy. The results show that our algorithm matches the performance of the current LabVIEW strategy in most cases, while in some cases outperforming it significantly.

1 Introduction

At their core, functional, data-flow programming and other single-assignment languages are free from side-effects, making it easier to write, parallelize, verify and optimize programs written in such languages. At the conceptual level, the side-effect free behavior implies that the involved variables are copied at each stage. Translated directly into an implementation this can result in programs that consume large amounts of time and space. Compiler transformations that recognize unnecessary copies and avoid them can significantly improve the

O. de Moor and M. Schwartzbach (Eds.): CC 2009, LNCS 5501, pp. 204–219, 2009.
© Springer-Verlag Berlin Heidelberg 2009

performance of programs in such languages. We call such copy avoidance transformations an in-placeness strategy, since data that is not copied is kept in-place. Unfortunately, the general problem of finding the minimum number of copies in a program involving aggregate data structures is NP-Complete [1].

In this paper (an extended version is given in [2]), we present an $O(T log T + E_W V + V^2)$ greedy in-placeness algorithm that significantly reduces the amount of copying of aggregate data structures for single assignment languages. Here, T is the number of in-placeness opportunities, E_W is the aggregate number of edges and V is the number of computational nodes in a program graph. This algorithm is general and can be applied to wide range of functional, data-flow and other single assignment languages. We have chosen to implement a prototype of the algorithm as an optimization phase in a compiler for LabVIEW^{TM}, a graphical data flow programming language from National Instruments Corporation (NI) [3], but it can be just as easily implemented in any other modern compiler infrastructure for other single assignment and functional languages. LabVIEW is a compiled, statically typed programming language widely used by scientists and engineers around the world. An integral part of its compilation process is its in-placeness strategy. Our experiments show that using the in-placeness strategy currently shipping with the LabVIEW compiler results in much faster and less memory intensive programs when compared to performing no computations in-place. The in-placeness algorithm presented in this paper results in a more robust performance, on par with the current LabVIEW strategy in most cases, while in some cases showing significant (orders of magnitude) performance improvement compared to the shipping LabVIEW compiler.

Our in-placeness algorithm saves both space and time in an executing program. It saves space by performing computations in-place. By performing in-place operations on aggregate data structures that only change a (small) part of the data structure, it saves the time needed for copying unchanged data.

The rest of the paper is organized as follows. Section 2 presents the LabVIEW data flow language and the in-placeness strategy used in its compiler. Section 3 states the in-placeness problem as a constrained optimization problem on a program graph. Section 4 describes our algorithm and analyzes its complexity. Section 5 presents the experimental results comparing our algorithm to the current LabVIEW strategy and program execution without any in-placeness optimizations. Section 6 describes the related work in register allocation and copy elimination in functional languages. Section 7 concludes the paper and suggests directions for future work.

2   The LabVIEW Language

LabVIEW is a graphical data flow programming language from National Instruments Corporation (NI), widely used in industry for implementation of control and measurement systems and embedded applications [3]. In this section we will briefly describe the semantics of LabVIEW, give an example of an in-placeness optimization, and the NI heuristic for determining in-placeness.

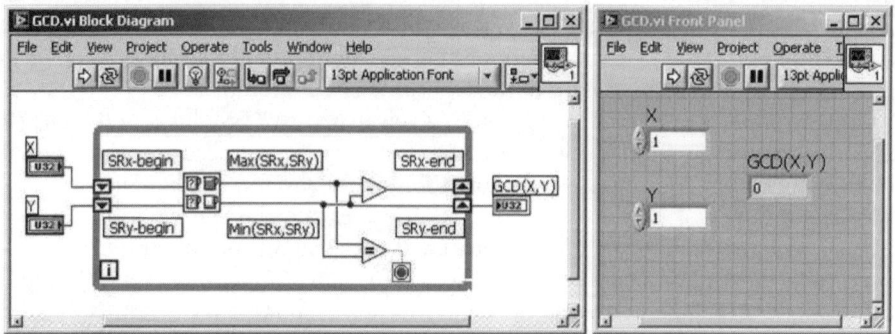

Fig. 1. A LabVIEW program for computing the greatest common divisor

2.1   Overview

A source program written in LabVIEW is referred to as a virtual instrument (VI). A VI consists of a front panel (graphical user interface) and a block diagram (a graphical data flow diagram) where icons and structures are used instead of textual instructions and wires are used instead of variables. Figure 1 shows a simple VI that computes the greatest common divisor (GCD) of the integer values provided to the controls (X and Y) on the front panel (on the right) or from a call to this VI from another VI, as part of a call chain.

When the VI is executed it copies the values into the two shift registers (labeled SRx-begin and SRy-begin) on the while loop (the box structure). On each iteration of the while loop the value of SRx-begin and SRy-begin are copied into the Min/Max node. It returns the maximum (minimum) value on the top (bottom) wire. The minimum value is copied back into shift register SRy-end, on the right hand side of the loop, and the difference between the minimum and maximum value is copied into shift register SRx-end. If the minimum and maximum values are different then the loop will execute another iteration; otherwise the value of SRy-end is copied to the front panel (or to the calling environment, if used as sub-VI) as the GCD of the provided values. Note that the program itself does not specify the order of the subtraction and the comparison nodes; in principle they can be executed in any order, including simultaneously.

The LabVIEW compiler uses a technique called "clumping", where a selected set of data-flow dependent nodes are combined into a single schedulable unit (a clump). This allows the run-time system to schedule VIs at the clump level, instead of at the individual node level. The nodes inside a clump are sorted topologically according to their data flow dependencies, resulting in a total (sequential) execution order within a clump. When defining the topological sort of a clump, the compiler applies a weight to each node that is proportional to the amount of data that the node may copy, so that non-copying nodes get scheduled ahead of copying nodes when they have no data flow dependency.

While the example VI above was explained in terms of copying values, it turns out that this VI can reuse the memory locations reserved for SRx-begin and SRy-begin for all intermediate integer results on the wires inside the while loop. This is achieved by statically scheduling the comparison node before the subtraction node, since the comparison node cannot make its outputs in-place to its inputs due to a type (size) mismatch. By reusing the memory locations reserved for SRx-begin and SRy-begin the VI will use less memory and also execute faster since it executes fewer copy instructions. These savings are more dramatic when dealing with complex data structures such as arrays, where the computational node may only change the values of a subset of the array.

2.2   The NI In-Placeness Heuristic

The in-place strategy currently used by LabVIEW is based on local and static decisions; binary operators, like the subtraction node in the GCD example, will make its output in-place to its top input if their types match. In the GCD example, this happened to be the best choice, but in general this approach is not optimal. The LabVIEW compiler is also hand-tuned for cases where this heuristic does not perform well. This ad-hoc implementation is difficult to maintain and requires expert knowledge to program applications and take full advantage of in-placeness opportunities available from the compiler. A more systematic approach to in-place computation is the main contribution of this paper.

3   Problem Description

First, we will formally encode in-placeness selection in LabVIEW as a constrained optimization problem on a program graph. We begin with a representation of the program as a directed acyclic graph (DAG). The input graph represents a set of data-flow dependent nodes that are part of a single schedulable unit (clump). The objective is to compute a schedule of the nodes of the clump in a single thread that maximizes the benefit from in-place computation.

3.1   Program Graph

We represent a LabVIEW program as a collection of two kinds of vertices. Let V be the set of computational nodes in the program and W be the collection of wires or memory locations. Each wire is the output of a single computational node but may be an input to an unbounded number of computational nodes. Thus we will assume that there are two sets of edges: E_V and E_W. $E_V \subseteq V \times W$ is the set of edges that connect a computational node to the wires that are produced as outputs from it. $E_W \subseteq W \times V$ is the set of edges that connect a wire to the computational nodes that use it as input. Note that the number of edges out of computational nodes is the same as the number of wires in total, since each wire is the output of a single computational node (i.e. $\|W\| = \|E_V\|$). As a notational convention, we will use the set names of the vertices and edges to represent both the set itself and the number of elements in the set, whenever the context is clear. Thus $O(E_W V)$ means the same as $O(\|E_W\| \, \|V\|)$.

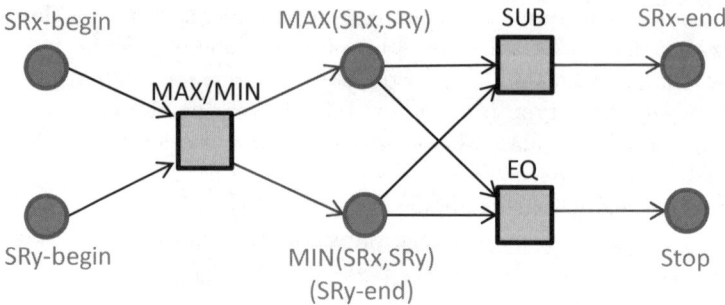

Fig. 2. Program graph for the LabVIEW program from Figure 1

Figure 2 shows the program graph for the LabVIEW program from Figure 1 for computing the GCD of two integers. The set V of computational nodes consists of the MAX/MIN, SUB, and EQ vertices (denoted by square vertices in Figure 2). The remaining vertices (denoted by circles) comprise the set W of wires or memory locations. Note that the wires $MIN(SRx, SRy)$ and $SRy-end$ correspond to the same memory location in the LabVIEW program in Figure 1, hence they are aggregated into one vertex in Figure 2. The edges preserve the data dependencies between the computational nodes in the LabVIEW program.

3.2   In-Placeness Opportunities

The algorithm begins by constructing a set of *in-placeness opportunities* T, where

$$T \subseteq \{(w_1, v, w_2) \in W \times V \times W \mid (w_1, v) \in E_W, (v, w_2) \in E_V\}.$$

In other words, each in-placeness opportunity is a triple $t = (w_1, v, w_2)$ where wire w_1 is the input to computational node v that could be overwritten in place by the contents of output wire w_2.

Since this overwriting is by definition destructive, choosing this triple for in-placing requires that all other consumers of w_1 be scheduled before it. Thus if there is a path in the original graph from v to another computational node v' that also consumes wire w_1, the triple t cannot be in-placed.

For each triple $t \in T$ that represents an in-placeness opportunity, there will be a *benefit* representing the value of in-placing t. The benefit measures the advantage gained by avoiding a memory copy and performing the computation in-place. We denote this as $B(t)$. For example, if a computational node v updates one element of an input array $A1$ to produce the array $A2$ then the benefit $B(t)$ of in-placing the triple $t = (A1, v, A2)$ is $size(A1) - 1$.

3.3   Optimization Objective and Constraints

The objective is to select in-placeness opportunities from the set T to maximize the total benefit, while adhering to the following constraints: (a) any wire $w \in W$

is an input to (similarly, output of) at most one selected in-placeness opportunity, and (b) if $(w_1, v, w_2) \in T$ is selected for in-placeness, then all other consumers of w_1 must be scheduled before v.

The inputs to the optimization problem are a LabVIEW program $G = (V, W, E_V, E_W)$, a set of in-placeness opportunities T, and a benefit function B. Let function $x : T \rightarrow \{0, 1\}$ denote whether $t \in T$ is selected for in-placeness. Also, let function $S : V \rightarrow \mathcal{Z}$ denote the position of $v \in V$ in a schedule of the program graph G. A valid solution to the optimization problem is characterized by functions x and S that satisfy the following four constraints:

$$(a) \ \forall t = (w_1, v, w_2), t' = (w'_1, v', w'_2) \in T, t \neq t', w_1 = w'_1,$$
$$x(t) = 1 \ \Rightarrow \ x(t') = 0 \text{ (unique input in-placeness)}$$
$$(b) \ \forall t = (w_1, v, w_2), t' = (w'_1, v', w'_2) \in T, t \neq t', w_2 = w'_2,$$
$$x(t) = 1 \ \Rightarrow \ x(t') = 0 \text{ (unique output in-placeness)}$$
$$(c) \ \forall (v_1, w_1) \in E_V, \forall (w_2, v_2) \in E_W,$$
$$w_1 = w_2 \ \Rightarrow \ S(v_2) > S(v_1) \text{ (program dependencies)}$$
$$(d) \ \forall t = (w_1, v, w_2) \in T, \forall (w_1, v') \in E_W, v' \neq v,$$
$$x(t) = 1 \ \Rightarrow \ S(v) > S(v') \text{ (ordering due to in-placeness)} .$$

Constraint (a) specifies that if $t = (w_1, v, w_2) \in T$ is selected for in-placeness, then the opportunities $t' \in T$ which have w_1 as input are not selected. Constraint (b) imposes a similar condition on the output wire of an in-placeness opportunity. Constraint (c) enforces the dependencies between computational nodes from the program graph in the resulting schedule. Finally, constraint (d) connects in-placeness selections to new scheduling constraints, which are not implied by the dependencies in the original program graph. In particular, if $t = (w_1, v, w_2) \in T$ is selected for in-placeness, the constraint ensures that the computational node v is scheduled only after all other computational nodes $v' \neq v$ which consume w_1 have been scheduled. The optimization objective is to compute valid solutions to x and S, such that the total benefit $\Sigma_{t \in T} B(t) x(t)$ is maximized.

4   Greedy In-Place Algorithm

The main contribution of this paper is an efficient heuristic algorithm for choosing pairs of inputs and outputs to compute in-place. The greedy algorithm selects the triple with maximum benefit for in-placing, tests whether the in-placing is legal, and marks it as in-placed. When a particular triple is in-placed, it creates new scheduling constraints that can make other in-place choices illegal.

We model these effects by creating a *scheduling graph* $G_S = (V, E)$ in which the vertex set V is the set of computational nodes as before and each $(x, y) \in E$ indicates that computational node x must be scheduled *before* computational node y. The initial version of the scheduling graph is a straightforward translation of the computed program graph. The scheduling graph is a Direct Acyclic Graph (DAG), since legal LabVIEW program cannot have cycles, and every step of our algorithm ensures that there are no cycles introduced in it.

In addition, to make the legality testing fast, we will compute a side data structure *Aft*, which represents the transitive closure of the scheduling graph at any point in the program. That is, $y \in Aft(x)$ if and only if y must be scheduled after x in the current scheduling graph.

The steps of the greedy in-placeness algorithm are:

– Compute a priority queue T of in-place opportunities.
– Compute the initial scheduling graph G_S and the initial *Aft* relationship from the program graph (V, W, E_V, E_W).
– While T is non-empty, iteratively remove the highest benefit triple t. If it is legal to in-place, mark the triple as in-placed and update both G_S and *Aft* to reflect the new scheduling constraints introduced by in-placing the triple.

4.1   Constructing the Opportunities Heap

While the number of in-placeness opportunities may be large (a loose upper bound is $E_V E_W = W E_W$), some pruning will reduce it. For example, it is not likely that computing an array in place with a much smaller array or a scalar will be useful. We can reorganize a pruned set of opportunities T into a heap in $O(T log T)$ time. Since the total number of triples that are *chosen* for in-placing will be far smaller than the number that are considered, it is very important that we be able to rapidly test for legality of in-placing a particular triple, and much of the machinery in this algorithm is designed to facilitate such a fast test.

4.2   Constructing the Initial Graph

The algorithm *InitGraph* in Figure 3 constructs the initial scheduling graph G_S along with the side data structure *Aft*, which is a transitive closure of the initial scheduling graph. The upper bound on the time spent in this initialization is fairly straightforward: L1 is entered $O(V)$ times and the body of L2 is executed $O(E_W)$ times (the header of L2 and the enclosing loop count as a single loop.) So the entire time spent in loop L1 is $O(E_W + V)$. The loop at L3, which implements a transitive closure, is entered V times, while the loop at L4 is executed once for each edge in E. Since the loop body contains a set operation taking at most $O(V)$ time, the time taken by the entire loop is $O(EV)$.

4.3   Selecting In-Placeness Opportunities

Once we have the priority queue T of triplets, organized by benefit B, we can iteratively select an in-placeness opportunity and test it for legality. A triple $t = (w_1, v, w_2)$ is legal to in-place if *neither* of the following conditions hold:

– There exists some $x \in suc[w_1] - \{v\}$ such that $x \in Aft[v]$. This would violate the requirement that v be scheduled after all other sinks of w_1.
– $w_1 \in I[v]$ or $w_2 \in I[v]$, where a wire is in $I[v]$ if it is either the input or output of a triple that has *already* been in-placed.

```
procedure InitGraph(V, E_V, E_W . E,
           suc, pred, Aft);
   for each v ∈ V do begin
      Aft[v] := ∅;
      count[v] := 0; pred[y] := suc[x] := ∅;
   end
   for each wire w ∈ W do
      for each v ∈ suc[w] do count[v]++;
   worklist := ∅; E := ∅;
   for each v ∈ V do
      if count[v] = 0 then worklist ∪ ={v};
L1: while worklist ≠ ∅ do begin
      remove element x from front of worklist;
      for each output wire w from x do begin
L2:      for each y ∈ suc[w] do begin
            if (x, y) ∉ E then begin
               E := E ∪ {(x, y)};
               pred[y] ∪ ={x}; suc[x] ∪ = {y};
            end
            count[y] − −;
            if count[y] = 0 then worklist ∪ = {y};
         end
      end
   end
   // Next compute the initial Aft
   // relationship, backing up through G_S
   for each v ∈ V do s_c[v] := 0;
   for each (x, y) ∈ E do s_c[x]++;
   for each v ∈ V do
      if s_c [v] = 0 then worklist ∪ = {v};
L3: while worklist ≠ ∅ do begin
      remove element y from front of worklist;
L4:   for each x ∈ pred[y] do begin
         Aft[x] ∪ =Aft[y]; s_c[x] := s_c[y] − 1;
         if s_c[x] = 0 then worklist ∪ ={x};
      end
   end
end InitGraph
```

```
procedure GreedyInplace(V, E_V, E_W . E,
           suc, pred, Aft);
   for each v ∈ V do I(v) := ∅;
   wire_used := ∅;
   while T ≠ ∅ do begin
      remove highest-benefit element t = (w_1, v, w_2)
         from the top of the heap, and reheap
      // Test for legality
      legal := true;
      if w_1 ∈ I[v] or w_2 ∈ I[v] then legal := false;
      if w_1 ∈ wire_used then legal := false;
      if legal then begin
         other_inputs := suc[w_1] − {v};
         while legal and other_inputs ≠ ∅ do begin
            remove an element x from other_inputs;
            if x ∈ Aft[v] then legal := false;
         end
      end
      if legal then begin
         mark t = (w_1, v, w_2) as in-placed;
         I[v] := I[v] ∪ {w_1} ∪ {w_2};
         wire_used = wire_used ∪{w_1};
         UpdateGraph(v, w_1, V, E, suc, pred, Aft);
      end
   end
end
```

```
procedure UpdateGraph(v, w_1, V, E, suc, pred, Aft);
// v: vertex where in-placing happens, w_1: input, G_S = (V, E): graph being updated
// Actual updates occur to E, suc, pred, The side data structure Aft is also updated,
// newAft[x] = the set of vertices added to the Aft set of x by this in-placing
// The set processed is used to ensure that a vertex goes on worklist at most once
   worklist := ∅; processed := ∅
L1: for each y ∈ suc[w_1] − {v} do begin
S1:   if (y, v) ∉ E then begin
         E ∪ = (y, v); suc[y] ∪ = {v}; pred[v] ∪ = {x}; newAft[y] := Aft[v] − Aft[y]; Aft[y] ∪ = Aft[v];
S2:      if newAft[y] ≠ ∅ then {worklist ∪ = {y}; processed ∪ = {y}; }
      end
   end
   // Update the Aft sets by backing up through the graph
L2: while worklist ≠ ∅ do begin
      remove an element y from the front of worklist;
L3:   for each x ∈ pred[y] − processed do begin
L4:      for each z ∈ newAft[y] do begin
S3:         if z ∉ Aft[x] then {Aft[x] ∪ = {z}; newAft[x] ∪ = {z}; }
S4:         newAft[x] ≠ ∅ then {worklist ∪ = {x}; processed ∪ = {x}; }
         end
      end
   end
end UpdateGraph;
```

Fig. 3. Algorithms

If in-placing the triple is legal, we introduce new scheduling constraints and update the side data structures. The pseuco code for this part is given in procedure *GreedyInplace* in Figure 3.

The execution time of this procedure, not counting the time spent in *InitGraph* and *UpdateGraph*, is $O(T log T + E_W V)$. The heap operations take $O(T log T)$. To avoid traversing the successors of an input wire w_1 every time a triple with that wire as an input is processed, we use the side data structure *wire_used*, containing all input wires that have already been in-placed (once a wire has been in-placed at some vertex, it cannot be in-placed at any other vertex, since that would create a scheduling cycle). Since we interrogate *wire_used* first, we traverse the successors of a wire at most once for every vertex to which it is an input that might be in-placed. Overall the total time spent traversing the successors of an input wire is $O(E_W V)$. Observe that if there is no pruning of the set of triples T, then $T = O(E_W V)$ so the entire process, aside from the graph updating, takes $O(T log T)$ time. However, assuming that significant pruning is done, it is useful to separate the two terms to yield $O(T log T + E_W V)$.

4.4   Updating the Scheduling Graph

We now turn to the process for updating the scheduling graph after in-placing $t = (w_1, v, w_2)$, perhaps the most complex part of the algorithm. The goal is to produce a time bound of $O(EV + V^2)$ time, where E is the number of edges in the scheduling graph G_S. Since $E \leq E_W$, this will give us the desired bound for the running time of the algorithm.

The procedure begins by inserting new edges between all the other computational nodes to which the input wire w_1 is also an input and updating the predecessor and successor lists. Then, the algorithm must update the *Aft* data structure. We add a new vertex to $Aft[v]$ only once for each v. This requires backing up through the predecessors *pred* of all the vertices with new edges (other inputs of w_1) while maintaining a new data structure called *newAft*, which gets reduced whenever there already exists a path to some element in *Aft* for the predecessor. The algorithm *UpdateGraph* in Figure 3 describes this process.

Since each wire w_1 is input to an in-placed triple only once, the body of loop L1 is executed only E_W times. Furthermore, since the conditional at S1 eliminates duplicate edges, the body of the conditional is executed at most E times over the entire program.

Even though E is smaller than E_W initially, it grows during the execution. However, we can still establish a bound on the size of E in terms of E_W after the algorithm is done, since at each in-placing step, the input wire w_1 can no longer be in-placed at any of its other inputs. So the total number of in-placings is bounded by the number of wires W. At each such in-placing we put edges into E for each vertex to which the wire w_1 is an input except the in-placed vertex, which is at most $E_W - W$ edges. The total number of edges in E after all in-placing steps is no more than $2E_W - W = O(E_W)$.

In loop L1, the most expensive operations are the set unions and differences, each taking $O(V)$ time, so the entire cost of loop L1 is $O(E_W + EV) = O(E_W V)$. Note that we limit, in statements S2 and S4, the number of times a vertex goes on the worklist to those times when it will actually add a vertex to its *Aft* set, which is not more than V times.

Now consider loop L2. Since a vertex y can only be added to the worklist at most V times, the body of L2 is executed an aggregate of V^2 times. However, if we count the number of times the body of loop L3 is executed, we want to charge the cost, including the cost of the loop iterator, to the edge (x, y). Given that each y can be on the worklist only V times, this means that the total number of times that we can process each edge is V, so the total number of executions of the body of L3 is EV. Even though the header of loop L4 is executed EV times, we can charge each execution of the body to a new element of the *Aft* set for y, which is only once per vertex. The total number of executions of the body of L4 is $O(V^2)$. Since the body of the *if* statement S3 takes constant time, the aggregate time over the entire algorithm for L4 is $O(V^2)$. The aggregate time for loop L2 is therefore $O(EV + V^2)$. Since $E = O(E_W)$, we have established that the running time for the entire algorithm is bounded by $O(T \log T + E_W V + V^2)$.

Note that the algorithm can be safely stopped at any time, since no node is ever *unmarked* for in-place computation. Running the algorithm to completion only affects the quality of the result, not the correctness.

4.5   Loops and Shift Registers

In LabVIEW, *shift registers* are used to represent the loop-carried dependences; they are equivalent to induction variables in an imperative language. Each shift register has a source and a sink and at the end of each iteration of a loop the value of the sink of the shift register is copied into the source of the same shift register. In the LabVIEW example in figure 1 there are two shift registers, labelled SRx and SRy. They are used to carry the state of the GCD computation from one iteration of the while loop to the next iteration.

The in-placeness algorithm as we have described it in this section so far only works on straight-line code. Since loops and shift registers (especially shift registers that transfer aggregate data structures) can have an enormous impact on performance, we treat loops and shift registers separately.

Our strategy is to make the in-placeness decisions for loops in three steps; First, all copies on the back edges of a loop are eliminated by in-placing the source of the shift register with its sink. Second, we apply the greedy in-placeness algorithm presented earlier in this section to the body of the loop. Finally, we replace the loop by dummy operations that model the input and output tunnels connecting the loop to the enclosing VI. Then we run our algorithm on the enclosing VI, using the dummy operations to decide on the in-placeness of the inputs and outputs of a loop. For the GCD example in figure 1 the input pairs is Y and SRy-begin and the output pair is SRy-end and GCD(X,Y). The input/output pairs of the dummy are added to the opportunities heap of the enclosing VI as in-placeness opportunities.

In-placing all the shift registers on the back edges of the loop may force some explicit copies to be inserted inside of the body of the loop. If there is a direct link from one shift register's source to a different shift register's sink, for example, then an explicit copy will have to be inserted along that edge. This does not affect the overall goal of the algorithm, as a copy involving that data structure would have to be performed anyway, either on the back edge or on some forward edge throughout the body of the loop.

5   Experimental Results

In our experimental study, we evaluated our heuristic for in-placeness optimization on two sets of benchmarks. The first set of benchmarks consisted on random program graphs in the form presented in Section 3. The second set of benchmarks consisted of 7 real-world LabVIEW applications. The platform we used for running these experiments was Intel (R), Pentium (R) 4 CPU 2.80 GHz. 2.79 GHz, 504 MB of RAM, running Microsoft window XP.

5.1   Random Graph Benchmarks

Our first set of benchmarks were random program graphs with a varying number of computational nodes. The largest instance in this set contained 75 computational nodes (which corresponds to the set V in the program graph from Section 3). This is a practical limit for what the optimal constraint-based solvers can handle in a reasonable amount of time. Figure 4 compares the percentage difference from the optimal in-placeness result of our heuristic and the NI LabVIEW heuristic on the random graph instances. The optimum results were computed using the Spear constraint solver that internally employs an exact branch-and-bound method to test satisfiability of problem constraints [4].

Figure 4 indicates that our greedy heuristic is consistently close to the optimal result across a varying number of vertices in the program graph. On average, our

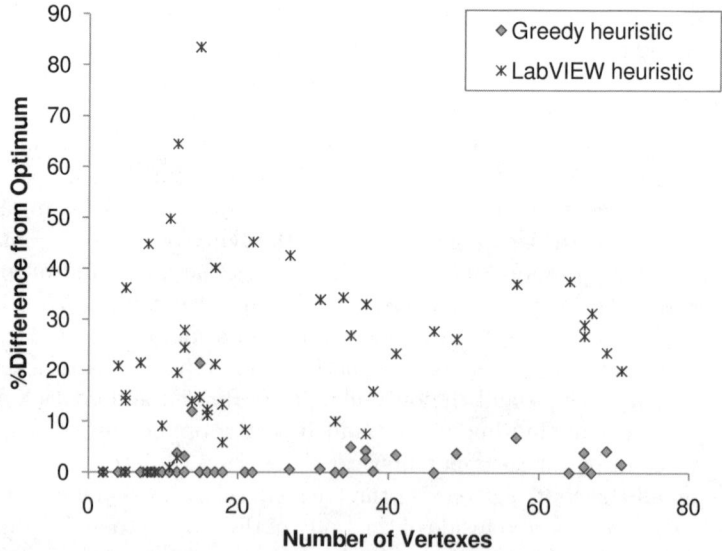

Fig. 4. Graph comparing the optimality gap of the LabVIEW heuristic and our heuristic for in-placeness on random program graphs. Lower is better.

heuristic is within 2% of the optimum for these instances, while the LabVIEW heuristic is over 25% below the optimum. The times taken to complete execution of the current LabVIEW heuristics and our algorithm are both on the order of milliseconds. In contrast, the exact solver method takes up to 3 minutes on some problem instances. Thus, our heuristic achieves a much higher quality of results while matching the efficiency of the NI LabVIEW heuristic for in-placeness.

5.2   LabVIEW Application Benchmarks

Tables 1 and 2 summarize the performance of programs compiled using our heuristic and the NI LabVIEW heuristic on several benchmarks. In four of the benchmarks our algorithm made the same in-placeness decisions as the Lab-VIEW compiler. The slight differences in the running times are due to different default schedules produced by the two algorithms. In the other programs, the code generated by our algorithm significantly outperforms the code generated by the current LabVIEW compiler.

The results presented in Tables 1 and 2 illustrate the importance of having a systematic in-place computation strategy in a LabVIEW implementation. For all the above programs, the difference in running times between no in-place

Table 1. Running times for a set of LabVIEW benchmarks

Sample VI	No In-placeness	NI In-placeness	Greedy In-placeness
1 Standard Div	110 ms	32 ms	32 ms
2 Original Unpack	> 8 hours	745 ms	733 ms
3 Simple Unpack	> 8 hours	695 ms	605 ms
4 Split Unpack	> 8 hours	353 ms	358 ms
5 Sine Generator	2,064,041 ms	94 ms	62 ms
6.a Updating Cluster	> 8 hours	132,796 ms	10 ms
6.b Tuned Updating Cluster	> 8 hours	10 ms	10 ms
7.a Mandelbrot	10,478,956 ms	44,425 ms	6,888 ms
7.b Rewired Mandelbrot	11,937,131 ms	42,958 ms	6,970 ms

Table 2. Speedup factors for the set of LabVIEW benchmarks from Table 1

Sample VI	NI In-placeness Vs. No In-placeness	Greedy In-placeness Vs. No In-placeness	Greedy In-placeness Vs. NI In-placeness
1 Standard Div	3	3	1.0
2 Original Unpack	$> 40,000$	$> 40,000$	1.016
3 Simple Unpack	$> 40,000$	$> 50,000$	1.149
4 Split Unpack	$> 80,000$	$> 80,000$	0.99
5 Sine Generator	21,958	33,291	1.516
6.a Updating Cluster	> 200	$> 300,000$	13,280
6.b Tuned Updating Cluster	$> 300,000$	$> 300,000$	1.0
7.a Mandelbrot	236	1,521	6.45
7.b Rewired Mandelbrot	278	1,713	6.16

computation and some in-place computation is enormous. Updating Cluster, for example, takes 10 milliseconds to compute using our in-place algorithm but it takes more than 8 hours (we terminate our experiments after 8 hours for practical reasons) with no in-place computation.

In summary, we have shown on a large collection of random graphs that our algorithm consistently finds a better solution, and on a collection of real-world LabVIEW programs it at least matches, and in several cases significantly outperforms the current LabVIEW compiler.

6   Related Work

Hudak and Bloss address the problem of updating aggregates in-place to avoid unnecessary copies in functional languages [5]. If the last use of an aggregate is a write, they perform the write in place. Our algorithm checks the legality of allowing a use to be done in-place before adding constraints, and uses a cost model to to in-place the uses that will be most beneficial to performance. Their algorithm relies on run-time reference counting to find the inplaceness opportunities, while we make all the decisions statically. In [6], Goyal and Paige gave a solution that combines dynamic reference counting and lazy copying. Their algorithm uses static analysis to enhance and improve the use of reference counting. They implement the optimization for the programming language SETL.

For fixed evaluation order, Bloss developed an algorithm that statically computes evaluation paths in non-strict functional programs [7], while Kirkham and Li developed a copy avoidance algorithm to improve the performance of the programming language *UFO* [8] and Gudjónsson and Winsborough developed an algorithm that introduces update-in-place operations to the logic programming language Prolog to allow it to update recursive data structures as in an imperative programming language [9]. These heuristics, as in the first step of Hudak and Bloss [5], update an aggregate in place if the last use is a write operation.

Sarkar and Cann built an optimized SISAL compiler that includes an update-in-place analysis phase that tackles the aggregate incremental update problem by extending the approach by Hudak and Bloss to additionally consider general iteration, function call boundaries, and nested aggregates [10]. However, as with Hudak and Bloss, they do not evaluate the benefits in choosing which nodes to modify in-place, and cannot make all the decisions during compilation.

Gopinath and Hennessy proposed "Targeting", an algorithm to reduce intermediate copies in divide and conquer problems [11] by properly selecting a storage area for expression evaluatiion. They eliminate copies in a given and fixed computing evaluation sequence. We allow changes to the evaluation sequence in order to find more opportunities for in-place updating. Unlike our heuristic, their algorithm constrains the arrays to have restricted bounds, and is unable to detect values whose lifetime cannot be computed at compile time.

Debray focuses on reusing dead data structures [1]. As in our algorithm, his heuristic chooses between interfering data structures based on a cost model, but does not describe how to derive these costs.

The problem of excessive copying appears in register allocation. The second stage of the Chaitin's [12] algorithm consists of coalescing nodes in the graph to use the same storage (machine register). If there is a copy from R_i to R_j, and R_i and R_j do not otherwise interfere, then R_i and R_j can share storage. Briggs *et al.* add a tradeoff between coalescing and spilling register values to memory [13]. In another related algorithm, Briggs *et al.* present an algorithm for inserting copies to replace ϕ-functions when translating SSA form to sequential code [14], which involves a similar problem with cycles of copies. lić *et al.* present an algorithm that performs coalescing without building an interference graph, but by using liveness and dominance information to model interference [15].

While copy avoidance problems are closely related to the one we are addressing in this paper, none of the results described above focus on a unique characteristic of the programs with aggregate data structures: it is much more profitable to perform an in-place computation on a data structure when such a computation only changes a small part of the data.

7   Conclusions and Future Work

Copy avoidance through in-place computation is extremely important for languages with copy semantics such as LabVIEW. The performance of LabVIEW programs with a methodical in-place computation strategy can improve by several orders of magnitude over programs with naïve implementations that allocate a new memory location for the result of every computation. This is especially true for programs with loops and aggregate (array and structure) data.

In this paper, we present a systematic greedy algorithm for deciding which computations should be performed in-place for LabVIEW programs. We show that our algorithm runs in $O(T log T + E_W V + V^2)$ time, where T is the number of in-placeness opportunities, E_W is the aggregate number of edges and V is the number of computational nodes in a program graph.

Our heuristic computes near-optimum (within 2% on average) solutions for a large collection of randomly generated graphs, compared to the current LabVIEW compiler heuristic which is more than 25% below the optimum. Our algorithm achieves this while still running in time competitive to the current LabVIEW compiler (order of milliseconds for random graphs of up to 75 nodes). It is much faster than optimal constraint-based solver strategies, which are impractical even for modestly large programs.

On a collection of LabVIEW programs, our algorithm produces in-placeness decisions that generate code that is at least competitive, and in several cases much faster than the code generated by the current LabVIEW compiler. This efficient and effective in-place computation strategy should prove itself a valuable addition to any implementation of languages with copy semantics.

In the future, we will investigate an adaptation of our algorithm to an interprocedural, modular compiler using the Telescoping Languages approach [16], which includes a size-inference algorithm that infers sizes of procedure variables in terms of the sizes of input arguments. This information will be important for determining benefits for in-placeness when the whole program is not available. This approach will summarize the in-placeness analysis results for each program and create different versions of programs based on different in-placeness contexts. Second, we will experiment with algorithms for splitting of aggregate data structures and in-place computation for parts of an aggregate data structure. Finally, we will explore heuristics for estimating the trade-off between more in-place computation and more parallelism available (especially for multicore platforms) that will attempt to balance the in-place computation, parallelism and scheduling to achieve faster running times.

Acknowledgments

This work was supported in part by National Instruments and by NSF grant CCF-0444465. We would like to thank Jeff Kodosky, Brent Schwan and Duncan Hudson for their comments and support during this project. We would also like to thank Keith Cooper and Tim Harvey for their insights and discussions concerning relevant register allocation topics, and Vivek Sarkar for his assistance in understanding copy elimination in SISAL and other data-flow languages.

References

1. Debray, S.K.: On copy avoidance in single assignment languages. In: International Conference on Logic Programming, pp. 393–407 (1993)
2. Abu-Mahmeed, S., McCosh, C., Budimlić, Z., Kennedy, K., Ravindran, K., Hogan, K., Austin, P., Rogers, S., Kornerup, J.: Scheduling tasks to maximize usage of aggregate variables in place. Technical report, Rice University, TR09-01 (2009)
3. National Instruments Corporation: LabVIEW™ User Manual (August 2007)
4. Babic, D., Hutter, F.: SPEAR theorem prover. In: Marques-Silva, J., Sakallah, K.A. (eds.) SAT 2007. LNCS, vol. 4501. Springer, Heidelberg (2007)
5. Hudak, P., Bloss, A.: The aggregate update problem in functional programming systems. In: POPL 1985: Proceedings of the 12th ACM SIGACT-SIGPLAN symposium on Principles of programming languages (1984)
6. Goyal, D., Paige, R.: A new solution to the hidden copy problem. In: Levi, G. (ed.) SAS 1998. LNCS, vol. 1503, pp. 327–348. Springer, Heidelberg (1998)
7. Bloss, A.: Update analysis and the efficient implementation of functional aggregates. In: FPCA 1989: Proceedings of the Fourth International Conference on Functional Programming Languages and Computer Architecture (1989)
8. Li, Z., Kirkham, C.: Efficient implementation of aggregates in united functions and objects. In: ACM-SE 33: Proceedings of the 33rd Annual Southeast Regional Conference (1995)
9. Gudjónsson, G., Winsborough, W.H.: Compile-time memory reuse in logic programming languages through update in place. ACM Trans. Program. Lang. Syst. (1999)
10. Sarkar, V., Cann, D.: Posc–a partitioning and optimizing sisal compiler. In: ICS 1990: Proceedings of the 4th international conference on Supercomputing, pp. 148–164. ACM Press, New York (1990)

11. Gopinath, K., Hennessy, J.L.: Copy elimination in functional languages. Technical report, Computer Systems Laboratory, CSL-TR-88-370. Stanford University, Stanford (1989)
12. Chaitin, G.J., Auslander, M.A., Chandra, A.K., Cocke, J., Hopkins, M.E., Markstein, P.W.: Register allocation via coloring. Computer Languages 6, 47–57 (1981)
13. Briggs, P., Cooper, K.D., Torczon, L.: Rematerialization. ACM SIGPLAN 1992 Conference on Programming Language Design and Implementation, 311–321, June 17-19 (1992)
14. Briggs, P., Cooper, K.D., Harvey, T.J., Taylor Simpson, L.: Practical improvements to the construction and destruction of static single assignment form. Software Practice and Experience (July 1998)
15. Budimlic, Z., Cooper, K.D., Harvey, T.J., Kennedy, K., Oberg, T.S., Reeves, S.W.: Fast copy coalescing and live-range identification. In: PLDI 2002: Proceedings of the ACM SIGPLAN 2002 Conference on Programming language design and implementation (2002)
16. Kennedy, K., Broom, B., Chauhan, A., Fowler, R., Garvin, J., Koelbel, C., McCosh, C., Mellor-Crummey, J.: Telescoping languages: a system for automatic generation of domain languages. Proceedings of the IEEE 93(2), 387–408 (2005)

Dynamic Look Ahead Compilation: A Technique to Hide JIT Compilation Latencies in Multicore Environment*

Simone Campanoni**, Martino Sykora, Giovanni Agosta, and Stefano Crespi Reghizzi

Politecnico di Milano, Milano 20133, Italy
{campanoni,sykora,agosta,crespi}@elet.polimi.it
http://compilergroup.elet.polimi.it

Abstract. Object-code virtualization, commonly used to achieve software portability, relies on a virtual execution environment, typically comprising an interpreter used for initial execution of methods, and a JIT for native code generation. The availability of multiple processors on current architectures makes it attractive to perform dynamic compilation in parallel with application execution. The major issue is to decide at runtime which methods to compile ahead of execution, and how much time to invest in their optimization. This research introduces an abstract model, termed Dynamic Look Ahead (DLA) compilation, which represents the available information on method calls and computational weight as a weighted graph. The graph dynamically evolves as computation proceeds. The model is then instantiated by specifying criteria for adaptively choosing the method compilation order. The DLA approach has been applied within our dynamic compiler for .NET. Experimental results are reported and analyzed, for both synthetic programs and benchmarks. The main finding is that a careful choice of method-selection criteria, based on light-weight program analysis and execution tracing, is essential to mask compilation times and to achieve higher overall performances. On multi-processors, the DLA approach is expected to challenge the traditional virtualization environments based on bytecode interpretation and JITing, thus bridging the gap between ahead-of-time and just-in-time translation.

1 Introduction

Portable, byte-code based, Object Oriented languages such as Java, Python and C# have achieved widespread adoption in both industry and academia. Modern Virtual Machines (VM) frequently include a dynamic translation system, the *Just In Time* (JIT) compiler. A JIT compiler translates a byte-code portion (typically a method) to native binary code, when needed. The generated binary code is then executed every time it is required. Dynamically compiled code can achieve large speedups, especially in the long run, since the execution time of a native method is dramatically lower than that of an interpreted one. However, the performance of a JIT-based VM is still lower than that of native code

---

* This work is supported in part by the European Commission under Framework Programme 7, OpenMedia Platform project.

** This author is supported in part by the ST Microelectronics.

O. de Moor and M. Schwartzbach (Eds.): CC 2009, LNCS 5501, pp. 220–235, 2009.

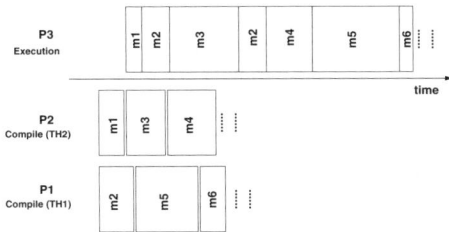

Fig. 1. An ideal case. Each invoked method has already been compiled and optimized.

produced by static byte-code compilation [23], or *Ahead Of Time* (AOT) compilation. The loss of performance is due to compilation overhead – often called *startup time* – and to the poor quality of the generated code, since the startup time minimization prevents the aggressive and costly optimizations usually performed by static compilers.

At the same time, multi-core technology is being employed in most recent high-performance architectures as a way to provide more computational power without relying on the reduction of the clock cycle, which is becoming increasingly difficult due to technology limitations.

Thus, we consider a multiprocessor environment and study how specialized threads of a dynamic compiler can compile bytecode portions in advance, in parallel with the application execution. In a best case scenario, there is no compilation overhead, because compilation fully overlaps with execution and methods are already compiled when they are invoked. Moreover, optimizations are applied to provide high quality code. Our goal is to prove that, given enough hardware resources, it is possible to effectively mask the compilation delays, approximating the ideal case shown in Figure 1, where compilation threads Th1 and Th2 – running on processors P_1 and P_2 – supply the requested native methods to the execution thread in advance. Compilation times depend both on method size and on the optimizations applied. To reach this ideal case, the dynamic compiler should predict the execution trace, and be able to recognize hot-spots. We call such a compiler a *Dynamic Look Ahead Compiler*.

While a processor is executing a method, compilation threads (running on different processors) *look ahead* into the call graph, detecting methods that have good chances to be executed in the next future. Moreover, they guess whether a method is an *hot spot* or not, and apply aggressive optimizations accordingly. Hence, DLA compilation dynamically exploits static code properties (call graph, structure of the method) for execution trace prediction and hot-spot optimization.

The DLA compilation paradigm, conceived for multiprocessor architectures and object-oriented languages, is the main contribution of this paper. In the rest of the paper, we outline the theoretical model in Section 2 and describe DLA compilation in Section 3. Section 4 reports the experimental results. Section 5 provides a survey of prior works, highlighting the distinctive aspects of the DLA compilation. Conclusions are discussed in the last Section.

2   Model

A DLA compiler examines the methods to be compiled with the aim of deciding:

Compilation order. In which order methods should be compiled. The *compilation order* quality is measured by its similarity to the actual execution order of the methods – considering only the first call of each method, since no compilation is required for further invocations.

Optimization level. Which optimizations should be applied in compiling. To this end, a *level of optimization* is assigned to each method.

Different platforms may use different criteria for dispatching and fine-tuning methods compilation. For a program, the basic concept is the *Static Call Graph SCG = (M, I)*, where M is the set of *methods* and I is the set of possible *invocations*. A direct arc $a = (m_i, m_j) \in I$ connects method m_i to m_j if the former may call the latter at run-time. The main method belongs to M and is named the *root*. The set of immediate successors of a method $m \in M$ is $S(m)$.

Initially, the SCG is not known to the DLA compiler, which progressively discovers it. We call this graph the *Dynamically Known Static Call Graph (DKSCG)*. Thus, the DKSCG is the portion of the SCG that is dynamically known: each time a method m is compiled, the DKSCG is updated with the subset of $S(m)$ not yet compiled.

Next we enrich the DKSCG with arcs and node weights, summarizing the relevant properties for deciding compilation order and optimization level. Figure 2 shows a portion of a generic DKSCG, where w and w' are the weights assigned to the arcs and nodes, respectively.

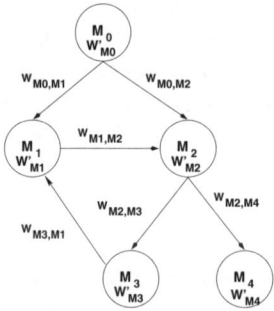

Fig. 2. Dynamically Known Static Call Graph

First consider the weight-less graph. Knowledge of the set of successors of a method gives some hints on the compilation order. It is obvious that, when a method is running, its immediate successors are likely to be executed soon. Following this assumption, the methods can be ordered according to their distance from the root. Let m be a method involved in the compilation process and n be the methods ordered so far; not yet compiled methods in $S(m)$ will be ordered starting from $n + 1$, as their appear in m body.

However such an ordering is rather unsatisfactory, as it neglects the effect of conditional branches – the execution order of the successors of a method depends on the control flow and input data. Adding information on the likelihood of the execution of each method, can improve the ordering quality. To this end, the model is enriched with weights. An arc $a = (m_i, m_j)$ of the DKSCG is characterized by two attributes: the *likelihood of invocation* λ, i.e. the likelihood that a is taken after execution reaches node

m_i; and the *estimated time distance* δ between the execution of the first instructions of m_i and of m_j, if that arc is taken.

The weight of an arc $a = (m_i, m_j)$ is defined as $w_a = f(\frac{1}{\lambda}, \delta)$ where f is a monotonic function of its parameters. Hence, given a method m, the not yet compiled methods in $S(m)$ can be ordered by increasing arc weights.

For a node m_i, let $\gamma(m, m_i)$ be the weighted distance from the executing method m. We here define the so called *Look Ahead Region* (LAR) as $LAR = \{m_i | \gamma(m, m_i) \leq Thr\}$, where Thr is an implementation dependent threshold. LAR should contain those methods having good chance to be executed in the next future. A method is a candidate for compilation if it belongs to the LAR. In this case it is enqueued for compilation, with an order depending on f. The weights on arcs dynamically change their values, as well as LAR. Details about LAR updating are provided in Section 3.

The weights on arcs must be combined with the information on the computational load of methods, providing hints on the most appropriate level of optimization. To achieve this, to each method m is given attribute indicating the computational load, t_{exc}. The weight of the node is a monotonic function of the attributes: $w'_m = f'(t_{exc})$ By convention, the higher w'_m, the higher is the benefit due to an aggressive optimization of m.

Note that the proposed general model may have different implementations, depending on: the definition of functions f and f'; the way the function arguments are computed. In the sequel, we present two model implementations, integrated in our DLA compilation framework [7]. A *naive* one, where λ, the likelihood of invocation, is dropped; δ is the order of appearance of a method into the bytecode and $f(\frac{1}{\lambda}, \delta) = \delta$. A more refined implementation, where static branch prediction techniques [5] are used to estimate the parameters λ, δ and the function f. For both models f' depends on hot-spot detection and is defined as $f'(t_{exc}) = t_{exc}$. Our implementation closely follows [5]. On the set of benchmarks used in Section 4 the branch predictor achieves a missrate of 18% comparable to the 20% declared in [5].

3 Dynamic Look Ahead Compilation

In this section, we focus on the DLA principle, presenting the application scenario and analyzing the main problems: execution trace prediction and hot spot detection. Specific choices concerning the definition of the main components of the model – functions and parameters – are also discussed.

Figure 3 shows the control flow of a DLA system, composed of several threads (shown as ovals) connected by queues and composing a compilation pipeline. First the methods are pushed into a compilation queue and translated from bytecode (BC) to an intermediate representation (IR). Then multiple threads, running onto multiple processors, optimize the IR methods and provide them for a final step of translation toward native code. Native methods, when ready, are installed in memory and invoked when needed. A method can be pushed for compilation in two cases: it is required for the execution but it has never been compiled (dashed arc in figure); it is detected by the DLA system as a method with high chances to be executed soon (bold arcs). The DLA decision is taken in the first stage, where the DKSCG is updated with new weighted nodes and the pipeline is supplied with new methods.

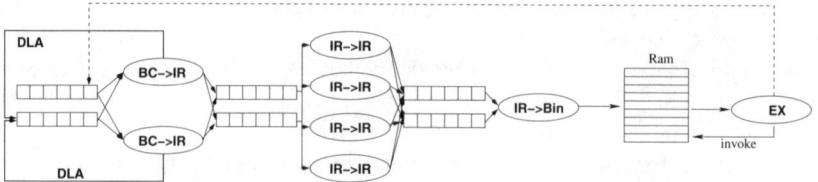

Fig. 3. DLA in a Pipelined Compilation Framework: the framework shown takes as input byte-code (BC) produced from source files, and uses an intermediate representation (*IR*) to perform machine independent optimization. The pipeline is based on a priority queue implemented by pairs of FIFO queues. Priorities of individual methods can change on information discovered at runtime. The execution goes through the trampoline if the called method has not been compiled yet.

Two queues with different priority are shown in Figure 3. The low priority queue contains those methods detected by the DLA engine as the most likely candidates for execution in the near future. The high priority one contains the method that is presently required for execution and the methods potentially invoked by it. Ideally, the high priority queue should always be empty, since all the invoked methods should be provided as native code in advance. However, the prioritization mechanism is useful when – due to wrong prediction or compilation delay – an invoked method has not yet been compiled (thus it has to be enqueued with high priority or moved from low to the high priority queue – *method prioritization*).

3.1   Applicative Scenario and Technique

DLA compilation is effective when the number of available processors is at least equal to the number of threads dedicated to execution, compilation and optimization, to avoid threads switching overhead. In this paper, for the sake of clarity, we focus on single thread applications. Thus, only one processor is dedicated to the execution and the remaining ones are exploited for compilation and optimization.

Let us consider the first invocation of a method in a typical JIT execution. The control flow jumps to a code fragment known as *trampoline*, which yields control to the dynamic compiler. The dynamic compiler, in turn, generates (and possibly optimizes) the native binary code, then replaces the trampoline with the address of the generated binary. In the DLA compilation the dynamic compiler also prepares other methods for parallel compilation. To this end, the compilation routine *looks ahead* into the portion of the SCG seen by the method it is currently processing, i.e. composed of its children methods. They are added to the DKSCG and, if they belong to the LAR, they are pushed into the *compilation queue*, in an order depending on the underlying model. Conceptually, it is equivalent to an assignment of weights to the DKSCG arcs, in accordance with the function presented in Section 2. The queue elements are consumed by one or more compilation and optimization threads, running in parallel with the execution flow and distributed over multiple processors. Each dequeued method is compiled and optimized, making it ready for the execution as soon as possible. During its compilation, the above process is iterated.

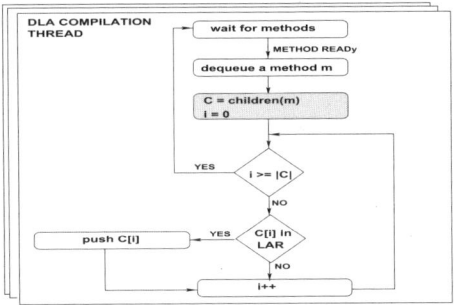

Fig. 4. DLA compilation thread(s), shown as multiple boxes. Each of them wait for methods in the compilation queue. When a method m is ready, it is dequeued and compiled. The set C of its children is then computed, as shown by the third stage (shaded in light grey), where the *look ahead* process is effectively performed. Elements of C belonging to the LAR and not yet compiled are pushed into the compilation queue. The update of the DKSCG is not explicitly shown in figure, as well as the pushing order is not highlighted.

If the DLA compilation is well tuned, the LAR is constantly updated, with the aim of (i) compiling methods in advance; (ii) controlling the pressure on the compilation queue. Figure 4 shows a DLA compilation thread in the large.

Summarizing, the DLA compilation tries to compile in advance (exploiting hardware parallelism) those methods that will be useful in the near future. To make predictions on the execution flow, compilation threads: (i) build and update the DKSCG; (ii) keep information about the Dynamic Call Graph (DCG), the SCG subgraph of the methods effectively executed; (iii) keep information about the execution trace, which is a linearization of the DCG. Both the execution trace and the DCG need a tracing mechanism (e.g. trampolines). In absence of this mechanism we observe a loss of information. (iv) update the LAR, which both limits the pressure on the compilation queue and drives the prediction. Figure 5 shows the relations between these concepts. Since a correct prediction of the methods to compile in advance depends on the ability to trace the execution flow, we devote the remaining part of this Section to it.

3.2 Execution Trace Prediction

The correct prediction of the execution flow is required to keep the Look Ahead Region (LAR) correctly updated. It needs two kinds of information: the DKSCG, built at compile time, and the past execution trace, monitored at runtime.

The execution can be traced via *code instrumentation, asynchronous call stack sampling* [10] or *trampoline instrumentation*. Code instrumentation – e.g. at each method call – introduces an overhead, while asynchronous access to the call stack is required to be thread-safe, and must thus stall the execution.

On the other hand, trampoline instrumentation reduces the cost of tracing, but can lead to a loss of trace information since once a method is translated, its native address replaces the trampoline. In DLA compilation, this effect is amplified by the early compilation, which potentially replaces a large number of trampolines before their execution. This loss of information can be observed in Figure 5, which is highlighted by a

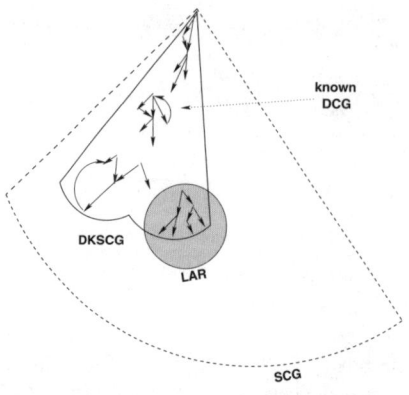

Fig. 5. Information exploited in DLA compilation. The SCG, unknown at run time, is the region bounded by dotted lines, while bold lines mark the DKSCG. This graph contains the DCG which is disconnected since, in the absence of a full execution tracing, this information is partial. The LAR is shaded in light grey.

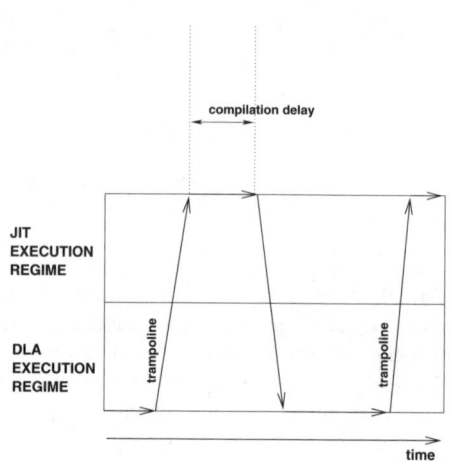

Fig. 6. DLA compilation falls into the worst application scenario (JIT) each time a trampoline is called

disconnected known-DCG. Figure 6 shows the working of the trampolines. The execution of trampoline code means that the system is invoking a method not yet compiled, hence it is not working in an optimum DLA compilation regime due to bad execution trace prediction. Figure 7 shows this case, where bold lines represent methods invocations, and dotted lines represent the DKSCG.

In Figure 8, a good prediction leads to the compilation of several methods, but also to the loss of tracing information, as the removed trampolines cannot be exploited for execution tracing. The bold line encloses the compiled methods, while the LAR is shown in grey. The execution trace is represented by an arrowed line. This execution trace is unknown, as it always passes through native methods, without invoking trampolines. Moreover, since it enters into the LAR boundary, it is correctly predicted. But, due to

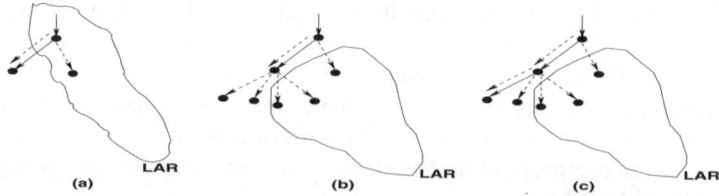

Fig. 7. Incorrect Execution Trace Prediction. (a) A method outside LAR is called through a trampoline. (b) LAR is updated, erroneously discarding two of the four children of the current method. (c) A method outside LAR – thus surely not yet compiled when invoked – is called through a trampoline.

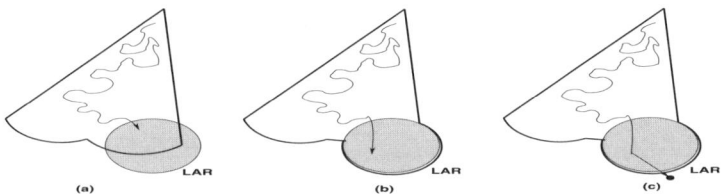

Fig. 8. Correct prediction with loss of tracing information. (a) (Unknown) execution trace stays inside the native methods region. (b) It enters into LAR, but the latter is not updated. (c) Trampoline call.

the loss of information, LAR is not updated (Figure 8.b) and the execution exits the boundary (Figure 8.c), thus a trampoline is invoked.

When a trampoline is taken, the compilation overhead can be very large, since the just invoked method must wait for the compilation of all methods in the compilation queue. A two-queues prioritization mechanism can be used to reduce this delay, as shown in the compilation framework of Figure 3. The invoked method is pushed into the high priority queue. The LAR is updated, and methods in the low priority queue, but not belonging to the new LAR, are dequeued.

Method Enqueueing Order. Each time the LAR is updated, all new methods belonging to the compilation boundary are moved into the compilation queue. The enqueueing order is driven by the prediction model, which takes into account the likelihood of execution of each method in the next future. Static branch prediction techniques can help in building an accurate model [19,9,5].

If enqueueing order differs from the invocation order, the compilation overhead can be dramatic. If the executor invokes a method that is still into the compilation queue, the execution stalls until the method is dequeued and compiled.

In our DLA implementation, we consider two kinds of methods enqueueing order. The first is a simple FIFO ordering. The second exploits static branch prediction techniques [5] to compute the likelihood of each invocation (by setting parameters λ and δ of the model in Section 2). The LAR is updated on using a rough DKSCG distance based criterion in the first case, while in the latter this criterion is coupled with the likelihood of invocation. Section 4 provides an experimental evaluation, showing how a fine tuned model can lead to a better prediction.

3.3 Hot-Spots Detection

The effectiveness of DLA compilation in the long run depends on the ability to generate high quality native code for the application *hot spots*. The DLA compiler estimates whether a method could be a hot spot before compiling it. It computes the node weight w' described by the model of Section 2. Specifically, the hot spot detection affects the parameter t_{exc}, which measures the time complexity of a method. For this purpose, the DLA compiler analyzes the method structure and the DKSCG.

The former provides clues on its run-time behavior, e.g indicators are number of instructions, presence of computationally intensive loops. This information is partial,

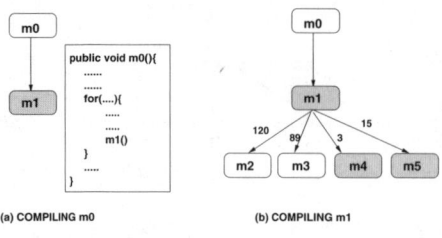

(a) COMPILING m0   (b) COMPILING m1

Fig. 9. Static hot spot detection based both on DKSCG and method structure. (a) While compiling m0, the DLA compiler discovers that it calls m1 into a loop. m1 is added to the DKSCG and marked as hot-spot. (b) While compiling m1, the DLA compiler marks as hot spots also its children that can be invoked through low weighted arcs.

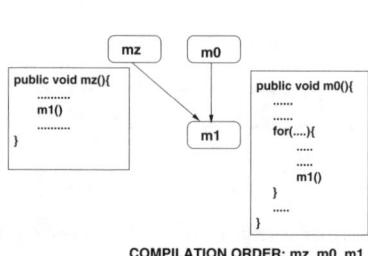

COMPILATION ORDER: mz, m0, m1

Fig. 10. Example of hot spot detection failure

but can be enough for hot-spot detection. More detailed overviews of static method time complexity evaluation can be found in [1,17]. For DKSCG contribution, consider the scenario shown in Figure 9, where the hot-spot marking is propagated through the DKSCG.

This approach, however, is not universally effective. Consider the example in Figure 10, where m1 can be called both by m0 and mz. In the latter case, the call is not within a loop. If mz is compiled before m0, then m1 will not be marked as hot spot. When hot spot detection fails, a recompilation mechanism can be exploited. When a method is recognized as hot-spot it is pushed again into the compilation queue, even though previously compiled. This approach is similar to what described in [14].

4   Experimental Results

To give a first evaluation of typical performance improvements achieved by the DLA compilation we have considered two well known scientific benchsuite (JavaGrande [16] and Scimark [20]) as target. The DLA technique has been implemented into our dynamic compiler, called Intermediate Language Distributed Just In Time (ILDJIT) [7], briefly described by Figure 3. It has three different working modes: AOT, JIT and DLA. The target platform is an 8 processor Xeon at 2G-Hz, with 16GB of RAM and a $4MB$ cache for each pair of processors.

To show the benefits due to DLA compilation w.r.t. the standard JIT compilation, we have considered the ILDJIT JIT working mode as the baseline. We do not compare with other JIT compilers such as Mono or the Microsoft .NET Framework, since the goal of the experimental study is to evaluate the DLA technique rather than comparing different JIT compilers. The results of an experiment using different JIT compilers would be affected primarily by the differences in the quality of the generated code, thus making it more difficult to understand the impact of the DLA technique. However the ILDJIT compiler currently outperforms Mono with full optimization enabled by 3% on the set of benchmarks considered in this work.

Table 1. DLA implementations

Name	Model	Priority queue	Execution tracing
DLA1	M1	Yes	Trampolines
DLA2	M2	Yes	Trampolines
DLA3	M1	Yes	Execution Stack Sampling
DLA4	M2	Yes	Execution Stack Sampling

Table 2. Characterization of the full benchmarks in terms of methods defined, static call points and number of method invocations performed at runtime

Benchmark	Methods defined	Call Points	Method invocations	Benchmark	Methods defined	Call Points	Method invocations
JGFArith	34	46	58	JGFFFT	58	1191	4191
JGFLoop	35	46	59	JGFSparseMatmult	54	1102	25094
JGFCast	34	46	58	JGFRayTracer	67	691	1678
JGFAssign	39	60	79	SciMarkSOR	47	2891	70267
JGFheapsort	54	67	35079	SciMarkMonteCarlo	45	4017	5600071
				SciMarkLU	55	10849	71367

To show the impact of the different choices in the abstract model parametrization, execution tracing technique, and prioritization of the compilation queues, we compare four versions of the DLA technique, shown in Table 1. In all versions, aggressive optimizations and hot-spot detection are used.

The two abstract models adopted use different definitions of the function f, which controls the enqueueing order (see Section 2):

M1. A *naive* implementation, where λ is dropped, δ is the order of appearance of a method in the parent body and $f(\frac{1}{\lambda}, \delta) = \delta$.

M2. A refined one, where λ and δ are estimated on the base of branch prediction analysis, as described in [5].

For both the models, a hot spot detector estimates the time complexity of the methods, t_{exc}, and the DKSCG node is weighted as $f'(t_{exc}) = t_{exc}$. Moreover, the LAR is updated following a fixed distance criterion over the DKSCG. We call this distance, the *boundary*. In model M2, this criterion is coupled with the information provided by the branch prediction technique; in this case, a method belongs to the LAR only if its distance is within the boundary *and* the branch prediction detects it as highly likely to be invoked.

Table 2 reports a characterization of the Java Grande and SciMark benchmarks in terms of methods defined and executed as well as of static call points. Since the DLA technique tries to compile methods before their invocation, the effectiveness of the prediction becomes more important when the number of invoked methods grows.

Table 3 reports the dynamic behavior of the different DLA approaches. The greater effectiveness of a well tuned prediction model can be explained in terms of the number of prioritized methods and taken trampolines. The lower these measures, the more precise the prediction of the execution flow. It means that the compilation threads are effectively able to provide in advance many native methods effectively executed in the near future.

Table 3. Dynamic execution characterization of JIT and DLA techniques. JIT1 and JIT2 (both reported as JIT) have the same behavior. AOT1 and AOT2 are neglected, since they have zeros for each column.

Benchmark	Compiler Technique	Methods translated	Trampolines taken	Methods prioritized	Classes analyzed	Benchmark	Compiler Technique	Methods translated	Trampolines taken	Methods prioritized	Classes analyzed
JGFArith	JIT	34	34	0	7	JGFSparseMatmult	JIT	54	54	0	16
	DLA1	48	43	14	15		DLA1	138	83	24	25
	DLA2	45	6	1	7		DLA2	108	4	4	18
	DLA3	47	43	31	14		DLA3	128	80	61	23
	DLA4	45	5	0	7		DLA4	108	3	3	18
JGFLoop	JIT	35	35	0	7	JGFRayTracer	JIT	67	67	0	52
	DLA1	55	37	13	13		DLA1	141	101	41	62
	DLA2	45	3	1	7		DLA2	121	11	7	54
	DLA3	49	37	29	12		DLA3	133	101	72	60
	DLA4	45	2	0	7		DLA4	119	9	5	54
JGFCast	JIT	34	34	0	7	SciMarkSOR	JIT	47	47	0	13
	DLA1	48	38	4	9		DLA1	69	51	13	17
	DLA2	45	4	1	7		DLA2	56	3	1	14
	DLA3	47	38	31	9		DLA3	66	51	42	16
	DLA4	45	4	1	7		DLA4	55	2	0	14
JGFAssign	JIT	39	39	0	13	SciMarkMonteCarlo	JIT	45	45	0	12
	DLA1	61	45	15	15		DLA1	69	46	10	18
	DLA2	52	3	1	13		DLA2	53	3	1	13
	DLA3	58	45	39	15		DLA3	66	46	37	17
	DLA4	52	2	0	13		DLA4	53	2	0	13
JGFheapsort	JIT	54	54	0	14	SciMarkLU	JIT	55	55	0	12
	DLA1	81	42	10	17		DLA1	81	51	25	16
	DLA2	64	8	3	14		DLA2	62	4	1	13
	DLA3	80	41	34	17		DLA3	78	51	43	16
	DLA4	64	6	1	14		DLA4	62	3	0	13
JGFFFT	JIT	58	58	0	18						
	DLA1	91	61	13	23						
	DLA2	74	9	4	20						
	DLA3	91	61	42	21						
	DLA4	72	7	2	20						

Table 4 shows the execution time for several settings of the system. JIT and AOT compilers are provided with and without optimizations, JIT1 and JIT2 (AOT, respectively). Their performance are compared to DLA1, DLA2, DLA3 and DLA4. Three main considerations arise. First, DLA2 is always faster than DLA1, as well as DLA4 is faster than DLA3; this proves that a fine-tuning of the prediction model is significant for making the DLA compilation effective. Second, the higher the number of different invocable methods that make up the benchmark, the more important the execution tracing becomes. For these benchmarks, execution tracing efficiently drives DLA compilation. Hence, DLA3 and DLA4 translate fewer methods than DLA1 and DLA2. Finally, these results show how DLA compilation is a successful technique, which effectively bridges the gap between JIT and AOT compilation – often reaching an execution time close to that obtained executing a statically compiled code.

The following experimental results describes the LAR boundary impact on the DLA compilation, as well as the scaling of this technique w.r.t. the number of available CPUs.

Table 5 shows how more methods will be promoted for compilation in advance, when the boundary increases. Increasing the boundary, DLA1 scales worse than DLA2. The latter is able to determine – thanks to branch prediction – which methods are effectively to be pushed for compilation, choosing them from the large number of methods within the boundary. Moreover, execution tracing leads to a speedup when the benchmark has a sufficient number of methods, introducing overheads otherwise. In fact DLA3 and DLA4 outperform DLA1 and DLA2 only for JGFheapsort, JGFFFT, JGFSparseMatmult and JGFRayTracer.

Table 4. Java Grande and SciMark benchmarks: Execution time

Benchmark	Metric	JIT1	JIT2	AOT1	AOT2	DLA1	DLA2	DLA3	DLA4
JGFArith	Total time	171.96	145.72	171.5	127.05	141.15	129.15	141.291	129.171
	Machine code execution time	171.5	127.05	171.05	127.05	127.05	127.05	127.05	127.05
	Compilation delay	0.46	18.67	0	0	14.1	2.1	14.241	2.121
JGFLoop	Total time	6.774	5.211	6.136	3.644	4.454	4	4.462	4.003
	Machine code execution time	6.136	3.644	6.136	3.644	3.644	3.644	3.644	3.644
	Compilation delay	0.638	1.567	0	0	0.81	0.356	0.818	0.36
JGFCast	Total time	21.302	17.159	21.256	14.62	15.938	15.53	15.952	15.539
	Machine code execution time	21.256	14.62	21.256	14.62	14.62	14.62	14.62	14.62
	Compilation delay	0.046	2.539	0	0	1.318	0.91	1.331	0.919
JGFAssign	Total time	167.655	146.059	167.551	131.476	143.98	136.08	144.105	136.126
	Machine code execution time	167.551	131.47	167.551	131.476	131.47	131.47	131.47	131.47
	Compilation delay	0.104	14.589	0	0	12.51	4.61	12.635	4.656
JGFheapsort	Total time	58.022	56.696	57.943	53.303	55.922	54.213	55.896	54.204
	Machine code execution time	57.943	53.303	57.943	53.303	53.303	53.303	53.303	53.303
	Compilation delay	0.079	3.393	0	0	2.619	0.91	2.593	0.901
JGFFFT	Total time	66.561	61.671	65.294	54.983	59.032	56.943	58.951	56.904
	Machine code execution time	65.294	54.983	65.294	54.983	54.983	54.983	54.983	54.983
	Compilation delay	1.267	6.688	0	0	4.048	1.96	3.967	1.921
JGFSparseMatmult	Total time	17.439	13.374	16.714	8.487	12.397	9.617	12.319	9.594
	Machine code execution time	16.714	8.487	16.714	8.487	8.487	8.487	8.487	8.487
	Compilation delay	0.725	4.887	0	0	3.91	1.13	3.832	1.107
JGFRayTracer	Total time	51.91	45.535	50.981	28.62	37.53	31.23	37.263	31.152
	Machine code execution time	50.981	28.62	50.981	28.62	28.62	28.62	28.62	28.62
	Compilation delay	0.929	16.915	0	0	8.91	2.61	8.643	2.532
SciMarkSOR	Total time	61.342	58.24	61.25	49.12	55.27	51.93	55.332	51.958
	Machine code execution time	61.25	49.12	61.25	49.12	49.12	49.12	49.12	49.12
	Compilation delay	0.092	9.12	0	0	6.15	2.81	6.212	2.838
SciMarkMonteCarlo	Total time	39.3	23.303	39.25	16.222	20.601	18.322	20.645	18.343
	Machine code execution time	39.25	16.222	39.25	16.222	16.222	16.222	16.222	16.222
	Compilation delay	0.05	7.081	0	0	4.379	2.1	4.423	2.121
SciMarkLU	Total time	31.131	23.13	31.1	18.92	22.73	20.04	23.061	20.051
	Machine code execution time	31.1	18.92	31.1	18.92	18.92	18.92	18.92	18.92
	Compilation delay	0.031	4.21	0	0	3.81	1.12	4.141	1.131

Finally, Table 6 provides a characterization of DLA approaches as a function of the number of CPUs, taking into account DLA2 and DLA4 only. As expected, we can see that the DLA technique is only effective when multiple CPUs are available, and then only for benchmarks with a high number of methods. The performance scaling is not linear, and the performance quickly converges to an asymptote, as the number of CPUs needed to perform the compilation steps is limited by the number of methods to compile. Thus, the scaling is expected to become more pronounced for large benchmarks, with many more methods. By the same token, we expected the difference

Table 5. DLA total execution time (in seconds) as a function of the maximum look-ahead distance from the executing method (Boundary)

Benchmark	DLA1 Boundary					DLA2 Boundary					DLA3 Boundary					DLA4 Boundary				
	1	2	3	4	5	1	2	3	4	5	1	2	3	4	5	1	2	3	4	5
JGFArith	141.15	144.15	143.966	143.941	143.941	140.56	137.15	135.46	129.15	129.15	141.291	144.321	144.135	144.11	144.11	140.695	137.251	135.544	129.171	129.171
JGFLoop	5	4.624	4.454	4.454	4.454	4.8	4.284	4	4	4	5.013	4.633	4.462	4.462	4.462	4.811	4.29	4.003	4.003	4.003
JGFCast	15.938	15.955	15.941	15.942	15.942	15.921	15.932	15.53	15.53	15.53	15.952	15.968	15.954	15.955	15.955	15.934	15.945	15.539	15.539	15.539
JGFAssign	145.59	145.28	143.98	145.62	145.62	141.78	138.62	136.08	136.08	136.08	145.731	145.418	144.105	145.762	145.762	141.883	138.692	136.126	136.126	136.126
JGFheapsort	55.922	56.696	56.684	56.513	56.543	55.922	55.915	55.821	54.613	54.213	55.896	56.662	56.65	56.481	56.511	55.896	55.889	55.796	54.6	54.204
JGFFFT	59.032	61.008	59.745	59.727	59.727	58.989	58.926	58.188	56.943	56.943	58.951	60.887	59.65	59.632	59.632	58.909	58.847	58.124	56.904	56.904
JGFSparseMatmult	13.197	12.637	12.497	12.397	12.397	13.167	12.497	11.697	9.637	9.617	13.103	12.554	12.417	12.319	12.319	13.073	12.417	11.633	9.614	9.594
JGFRayTracer	37.797	38.87	37.645	37.53	37.53	37.796	37.686	37.537	31.56	31.23	37.522	38.563	37.374	37.263	37.263	37.521	37.414	37.269	31.472	31.152
SciMarkSOR	58.13	55.27	57.22	56.94	56.94	57.24	52.24	51.93	51.93	51.93	58.22	55.332	57.301	57.018	57.018	57.321	52.271	51.958	51.958	51.958
SciMarkMonteCarlo	20.601	21.132	21.372	21.472	21.472	20.232	19.626	18.322	18.322	18.322	20.645	21.181	21.423	21.524	21.524	20.272	19.66	18.343	18.343	18.343
SciMarkLU	23.02	22.73	23.02	23.02	23.02	22.04	21.16	20.04	20.04	20.04	23.061	22.768	23.061	23.061	23.061	22.071	21.182	20.051	20.051	20.051

Table 6. DLA characterization over the number of CPUs; results are in seconds and they are the total execution time of the compiler

Benchmark	JIT CPUs 1	DLA2 CPUs 1	2	3	4	5	6	7	8	DLA4 CPUs 1	2	3	4	5	6	7	8
JGFArith	171.96	182.684	137.147	129.214	129.15	129.15	129.15	129.15	129.15	191.604	138.745	130.8	129.171	129.171	129.171	129.171	129.171
JGFLoop	6.774	7.257	4.247	4.002	4	4	4	4	4	9.817	4.503	4.317	4.003	4.003	4.003	4.003	4.003
JGFCast	21.302	22.744	16.492	15.538	15.53	15.53	15.53	15.53	15.53	28.254	17.744	16.55	15.539	15.539	15.539	15.539	15.539
JGFAssign	167.655	183.761	150.826	136.197	136.08	136.08	136.08	136.08	136.08	200.291	152.082	137.396	136.126	136.126	136.126	136.126	136.126
JGFheapsort	58.022	134.438	57.497	54.902	54.268	54.213	54.213	54.213	54.213	146.998	57.372	54.79	54.266	54.204	54.204	54.204	54.204
JGFFFT	66.561	171.745	62.374	57.168	56.944	56.943	56.943	56.943	56.943	190.275	62.123	57.047	56.904	56.904	56.904	56.904	56.904
JGFSparseMatmult	17.439	28.521	13.339	9.647	9.617	9.617	9.617	9.617	9.617	37.721	13.214	9.635	9.594	9.594	9.594	9.594	9.594
JGFRayTracer	51.91	161.373	50.607	40.803	37.476	36.851	35.915	34.353	31.23	174.688	49.351	39.878	37.376	36.839	35.894	33.432	31.152
SciMarkSOR	61.342	89.431	57.188	52.013	51.93	51.93	51.93	51.93	51.93	96.851	57.176	52.013	51.958	51.958	51.958	51.958	51.958
SciMarkMonteCarlo	39.3	42.28	20.875	18.342	18.322	18.322	18.322	18.322	18.322	45.53	20.851	18.343	18.343	18.343	18.343	18.343	18.343
SciMarkLU	31.131	35.797	23.142	20.065	20.04	20.04	20.04	20.04	20.04	37.953	23.127	20.065	20.051	20.051	20.051	20.051	20.051

between DLA2 and DLA4 to increase for larger benchmarks, as precision loss due to execution stack tracing would have a greater impact on the DLA performance.

Due to space constraints, we omit discussion about the negligible memory overhead due to DKSCG storage needed by the DLA compiler. We note, however, that the computation of DKSCG is performed using information that is required for the usual operation of the dynamic compiler, thus not resulting in significant performance overhead.

5   Related Works

A wide survey of *Just in Time* (JIT) and *Ahead of Time* (AOT) compilation can be found in [3] and [21].

Continuous Program Optimization [13] allows periodic code recompilation for adapting it to different workloads. In BEA's JRockit [6], methods are first compiled without optimizations. A single thread is used both for compilation and execution, while a parallel one samples the execution and triggers aggressive recompilation of "hot" methods. While this paper focuses on the DLA technique itself, continuous optimization is just as easily implemented in a DLA compiler as in a traditional JIT. A method that needs recompilation is treated as a new method by the DLA compiler.

Selective Compilation is used to minimize compilation overheads while still achieving the largest part of the beneficial effects of JIT compilation. The Sun Microsystems Java HotSpot Virtual Machine [24] runs both an interpreter and a compiler, the latter invoked on hot-spots [18]. In [1], an evaluation of several techniques for *hot spot* detection is presented. The main difference between DLA and Selective Compilation is that the former aims at predicting in advance which methods are hot spot and which not, both hiding the compilation time and ensuring good quality binary code. Moreover, DLA compilation is based on prediction techniques that analyzes the static code properties, even though they are applied dynamically; conversely, selective compilation is mainly based on dynamic profiling, which requires code instrumentation. However, the two techniques could be adapted to work together.

Adaptive Optimization merges *Continuous Program Optimization* and *Selective Compilation*. A complete survey can be found in [2], while further considerations are presented by Kulkarny *et al.* [15]. This approach exploits a dedicated thread to detect hot spots and optimize them. The optimizer thread is run asynchronously w.r.t. the execution flow. In a multiprocessor environment, the optimization time can be masked.

Background Compilation [14] is directly related to DLA compilation. Optimization is performed on dedicated hardware, on the base of an off-line profiling phase. If a method still lies into the optimization queue at its invocation, lazy compilation is employed. This is the main difference w.r.t. DLA compilation. However, these techniques could be coupled since DLA compilation is orthogonal w.r.t dynamic code profiling. A more distantly related approach has been proposed in [12], involving the use of a compilation thread to guarantee an upper bound to the occupation of processor by the compiler by means of earliest deadline first scheduling.

Another work partially matching the DLA compilation is presented by Unnikrishnan *et al.* in [25]. Multiple threads on multiple processors re-compile and optimize in advance those code portions with high chances to be executed soon or requiring further improvements. The main difference w.r.t DLA compilation is that two kinds of run-time information are required in this case: the sampling of the execution trace and the profiling of properties such as time or energy consumption. Code instrumentation is needed to collect this information, which would impact the performance. Moreover, a method is only optimized after it has been invoked several times.

To be really effective, the DLA compilation has to follow a precise prediction model, described in Section 2 and based on the assignment of merit factors to the vertices and the arcs of a call-graph portion. These are computed in the *Look Ahead* phase on the base of structural parameters. State of the art branch prediction techniques are described in [19,9,5]. An approach for fast hot spot estimation/detection is reported in [1]; another method-time-complexity evaluation can be found in [17]. Sophisticated techniques for optimization profit estimation are described in [26] and [4].

Last but not least, some considerations on polymorphism in OO languages are needed, since we claim that DLA compilation is most effective for those applications characterized by large static and dynamic call graphs, in terms of number of methods. These call graphs are typical of OO application, as also underlined in the DaCapo[1] benchmark suite [11]. Polymorphism introduces an uncertainty in method naming, thus making the run-time alias analysis a costly but effective optimization, as pointed in [22,8]. On-line method versioning explicit the uncertain on the method to invoke producing several versions of the same method.

6 Conclusions

We have introduced the DLA compilation technique, covering theoretical and practical problems related to it and showing how DLA compilation can be a powerful technique to reduce the impact of dynamic compilation time and to generate high quality native code. Its effectiveness proves to be strictly related to the ability both to correctly predict the execution flow and to apply the right set of optimizations to each code region. A more precise matching of the DLA compiled methods set to the execution trace directly results into a reduction of the compilation delay, while the optimization of the hot spots should guarantee the execution of good quality code. On the Java Grande and SciMark benchmark set (not a favourable one, since it has a reduced use of polymorphism) we obtain an average speedup of 15%, and an average reduction of the overhead to less than

---

[1] We do not take DaCapo benchmarks into consideration in the experimental evaluation because ILDJIT does not support generics at this time.

1% of the JIT compilation time. It is to be expected that the benefits of DLA compilation will be higher for applications characterized by large call graphs, which are typical of Object Oriented highly polymorphic applications. This will be investigated in the future.

References

1. Agosta, G., Crespi Reghizzi, S., Palumbo, P., Sykora, M.: Selective compilation via fast code analysis and bytecode tracing. In: SAC 2006, pp. 906–911. ACM, New York (2006)
2. Arnold, M., Fink, S.J., Grove, D., Hind, M., Sweeney, P.F.: A Survey of Adaptive Optimization in Virtual Machines. Proceedings of the IEEE 93(2), 449–466 (2005)
3. Aycock, J.: A Brief History of Just-In-Time. ACM Comp. Surveys 35(2), 97–113 (2003)
4. Bacon, D.F., Graham, S.L., Sharp, O.J.: Compiler Transformations for High-Performance Computing. ACM Computing Surveys 26(4), 345–420 (1994)
5. Ball, T., Larus, J.R.: Branch Prediction For Free. In: SIGPLAN Conference on Programming Language Design and Implementation, pp. 300–313 (1993)
6. BEA JRockit: Java for the enterprise technical white paper (2006)
7. Campanoni, S., Agosta, G., Crespi Reghizzi, S.: A parallel dynamic compiler for CIL byte-code. SIGPLAN Not. 43(4), 11–20 (2008)
8. Dean, J., Grove, D., Chambers, C.: Optimization of Object-Oriented Programs Using Static Class Hierarchy Analysis. In: Olthoff, W. (ed.) ECOOP 1995. LNCS, vol. 952, pp. 77–101. Springer, Heidelberg (1995)
9. Deitrich, B.L., Cheng, B.-C., Hwu, W.-M.W.: Improving Static Branch Prediction in a Compiler. In: IEEE PACT, pp. 214–221 (1998)
10. Dunlavey, M.: Performance tuning with instruction-level cost derived from call-stack sampling. SIGPLAN Not. 42(8), 4–8 (2007)
11. Blackburn, S.M., et al.: The DaCapo benchmarks: java benchmarking development and analysis. In: OOPSLA, pp. 169–190 (2006)
12. Harris, T.: Controlling run-time compilation. In: Procedings of the IEEE Workshop on Programming Languages for Real-Time Industrial Applications, pp. 75–84 (1998)
13. Kistler, T., Franz, M.: Continuous program optimization: A case study. ACM Trans. Program. Lang. Syst. 25(4), 500–548 (2003)
14. Krintz, C.J., Grove, D., Sarkar, V., Calder, B.: Reducing the overhead of dynamic compilation. Software Practice and Experience 31(8), 717–738 (2001)
15. Kulkarni, P., Arnold, M., Hind, M.: Dynamic compilation: the benefits of early investing. In: VEE, pp. 94–104 (2007)
16. Mathew, J.A., Coddington, P.D., Hawick, K.A.: Analysis and development of Java Grande benchmarks. In: JAVA 1999: Proceedings of the ACM 1999 conference on Java Grande, pp. 72–80. ACM Press, New York (1999)
17. Le Métayer, D.: ACE: an automatic complexity evaluator. ACM Trans. Program. Lang. Syst. 10(2), 248–266 (1988)
18. Paleczny, M., Vick, C.A., Click, C.: The Java HotSpot Server Compiler. In: Java Virtual Machine Research and Technology Symposium (2001)
19. Patterson, J.R.C.: Accurate Static Branch Prediction by Value Range Propagation. In: SIGPLAN Conf. on Programming Language Design and Implementation, pp. 67–78 (1995)
20. Pozo, R., Miller, B.: SciMark benchmark, http://math.nist.gov/scimark2
21. Proebsting, T.A., Townsend, G., Bridges, P., Hartman, J.H., Newsham, T., Watterson, S.A.: Toba: Java For Applications, A Way Ahead of Time (WAT) Compiler. In: Proc. of the Third Conference on Object-Oriented Technologies and Systems (June 1997)
22. Rayside, D.: Polymorphism is a Problem. In: Panel on Reverse Engineering and Architecture (CSMR 2002) (March 2002)

23. Shudo, K.: Performance comparison of java/.net runtimes (2005),
    `http://www.shudo.net/jit/perf`
24. Sun Microsystems Java team. The Java HotSpot Virtual Machine, v1.4.1
25. Unnikrishnan, P., Kandemir, M., Li, F.: Reducing dynamic compilation overhead by over-lapping compilation and execution. In: ASP-DAC 2006: Proceedings of the 2006 conference on Asia South Pacific design automation, Piscataway, NJ, USA, pp. 929–934. IEEE, Los Alamitos (2006)
26. Zhao, M., Childers, B.R., Soffa, M.L.: An approach toward profit-driven optimization. ACM Trans. Archit. Code Optim. 3(3), 231–262 (2006)

Precise Management of Scratchpad Memories for Localising Array Accesses in Scientific Codes

Armin Größlinger

University of Passau
Department of Informatics and Mathematics
Innstraße 33, 94032 Passau, Germany
armin.groesslinger@uni-passau.de

Abstract. Unlike desktop and server CPUs, special-purpose processors found in embedded systems and on graphics cards often do not have a cache memory which is managed automatically by hardware logic. Instead, they offer a so-called scratchpad memory which is fast like a cache but, unlike a cache, has to be managed explicitly, i.e., the burden of its efficient use is imposed on the software. We present a method for computing precisely which memory cells are reused due to temporal locality of a certain class of codes, namely codes which can be modelled in the well-known polyhedron model. We present some examples demonstrating the effectiveness of our method for scientific codes.

Keywords: scratchpad memory, software-managed data cache, array localisation, polyhedron model, embedded systems.

1 Introduction

The success of parallelising an algorithm depends on two factors. First, the computations must be arranged suitably to exploit the available computational power efficiently. Second, data transport between the computing entities must not spoil the efficiency of the execution by consuming a considerable amount of the total execution time. With current architectures, several levels of data storage are available: registers, caches, CPU-local main memory, main memory of remote CPUs, remote network storage. Due to the dramatic difference in their performance, which is, for technical and economic reasons, reflected in the smaller sizes of faster storages, the data accessed often must be kept in the fastest memory. Program transformations which increase locality have been widely studied (cf. Section 2). On special-purpose architectures like embedded systems and graphics processors, fast cache memory is not managed automatically by hardware but has to be managed explicitly by software. We aim at an automatic explicit management of so-called scratchpad memories present in such architectures.

Since we aim at full automation, the techniques are not applicable to arbitrary programs. They must be loop nests with bounds linear in the surrounding loops

O. de Moor and M. Schwartzbach (Eds.): CC 2009, LNCS 5501, pp. 236–250, 2009.

```
                              for (x=0; x<=n-1; x++)
                                 L[x] = A[x+1];
                              for (t=0; t<=n; t++) {
                                 L[n] = A[t+n+1];
   for (t=0; t<=n; t++)          parfor (p=0; p<=n; p++)
      parfor (p=0; p<=n; p++)       L[p] = f(L[p]);
         A[t+p+1] = f(A[t+p+1]);  A[t+1] = L[0];
                                 syncparfor (x=1; x<=n; x++)
      (a) original program          L[x-1] = L[x];
                              }
                              parfor (x=0; x<=n-1; x++)
                                 A[n+x+2] = L[x];
                                 (b) localised version
```

Fig. 1. Locality-improving transformation on a simple parallel program

and structure parameters containing bodies with array accesses with affine sub-
scripts, i.e., we are working with programs that are being studied in the context
of the polytope/polyhedron model [12,13,14].

As an example of the desired transformation, let us look at the example program in Figure 1(a). It consists of an outer sequential time loop and an inner
parallel loop. Each iteration (t, p) updates an array element $A[t+p+1]$. Since every time step t accesses array elements $A[t+1], \ldots, A[t+n+1]$, there is considerable
overlap in the array elements used in successive time steps, namely n elements.
For example, the first time step $t = 0$ accesses the elements $A[1], \ldots, A[n+1]$,
the second time step $t = 1$ accesses $A[2], \ldots, A[n+2]$ and uses $A[2], \ldots, A[n+1]$
again. If the access of array A has high latency, i.e., it is not stored in the fastest
available memory, the execution of the program can be accelerated by keeping
the relevant parts of A in a faster memory. One possible way to achieve this
localisation is shown in Figure 1(b). The array L is assumed to be stored in fast
memory. In every iteration of the loop on t, the element $A[t+n+1]$ of A, which
has not been accessed in the previous iteration, is brought into L at $L[n]$. After
the computation, $L[0]$ is exported to $A[t+1]$, because it is not needed in the
next iteration, and the elements of L are shifted inside L to bring them into the
right position for the next iteration. In addition, elements are moved to/from L
before and after the loop on t, respectively. Having to move all (but one) elements of L can be costly depending on the architecture. With memory local to
the computing cores (which may require only one cycle per memory access) the
overall positive effect of the transformation outweighs this additional cost. As
the `syncparfor` statement in the code shown suggests, this reorganisation can
be executed synchronously in parallel.

We propose a way of computing the array elements which have to be moved
into L before each time step, exported from L and reorganised in L after each
time step. The reorganisation step requires particular attention because, as can
be seen in the above example, it overwrites elements of L. Therefore, an in-situ
reuse of the same L requires an ordering of the overwriting operations that does
not destroy data elements before they have been copied.

This paper is organised as follows. After discussing related work in Section 2, we sketch a few concepts of the polyhedron model in Section 3. We present our technique of computing the desired information about the memory accesses in Section 4. We show some examples in Section 5 before Section 6 concludes.

2   Related Work

Improving data locality by transforming a loop nest to obtain temporal or spatial locality by reordering the loop iterations and/or changing the data layout has long been a subject of study [19,10,5]. Earlier work relies on partitioning program data [16]. Loop transformations have been used to partition the program operations such that each partition's accessed data fits into cache memory [4] or to simplify the reuse pattern in order to store the reused data compactly in scratchpad memory [11,9] if such a transformation is permitted by the dependences. Later work [8] improves the situation by partitioning according to the coefficients of the array index expressions, thus reducing the size of the blocks stored in scratchpad memory considerably. Chen et. al [6] present a method to minimise off-chip memory accesses by restructuring parallel code according to data tiles to create temporal locality across processors.

Ehrhart polynomials have been used to compactly store only the elements of an array used by the code after applying a transformation [7,15] or to compute the number of accessed memory elements, cache misses, etc. [17].

For our technique to be effective, locality improving transformations described in the previous work cited are desirable. Baskaran et al. [2] execute tiled loop code on a graphics card with scratchpad memory. They approximate the local data of a tile by a rectangular superset, load the respective data into scratchpad memory before executing a tile and store it to global memory afterwards, but they do not compute the used data set precisely nor do they try to retain reused data in the scratchpad between tiles.

3   Prerequisites

3.1   The Polyhedron Model

Definition 1. *An* access *is an array reference* $A[x]$ *in a loop body. An* instance *of an access is its execution for particular values of the variables of the surrounding loops.*

Definition 2. *A* dependence *is a relation between access instances which refer to the same memory cell. An access instance* a_2 *is said to depend* directly *on an access instance* a_1, *written* $a_1 \rightarrow a_2$, *if both* a_1 *and* a_2 *access the same memory cell,* a_2 *is executed after* a_1 *and there is no access* a_3 *referring to the same memory cell executed between* a_1 *and* a_2. *A dependence is called an* input *dependence if both access are reads, an* output *dependence if both accesses are writes, a* flow *dependence if* a_1 *writes and* a_2 *reads, and an* anti *dependence if* a_1 *reads and* a_2 *writes. The array index referred to by an access* a *is denoted by* $accelem(a)$.

We require precise dependence information, i.e., there must not be dependences which follow from other dependences by transitivity. Note that our definition of dependences is a bit different from the usual, statement-based definition. With our definition, there are two dependences in the statement

```
A[i] = A[i] + A[i] ,
```

namely an input dependence from one of the read accesses to the other (the choice of the direction is arbitrary) and an anti dependence from the later read access to the write access. With the usual definition, there are no dependences inside one statement instance. We require this finer granularity of dependences to capture that, in this example, all three accesses in the above statement refer to the same memory cell and, hence, it is sufficient to fetch $A[i]$ once from global memory for both read accesses and that $A[i]$ is immediately overwritten again, so the fetched value must not be cached for following statements.

3.2 Z-Polyhedra

Definition 3. *A Z-polyhedron $Z \subseteq \mathbb{Z}^m$ is the image of the integral points of a polyhedron $P \subseteq \mathbb{R}^n$ under an integral affine mapping $f : \mathbb{Z}^n \to \mathbb{Z}^m$, i.e., $Z = \{f(\boldsymbol{x}) \,|\, \boldsymbol{x} \in P \cap \mathbb{Z}^n\}$.*

For example, the Z-polyhedron containing the even numbers can be defined by $P = \mathbb{R}$ and $f(x) = 2x$.

Our main operation on Z-polyhedra is the counting of the integral points in a (parametric) Z-polyhedron. There are algorithms [18] which compute, from the description of a Z-polyhedron $Z(\boldsymbol{p})$, a set of condition/quasi-polynomial pairs (c_i, ρ_i) such that the value $\rho_i(\boldsymbol{p})$ of the quasi-polynomial ρ_i gives the number of integral points in $Z(\boldsymbol{p})$ if $c_i(\boldsymbol{p})$ holds. For example, the number of integral points in the parametric Z-polyhedron $Z(p, q) = \{2 \cdot i \,|\, 0 \leq i \leq \min(\frac{p}{2}, q) \wedge i \in \mathbb{Z}\}$ is given by:

$$|Z(p,q)| = \begin{cases} \frac{p}{2} + [1, \frac{1}{2}]_p & \text{if } 0 \leq p \leq 2q \\ q + 1 & \text{if } p \geq 2q \geq 0 \\ 0 & \text{otherwise} \end{cases}$$

Counting the integral points in a union of Z-polyhedra is possible, too, by computing a disjoint union of the Z-polyhedra first.

4   Locality Transformation

We consider codes of the form shown in Figure 2, i.e., there is one outer sequential loop on t enumerating the *time steps* of the program and there are zero, one, or several sequential and/or parallel loops on $\boldsymbol{i}$ inside (which need not be perfectly nested, even though the code fragment shown in the figure is). The computation statements inside the loops on $\boldsymbol{i}$ contain accesses $A[f_j(\boldsymbol{i})]$ $(1 \leq j \leq n)$ to an

```
for (t ∈ T) {
    (par)for (i ∈ D(t)) { body with A[f₁(i,t)],..., A[fₙ(i,t)] }
}
```

Fig. 2. Program to be transformed with one outer sequential time loop

array A. The transformation can be applied successively for several different arrays, but we restrict our presentation to the case of a single array.

Each array access $A[f_j(\boldsymbol{i}, t)]$ is part of a statement with an iteration domain $D_j(t)$, which depends on the point in time t, i.e., the access is executed for every $\boldsymbol{i} \in D_j(t)$ for given t. To make our technique applicable, $D_j(t)$ must be a (parametric) Z-polyhedron. The aim of the proposed transformation is to achieve that some or all array elements accessed at time t are loaded into the local memory L of the compute node before the execution of the operations at time t. This requires three questions to be answered:

1. Where (at which index) do we place elements to be stored in L?
2. Which elements are present at time t and which elements are loaded into and which are removed from L before/during/after time t?
3. What happens to the elements in L between time t and time $t+1$?

Answers to these questions are given in the following sections. In Section 4.1, we present how we map elements from A to L, assuming that we known already which elements from A are to be mapped to L. Sections 4.2 and 4.3 present two answers to the second question. Finally, we discuss answers to the third question (applicable to both previous answers to Question 2) in Section 4.4.

4.1   The New Location of Array Elements

The local storage caches some elements of A at a given time to accelerate their access. Let $C(t)$ be the indices of the elements of A to be cached in L at time t, i.e., $\boldsymbol{x} \in C(t)$ means that $A[\boldsymbol{x}]$ is available in L. We require $C(t)$ to be a Z-polyhedron.

We map the elements of A, which are present in L at a given time to L such that $L[0], L[1], \ldots$ contain the cached elements of A in ascending order, i.e., if $A[x_1]$ and $A[x_2]$ are mapped to $L[y_1]$ and $L[y_2]$, respectively, then $x_1 < x_2$ implies $y_1 < y_2$. This way, we can determine the index of an element $A[\boldsymbol{x}]$ in L by the number of elements $\boldsymbol{y} \in C(t)$ which precede $\boldsymbol{x}$ in lexicographic order. To this end, we consider the union of parametric Z-polyhedra defined by

$$A_{\prec}(\boldsymbol{x}, t) := \{\boldsymbol{y} \mid \boldsymbol{y} \in C(t) \wedge \boldsymbol{y} \prec \boldsymbol{x}\}.$$

The number of integral points in $A_{\prec}(\boldsymbol{x}, t)$ is the number of array indices in $C(t)$ up to, but not including, $\boldsymbol{x}$ (at time t). Computing the number of integral points in $A_{\prec}(\boldsymbol{x}, t)$ (cf. Section 3.2) yields a set $\{(c_1, \rho_1), \ldots, (c_q, \rho_q)\}$ of conditions c_j on the parameters (including $\boldsymbol{x}$ and t) and quasi-polynomials ρ_j, where $\rho_j(\boldsymbol{x}, t)$ evaluates to the number of integral points in $A_{\prec}(\boldsymbol{x}, t)$ if $c_j(\boldsymbol{x}, t)$ holds. If we combine the c_j and ρ_j to a conditional expression ρ, which evaluates to ρ_j if c_j holds, then the location of an element $A[\boldsymbol{x}]$ in the local storage at time t is given by $L[\rho(\boldsymbol{x}, t)]$ (provided that $\boldsymbol{x} \in C(t)$).

By construction, we have the ordering property stated in the following lemma.

Lemma 1. *Let $t \in \mathbb{Z}$ and $\boldsymbol{x}_1, \boldsymbol{x}_2 \in C(t)$. Then $\boldsymbol{x}_1 \prec \boldsymbol{x}_2 \Leftrightarrow \rho(\boldsymbol{x}_1, t) < \rho(\boldsymbol{x}_2, t)$.*

The total amount of local storage needed can be computed by counting $C(t)$ and maximising w.r.t to t.

4.2   Localisation Based on Access Instances

Localisation can be achieved without dependence information if we perform it based on access instances only. The set of array elements accessed by an access $A[f_j(\boldsymbol{i}, t)]$, with iteration domain $D_j(t)$ at time t, is given by the parametric Z-polyhedron $C_j(t) = \{f_j(\boldsymbol{i}, t) \mid \boldsymbol{i} \in D_j(t)\}$. The set of all array elements accessed at time t is given by the union of the $C_j(t)$. The most obvious choice of $C(t)$ to be stored in L is the set of exactly the elements accessed at a given time step, but, since any superset represents a correct transformation, it is worthwhile to add another degree of freedom. Often, we encounter algorithms which have an alternating access pattern, for example, at even time steps one part of the data is accessed and at odd time steps a different part of the data. With the obvious choice of $C(t)$, we would transform the program such that the contents of L is replaced completely at every time step. Such situations are remedied by introducing a *localisation window*, i.e., permitting the scope of elements kept in L to be larger than the current time point. We describe the localisation window by its width w ($w \geq 1$) which denotes the number of successive time steps considered part of the window. We now define $C(t)$ by

$$C(t) := \bigcup_{j=1}^{n} \bigcup_{\tau=0}^{w-1} C_j(t + \tau).$$

Note that $w = 1$ is the case in which $C(t)$ contains only the elements accessed at the current time t. From $C(t)$, one can compute $\rho(\boldsymbol{x}, t)$ as described in Section 4.1. Let us now address the question of data movement, i.e., which elements to move in/out and around (within L) at a given time step. There are three parts involved:

1. a "move in" phase which loads data not present in local storage before the computation of the current time step,
2. a "move out" phase which removes data not need at the next time step from local storage and saves it to the global memory,
3. a "reorganisation" phase between two successive time steps, in which the data in local storage is reorganised such that the data retained in local storage is in the correct location for the next computation.

The array elements relevant for each of these three phases are given by the following sets:

$$I(t) := C(t) - C(t-1), \quad O(t) := C(t) - C(t+1), \quad G(t) := C(t) \cap C(t+1).$$

$I(t)$ contains the indices of elements used at t but not at $t-1$, i.e., the elements to be moved to local storage for step t; $O(t)$ contains the indices of elements used only at t but not at $t+1$, i.e., the elements to be moved out after step t; and $G(t)$ contains the elements used at both t and $t+1$, i.e., the elements which must remain in local storage and have to be reorganised between t and $t+1$. Each of these three sets is a union of Z-polyhedra.

It is tempting to try to optimise the move-in and move-out sets by, for example, moving out only the elements in $O(t)$ that have actually been written to at time t. But this "optimisation" is incorrect, since an element may have been written several time steps before it is moved out (and may only have been read in between). A correct and exact optimisation of data move in and out requires dependence analysis techniques and is presented in Section 4.3.

During the reorganisation phase, care has to be taken not to overwrite data which must still be moved before the next time step begins. A simple way to avoid this problem is to use a second local storage to which the reorganised data is written and swap the two storage areas after reorganisation. Using pointer exchange for efficiency, this approach has little run-time overhead, but uses twice as much local storage. This may be sufficient, but the amount of local storage is often limited, e.g., in embedded devices. We present techniques for remedying this drawback in Section 4.4.

```
for (t ∈ T) {
    for (x ∈ I(t))  L₁[ρ(x,t)] = A[x];                    // move in
    (par)for (i ∈ D(t)) { body with L₁[ρ(fⱼ(i,t))] instead of A[fⱼ(i,t)] }
    for (x ∈ O(t))  A[x] = L₁[ρ(x,t)];                    // move out
    for (x ∈ G(t))  L₂[ρ(x,t+1)] = L₁[ρ(x,t)];            // reorg
    swap(L₁, L₂);
}
```

Fig. 3. Preliminary localised code based on access instances with two local storages

A sketch of the code after the localising transformation is shown in Figure 3. The array accesses $A[f_j(\boldsymbol{i},t)]$ in the body (cf. Figure 2) have been replaced by $L_1[\rho(f(\boldsymbol{i},t))]$. In Section 4.4, we show why a single area of local storage is sufficient.

4.3   Localisation Based on Dependences

The access-based localisation of memory accesses presented in Section 4.2 is simple in the sense that no dependence information is required by the localising transformation. On the other hand, this simplicity leads to overhead in the data movement, for example by loading elements into local storage which are never read but only written to. A dependence-based approach can remedy this situation. Provided that an exact dependence analysis of the loop nest is available, we can mark each access as global or local. Whether to access global or local memory depends on whether the desired value is present in local storage or not. This way, there are no separate move-in and move-out statements which precede and succeed the computation statements, respectively. Instead, they are integrated into (or placed next to) the computations themselves.

Let $\mathcal{R}$ be the set of read access instances and $\mathcal{W}$ the set of write access instances of the program. We write $win(a_1, a_2)$ to denote that an access instance a_2 is inside the localisation window starting at a_1, i.e., a_2 is at most w time steps after a_1. We define global writes $\mathcal{W}_g$ and local writes $\mathcal{W}_l$ as follows:

$$\mathcal{W}_g = \{w \in \mathcal{W} \mid \neg(\exists w' : w' \in \mathcal{W} : w \xrightarrow{\text{out}} w' \wedge win(w, w'))\}$$
$$\mathcal{W}_l = \{w \in \mathcal{W} \mid (\exists r : r \in \mathcal{R} : w \xrightarrow{\text{flow}} r \wedge win(w, r))\}$$

A write is global if the value is not overwritten inside the localisation window. A write is local if the value is read later inside the localisation window. Note that, by this definition, there can be a write that is global and local. This happens when the value is not overwritten in the localisation window and, therefore, has to be written to global memory at some point (and we choose to do it immediately), but it is read again later, so we also keep the value in local memory. It is also possible for a write to be neither global nor local; this means that the value will be overwritten and not read in between and, hence, we can drop the write entirely.

Reads have to be partitioned into three groups. A read is local ($\mathcal{R}_l$) if the value accessed is present in local storage because it has been read or written to earlier in the localisation window. A read is global ($\mathcal{R}_g$) if no prior access in the localisation window has been made and no later access will be made. A read is from global memory with a successive store to local memory ($\mathcal{R}_{gl}$) if no prior access has been made but, later in the localisation window, the value will be read again.

$$\mathcal{R}_l = \{r \in \mathcal{R} \mid (\exists w : w \in \mathcal{W} : w \xrightarrow{\text{flow}} r \wedge win(w, r)) \vee$$
$$(\exists r' : r' \in \mathcal{R} : r' \xrightarrow{\text{in}} r \wedge win(r', r))\}$$
$$\mathcal{R}_g = \{r \in \mathcal{R} \mid \neg(\exists r' : r' \in \mathcal{R} : r \xrightarrow{\text{in}} r' \wedge win(r, r'))\} - \mathcal{R}_l$$
$$\mathcal{R}_{gl} = \{r \in \mathcal{R} \mid (\exists r' : r' \in \mathcal{R} : r \xrightarrow{\text{in}} r' \wedge win(r, r'))\} - \mathcal{R}_l$$

The elements that are present in local storage are given by

$$C(t) = \{accelem(a) \mid a \in \mathcal{R}_l \cup \mathcal{R}_{gl} \cup \mathcal{W}_l, t \leq time(a) \leq t + w\}.$$

From $C(t)$ we can again compute $\rho(\boldsymbol{x}, t)$ (cf. Section 4.1), which gives the location of an element $A[\boldsymbol{x}]$ in L at a given time t. The reorganisation of L between time steps is described by the set $G(t) = C(t) \cap C(t + 1)$ as in Section 4.2.

There is one detail we have to consider with this approach. Scheduling a parallel program usually does not impose restrictions on input dependences. This allows the case that an input dependence $r_1 \xrightarrow{\text{in}} r_2$ with $r_1 \in \mathcal{R}_{gl}$ is not carried by a sequential loop and r_1 and r_2 reside on different processors. In this case, it is possible that the read from global memory and the following write to the local memory cell for r_1 are, in fact, executed *after* r_2, which is supposed to read the same value as r_1 from local memory, because the ordering of operations between the two involved processors in not determined. To guarantee correct execution of transformed programs we have either to require that input dependences respect the same restrictions as the other dependence types or we have to emit a barrier synchronisation statement which makes sure the write to local memory at r_1 is executed before the read from local memory at r_2. In the examples we present in Section 5, we choose to introduce synchronisations when needed as synchronisation is rather cheap on the platform we use.

4.4   Ordering the Reorganisation

As has been outlined in Section 4.2, a straight-forward implementation of the reorganisation phase requires two areas of local storage to avoid overwriting elements which have not been moved, yet. We will now prove that a single storage area is sufficient, i.e., the reorganisation can always be performed in-situ by adhering to a certain order in the intra-storage element moves. The key observation is that, if an element $L[y_1]$ has to be moved to $L[y_2]$ $(y_1 \neq y_2)$ and $L[y_2]$ has in turn to be moved to $L[y_3]$, then $y_2 \neq y_3$ and $L[y_1]$ and $L[y_2]$ move in the same direction, i.e., $y_1 < y_2 \Leftrightarrow y_2 < y_3$.

Definition 4. *Let $t \in \mathbb{Z}$ and $\boldsymbol{x} \in G(t)$. The* drift $\delta(\boldsymbol{x}, t)$ *of the element $L[\rho(\boldsymbol{x}, t)]$ is defined as $\delta(\boldsymbol{x}, t) := \rho(\boldsymbol{x}, t+1) - \rho(\boldsymbol{x}, t)$. We say that $L[\rho(\boldsymbol{x}, t)]$ moves* forward, *if $\delta(\boldsymbol{x}, t) > 0$, and* backward *if $\delta(\boldsymbol{x}, t) < 0$.*

We now present the key idea introduced above formally and prove that, if an element moves from $L[y_1]$ to $L[y_2]$, the contents of $L[y_2]$ moves in the same direction as the contents of $L[y_1]$ (provided that $L[y_2]$ moves at all).

Proposition 1. *Let $t \in \mathbb{Z}$ and $\boldsymbol{x}_1, \boldsymbol{x}_2 \in G(t)$ such that $\rho(\boldsymbol{x}_1, t+1) = \rho(\boldsymbol{x}_2, t)$. This validates the following two implications:*

$$\delta(\boldsymbol{x}_1, t) > 0 \Rightarrow \delta(\boldsymbol{x}_2, t) > 0$$
$$\delta(\boldsymbol{x}_1, t) < 0 \Rightarrow \delta(\boldsymbol{x}_2, t) < 0$$

Proof. Let $t, \boldsymbol{x}_1, \boldsymbol{x}_2$ be as stated and $\delta(\boldsymbol{x}_1, t) > 0$, i.e., $\rho(\boldsymbol{x}_1, t+1) > \rho(\boldsymbol{x}_1, t)$. Since $\rho(\boldsymbol{x}_1, t+1) = \rho(\boldsymbol{x}_2, t)$ and $\boldsymbol{x}_1, \boldsymbol{x}_2 \in C(t)$, this implies (by Lemma 1) that $\boldsymbol{x}_1 \prec \boldsymbol{x}_2$. Again by Lemma 1 and since $\boldsymbol{x}_1, \boldsymbol{x}_2 \in C(t+1)$, this implies $\rho(\boldsymbol{x}_1, t+1) < \rho(\boldsymbol{x}_2, t+1)$ and, because of $\rho(\boldsymbol{x}_1, t+1) = \rho(\boldsymbol{x}_2, t)$, we get $\delta(\boldsymbol{x}_2, t) > 0$. Analogous reasoning applies to the second case with < 0 instead of > 0.

From this proposition, a way to reorganise local storage in-situ is quite obvious.

Corollary 1. *The reordering of elements in local storage L at the end of time step t can be achieved in-situ by a two-pass sweep over L.*

The in-situ reorganisation works by scanning $G(t)$ once in ascending lexicographic order and once in descending lexicographic order. In the ascending pass, it is guaranteed that, if $\delta(\boldsymbol{x}, t) < 0$ holds for an $\boldsymbol{x} \in G(t)$ scanned, then its value (which corresponds to $A[\boldsymbol{x}]$) can safely be moved from $L[\rho(\boldsymbol{x}, t)]$ to $L[\rho(\boldsymbol{x}, t+1)]$, since the target entry in L is either empty (because it contained an element from A which is not used at time step t) or it has been moved already, because its drift is negative, too. The descending scan, in turn, can safely move all the elements with a positive drift.

Modulo Addressing. In the very regular cases that the drift is identical for all elements of local storage, there exists an alternative to moving the data around. We can change the addressing of the local storage to accomplish the same effect. Accesses $L[\rho(\boldsymbol{x}, t)]$ are replaced by $L[(\rho(\boldsymbol{x}, t) + o) \bmod s]$, where s is the size of the local storage and o is an offset which is initialised to 0 and incremented by $-\delta(t)$ at the end of every time step.

This round-robin addressing achieves the same effect as continuous movement by $\delta(t)$. It is, of course, costly. It depends on the architecture whether moving the data or paying additional addressing costs is more efficient. If $\delta(t)$ is constant, i.e., independent of t, the increment to o is the same in each iteration of the loop on t and the costly modulo operation may be replaced by less costly constructs like a conditional increment-or-zero.

4.5   Code Generation Considerations

Since the iteration domains of the computation statements and the move in, move out, and reorganisation statements are Z-polyhedra, we can use a polyhedral code generator like CLooG [3] to generate the transformed code. To obtain efficient code, we have to take care of the conditionals contained in the new access functions $L[\rho(\ldots)]$. In general, ρ is a case distinction on several conditions $c_1, \ldots, c_q$. To avoid evaluating the conditions at every access, we split the iteration domain D of the statement by the conditions, i.e., we replace D by $D_i := \{\boldsymbol{x} \mid \boldsymbol{x} \in D, c_i(\boldsymbol{x})\}$. This increases the number of iteration domains, but in each D_i no conditional has to evaluated in the access function.

At present, we have an implemented prototype of the localisation based on access instances. We have used this prototype to compute the examples presented in Section 5; the examples for the localisation based on dependences have been derived by hand from the localisation based on access instances.

5   Examples

Let us now present some examples demonstrating the effectiveness of our transformation. In order not to bother the reader with long, complicated code resulting from the transformation, we show shortened versions of the code which illustrate the transformation but may be less efficient w.r.t. control flow than the codes used in the benchmarks.

The parallel benchmarks have been performed on an NVIDIA graphics card with a GTX9800 GPU, a 1944 MHz shader clock and a 1150 MHz memory clock. The programming environment is NVIDIA's CUDA technology [1]. The graphics card consists of 16 *streaming multi-processors*. Each multi-processor executes one instruction of 32 threads in 4 clock cycles provided that all 32 threads (called a *warp*) take the same execution path. When the threads of a warp *diverge*, i.e., take different execution paths, their execution is sequential. A multiprocessor has 16 KB of local memory which can be accessed within one clock cycle simultaneously by the threads of a warp provided that some alignment restrictions are obeyed. Access to main memory is much slower, but the thread scheduler in a multiprocessor tries to hide memory latency by overlapping computation and memory access. Therefore, the higher latency of the main memory can be hidden partly if enough threads are available. Our experiments use only one multiprocessor at a time since there is no way to share scratchpad memory between multiprocessors.

Example 1 (1d-SOR). As an example of a scientific code, let us look at one-dimensional successive over-relaxation (1d-SOR). The code of a sequential implementation is given in Figure 4(a). 1d-SOR scans the elements of an array A repeatedly and replaces every element $A[i]$ by the average of its two neighbours. A parallel version of the code is shown in Figure 5(a). Notice the synchronous parallelism expressed by the parallel loop on p inside the sequential loop on t. Before we apply our techniques to the parallel code, we briefly note that the sequential code can be improved slightly using the localisation transformation. We also use this example to compare the localisation based on access instances and on dependences.

Localisation based on access instances. Considering the loop on i in the sequential code as the time loop, we obtain $C(i) = \{i-1, i, i+1\}$, i.e., at time i the accessed elements are $A[i-1]$, $A[i]$, and $A[i+1]$. This yields $\rho(x,i) = x-i+1$, i.e., $A[i-1]$ is mapped to $L[0]$, $A[i]$ to $L[1]$, and $A[i+1]$ to $L[2]$. Since the drift $\delta(x,i) = \rho(x,i+1) - \rho(x,i)$ is constantly -1, we obtain the simple transformed code shown in Figure 4(b). Since the indices into L are fixed at 0, 1, 2, the array L can be replaced by three local variables for the array elements.

Localisation based on dependences. Localisation based on dependences takes into account which elements are reused, i.e., which are read again after

Table 1. 1d-SOR: benchmark for sequential codes for $n = 10^6$ on AMD Opteron 2.2 GHz with GCC 4.2, runtimes in milliseconds

$m =$	128	256	384	512
original	1095	2168	3111	4139
localised	723	1595	2150	2865
speed-up	1.52	1.36	1.45	1.44

Table 2. 1d-SOR: benchmark for parallel codes, $n = 10^6$ on GPU, number of threads equal to m, runtimes in milliseconds. "X" means code could not be executed due to too many divergent threads.

$m =$	1	32	64	128	192	256	320	384	448	512
parallel code	381	511	709	1089	1456	1759	2135	2416	2807	3082
intra-thread localised	–	433	545	758	964	1125	1322	1515	1766	2019
inter-thread localised	–	529	525	539	587	652	684	784	856	1002
fully localised with moves	–	509	504	518	559	611	647	735	800	X
fully localised with modulo addr.	–	577	498	534	621	710	789	905	X	X

having been read or written. In this example, this reveals that the write to $A[i]$ is local, since it is reused at the next time step, and global, since it is not overwritten later. $A[i-1]$ is in the local read set for $i \geq 2$. It is in the global read set for $i = 1$ since no input dependence to $A[i-1]$ for $i = 1$ exists. Since there is no relevant input dependence, the global-local read set $\mathcal{R}_{gl}$ is empty. The code obtained (we again exploit the fact that the indices into L turn out to be constants) is shown in Figure 4(c). A polyhedral code generator can unroll the first iteration of the loop on i to avoid the conditionals $i = 1$ and $i \geq 2$; additionally, traditional compiler data flow analysis reveals that l_0 and l_1 can be stored in the same memory cell l (likely a register), thereby saving the reorganisation. The resulting code is shown in Figure 4(d). Running the sequential code and the transformed code on an AMD Opteron machine yields the runtimes shown in Table 1. The

```
for (k=1; k<=m; k++)
  for (i=1; i<=n-1; i++)
    A[i] = (A[i-1]+A[i+1])*0.5;
         (a) original code
```

```
for (k=1; k<=m; k++) {
  l0 = A[0];              // move in
  for (i=1; i<=n-1; i++) {
    l2 = A[i+1];          // move in
    l1 = (l0 + l2) * 0.5;
    A[i-1] = l0;          // move out
    l0 = l1;              // reorganise
  }
  A[n-1]=l0; A[n]=l1; // move out
}
```
(b) access-based localisation

```
for (k=1; k<=m; k++) {
  for (i=1; i<=n-1; i++) {
    (i==1 ? l0:l1) = A[i] =
      ((i==1 ? A[i-1] : l0)
        + A[i+1]) * 0.5;
    if (i >= 2) l0 = l1;
  }
}
```
(c) dependence-based localisation

```
for (k=1; k<=m; k++) {
  l = (A[0]+A[2])*0.5;
  for (i=2; i<=n-1; i++)
    l = A[i] = (l+A[i+1])*0.5;
}
```
(d) dependence-based localisation with loop optimisations

Fig. 4. One-dimensional successive over-relaxation: sequential codes

```
for (t=0; t<=n+2*m-4; t++) {
  parfor (p=max(0,(t-n+3)/2); p<=min(m-1,t/2); p++) {
    int i = t+1-2*p;
    A[i] = (A[i-1] + A[i+1]) * 0.5;
  }
}
```

(a) parallel code

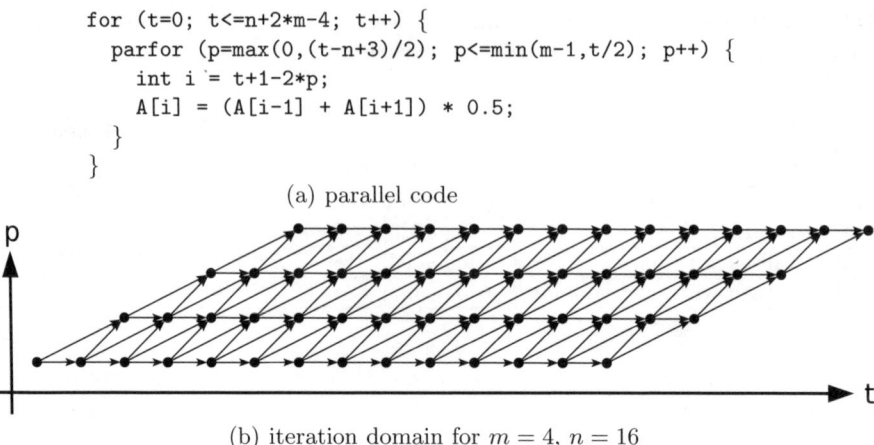

(b) iteration domain for $m = 4$, $n = 16$

Fig. 5. One-dimensional successive over-relaxation: parallel version

transformed code runs faster because localisation and traditional optimisation techniques together save one of the three accesses to array A.

The parallel code is shown in Figure 5(a) and depicted in Figure 5(b). Note that the number of parallel threads that can be used equals the parameter m. We can localise twice. First, we can do localisation for each thread of the inner parallel loop w.r.t. the loop on t, i.e., exploit the intra-thread reuse of data (similar to the localisation of the sequential code). We find by the dependence-based localisation that the value written by $A[i]$ in iteration t is read again by $A[i-1]$ in the iteration $t+1$ in the same thread.

The second localisation is again w.r.t the loop on t for all threads, i.e., to exploit inter-thread data reuse, too. With all m threads active, $2m+1$ array elements are accessed in one iteration of the t loop and there is an overlap of $2m-1$ elements to the next iteration. The code resulting from this transformation with about 60 lines of code is not shown for lack of space. Table 2 shows the runtimes of the unlocalised and the localised codes. As can be seen, the fully localised code (both localisations applied) performs best with speedups up to 3.5; explicit data moves in the reorganisation phase outperform modulo addressing. On a GPU with slower main memory (NVIDIA Quadro NVS 135m, 800 MHz shader clock, 600 MHz memory clock), we observed speedups up to 4.7.

Example 2 (2d-Gauss-Seidel). Let us now consider a two-dimensional Gauss-Seidel algorithm with row-wise alternating even-odd updates on an $(n+1)^2$ matrix

Table 3. 2d-Gauss-Seidel: runtimes in seconds for $m = 1000$, $n = 2p + 1$ on GPU

$p =$	64	128	192	256	320	384
parallel code	0.29	0.99	2.10	3.54	5.42	8.03
fully localised parallel code with moves	0.30	0.74	1.42	2.18	3.10	4.21
speedup	0.99	1.35	1.48	1.62	1.75	1.91

with m iterations and p parallel threads. The localisation based on dependences is performed with a localisation window encompassing both the updates to even and odd elements of a row. The localised part of the matrix consists of two successive rows progressing row by row with the computation. The comparison of the runtimes of the original and localised codes is shown in Table 3.

6   Conclusions

By way of precise data dependence information we are able to compute precisely which data items to copy to fast memory (e.g., scratchpad memory) to exploit temporal locality. We determine exactly when to copy a value to fast memory, when to copy an updated value back to main memory and when to relocate a value in fast memory. Our technique is applicable to all codes which can be modelled in the polyhedron model, i.e., loop programs with bounds and array index expressions linear in the variables and structure parameters. Since the data held in fast storage is stored in a compact fashion without holes, the access functions can be complex (piecewise conditional quasi-polynomials), but our experiments suggest that, by using advanced code generation techniques, the overhead can be eliminated by partitioning the iteration domains according to the conditions in the new access functions. In our experiments on a GPU, we observed accelerations of factors up to 3.5 compared to parallel code which uses main memory only. If no dependence information is available, a simpler transformation based on access instances which may move more elements to fast storage than necessary can be applied.

References

1. NVIDIA CUDA. http://www.nvidia.com/cuda
2. Baskaran, M.M., Bondhugula, U., Krishnamoorthy, S., Ramanujam, J., Rountev, A., Sadayappan, P.: Automatic data movement and computation mapping for multi-level parallel architectures with explicitly managed memories. In: PPoPP 2008: Proc. of the 13th ACM SIGPLAN Symposium on Principles and Practice of Parallel Programming, pp. 1–10. ACM Press, New York (2008)
3. Bastoul, C.: Code generation in the polyhedral model is easier than you think. In: PACT 2004: Proc. of the 13th Int. Conf. on Parallel Architectures and Compilation Techniques, Washington, DC, USA, pp. 7–16. IEEE Computer Society Press, Los Alamitos (2004)
4. Bastoul, C., Feautrier, P.: Improving data locality by chunking. In: Hedin, G. (ed.) CC 2003. LNCS, vol. 2622, pp. 320–335. Springer, Heidelberg (2003)
5. Bondhugula, U., Baskaran, M.M., Krishnamoorthy, S., Ramanujam, J., Rountev, A., Sadayappan, P.: Automatic transformations for communication-minimized parallelization and locality optimization in the polyhedral model. In: Hendren, L. (ed.) CC 2008. LNCS, vol. 4959, pp. 132–146. Springer, Heidelberg (2008)
6. Chen, G., Kandemir, M.: Compiler-directed code restructuring for improving performance of MPSoCs. IEEE Transactions on Parallel and Distributed Systems 19(9), 1201–1214 (2008)

7. Clauss, P., Meister, B.: Automatic memory layout transformations to optimize spatial locality in parameterized loop nests. In: 4th Annual Workshop on Interaction between Compilers and Computer Architectures, INTERACT-4, Toulouse, France (January 2000)

8. Issenin, I., Brockmeyer, E., Miranda, M., Dutt, N.: Data reuse analysis technique for software-controlled memory hierarchies. In: DATE 2004: Proc. of the Conf. on Design, Automation and Test in Europe, Washington, DC, USA, pp. 202–207. IEEE Computer Society Press, Los Alamitos (2004)

9. Kandemir, M., Choudhary, A.: Compiler-directed scratch pad memory hierarchy design and management. In: DAC 2002: Proc. of the 39th Conf. on Design Automation, pp. 628–633. ACM Press, New York (2002)

10. Kandemir, M., Ramanujam, J., Choudhary, A.: A compiler algorithm for optimizing locality in loop nests. In: Proc. of the 11th Int. Conf. on Supercomputing (ICS), July 1997, pp. 269–276 (1997)

11. Kandemir, M., Ramanujam, J., Irwin, J., Vijaykrishnan, N., Kadayif, I., Parikh, A.: Dynamic management of scratch-pad memory space. In: DAC 2001: Proc. of the 38th Conf. on Design Automation, pp. 690–695. ACM, New York (2001)

12. Karp, R.M., Miller, R.E., Winograd, S.: The organization of computations for uniform recurrence equations. Journal of the ACM 14(3), 563–590 (1967)

13. Lamport, L.: The parallel execution of DO loops. Communications of the ACM 17(2), 83–93 (1974)

14. Lengauer, C.: Loop parallelization in the polytope model. In: Best, E. (ed.) CONCUR 1993. LNCS, vol. 715, pp. 398–416. Springer, Heidelberg (1993)

15. Loechner, V., Meister, B., Clauss, P.: Precise data locality optimization of nested loops. J. Supercomput. 21(1), 37–76 (2002)

16. Panda, P.R., Dutt, N.D., Nicolau, A.: Efficient utilization of scratch-pad memory in embedded processor applications. In: EDTC 1997: Proc. of the 1997 European Conf. on Design and Test, Washington, DC, USA, p. 7. IEEE Computer Society Press, Los Alamitos (1997)

17. Verdoolaege, S., Seghir, R., Beyls, K., Loechner, V., Bruynooghe, M.: Analytical computation of ehrhart polynomials: Enabling more compiler analyses and optimizations. In: Irwin, M.J., Zhao, W., Lavagno, L., Mahlke, S. (eds.) Proc. of the 2004 Int. Conf. on Compilers, Architecture, and Synthesis for Embedded Systems (CASES), Washington DC, USA, pp. 248–258. ACM Press, New York (2004)

18. Verdoolaege, S., Seghir, R., Beyls, K., Loechner, V., Bruynooghe, M.: Counting integer points in parametric polytopes using Barvinok's rational functions. Algorithmica 48(1), 37–66 (2007)

19. Wolf, M.E., Lam, M.S.: A data locality optimizing algorithm. In: PLDI 1991: Proc. of the ACM SIGPLAN 1991 Conf. on Programming Language Design and Implementation, pp. 30–44. ACM Press, New York (1991)

Blind Optimization for Exploiting Hardware Features

Dan Knights, Todd Mytkowicz, Peter F. Sweeney,
Michael C. Mozer, and Amer Diwan*

Department of Computer Science
University of Colorado, Boulder

Abstract. Software systems typically exploit only a small fraction of the realizable performance from the underlying microprocessors. While there has been much work on hardware-aware optimizations, two factors limit their benefit. First, microprocessors are so complex that it is unlikely that even an aggressively optimizing compiler will be able to satisfy all the constraints necessary to obtain the best performance. Thus, most optimizations use a simplified model of the hardware (e.g., they may be cache-aware but they may ignore other hardware structures, such as TLBs, etc.). Second, hardware manufacturers do not reveal all details of their microprocessors so even if the authors of optimizations wanted to simultaneously optimize for all components of the hardware, they may be unable to do so because they are working with limited knowledge. This paper presents and evaluates our blind optimization approach which provides a way to get around these issues.

Blind optimization uses the insight that we can generate many variants of an application by altering semantic preserving parameters of an application; for example our variants can cover the space of code and data layout by shifting the positions of code and data in memory. Our optimization strategy attempts to find a variant that performs well with respect to an optimization objective. We show that even our first implementation of blind optimization speeds up a number of programs from the SPECint 2006 benchmark suite.

1 Introduction

Computer systems rarely exploit the underlying hardware to its fullest potential. For example, even though many microprocessors can execute 4 or more instructions per cycle per core, it is rare for applications to execute more than 1 instruction per cycle even for brief periods [10] of time. Thus, there is an enormous potential for improving performance: in theory, at least, we should be able

---

* This work is supported by NSF CSE-0509521, NSF ITR grant CCR-0085792, NSF grant ST-CRTS 0540997, and the Defense Advanced Research Projects Agency under its Agreement No. HR0011-07-9-0002. Any opinions, findings and conclusions or recommendations expressed in this material are the authors' and do not necessarily reflect those of the sponsors.

O. de Moor and M. Schwartzbach (Eds.): CC 2009, LNCS 5501, pp. 251–265, 2009.

to obtain multi-fold speedup for many applications without counting on any advances from hardware. Unfortunately, this potential is not easy to realize: modern microprocessors are incredibly complex and worse, hardware manufacturers do not reveal full details of their hardware. As a consequence even if compiler writers were extremely knowledgeable about microprocessors in general, they would not be able to fully exploit any particular microprocessor because they do not know all the details of that microprocessor.

For example, code layout affects how the code ends up in the many different hardware structures inside a microprocessor. These hardware structures include instruction queues, L1 instruction cache, L2 cache, instruction TLB, buffers for issuing prefetches, buffers for predicting branches, etc. Given this plethora of hardware structures, even if we knew exactly how they all worked (which we usually do not), it would require tremendous effort to implement an optimization that lays out the program code so that it interacts well with all of them. To address such situations, this paper proposes and evaluates *blind optimization*, a new model for compiler optimizations.

The key insight behind blind optimization is that an optimization can be ignorant of—or "blind" to—the details of the hardware architecture and yet still offer significant performance improvements. Understanding why the performance has improved is not essential, as long as the improvement is significant and reproducible. In contrast, existing compiler optimizations are "knowledge-based" because they exploit domain knowledge of the underlying machine.

To specify an instance of blind optimization, we specify three elements: an *optimization objective*, the space of *program variants*, and an *optimization strategy*. The optimization objective is the metric that we wish to optimize (e.g., run time of the program). The space of program variants is an n-dimensional space in which each point is a variant of the program being optimized. We pick the dimensions so that they only affect the optimization objective and not the program's correctness. The optimization strategy explores the variant space in an attempt to identify a variant that has the best optimization objective. Thus, with blind optimization we can find a variant that performs well without knowing why it performs well. This is why these optimizations are "blind".

This paper makes two main contributions. First, this paper introduces the concept of blind optimization and discusses how one can implement them. Second, this paper demonstrates that one blind optimization, improving code and global data layout, improves the performance of several programs from the SPECint 2006 suite with a maximum speedup of over 12% and an average speedup of 1.58%.

2   Motivation

Predicting the performance of a program run is nearly hopeless because it requires us to correctly answer numerous questions. Should we assume that a load will hit in the L1 cache, L2 cache, or L3 cache? Should we assume that an instruction reference will hit in the L1 cache, L2 cache, or L3 cache? Should we assume that the load or next instruction's address is going to hit in the TLB and if not which level of the hierarchical page table will it hit on? Will the branch predictor correctly predict a particular branch? Will we even need to access the branch predictor for a particular branch or will the loop-stream detector avoid that access? These and many other factors determine the overall performance of a program. Given that hardware manufacturers do not reveal all information about their microprocessors some of these questions may be unanswerable.

The difficulty of accurately predicting performance does not bode well for compiler optimizations. To effectively optimize a program, an optimization must predict, using *predictive heuristics*, how code will interact with hardware structures. Because predicting performance is so hard, most predictive heuristics are simple (e.g., they consider the L1 caches but ignore other aspects of the memory hierarchy) and attempt to be a best-guess; others, e.g., Triantafyllis *et al.* [24], have written about the difficulty of coming up with reasonable heuristics. Perhaps, for this reason, it is not surprising that most compiler optimizations offer only modest benefit [13].

For the above reasons, this paper proposes and evaluates blind optimizations, a new technique that does not rely on predictive heuristics.

3   Approach

To specify an instance of blind optimization, we need to specify three elements: the space of program variants, an optimization objective, and an optimization strategy (Figure 1). Intuitively, our approach uses the insight that a program has variants that are behaviorally equivalent but differ in their performance with respect to the optimization objective, e.g., execution time. The optimization strategy navigates this space in an attempt to identify the best variant. This section describes our approach abstractly and Section 4 gives a concrete example of our approach.

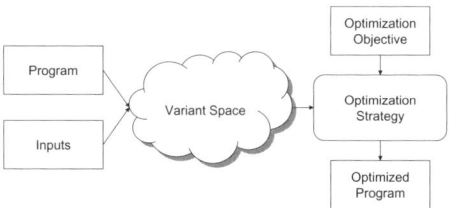

Fig. 1. The blind optimization approach

3.1   Space of Program Variants

A *program variant*, P', is a variant of the program being optimized, P, such that P and P' differ only in performance (if at all). Specifically, P and P' always produce the same answer. By specifying a set of dimensions along which the program can vary, we can define a multidimensional space of program variants—hereafter, *variant space*. Each variant corresponds to a point in this space and thus we can represent it by a discrete-valued vector. Figure 2A shows a two-dimensional variant space. Each point in the grid represents a variant.

The nature of the optimization that we wish to perform determines the dimensions for the variant space. Specifically, we want the dimensions that are actually relevant to our optimization. For example, if we wish to optimize code layout then there may be one dimension for the address (absolute or relative) of each function, loop, or basic block. The dimensions are obviously relevant: changing the address of code blocks clearly affects code layout. To generate a variant (and thus a point in the variant space) we transform the original program.

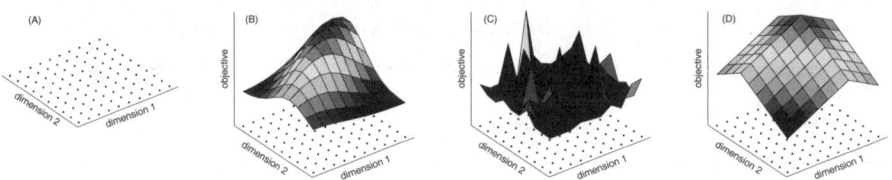

Fig. 2. (A) optimization search space. (B)-(D) potential optimization objective functions.

3.2   Optimization Objective

The optimization objective is the metric that we wish to optimize. The obvious objective is to optimize program run time, but one could use other objectives such as program size, number of cache misses or branch prediction accuracy. If we expect that a program's performance will vary significantly with program input, rather than using data from a single execution for each variant, we should use a *mean* execution time from many different inputs.

Figure 2B adds a third dimension, the optimization objective, to the plot in Figure 2A. Specifically, the *objective* value for a point $(d1, d2)$ gives the value of the optimization objective when dimension 1 is $d1$ and dimension 2 is $d2$.

3.3   Optimization Strategy

The optimization strategy navigates the variant space in an attempt to identify the most efficient variant. We can exploit techniques from the numerical optimization, machine learning, and operations research literatures to identify possible optimization strategies. However, unlike many optimization problems in those domains, the space we are optimizing over is intrinsically discrete, and therefore we cannot use continuous optimization techniques.

If the variant space is small then we can use exhaustive variant generation: i.e., try all the variants and pick the best one. However, variant spaces in our domain are rarely small enough to allow an exhaustive approach. If the optimization objective has structure then we can use smarter approaches (described below). If it has no structure (e.g., Figure 2C) then the best we can do is to use random search; i.e., pick variants at random and use the best one. On the other hand, if the optimization surface is relatively smooth (e.g., Figure 2B), we can use hill climbing approaches such as genetic algorithms. Unfortunately, our prior work has shown that the optimization surface is rarely smooth: a small change in one dimension can significantly change the optimization objective [18].

From the techniques described above, only the random approach seems feasible. Fortunately, in some cases we can actually do better. For example, if we have reason to believe that the dimensions contribute independently to the optimization objective (e.g., Figure 2D) we can explore one dimension at a time and then combine the results to obtain a variant that performs well. Specifically, this situation corresponds to the case where the optimization objective is a linear combination of functions of the individual dimensions, i.e., $o(\mathbf{x}) = \sum_i f_i(x_i)$, where $o(.)$ is the objective function, $\mathbf{x}$ is the vector corresponding to a variant, and the f_i are a set of functions specifying the relationship between the variant's value on dimension i and the optimization objective. Exploiting this relationship turns a $\mathcal{O}(D^V)$ search into an $\mathcal{O}(DV)$ search, where D is the number of dimensions and V is the number of distinct points along each dimension.

As discussed later (Section 4), the assumption behind the above approach hold for at least some blind optimization scenarios. However, even if the assumption behind the above approach does not hold (we show that sometimes it does not), we may have sufficient domain knowledge to express $o(\mathbf{x})$ as a function of lower order terms, e.g., involving pairs of dimensions. In this paper, we explore blind optimization and thus we do not inject any domain knowledge into our approach. It may eventually turn out that some domain knowledge is beneficial.

4   Implementation

Memory system performance is well known to be one of the main bottlenecks for program performance. Thus, our first use of blind optimization is to improve the memory behavior of programs. Specifically, our optimization aligns code and global data to improve program performance. Such alignment can affect how the code and data interact with many different hardware structures. For example, if a cache block is 64 bytes and a hot loop is less than 64 bytes, then the loop fits in a cache block if it is aligned correctly; however, if the loop starts in the middle of the cache block then it may spill over to the next cache block which may be detrimental to performance. Because there are many different hardware structures that may be affected by this alignment, it will be difficult to analytically determine the ideal alignment for code and data. Thus, this optimization is a perfect candidate for the blind approach.

As described in Section 3, blind optimization requires us to specify the following components: a variant space, an optimization objective, and an optimization strategy. We now describe these components in detail.

4.1   Variant Space

Our variants differ in the alignment of code and global data to a 64-byte bound-ary. Our implementation generates variants by shifting functions and global vari-ables. To keep the variant space manageable, we changed the alignment of only hot functions (functions that account for 95% of the total execution time in our training run) and up to 10 randomly picked global variables.

Even within the limited scope of code and global variable alignment, there are many alternatives that we could have pursued. For example, we could have aligned to a 4K boundary instead of a 64 byte boundary to get better alignment to page-level structures. Also, we could have moved code at different granularities (e.g., basic blocks or loops). We will explore these variants in future work.

The variant space has one dimension for each function and global variable, and the values along that dimension are the integers between 0 and 63 (i.e., we use the address of the function or variable modulo 64). We represent a particular variant in this space using a D-dimensional integer vector, where D is the number of functions and global variables that we used.

To generate a particular variant, we first compile the program using gcc (with optimization level -O3) to generate a single assembly file for the entire program (using -combine -S)[1]. Then, we insert `.p2align` and `.byte` directives in the assembly file to affect an alignment. For example, if we want the alignment of function G to be 1 byte off from a 64 byte boundary, we insert `.p2align 8` and `.byte 1` before the start of the function. The `.p2align` forces alignment to a 64 byte boundary and the `.byte` directive shifts the following code by 1 byte; thus, G's address modulo 64 will be 1. Finally, use gcc to generate the executable from the instrumented assembly file. We use a similar technique to adjust the alignment of global variables. Using this technique, we can independently control the alignment of each function and global variable.

4.2   Optimization Objective

We used the program runtime as the optimization objective. We measured the runtime using hardware-performance monitors and used multiple runs to obtain statistically significant results (Section 5).

4.3   Optimization Strategy

As we discussed in Section 3 we can either use an exhaustive approach or an approach that relies on some structure in the variant space (e.g., linearity). We first show that at least some programs exhibit structure that we can exploit and then describe the two approaches.

---

[1] In order to get the entire suite of SPEC C INT 2006 programs to compile with the -combine gcc mode we had to alter a few function headers for most of the programs. We did not change any logic of the code.

Do dimensions independently affect run time? To see if the variant space
has structure that we can exploit, we tested if the assumption in Section 3.3
holds: i.e., do the dimensions contribute independently to the runtime (e.g.,
Figure 2D) or do they interact with one another and their interactions affect
the runtime (e.g., Figure 2B,C). Independence allows for efficient optimization
strategies (linear in the number of dimensions) whereas interactions may require
exponential search. We show that we can assume independence at least for some
of our benchmark programs.

To test for independence, we produced and evaluated a large number, R, of
random points in the variant space. For each run, r, we obtained a runtime,
t_r and a vector $\mathbf{v}_r = \{v_{r,1}, v_{r,2}, ..., v_{r,D}\}$ where $v_{r,i}$ gives the value of the ith
dimension in run r.

Next, we classified variant runtimes. Specifically, as we change the alignment
of a function or global variable we do not see a smooth change in the runtime;
instead, we may see only a few different runtimes (usually 2 to 5) and many
different alignments can produce the same runtime. For example, the odd alignments of a function may all yield a "fast" run and the "even" alignments all yield
a "slow" run, with nothing in between. This classification induces a clustering
on the alignment of each function or global variable; in the above example, the
odd alignments will be in one cluster and even alignments in another cluster.
Our clusters were often surprising: for example some clusters included a mixture
of odd and even alignments (e.g. function `foo` aligned to a 13 byte boundary);
we would probably not have guessed these clusters using a knowledge-based
approach.

We then used the clustering to convert the variant vectors into vectors of
indicator variables, $\mathbf{q}_r = \{q_{r,1}, q_{r,2}, ..., q_{r,D}\}$, where $q_{r,i}$ is 1 if $v_{r,i}$ was in cluster
1 and 0 otherwise. The linear model we wish to produce is now:

$$\hat{t}_r = \sum_d w_d \, q_{r,d}$$

where $\mathbf{w}$ is a vector of weights (coefficients) and d spans D, the number of
dimensions in the vector space. If $\hat{t}_r$ predicts the actual t_r accurately for a
large number of runs $R >> D$, it implies that function and global variable
alignments contribute independently to the total runtime. The constraint $R >>
D$ is necessary to ensure that the model, which has D free parameters, is simple
relative to the number of data points, R, that it explains.

We develop the simplest linear model via a greedy add-one-in regression. In
other words, at each step, we add the dimension that yields the best improvement
in the squared error between $\hat{t}_r$ and t_r. We stop when adding another dimension
does not yield a significant improvement in squared error.

Figure 3 compares actual runtime, t_r, to the model's prediction, $\hat{t}_r$. Each point
on the scatter-plot corresponds to a single run, r. We see that we get a good
linear fit for libquantum while the fit is much worse for bzip2. Thus, while some
of our programs are amenable to a linear model, others are not. For this reason,
we explore two approaches in our experiments: (i) *random search* assumes that
the optimization objective does not exhibit a structure that we can exploit; and

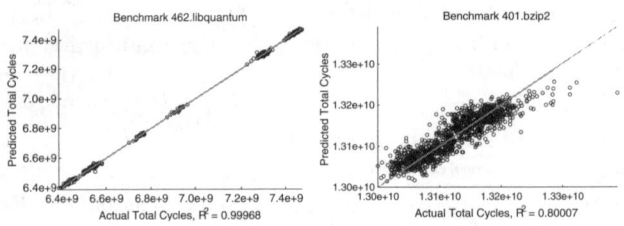

Fig. 3. Predicted versus actual runtimes

(ii) *independent dimension search* assumes that the dimensions independently contribute to the optimization objective.

Approach for random search. Random search simply tries many variants and chooses fastest variant as the optimized program. Random search is not as naive as it might sound. Ordinarily, one would not expect a random search in a space of 64^D variants to turn up anything close to the optimal variant. However, our earlier clustering results suggest that the real space is actually much smaller than 64^D and thus random search with even a modest number of variants may actually produce good results.

Approach for independent dimension search. Unlike random search, independent dimension search does not simply pick the best variant out of the ones that it has tried; instead it synthesizes a (possibly as yet untried) variant by analyzing the variants it has seen. It works as follows:

1. For a program whose variant space has D dimensions, and each dimension has 64 possible alignments, randomly select a set of $64D$ variants in the variant space subject to the constraint that over the set, all 64 alignments for each dimension occur with equal frequency.
2. Measure the runtime of each variant.
3. For each dimension, d, compute the mean runtime for each possible alignment. This involves computing the average runtime over all random variants whose value for dimension d is a, for $d = 1, ...D$ and $a = 0, 1, 2, ..., 63$. Let $\bar{t}_{d,a}$ denote the mean runtime for dimension d aligned to byte a.
4. For each dimension d, choose the best alignment $a_d^* = \arg\min_a \bar{t}_{d,a}$.
5. Form a new variant in which each dimension's value is a_d^*. This variant will be the optimized program under the assumption of independence.

In future work, we will likely opt for hill climbing search which is based on a small number of equivalence classes instead of 64 possible alignments.

5 Methodology

With all aspects of our measurements, we followed best practices so as to avoid perturbing our data. Specifically, we conducted all our experiments on

Table 1. Benchmark programs

Benchmark	Description	# Inputs	# Variants
bzip2	Compression algorithm	10	100
gcc	C Compiler	10	100
gobmk	Go game	7	100
hmmer	Computational biology DNA search	4	100
h264ref	Video encoding	10	100
lbm	3D Fluid dynamics	3	100
libquantum	Quantum computer simulator	10	100
mcf	Single-depot vehicle scheduler	3	100
milc	4D Lattice simulations	3	100
perlbench	Scripting language interpreter	5	100
sjeng	Chess program	3	100

minimally-loaded machines and used only local disks. We ran each benchmark N times—where N is such that the 95% confidence interval of the mean is 0.5% of the mean itself. N was 3 for most of our benchmarks. We used PAPI [3] (version 3.5.0) to capture the cycle counter before and after a benchmark runs. We used the default (as per SPEC) linking order for all benchmarks. We used *gcc* version 4.2.1 and optimization level *O3* to compile our benchmarks. Finally, we ran our programs in an empty environment (`env -i`) and turned off the kernel's address randomization.

Table 1 presents SPECint 2006 [22] benchmarks that we use (we omitted benchmarks not written in C). For each benchmark, Table 1 gives the number of variants that we generated and the number of inputs that we used. We used the *ref* and *train* inputs provided by SPEC.

Because of the large running times of the SPEC programs (total machine time was over 525 hours) and the large number of program variants required by blind optimization we used three similar Intel Core 2 workstations. Each workstation runs the Linux operating system on a Core 2 processor. We ran all experiments for a particular benchmark on the same machine to remove the possibility of introducing a confounding variable into our analysis.

6   Results

In this section, we evaluate our first instantiation of blind optimization.

6.1   Are Programs Amenable to Code- and Global Data-Layout Optimization?

Figure 4 shows that improving code- and global data-layout can significantly affect program performance. The height of a bar gives the number of variants that have a particular execution time (indicated by the x-axis label). We normalize all execution times to the execution time of the default variant. We present the histograms only for three benchmarks due to space limitations: libquantum and perlbench with a wide range of 17.4% and 9.5% respectively, and mcf with its narrow range of 0.3%. From these histograms we conclude that depending on

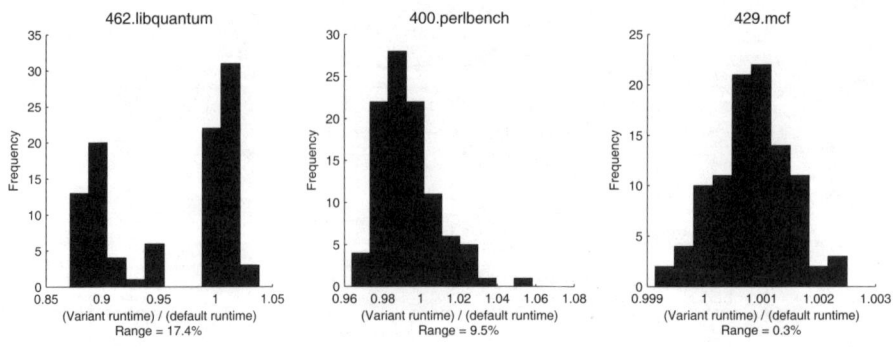

Fig. 4. Distribution of run-times

which variant *gcc -O3* actually generates, our approach may be able to speed up these programs by up to 17.4%. On the other hand, our optimization will not help some benchmarks, such as *mcf.*

In general, we have found that *gcc -O3* does only slightly better than a randomly chosen program variant. When averaged across all inputs for all benchmarks, we found that *gcc -O3* was slower than the average variant for five out of the eleven benchmarks. This is remarkable, since it suggests that *gcc*'s domain knowledge is not helpful; thus blind optimization is a promising alternative.

Table 2 presents the benefit due to blind optimization of code- and global data-layout for each benchmark. The "random: % observed improvement" and "indep: % observed improvement" give percentage speedups (over the default variant) using random search and independent dimensions search respectively. We obtained these speedups using n-fold cross-validation. For each of the n inputs of a given benchmark (shown in the "# inputs" column in Table 1), we used the remaining $n - 1$ inputs to choose (random search) or produce (independent dimensions search) the best program variant, and then measured the speedup obtained on the nth hold-out input. We present the average speedup over all n

Table 2. Cross-validation results for random and independent models on all benchmarks

Benchmark	random: potential % speedup	random: observed % speedup	indep.: observed % speedup
bzip2	1.04	0.93	0.81
gcc	0.23	0.20	-2.19
gobmk	0.49	0.47	-0.48
hmmer	2.72	0.32	0.76
h264ref	0.12	0.05	0.04
lbm	0.70	-0.14	0.17
libquantum	12.61	12.61	12.46
mcf	0.51	-0.26	0.02
milc	2.24	1.93	1.43
perlbench	1.17	0.24	-0.29
sjeng	1.10	1.10	0.53

folds. This methodology, commonly used in the statistics literature, ensures that we do not use the same inputs for training as for evaluation.

From Table 2 we see that random search speeds up 9 of the 11 benchmarks and slightly slows down two benchmarks (lbm and mcf). Moreover, three programs show significant (more than 1%) speedups: libquantum, milc, and sjeng. These speedups are significant because they come on top of code that *gcc* has already optimized.

From the data for independent dimensions search (Column "indep: observed % speedup") we see that it outperforms random search for only three benchmarks (hmmer, lbm, and mcf). This is not surprising; as Figure 3 shows the independent dimensions assumption does not always hold.

6.2   Is the Fastest Variant on One Input the Fastest Variant on Another?

So far, all our results use cross-validation; i.e., we evaluate and train on different inputs. The "random: % potential improvement" column shows the speedup we would get if we trained and evaluated on the same input. In other words, it gives the upper-bound for how well random search can do. Comparing the "random: % potential improvement" and "random: % observed improvement" columns tells us the extent to which the optimization generalizes across inputs. We see that for many benchmarks it does but for some benchmarks (particularly hmmer, lbm, mcf, and perlbench) it does not. In other words, the inputs for these benchmarks behave differently enough from each other that we cannot fully translate results from one input to another input. This underlies the need to have a good set of training inputs for blind (or any profile-guided) optimization.

6.3   Do Our Results Generalize across Machines?

To answer this question, we used random search to find the best variant on one (training) machine and then compared that variant to the default variant on another (test) machine. Both machines use the Core2 chip, but with different amounts of memory and different clock speeds. The random model for the libquantum, for example, achieved a 12.61% improvement over *gcc* on the training machine and a 12.51% improvement on the test machine. Thus, at least in some cases, our results generalize across machines.

6.4   Do Our Results Generalize across Compilers?

To see if the benefit due to blind optimization was an artifact of something in *gcc*, we repeated the experiments for libquantum (the benchmark with the greatest speedup) using Intel's *icc* compiler. Blind optimization was able to speed up libquantum by 4.63%; while this speedup is smaller than what we observed with *gcc* it is still significant. Thus, blind optimization is useful even for code compiled using *icc*.

7   Discussion

The performance of a program depends not just on characteristics of the program but also on characteristics of the underlying system. Thus, we do not view blind optimizations as something that software manufacturers do just before they ship out their code; instead it is something that occurs at installation time. Indeed, it may be worthwhile to treat blind optimizations analogously to "disk defragmentation": periodically, when the machine is idle, we can rerun blind optimizations on the most performance critical applications. Because blind optimizations do not need the source code, this approach is feasible; moreover, as clients of the software use the system, we can record client inputs and use those inputs to explore the variant space. In this way, the re-optimization will be customized to how clients actually use the software.

8   Related Work

Compiler optimizations have obviously been an active area of research for several decades. Broadly speaking, prior work falls in four categories: optimization-space exploration, machine learning to derive predictive heuristics, search-based optimizations, and knowledge-based optimizations.

8.1   Optimization Space Exploration

This area solves the following problem: given the following set of optimizations, which ones should we use and in what order should we apply them? For the most part, once they have picked the set and order of optimizations, that order is used unchanged for all programs.

Pan et al. [19] use an offline search to find an optimization combination that works well for a training set; this combination is used to optimize subsequent programs. Triantafyllis et al. [24] uses trials at compiler-construction time that produces a hopefully small set of configurations that perform well for a set of training benchmarks. When compiling a new program, they pick one of the configurations from this set; this set is organized hierarchically which helps to quickly identify the best one for the current program.

Given a set of optimizations and underlying system (microprocessor, OS, etc.), work in this area is invaluable for picking combinations that work well together on that system. Blind optimization compliments this area by refining the optimized binaries at a fine-grained level (i.e., applications of individual transformations).

8.2   Machine Learning to Derive Predictive Heuristics

This area uses machine learning to learn predictive heuristics which the compiler uses when optimizing programs.

Cavazos and Moss [5] use supervised learning to learn heuristics for whether or not a basic block is worth scheduling. This heuristic helps focus scheduling effort on blocks that may actually benefit from it. This approach depends on a simulator that can evaluate different schedules; thus the simulator is the "supervisor". Cavazos and O'Boyle [6] use genetic algorithms to find the setting of inlining parameters; they use these settings for subsequent compilations. Singer *et al.* [21] build decision trees to decide which garbage collection to use for an as-yet unseen application. To pick the garbage collector for an unseen application, they identify training applications that were similar to this application and use the garbage collector that performed best for the training application.

These techniques free the compiler writer from having to come up with heuristics. However, they assume that program-independent features are enough to base predictive heuristics on. In contrast, blind optimization does not depend on predictive heuristics.

8.3 Search-Based Optimizations

Search-based optimizations attempt to obtain good performance by exploring a space of optimizations and picking the best point in the space for a given piece of code. Blind-optimization is a search-based optimization technique.

Massalin's superoptimizer [14], for example, exhaustively explores instruction combinations to find the shortest sequence that behaves the same as the sequence being optimized. McGovern *et al.* [17] try many different schedules of one basic block at a time and pick the one that gives the best performance. Because McGovern *et al.*'s technique works on one basic block at a time, it requires a simulator to estimate the performance of the basic block. Cooper *et al.* [7] use biased random sampling to try many different compilation sequences (i.e., different orders for optimizations) to identify an order that gives the best performance for the program being compiled. Lau *et al.* [12] effectively implement Cooper *et al.*'s approach in an online setting. Given multiple versions of a method (variants), each optimized differently, Lau's approach uses sampling to pick the best variant. It uses exhaustive search since it collects data on all the variants.

All of the above work can be thought of as examples of the blind optimization approach. For example, the Massalin's superoptimizer uses program size as the optimization objective and the machine's instruction set as the variant space. In contrast, our instantiation of the blind optimization approach either (i) uses a much larger variant space where exhaustive search is simply not possible; or (ii) attempts to identify structure in the variant space which enables us to efficiently search the space.

8.4 Knowledge-Based Optimizations

Knowledge-based optimizations attempt to improve performance by incorporating significant domain knowledge about what makes code efficient or inefficient on the underlying system. This work falls in two categories: dynamic and static.

Dynamic knowledge-based optimizations improve the performance of code while it is running. Adaptive optimizations [1] track which code is hot and optimize only that code. Feedback-directed optimizations [2] continually reevaluate optimization decisions while the optimized program is running. Both adaptive and feedback-directed optimizations avoid having to predict which code is slow: they know which code is slow since they have measured it recently. However, unlike blind optimization, they still need to predict the benefit of an optimization on the subsequent performance of the code.

Static knowledge-based optimizations requires deep knowledge of the underlying system to optimize code using profiling data. Required knowledge of the underlying system for these approaches to work include: knowledge that the instruction cache is direct-mapped [15,8], knowledge of the size of the instruction cache [9,16] knowledge of the branch predictor [11,20,23,4]. In contrast, blind optimization requires no knowledge of the underlying hardware.

9 Conclusions

We have introduced blind optimization, a useful new approach for optimizing programs to better utilize the underlying hardware. We have demonstrated this approach with a single example: improving code and global-data layout. We have shown that even this single example yields statistically significant speedups (average 1.58%) and in one benchmark, large (12%) speedup. These results are exciting since we are improving code that *gcc* has already optimized (even with respect to its alignment) to the best of its ability.

References

1. Arnold, M., Fink, S., Grove, D., Hind, M., Sweeney, P.F.: Adaptive optimization in the Jalapeño JVM. ACM SIGPLAN Notices 35(10), 47–65 (2000)
2. Arnold, M., Hind, M., Ryder, B.G.: Online feedback-directed optimization of java. SIGPLAN Not. 37(11), 111–129 (2002)
3. Browne, S., Dongarra, J., Garner, N., London, K., Mucci, P.: A scalable cross-platform infrastructure for application performance tuning using hardware counters. In: SC, Dallas, Texas (November 2000)
4. Calder, B., Grunwald, D.: Reducing branch costs via branch alignment. In: ASPLOS (October 1994)
5. Cavazos, J., Moss, J.E.B.: Inducing heuristics to decide whether to schedule. In: PLDI, pp. 183–194. ACM Press, New York (2004)
6. Cavazos, J., O'Boyle, M.F.P.: Automatic tuning of inlining heuristics. In: SC, Washington, DC, USA, p. 14. IEEE Computer Society, Los Alamitos (2005)
7. Cooper, K.D., Subramanian, D., Torczon, L.: Adaptive optimizing compilers for the 21st century. J. Supercomput. 23(1), 7–22 (2002)
8. Gloy, N., Blackwell, T., Smith, M.D., Calder, B.: Procedure placement using temporal ordering information. In: MICRO, pp. 303–313 (1997)
9. Hashemi, A.H., Kaeli, D.R., Calder, B.: Efficient procedure mapping using cache line coloring. In: PLDI, pp. 171–182 (1997)

10. Hauswirth, M., Sweeney, P.F., Diwan, A., Hind, M.: Vertical profiling: Understanding the behavior of object-oriented applications. In: OOPSLA (2004)
11. Jiménez, D.A.: Code placement for improving dynamic branch prediction accuracy. In: PLDI, pp. 107–116. ACM Press, New York (2005)
12. Lau, J., Arnold, M., Hind, M., Calder, B.: Online performance auditing: using hot optimizations without getting burned. SIGPLAN Not. 41(6), 239–251 (2006)
13. Lee, H., von Dincklage, D., Diwan, A., Eliot, J., Moss, B.: Understanding the behavior of compiler optimizations. Softw. Pract. Exper. 36(8), 835–844 (2006)
14. Massalin, H.: Superoptimizer: a look at the smallest program. SIGPLAN Not. 22(10), 122–126 (1987)
15. Mcfarling, S.: Program optimization for instruction caches. In: ASPLOS, pp. 183–191. ACM, New York (1989)
16. Mcfarling, S.: Procedure merging with instruction caches. In: PLDI, pp. 71–79 (1991)
17. McGovern, A., Moss, E., Barto, A.G.: Building a basic block instruction scheduler with reinforcement learning and rollouts. Mach. Learn. 49(2-3), 141–160 (2002)
18. Mytkowicz, T., Diwan, A., Hauswirth, M., Sweeney, P.F.: Producing wrong data without doing anything obviously wrong? In: ASPLOS (2009)
19. Pan, Z., Eigenmann, R.: Fast and effective orchestration of compiler optimizations for automatic performance tuning. In: CGO, Washington, DC, USA, pp. 319–332. IEEE Computer Society, Los Alamitos (2006)
20. Pettis, K., Hansen, R.C.: Profile guided code positioning. In: PLDI, pp. 16–27 (June 1990)
21. Singer, J., Brown, G., Watson, I., Cavazos, J.: Intelligent selection of application-specific garbage collectors. In: ISMM, pp. 91–102. ACM Press, New York (2007)
22. Standard Performance Evaluation Corporation. SPEC CPU2006 Benchmarks, http://www.spec.org/cpu2006/
23. Tomiyama, H., Yasuura, H.: Code placement techniques for cache miss rate reduction. ACM Trans. Des. Autom. Electron. Syst. 2(4), 410–429 (1997)
24. Triantafyllis, S., Vachharajani, M., Vachharajani, N., August, D.I.: Compiler optimization-space exploration. In: CGO, Washington, DC, USA, pp. 204–215. IEEE Computer Society Press, Los Alamitos (2003)

How to CPS Transform a Monad

Annette Bieniusa and Peter Thiemann

Institut für Informatik, Universität Freiburg, Georges-Köhler-Allee 079
79110 Freiburg, Germany
{bieniusa,thiemann}@informatik.uni-freiburg.de

Abstract. CPS transformation is an important tool in the compilation of functional programming languages. For strict languages, such as our web programming language "Rinso" or Microsoft's F#, monadic expressions can help with structuring and composing computations.

To apply a CPS transformation in the compilation process of such a language, we integrate explicit monadic abstraction in a call-by-value source language, present a Danvy-Filinski-style CPS transformation for this extension, and verify that the translation preserves simple typing. We establish the simulation properties of this transformation in an untyped setting and relate it to a two stage transformation that implements the monadic abstraction with thunks and introduces continuations in a second step. Furthermore, we give a direct style translation which corresponds to the monadic translation.

1   Introduction

A monad [21] is a powerful abstraction for a computation that may involve side effects. Programming languages that support monads are often of the lazy functional kind. For example, in Haskell [25] monads serve to integrate side-effecting computations like I/O operations, exceptions, operations on references and mutable arrays, and concurrency primitives [26,27,28,29].

However, monads do not only serve to encapsulate computation but also to structure it. The basic operations of a monad are the creation of a trivial computation (the "return" operator, which just returns a value) and the composition of computations (the "bind" operator). Thus, a computation expressed using a monad can be assembled declaratively (and compositionally) from some primitive computations. This compositionality aspect has proven its relevance, for example, in the Kleisli database query system where a monad abstracts over different collection types and its laws serve as simplification rules for queries [41].

Monadic structure also plays a role in strict languages (see Danvy and Hatcliff's factorization of CPS translations [14], Wadler's marriage of monads and effects [39], or the work on monadic regions [12]) and there are less obvious applications like the monads representing probability distributions in the work of Ramsey and Pfeffer [31] or Park and others [24].

We are currently running two projects in the context of call-by-value functional programming languages that both benefit from the structuring aspect of

O. de Moor and M. Schwartzbach (Eds.): CC 2009, LNCS 5501, pp. 266–280, 2009.

a monad and the compositionality of monadic computations. The first project concerns the implementation of a web programming language inspired by the second author's work on the WASH system [38], the Links project [6], Hop [35], and generally the idea of tierless web programming [22]. The second project deals with the efficient implementation of Park's work [24] on representing probability distributions by sampling functions (of monadic type).

Another indication for the importance of monads in strict languages is the recent addition of *workflow expressions* to the F# language[37]. These workflow expressions (or computation expressions) are nothing but monad comprehensions [40] which admit some additional operators for monads that support them. F# supports list and sequence operations, database operations, asynchronous operations, manipulation of probability distributions as in Ramsey and Pfeffer's work [31], and a few more monadic computations through workflow expressions. Interestingly, the concrete syntax chosen in F# closely matches our calculus in Sec.3.1. Thus, our results are applicable to compiling F#.

The suitability of the CPS transformation for compilation has been disputed [11,5] but is now receiving renewed attention and is successfully competing with other approaches like ANF or monadic languages [17]. Our projects and in particular the work reported here may yield additional evidence in favor of CPS.

The projects have two commonalities. First, both source languages are strict functional languages with linguistic support for monads (see Sec. 2). Both languages restrict side effects to monadic computations, so we are after encapsulation of both, effects and compositionality.[1] Second, both implementations involve a CPS translation, a well-established implementation path for such languages. These two requirements lead directly to the present work.

The main contributions of this work are as follows. We define Λ^M, a call-by-value lambda calculus with explicit monadic constructs (a strict variant of the monadic metalanguage). We specify an optimizing CPS translation from Λ^M to the lambda calculus and prove its simulation and translation properties. We define the corresponding direct-style translation and prove simulation for it. We briefly investigate an alternative transformation that first performs thunkification and then runs a standard CPS transformation. We state a type system based on simple types for Λ^M and prove that the transformation preserves typing.

2   Two Strict Languages with Monads

In two seemingly unrelated projects, we have arrived at using a strict language with a monadic sublanguage as a good match for the problem domain. In both projects there is also the need of applying the CPS transformation to programs. This section briefly introduces the projects and explains the role of the CPS transformation in their implementation.

Rinso. Rinso is an experimental programming language for writing client-side web applications. Rinso compiles to JavaScript and provides convenient monadic

---

[1] Another option would be to structure side effects using a hierarchy of effect-indexed monads [10], but we stick with the simpler scenario for this paper.

```
// producer : MVar Int * Int * Int -> IO ()
producer (mvar, a, b)
  if (a <= b) {
    exec (putMVar (mvar, a));
    exec (producer (mvar, a+1, b))
  } else {
    return ()
  }
// consumer : MVar Int -> IO ()
consumer (mvar) {
  x = exec (readMVar (mvar));
  exec (print (x));
  consumer (mvar)
}
// main : Unit -> IO ()
main () {
  mvar = exec newEmptyMVar;
  exec (fork (producer (mvar, 1, 100)));
  exec (consumer (mvar))
}
```

Fig. 1. Producer and consumer in Rinso

abstractions to protect programmers from the idiosyncrasies of the target language as much as possible. The current prototype implementation supports a monadic interface to I/O, references, and concurrency via thread creation. Before getting to an actual example program, we take a short digression and explain the underlying concurrency primitives.

Rinso's concurrency library is based on Concurrent Haskell's MVar abstraction [26]. An MVar is a mutable variable with two distinct states. It is either empty or it is full and holds a value of a fixed type. An MVar supports the following operations in the IO monad:

```
newEmptyMVar : IO (MVar a)
putMVar      : MVar a * a -> IO ()
readMVar     : MVar a -> IO a
```

An MVar starts its life cycle with an invocation of **newEmptyMVar**, which creates a fresh, empty MVar. The execution of **readMVar** (mv) blocks while mv is empty. If mv is full, then **readMVar** mv empties mv and returns its value. The execution of putMVar (mv, v) blocks while mv is full. If mv is empty, then putMVar (mv, v) fills mv with v and returns the unit value. Multiple **readMVar** (putMVar) may block on the same empty (full) MVar, only one will be chosen by the run-time system to proceed. The operations putMVar and readMVar are atomic.

Figure 1 shows an excerpt of Rinso code implementing a producer/consumer abstraction. Rinso marks monadic computations by curly braces, that is, $\{m\}$ is a computation defined by the statement sequence m (which is quite similar to Haskell's do-notation [25]). A statement can be a binding $x = e$; (where the

```
// bernoulli : double -> P bool
bernoulli (p) {
  x = exec sample;
  return (x <= p)
}
// uniform : double * double -> P double
uniform (a, b) {
  x = exec sample;
  return (a + x * (b-a))
}
// gaussian : double * double -> P double
gaussian (m, sigma) {
  x1 = exec sample;
  x2 = exec sample;
  ...
  x12 = exec sample;
  return (m + sigma * (x1 + x2 + ... + x12 - 6.0))
}
```

Fig. 2. Encodings of distributions

$x =$ part may be omitted) or a return statement **return** e. In both cases, e is evaluated. Ordinary binding is free of side effects, whereas a binding $x =$ **exec** e; expects e to evaluate to a monadic value which is then executed immediately.

The prototype implementation of Rinso performs lambda lifting, CPS transformation, and closure conversion. The resulting first-order program is translated to JavaScript. The CPS transformation must be involved for two reasons. First, the target technology (your friendly web browser) stops programs that run "too long". Hence, the program has to be chopped in pieces that invoke each others indirectly. Cooper et al. report a similar approach [6].

Second, as Rinso is supposed to be used on the client side of a web application, it needs facilities for implementing user interfaces. One important ingredient here is concurrency where Rinso supports a thread model similar to concurrent Haskell. The implementation of such a thread model is much facilitated if programs are translated to CPS.

A planned extension of Rinso to also include server-side computation would add yet another reason for using the CPS transformation. As Graunke et al. [19] point out, compiling interactive programs for server-side execution requires a CPS transformation.

Stochastic Computation. Our second project concerns sensor-based technical devices. These devices perform stochastic processing of their sensor data close to the sensors themselves to avoid network congestion with bulk data and also to save power by keeping network transmitters powered down as long as possible.

To cut down on power and cost, as well as to lower the likelihood of errors, part of this processing is implemented in hardware. Thus, this hardware implements computation-intensive tasks which remain fixed over the lifetime of the system.

It is often co-designed with the software that performs higher level processing tasks which are more likely to change over time.

Our project investigates an approach to specifying such systems in a single linguistic framework. One core aspect is the modeling of probability distributions using a sampling monad as inspired by Park et al.'s work [24]. One obstacle in putting this work into practice is its limited performance if implemented purely in software. Thus, we aim at implementing the stochastic processing in hardware. The implementation follows one of the standard paths in functional language compilation, CPS transformation and closure conversion, before mapping the program to hardware via VHDL [34].

Figure 2 contains some distributions which are encoded using a Rinso-like syntax. They are transcribed from Park et al. [24]. The basic computation is `sample` of type P `double` (where P is the probability monad), which models a 0-1 uniformly distributed random variable. `bernoulli(p)` implements a Bernoulli distribution with probability p, `uniform(a,b)` implements a uniform distribution over the interval (a,b), and `gaussian(m,sigma)` implements an (approximation of a) Gaussian distribution using the 12-rule.

3   CPS Transformation

3.1   The Source Language

Figure 3 shows the syntax of Λ^M, a call-by-value lambda calculus extended with monadic expressions. In addition to constants, variables, lambda abstractions, and function applications (marked with infix @) there are also monadic computations $\{m\}$, which open a new binding scope with the $x = \ldots$ statements as binding operations. Side effects can only occur in computations. Computations can be bound to variables as in $x = \{m\}$ because they are values. Their evaluation must be triggered via the keyword `exec`. The monadic statement $x = e \, ; m$ behaves like $x = $ `exec` $\{$`return` $e\} \, ; m$. We use fv to denote the set of free variables in an expression or computation, and bv for variable bound by a binding operation m_i. The `print` operation which displays integers serves as an example for a side effecting operation.

The figure further defines the semantics of Λ^M. Monadic reduction $\mapsto_m$ is the top-level notion of reduction. $\mathcal{M}$ denotes the evaluation context for monadic statements, $\mathcal{E}$ the corresponding one for expressions. The superscript on the reduction can be i representing the printed value or ε if no output happens. The annotation $\mathcal{A}$ on the transitive closure of reduction stands for a (potentially empty) sequence of integers. Computation stops with `return` v at the top level.

Figure 4 presents a simple type system for Λ^M inspired by Moggi's meta-language [21]. The unary type constructor T represents the monad. Hence, a computation returning a value of type τ has type $T\tau$.

Theorem 1. *The type system in Fig. 4 is sound with respect to the semantics of Λ^M in Fig. 3.*

Syntax:

$$\begin{array}{llll}
\text{expressions} & e & ::= c \mid x \mid \lambda x.e \mid e@e \mid \{m\} \\
\text{statements} & m & ::= \mathbf{return}\ e \mid x = \mathbf{exec}\ e\,;m \mid x = e\,;m \\
\text{constants} & c & ::= \ulcorner i \urcorner \mid \mathbf{print} \\
\text{values} & v & ::= \ulcorner i \urcorner \mid \lambda x.e \mid \{m\} \mid \mathbf{print} \\
\text{output} & a & ::= \varepsilon \mid i & i \in \mathbb{Z} \\
\text{variables} & x & \in Var
\end{array}$$

Evaluation contexts:

$$\mathcal{M} ::= x = \mathbf{exec}\ \mathcal{E}\,;m \mid x = \mathcal{E}\,;m \mid \mathbf{return}\ \mathcal{E}$$
$$\mathcal{E} ::= [\,] \mid \mathcal{E}@e \mid v@\mathcal{E}$$

Evaluation:

$$(\lambda x.e)@v \mapsto_e e[x \mapsto v]$$
$$x = v\,;m \overset{\varepsilon}{\mapsto}_m m[x \mapsto v]$$
$$x = \mathbf{exec}\ (\mathbf{print}@\ulcorner i \urcorner)\,;m \overset{i}{\mapsto}_m m[x \mapsto \ulcorner i \urcorner]$$
$$x = \mathbf{exec}\ \{m_1;\ldots;m_n;\mathbf{return}\ e\}\,;m \overset{\varepsilon}{\mapsto}_m m_1;\ldots;m_n;x = e\,;m$$
$$\text{if } fv(m) \cap bv(m_1,\ldots,m_n) = \emptyset$$

$$\frac{e \mapsto_e e'}{\mathcal{E}[e] \mapsto_e \mathcal{E}[e']} \qquad e \mapsto_e^* e \qquad \frac{e \mapsto_e^* e' \quad e' \mapsto_e e''}{e \mapsto_e^* e''} \qquad \frac{e \mapsto_e e'}{\mathcal{M}[e] \overset{\varepsilon}{\mapsto}_m \mathcal{M}[e']}$$

$$\frac{m \overset{a}{\mapsto}_m m'}{\mathcal{M}[m] \overset{a}{\mapsto}_m \mathcal{M}[m']} \qquad m \overset{\varepsilon}{\mapsto}_m^* m \qquad \frac{m \overset{\mathcal{A},*}{\mapsto}_m m' \quad m' \overset{a}{\mapsto}_m m''}{m \overset{\mathcal{A}a,*}{\mapsto}_m m''}$$

Fig. 3. Syntax and semantics of the source language Λ^M

$$\begin{array}{ll}
\text{types} & \tau,\sigma ::= \mathbf{int} \mid \tau \to \tau \mid \mathbf{T}\,\tau \\
\text{contexts} & \Gamma ::= \cdot \mid \Gamma, x:\tau
\end{array}$$

Typing rules:

$$\overline{\Gamma \vdash_e \mathbf{print} : \mathbf{int} \to \mathbf{T}\,\mathbf{int}} \qquad \overline{\Gamma \vdash_e \ulcorner i \urcorner : \mathbf{int}} \qquad \frac{\Gamma(x) = \tau}{\Gamma \vdash_e x : \tau}$$

$$\frac{\Gamma, x:\tau_1 \vdash_e e : \tau_2}{\Gamma \vdash_e \lambda x.e : \tau_1 \to \tau_2} \qquad \frac{\Gamma \vdash_e e_1 : \tau_1 \to \tau_2 \quad \Gamma \vdash_e e_2 : \tau_1}{\Gamma \vdash_e e_1@e_2 : \tau_2}$$

$$\frac{\Gamma \vdash_m m : \mathbf{T}\,\tau}{\Gamma \vdash_e \{m\} : \mathbf{T}\,\tau} \qquad \frac{\Gamma \vdash_e e : \tau}{\Gamma \vdash_m \mathbf{return}\ e : \mathbf{T}\,\tau} \qquad \frac{\Gamma \vdash_e e : \tau \quad \Gamma, x:\tau \vdash_m m : \mathbf{T}\,\tau'}{\Gamma \vdash_m x = e;m : \mathbf{T}\,\tau'}$$

$$\frac{\Gamma \vdash_e e : \mathbf{T}\,\tau \quad \Gamma, x:\tau \vdash_m m : \mathbf{T}\,\tau'}{\Gamma \vdash_m x = \mathbf{exec}\ e;m : \mathbf{T}\,\tau'}$$

Fig. 4. Simple type system for Λ^M

3.2 CPS Transformation of Monadic Expressions

Our CPS transformation on Λ^M terms extends Danvy and Filinski's one-pass optimizing call-by-value CPS transformation [8] with transformation rules for

Syntax:

$$\text{expressions} \quad E, F ::= C \mid x \mid \lambda x.E \mid F@E$$
$$\text{constants} \quad C \quad ::= \text{print}_c \mid \ulcorner i \urcorner$$
$$\text{values} \quad V \quad ::= C \mid \lambda x.E$$

where $i \in \mathbb{Z}$ and $x \in Var$, an infinite set of variables

Reduction contexts for call-by-value ($\mathcal{E}_v$) and call-by-name ($\mathcal{E}_n$):

$$\mathcal{E}_v ::= [] \mid \mathcal{E}_v@E \mid V@\mathcal{E}_v \qquad \mathcal{E}_n ::= [] \mid \mathcal{E}_n@E$$

Reduction (for $j \in \{v, n\}$):

$$(\lambda x.E)@F \overset{\varepsilon}{\mapsto}_\beta E[F/x] \qquad (\lambda x.E)@V \overset{\varepsilon}{\mapsto}_{\beta V} E[V/x] \qquad (\text{print}_c@\ulcorner i \urcorner)@F \overset{i}{\mapsto}_\gamma F@\ulcorner i \urcorner$$

$$\frac{E \overset{a}{\mapsto}_{\beta V, \gamma} E'}{\mathcal{E}_v[E] \overset{a}{\mapsto}_v \mathcal{E}_v[E']} \qquad \frac{E \overset{a}{\mapsto}_{\beta, \gamma} E'}{\mathcal{E}_n[E] \overset{a}{\mapsto}_n \mathcal{E}_n[E']} \qquad E \overset{\varepsilon,*}{\longmapsto}_j E \qquad \frac{E \overset{A,*}{\longmapsto}_j E' \quad E' \overset{a}{\longmapsto}_j E''}{E \overset{Aa,*}{\longmapsto}_j E''}$$

Fig. 5. The target language Λ

monadic expressions and statements. The result is a one-pass CPS transformation which does not introduce any administrative β-redexes. In addition, potential η-redexes around tail calls are avoided by using auxiliary transformations $\mathcal{C}'_e$ and $\mathcal{C}'_m$.

The transformation is defined in a two-level lambda calculus [23] which distinguishes between abstractions and applications at transformation time ($\overline{\lambda}x.e$ and $f\overline{@}e$) and at run time ($\underline{\lambda}x.e$ and $f\underline{@}e$). The former reduce during transformation whereas the latter generate target code.

Figure 5 defines syntax and semantics of the target language of the transformation. There are two semantics, call-by-value given by the relation $\mapsto_v$ and call-by-name given by $\mapsto_n$. The print operation is provided in terms of a CPS primitive print_c.

Figure 6 defines the CPS transformation for Λ^M. The result of transforming an expression e to CPS in an empty context is given by $\mathcal{C}_e[\![e]\!]\overline{@}(\underline{\lambda}z.z)$, and in a dynamic context by $\underline{\lambda}k.\mathcal{C}_e[\![e]\!]\overline{@}(\underline{\lambda}z.k\underline{@}z)$. The same holds for the transformation of monadic expressions m. The latter are only transformed in a dynamic context, so the corresponding transformation $\mathcal{C}_m[\![\_]\!]$ for static contexts has been elided.

The type transformation corresponding to our call-by-value CPS transformation is defined in two steps with a value type transformation * and a computation type transformation $\_^\sharp$. The type X is the answer type of all continuations.

$$\text{int}^* = \text{int}$$
$$(\tau \to \sigma)^* = \tau^* \to \sigma^\sharp$$
$$(\mathrm{T}\,\tau)^* = \tau^\sharp$$
$$\tau^\sharp = (\tau^* \to X) \to X$$

Theorem 2. *If* $\Gamma \vdash_e e : \tau$, *then* $\Gamma^*, k : \tau^* \to X \vdash_e (\mathcal{C}'_e[\![e]\!])\overline{@}k : \tau^\sharp$.
  If $\Gamma \vdash_m m : \tau$, *then* $\Gamma^*, k : \tau^* \to X \vdash_e (\mathcal{C}'_m[\![m]\!])\overline{@}k : \tau^\sharp$.

Danvy and Filinski's optimizing call-by-value CPS transformation [8]

$$\mathcal{C}_e[\![\ulcorner i \urcorner]\!] = \overline{\lambda}\kappa.\kappa\overline{@}\ulcorner i \urcorner$$

$$\mathcal{C}_e[\![x]\!] = \overline{\lambda}\kappa.\kappa\overline{@}x$$

$$\mathcal{C}_e[\![\lambda x.e]\!] = \overline{\lambda}\kappa.\kappa\overline{@}(\underline{\lambda}x.\underline{\lambda}k.\mathcal{C}'_e[\![e]\!]\overline{@}k)$$

$$\mathcal{C}_e[\![e_0 @ e_1]\!] = \overline{\lambda}\kappa.\mathcal{C}_e[\![e_0]\!]\overline{@}(\overline{\lambda}v_0.\mathcal{C}_e[\![e_1]\!]\overline{@}(\overline{\lambda}v_1.(v_0\underline{@}v_1)\underline{@}(\underline{\lambda}a.\kappa\overline{@}a)))$$

$$\mathcal{C}'_e[\![\ulcorner i \urcorner]\!] = \overline{\lambda}k.k\underline{@}\ulcorner i \urcorner$$

$$\mathcal{C}'_e[\![x]\!] = \overline{\lambda}k.k\underline{@}x$$

$$\mathcal{C}'_e[\![\lambda x.e]\!] = \overline{\lambda}k.k\underline{@}(\underline{\lambda}x.\underline{\lambda}k.\mathcal{C}'_e[\![e]\!]\overline{@}k)$$

$$\mathcal{C}'_e[\![e_0 @ e_1]\!] = \overline{\lambda}k.\mathcal{C}_e[\![e_0]\!]\overline{@}(\overline{\lambda}v_0.\mathcal{C}_e[\![e_1]\!]\overline{@}(\overline{\lambda}v_1.(v_0\underline{@}v_1)\underline{@}k))$$

Extension to monadic expressions and statements

$$\mathcal{C}_e[\![\mathtt{print}]\!] = \overline{\lambda}\kappa.\kappa\overline{@}(\underline{\lambda}x.\underline{\lambda}k.k\underline{@}(\mathtt{print}_c\underline{@}x))$$

$$\mathcal{C}_e[\![\{m\}]\!] = \overline{\lambda}\kappa.\kappa\overline{@}(\underline{\lambda}k.\mathcal{C}'_m[\![m]\!]\overline{@}k)$$

$$\mathcal{C}'_e[\![\mathtt{print}]\!] = \overline{\lambda}k.k\underline{@}(\underline{\lambda}x.\underline{\lambda}k.k\underline{@}(\mathtt{print}_c\underline{@}x))$$

$$\mathcal{C}'_e[\![\{m\}]\!] = \overline{\lambda}k.k\underline{@}(\underline{\lambda}n.\mathcal{C}'_m[\![m]\!]\overline{@}n)$$

$$\mathcal{C}'_m[\![\mathtt{return}\ e]\!] = \mathcal{C}'_e[\![e]\!]$$

$$\mathcal{C}'_m[\![x = e\ ;m]\!] = \overline{\lambda}k.\mathcal{C}'_e[\![e]\!]\overline{@}(\underline{\lambda}x.\mathcal{C}'_m[\![m]\!]\overline{@}k)$$

$$\mathcal{C}'_m[\![x = \mathtt{exec}\ e\ ;m]\!] = \overline{\lambda}k.\mathcal{C}_e[\![e]\!]\overline{@}(\overline{\lambda}v.v\underline{@}(\underline{\lambda}x.\mathcal{C}'_m[\![m]\!]\overline{@}k))$$

Fig. 6. CPS transformation

Proof. The proof works by ignoring the annotations, performing induction on the translated terms, and then invoking subject reduction for the simply typed lambda calculus to see that the overlined reductions do not change the type.

3.3 Simulation and Indifference

Danvy and Filinski [8] have shown that the upper half of the rules in Fig. 6 transforms a source term to a result which is $\beta\eta$-equivalent to applying Plotkin's call-by-value CPS transformation to the same source term. Like Plotkin, they prove simulation and indifference results and we follow their lead closely in extending the simulation and indifference results to our setting.

For values v let $\Psi(v) = \mathcal{C}_e[\![v]\!]\overline{@}(\overline{\lambda}x.x)$. It is straightforward to show that $\Psi(v)$ is a value and that the following equations hold:

$$\mathcal{C}_e[\![v]\!]\overline{@}\kappa = \kappa\overline{@}(\Psi(v))$$

$$\mathcal{C}'_e[\![v]\!]\overline{@}k = k\underline{@}(\Psi(v))$$

$$\mathcal{C}_e[\![w]\!]\overline{@}\kappa = \mathcal{C}'_e[\![w]\!]\overline{@}(\underline{\lambda}n.\kappa\overline{@}n)$$

where v denotes a value and w a term that is not a value.

A variable x occurs free in a static continuation κ if for some term p it occurs free in $\kappa\overline{@}p$ but not in p. An expression κ is *schematic* if for any terms p and q and any variable x not occurring free in κ,

$$(\kappa\overline{@}p)[x \mapsto q] = \kappa\overline{@}(p[x \mapsto q]).$$

Lemma 1. *Let p be a term, v a value, x a variable, x' a fresh variable, and let κ be a schematic continuation and k any term. Then*

$$\mathcal{C}_e[\![p[x \mapsto v]]\!]\overline{@}\kappa = (\mathcal{C}_e[\![p[x \mapsto x']]\!]\overline{@}\kappa)[x' \mapsto \Psi(v)]$$
$$\mathcal{C}'_{e/m}[\![p[x \mapsto v]]\!]\overline{@}k = (\mathcal{C}'_{e/m}[\![p[x \mapsto x']]\!]\overline{@}k)[x' \mapsto \Psi(v)]$$

Proof. By induction on p.

The next lemma extends the indifference theorem to Λ^M. All reductions are independent of the choice of the reduction strategy j for the target language: Each argument of an application is a value from the beginning, hence the $V@\mathcal{E}_v$ evaluation context is never needed and the rule βV is sufficient for all reductions. The relation $\overset{a,+}{\mapsto}_j$ denotes the transitive closure of the respective relation $\overset{a}{\mapsto}_j$.

Lemma 2. *Let κ be a schematic continuation and $j \in \{v, n\}$.*
If $p \mapsto_e q$, then $\mathcal{C}_e[\![p]\!]\overline{@}\kappa \overset{\varepsilon,+}{\mapsto}_j \mathcal{C}_e[\![q]\!]\overline{@}\kappa$ and $\mathcal{C}'_e[\![p]\!]@k \overset{\varepsilon,+}{\mapsto}_j \mathcal{C}'_e[\![q]\!]@k$.
If $p \overset{a}{\mapsto}_m q$, then $\mathcal{C}'_m[\![p]\!]@k \overset{a,+}{\mapsto}_j \mathcal{C}'_m[\![q]\!]@k$.
Each source reduction gives rise to at most five target reduction steps.

Proof. Induction on the derivation of $\mapsto_e$ and $\overset{i}{\mapsto}_m$. The case for reducing $x = $ exec $(\text{print}@\ulcorner i\urcorner)$; takes five steps in the target language. All other cases take fewer steps.

Inductive application of Lemma 2 to a multi-step reduction yields the indifference and simulation theorem.

Theorem 3. *Let m be a well-typed term and v be a value such that $m \overset{\mathcal{A}}{\mapsto}_m$* return v. *Then*

$$\mathcal{C}'_m[\![m]\!]\overline{@}(\underline{\lambda}x.x) \overset{\mathcal{A},*}{\mapsto}_j \Psi(v)$$

in at most five times as many reduction steps for $j \in \{v, n\}$.

4   Alternative CPS Transformation

An obvious alternative to the discussed CPS transformation works in two stages, thunkification followed by CPS transformation. Thunkification defers the evaluation of a monadic expression by wrapping its body into a thunk. The transformation of exec forces the thunk's evaluation by providing a dummy argument.

We extend Λ^M (and its CPS transformation) with a new direct-style print operator print_d as indicated in Fig. 7. Figure 8 gives the thunkification as a transformation on Λ^M. It maps print to a function that accepts an output

$$c ::= \cdots \mid \text{print}_d \qquad \text{print}_d @^\ulcorner i^\urcorner \overset{i}{\mapsto}_e {}^\ulcorner i^\urcorner$$
$$v ::= \cdots \mid \text{print}_d \qquad \mathcal{C}_e[\![\text{print}_d]\!] = \overline{\lambda}\kappa.\kappa\overline{@}\text{print}_c$$

Fig. 7. Extension of the source language

$$
\begin{aligned}
\mathcal{T}_e[\![^\ulcorner i^\urcorner]\!] &= {}^\ulcorner i^\urcorner \\
\mathcal{T}_e[\![\text{print}]\!] &= \lambda x.\lambda z.\text{print}_d @x \qquad z \neq x \\
\mathcal{T}_e[\![x]\!] &= x \\
\mathcal{T}_e[\![\lambda x.e]\!] &= \lambda x.\mathcal{T}_e[\![e]\!] \\
\mathcal{T}_e[\![e_1 @ e_2]\!] &= (\mathcal{T}_e[\![e_1]\!]) @ (\mathcal{T}_e[\![e_2]\!]) \\
\mathcal{T}_e[\![\{m\}]\!] &= \lambda z.\mathcal{T}_m[\![m]\!] \qquad z \notin \mathit{fv}(m) \\
\mathcal{T}_m[\![\text{return } e]\!] &= \mathcal{T}_e[\![e]\!] \\
\mathcal{T}_m[\![x = e \,;\, m]\!] &= (\lambda x.\mathcal{T}_m[\![m]\!]) @ (\mathcal{T}_e[\![e]\!]) \\
\mathcal{T}_m[\![x = \text{exec } e \,;\, m]\!] &= (\lambda x.\mathcal{T}_m[\![m]\!]) @ ((\mathcal{T}_e[\![e]\!]) @^\ulcorner 0^\urcorner)
\end{aligned}
$$

Fig. 8. Thunkification

value and a dummy argument and calls print_d if the dummy argument is provided. The value $^\ulcorner 0^\urcorner$ serves as a dummy argument to force the evaluation of the expression following an exec. The transformed program does not use the monadic constructs anymore.[2]

We now get a one-pass CPS transformation as the combination of two transformations:

$$\tilde{\mathcal{C}}_e[\![p]\!] = \mathcal{C}_e[\![\mathcal{T}_e[\![p]\!]]\!] \quad \text{and} \quad \tilde{\mathcal{C}}'_{e/m}[\![p]\!] = \mathcal{C}'_e[\![\mathcal{T}_{e/m}[\![p]\!]]\!]$$

The result is a set of somewhat more complicated transformation rules for the monadic expressions (all other transformation rules remain unchanged as they are not affected by thunkification).

$$
\begin{aligned}
\tilde{\mathcal{C}}_e[\![\text{print}]\!] &= \overline{\lambda}\kappa.\kappa\overline{@}\underline{\lambda}k.\lambda k.k\underline{@}(\underline{\lambda}z.\underline{\lambda}k.(\text{print}_c @x)\underline{@}k) \\
\tilde{\mathcal{C}}_e[\![\{m\}]\!] &= \overline{\lambda}\kappa.\kappa\overline{@}\underline{\lambda}z.(\underline{\lambda}k.\tilde{\mathcal{C}}'_m[\![m]\!]\overline{@}k) \\
\tilde{\mathcal{C}}'_m[\![\text{return } e]\!] &= \mathcal{C}'_e[\![e]\!] = \mathcal{C}'_m[\![\text{return } e]\!] \\
\tilde{\mathcal{C}}'_m[\![x = e \,;\, m]\!] &= \overline{\lambda}k.\tilde{\mathcal{C}}_e[\![e]\!]\overline{@}(\overline{\lambda}v_1.((\underline{\lambda}x.\underline{\lambda}k.\tilde{\mathcal{C}}'_m[\![m]\!]\overline{@}k)\underline{@}v_1)\underline{@}k) \\
\tilde{\mathcal{C}}'_m[\![x = \text{exec } e \,;\, m]\!] &= \\
\overline{\lambda}k.\tilde{\mathcal{C}}_e&[\![e]\!]\overline{@}(\overline{\lambda}w_0.(w_0\underline{@}^\ulcorner 0^\urcorner)\underline{@}(\underline{\lambda}a.((\underline{\lambda}x.\underline{\lambda}k.\tilde{\mathcal{C}}'_m[\![m]\!]\overline{@}k)\underline{@}a)\underline{@}k))
\end{aligned}
$$

As one can easily show, this more intuitive ansatz is $\beta\eta$ equivalent, but less efficient for the monadic constructs as the one in Fig. 6. Indeed, of the most frequently used monadic operations the $x = v$ binding requires one additional reduction step and the $x = \text{exec } \{m\}$ binding requires three additional reduction steps.

---

[2] Park's implementation of the probability monad [24] works in a similar way.

5 Direct-Style Translation

To obtain the direct-style translation in Fig.9 corresponding to the monadic translation in Fig.6, we first have to find a suitable grammar for the resulting CPS terms. The nonterminals cv, cc, and ck stand for CPS values, computations, and continuations. Their definitions are familiar from direct-style translations for the lambda calculus [7]. The last two cases for cv are specific to the monadic case. They involve mc (monadic computations), which in turn involve monadic continuations mk. The translation inserts $\texttt{let}\, x = e\,\texttt{in}\, f$ expressions which are interpreted as $(\lambda x.f)@e$.

The special cases are as follows. The new value $\lambda k.mc$ corresponds to a monadic computation. The computation $cv@mk$ stands for the activation of a delayed computation and is hence mapped to an $\texttt{exec}$ statement in the monad.

The direct style transformation is given for each CPS term. To obtain better readability, $\mathcal{D}^e_{mk}[\![\_]\!]$ denotes the translation that results in a monadic binding with $\texttt{exec}$. The expected simulation result holds:

Lemma 3. *Suppose that* $mc \stackrel{A,*}{\longmapsto}_j k@cv$. *Then* $\mathcal{D}_{mc}[\![mc]\!] \stackrel{A,*}{\longrightarrow}_m \mathcal{D}_{mc}[\![k@cv]\!]$.

However, the pair of transformations $\mathcal{C}'_m$ and $\mathcal{D}_{mc}$ does not form an equational correspondence (let alone a reduction correspondence or a reflection) because the source language Λ^M lacks reductions that perform $\texttt{let}$ insertion and $\texttt{let}$ normalization. Such reductions are added in the work of Sabry, Wadler, and Felleisen [33,32] and lead directly to the existence of such correspondences. The same reductions could be added to Λ^M with the same effect, but we refrained from doing so because it yields no new insights.

6 Related Work

Since Plotkin's seminal paper [30] CPS transformations have been described and characterized in many different flavors. Danvy and Filinski [8] describe an optimizing one-pass transformation for an applied call-by-value lambda calculus that elides administrative reductions by making them static reductions which are performed at transformation time. Our transformation extends their results for a source language with an explicit monad.

Danvy and Hatcliff [9] present a CPS transformation that exploits the results of strictness analysis. Our transformation of the explicit monad is inspired by their treatment of $\texttt{force}$ and $\texttt{delay}$, but adds the one-pass machinery.

Hatcliff and Danvy's generic account of continuation-passing styles [14] factorizes CPS transformations in two strata. The first stratum transforms the source language into Moggi's computational meta-language [21] encoding different evaluation strategies. The second stratum "continuation introduction" is independent from the source language and maps the meta-language into the CPS sublanguage of lambda calculus. Our transformation is reminiscent of the second stratum, but our source language is call-by-value lambda calculus with an explicit monad and our transformation optimizes administrative reductions.

Grammar of CPS terms

$$cv ::= \ulcorner i \urcorner \mid x \mid \lambda x.\lambda k.cc \mid \lambda k.mc \mid \mathtt{print}_c @x$$
$$cc ::= cv@cv@ck \mid ck@cv$$
$$ck ::= \lambda a.cc \mid k$$
$$mc ::= cv@cv@mk \mid mk@cv \mid cv@mk$$
$$mk ::= \lambda x.mc \mid k$$

Lambda calculus cases

$$\mathcal{D}_{cv}\llbracket \ulcorner i \urcorner \rrbracket = \ulcorner i \urcorner \qquad\qquad \mathcal{D}_{cc}\llbracket ck@cv \rrbracket = \mathcal{D}_{ck}\llbracket ck \rrbracket [\mathcal{D}_{cv}\llbracket cv \rrbracket]$$
$$\mathcal{D}_{cv}\llbracket x \rrbracket = x \qquad\qquad\qquad\qquad \mathcal{D}_{ck}\llbracket k \rrbracket = [\,]$$
$$\mathcal{D}_{cv}\llbracket \lambda x.\lambda k.cc \rrbracket = \lambda x.\mathcal{D}_{cc}\llbracket cc \rrbracket \qquad \mathcal{D}_{ck}\llbracket \lambda a.cc \rrbracket = \mathtt{let}\ a = [\,]\ \mathtt{in}\ \mathcal{D}_{cc}\llbracket cc \rrbracket$$
$$\mathcal{D}_{cc}\llbracket cv_1@cv_2@ck \rrbracket = \mathcal{D}_{ck}\llbracket ck \rrbracket [\mathcal{D}_{cv}\llbracket cv_1 \rrbracket @ \mathcal{D}_{cv}\llbracket cv_2 \rrbracket]$$

Monadic cases

$$\mathcal{D}_{cv}\llbracket \lambda k.mc \rrbracket = \{\mathcal{D}_{mc}\llbracket mc \rrbracket\} \qquad \mathcal{D}_{mk}^e\llbracket \lambda x.mc \rrbracket = x = \mathtt{exec}\ [\,]\ ; \mathcal{D}_{mc}\llbracket mc \rrbracket$$
$$\mathcal{D}_{cv}\llbracket \mathtt{print}_c@x \rrbracket = \mathtt{print}@x \qquad \mathcal{D}_{mk}^e\llbracket k \rrbracket = x = \mathtt{exec}\ [\,] ; \mathtt{return}\ x$$
$$\mathcal{D}_{mc}\llbracket mk@cv \rrbracket = \mathcal{D}_{mk}\llbracket mk \rrbracket [\mathcal{D}_{cv}\llbracket cv \rrbracket] \qquad \mathcal{D}_{mk}\llbracket \lambda x.mc \rrbracket = x = [\,]\ ; \mathcal{D}_{mc}\llbracket mc \rrbracket$$
$$\mathcal{D}_{mc}\llbracket cv@mk \rrbracket = \mathcal{D}_{mk}^e\llbracket mk \rrbracket [\mathcal{D}_{cv}\llbracket cv \rrbracket] \qquad \mathcal{D}_{mk}\llbracket k \rrbracket = \mathtt{return}\ [\,]$$
$$\mathcal{D}_{mc}\llbracket cv_1@cv_2@mk \rrbracket = \mathcal{D}_{mk}\llbracket mk \rrbracket [\mathcal{D}_{cv}\llbracket cv_1 \rrbracket @ \mathcal{D}_{cv}\llbracket cv_2 \rrbracket]$$

Fig. 9. Direct style translation

An unoptimized version of our transformation could likely be factored through the computational meta-language, but we have not investigated this issue, yet.

Danvy and Hatcliff [15] study an alternative presentation of the call-by-name CPS transformation by factoring it into a thunkification transformation that inserts `delays` around all function arguments and `forces` all variables and a call-by-value CPS transformation extended to deal with `delay` and `force`. In addition, the paper also investigates an optimizing one-pass transformation but the details are different because our monadic brackets do not contain expressions but monadic statements.

Ager et al. [2] employ another path for transforming monadic code to CPS, which is a key step in their work to derive an abstract machine from a monadic evaluator. The authors first replace the monadic operations in the interpreter with their functional definitions. Then they transform the resulting monad-free evaluator to CPS using a standard call-by-value CPS transformation. It turns out that our thunkification transformation can be seen as expansion of the monadic operations. In fact, the transformation maps the monad type $(\mathrm{T}\,\tau)^\natural$ to $() \to \tau^\natural$ with the obvious return and bind operations. However, as we have demonstrated in Section 4, the combined transformation misses opportunities for optimization that our one-pass transformation exploits. One way to obtain a better transformation via thunkification might be to apply Millikin's idea of using shortcut deforestation with a normalization pass to create a one-pass transformation [20], but we have not yet explored this idea further.

Sabry and Felleisen [32] describe their source calculus via an axiom set which extends the call-by-value lambda calculus. Using an compactifying CPS transformation they present an inverse mapping which yields equational correspondence of terms in source and target calculi of Fischer-style call-by-value CPS transformations. Sabry and Wadler [33] show that Plotkin's CPS transformation is a reflection on Moggi's computational lambda calculus. Barthe et al. [4] propose the weaker notion of reduction correspondence for reasoning about translations. An initial investigation shows some promise for embedding our CPS transformation into this framework.

On the practical side, Appel's book [3] presents all the machinery necessary for compiling with continuations and applies it to the full ML language. The main impact for compilation is that CPS names each intermediate value, sequentializes all computations, and yields an evaluation-order independent intermediate representation that is closed under β reduction. The latter is important as it simplifies the optimization phase of the compiler: It can perform unrestricted β reduction wherever that is desirable. Steele [36] was the first to exploit this insight in his Rabbit compiler for Scheme, Kelsey and others [18,16] later extended the techniques to work with procedural languages in general. Unlike some of his precursors, Appel uses a one-pass CPS transformation which reduces some administrative reductions. He relies on another optimizing pass for eliminating η reductions. An optimizing transformation, like ours, avoids this burden and leads to more efficient compilation.

Another point in favor of CPS-based compilation is the ease with which control operators can be supported in the source language. Friedman et al. [13] make a compelling point of this fact. This may be important in the further development of our Rinso language as control operators are well suited to implement cooperative concurrency.

7   Conclusion

There is evidence that a call-by-value language with an explicit monad is a design option for certain applications. Working towards compilation of such a language, we have developed an optimizing one-pass CPS transformation for this language and proven simulation and indifference for it. We present a direct style transformation for the CPS terms. We have demonstrated that our CPS transformation is preferable to an indirect one via thunkification. Finally, the transformation is compatible with simple typing.

References

1. Abadi, M. (ed.): Proc. 32nd ACM Symp. POPL, Long Beach, CA, USA, January 2005. ACM Press, New York (2005)
2. Ager, M.S., Danvy, O., Midtgaard, J.: A functional correspondence between monadic evaluators and abstract machines for languages with computational effects. Theoretical Computer Science 342(1), 149–172 (2005)
3. Appel, A.W.: Compiling with Continuations. Cambridge University Press, Cambridge (1992)

4. Barthe, G., Hatcliff, J., Sørensen, M.H.: Reflections on reflections. In: Hartel, P.H., Kuchen, H. (eds.) PLILP 1997. LNCS, vol. 1292, pp. 241–258. Springer, Heidelberg (1997)

5. Benton, N., Kennedy, A., Russell, G.: Compiling Standard ML to Java bytecodes. In: Hudak, P. (ed.) Proc. ICFP 1998, Baltimore, MD, USA. ACM Press, New York (1998)

6. Cooper, E., Lindley, S., Wadler, P., Yallop, J.: Links: Web programming without tiers. In: de Boer, F.S., Bonsangue, M.M., Graf, S., de Roever, W.-P. (eds.) FMCO 2006. LNCS, vol. 4709, pp. 266–296. Springer, Heidelberg (2007)

7. Danvy, O.: Back to direct style. Science of Computer Programming 22, 183–195 (1994)

8. Danvy, O., Filinski, A.: Representing control: A study of the CPS transformation. Mathematical Structures in Computer Science 2, 361–391 (1992)

9. Danvy, O., Hatcliff, J.: CPS transformation after strictness analysis. Letters on Programming Languages and Systems 1(3), 195–212 (1993)

10. Filinski, A.: Representing layered monads. In: Aiken, A. (ed.) Proc. 26th ACM Symp. POPL, San Antonio, Texas, USA, pp. 175–188. ACM Press, New York (1999)

11. Flanagan, C., Sabry, A., Duba, B.F., Felleisen, M.: The essence of compiling with continuations. In: Proc. 1993 PLDI, Albuquerque, NM, USA, pp. 237–247 (June 1993)

12. Fluet, M., Morrisett, G.: Monadic regions. J. Funct. Program. 16(4-5), 485–545 (2006)

13. Friedman, D.P., Wand, M.: Essentials of Programming Languages, 3rd edn. MIT Press and McGraw-Hill (2008)

14. Hatcliff, J., Danvy, O.: A generic account of continuation-passing styles. In: Proc. 1994 ACM Symp. POPL, Portland, OR, USA, pp. 458–471. ACM Press, New York (1994)

15. Hatcliff, J., Danvy, O.: Thunks and the λ-calculus. J. Funct. Program. 7(3), 303–319 (1997)

16. Kelsey, R., Hudak, P.: Realistic compilation by program transformation. In: Proc. 16th ACM Symp. POPL, Austin, Texas, pp. 281–292. ACM Press, New York (1989)

17. Kennedy, A.: Compiling with continuations, continued. In: Ramsey, N. (ed.) Proc. ICFP 2007, Freiburg, Germany, pp. 177–190. ACM Press, New York (2007)

18. Kranz, D., Kelsey, R., Rees, J., Hudak, P., Philbin, J., Adams, N.: ORBIT: An optimizing compiler for Scheme. SIGPLAN Notices 21(7), 219–233 (1986); Proc. Sigplan 1986 Symp. on Compiler Construction

19. Matthews, J., Findler, R.B., Graunke, P., Krishnamurthi, S., Felleisen, M.: Automatically restructuring programs for the web. Automated Software Engineering 11(4), 337–364 (2004)

20. Millikin, K.: A new approach to one-pass transformations. In: van Eekelen, M. (ed.) Trends in Functional Programming, September 2007, vol. 6 (2007), intellectbooks.co.uk

21. Moggi, E.: Notions of computations and monads. Information and Computation 93, 55–92 (1991)

22. Neubauer, M., Thiemann, P.: From sequential programs to multi-tier applications by program transformation. In: Abadi [1], pp. 221–232

23. Nielson, F., Nielson, H.R.: Two-Level Functional Languages. Cambridge Tracts in Theoretical Computer Science, vol. 34. Cambridge University Press, Cambridge (1992)

24. Park, S., Pfenning, F., Thrun, S.: A probabilistic language based upon sampling functions. In Abadi [1], pp. 171–182
25. Peyton Jones, S. (ed.): Haskell 98 Language and Libraries, The Revised Report. Cambridge University Press, Cambridge (2003)
26. Peyton Jones, S., Gordon, A., Finne, S.: Concurrent Haskell. In: Proc. 1996 ACM Symp. PQPL, St. Petersburg, FL, USA, pp. 295–308. ACM Press, New York (1996)
27. Peyton Jones, S., Reid, A., Hoare, T., Marlow, S., Henderson, F.: A semantics for imprecise exceptions. In: Proc. 1999 PLDI, Atlanta, Georgia, USA (May 1999); volume 34(5) of SIGPLAN Notices
28. Peyton Jones, S.L.: Tackling the awkward squad: Monadic input/output, concurrency, exceptions, and foreign-language calls in Haskell. In: Hoare, T., Broy, M., Steinbruggen, R. (eds.) Engineering Theories of Software Construction, pp. 47–96. IOS Press, Amsterdam (2001)
29. Peyton Jones, S.L., Wadler, P.L.: Imperative functional programming. In: Proc. 1993 ACM Symp. POPL, Charleston, South Carolina, pp. 71–84. ACM Press, New York (1993)
30. Plotkin, G.: Call-by-name, call-by-value and the λ-calculus. Theoretical Computer Science 1, 125–159 (1975)
31. Ramsey, N., Pfeffer, A.: Stochastic lambda calculus and monads of probability distributions. In: Mitchell, J. (ed.) Proc. 29th ACM Symp. POPL, Portland, OR, USA. ACM Press, New York (2002)
32. Sabry, A., Felleisen, M.: Reasoning about programs in continuation-passing style. Lisp and Symbolic Computation 6(3/4), 289–360 (1993)
33. Sabry, A., Wadler, P.: A reflection on call-by-value. ACM Trans. Prog. Lang. and Systems 19(6), 916–941 (1997)
34. Saint-Mleux, X., Feeley, M., David, J.-P.: SHard: A Scheme to hardware compiler. In: Proc. 2006 Scheme and Functional Programming Workshop, pp. 39–49. Univ. of Chicago Press (2006)
35. Serrano, M., Gallesio, E., Loitsch, F.: HOP, a language for programming the Web 2.0. In: Proceedings of the First Dynamic Languages Symposium, Portland, OR, USA (October 2006)
36. Steele, G.L.: Rabbit: a compiler for Scheme. Technical Report AI-TR-474, MIT, Cambridge, MA (1978)
37. Syme, D., Granicz, A., Cisternino, A.: Expert F#. Apress (2007)
38. Thiemann, P.: An embedded domain-specific language for type-safe server-side Web-scripting. ACM Trans. Internet Technology 5(1), 1–46 (2005)
39. Wadler, P., Thiemann, P.: The marriage of monads and effects. ACM Trans. Computational Logic 4(1), 1–32 (2003)
40. Wadler, P.L.: Comprehending monads. In: Proc. ACM Conference on Lisp and Functional Programming, Nice, France, pp. 61–78. ACM Press, New York (1990)
41. Wong, L.: Kleisli, a functional query system. J. Funct. Program. 10(1), 19–56 (2000)

Author Index

Printing: Mercedes-Druck, Berlin
Binding: Stein+Lehmann, Berlin